True Stories
from the American Past

Volume I: To 1865

TRUE STORIES FROM THE AMERICAN PAST

VOLUME I: TO 1865

EDITED BY

Altina L. Waller
University of Connecticut, Storrs

William Graebner
State University of New York
College at Fredonia

THE McGRAW-HILL COMPANIES, INC.

New York St. Louis San Francisco Auckland Bogotá Caracas Lisbon
London Madrid Mexico City Milan Montreal New Delhi
San Juan Singapore Sydney Tokyo Toronto

McGraw-Hill

*A Division of The **McGraw·Hill** Companies*

TRUE STORIES FROM THE AMERICAN PAST
VOLUME I: TO 1865

This book is printed on acid-free paper.

1 2 3 4 5 6 7 8 9 0 FGR FGR 9 0 9 8 7 6

ISBN 0-07-067954-1

This book was set in Plantin by ComCom, Inc.
The editors were Lyn Uhl and Monica Freedman;
the production supervisor was Diane Ficarra.
The cover was designed by Joseph A. Piliero.
The photo editor was Anne Manning.
Project supervision was done by The Total Book.
Quebecor Printing/Fairfield was printer and binder.

Library of Congress Cataloging-in-Publication Data

Waller, Altina L. (Altina Laura), (date)
True stories from the American past / edited by Altina L. Waller,
William Graebner.—2nd ed.
p.   cm.

Contents: v. 1. To 1865—v. 2. Since 1865.
ISBN 0-07-067954-1 (alk. paper : v. 1).—ISBN 0-07-023015-3 (v.   2)
1. United States—History.   I. Graebner, William.   II. Title.
E178.W265   1997
973—dc20   96-9569

About the Authors

BERNARD BAILYN is Adams University Professor and James Duncan Phillips Professor of Early American History emeritus at Harvard University. He is the author or editor of more than twenty-five books including *New England Merchants in the Seventeenth Century* (1955); *The Ideological Origins of the American Revolution* (1967) which won the Pulitzer and Bancroft Prizes; *The Ordeal of Thomas Hutchinson* (1974) which won the National Book Award in History; *Voyagers to the West* (1986) which won the Pulitzer Prize and the Saloutos Award of the Immigration History Society; *Faces of Revolution* (1990); and *On the Teaching and Writing of History* (1994). In 1993 he received the Thomas Jefferson Medal of the American Philosophical Society for his work in history. He is Director of Harvard's International Seminar on the History of the Atlantic World.

MICHAEL A. BELLESILES teaches legal history at Emory University. He is the author of *Revolutionary Outlaws: Ethan Allen and the Struggle for Independence on the Early American Frontier* (University of Virginia Press, 1993). Currently, he is working on a history of gun laws in America.

THOMAS J. DAVIS is professor of African American Studies and History at the State University of New York in Buffalo. A historian and lawyer, he is editor of *The New York Conspiracy* (Boston: Beacon Press 1971) and author of *A Rumor of Revolt: The 'Great Negro Plot' in Colonial New York* (New York: Free Press/Macmillan 1985), paperback edition (Amherst: University of Massachusetts Press 1990) and most recently with Michael L. Conniff, of *Africans in the Americas: A History of the Black Diaspora* (New York: St. Martin's Press 1994).

R. DAVID EDMUNDS is professor of history at Indiana University. He is the author of *The Potawatomis: Keepers of the Fire* (Norman: University of Oklahoma Press 1978), *The Shawnee Prophet* (Lincoln: University of Nebraska Press 1983), *Tecumseh and the Quest for Indian Leadership* (Boston: Little, Brown and Co., 1984). He has co-authored *The Fox Wars: The Mesquakie Challenge to New France* (Norman: University of Oklahoma Press 1993) with Joseph L. Peyser, and has edited *American Indian Leaders: Studies in Diversity* (Lincoln: University of Nebraska Press 1980). Edmunds is of Cherokee descent and has served as the Acting Director of the McNickle Center for Indian History at the Newberry Library. He has held Ford Foundation and Guggenheim fellowships.

WILLIAM GRAEBNER is professor of history at the State University of New York, College at Fredonia. He has written on a variety of aspects of twentieth-century American history. His books include *A History of Retirement* (New Haven: Yale University Press, 1980), *The Engineering of Consent: Democracy and Authority in Twentieth-Century America* (Madison: University of Wisconsin Press, 1987), *Coming of Age in Buffalo* (Philadelphia: Temple University Press, 1990), and *The Age of Doubt: American Thought and Culture in the 1940s* (Boston: Twayne, 1991). He is Associate Editor of *American Studies*.

KAREN ORDAHL KUPPERMAN: Professor of History at New York University, holds a Ph.D. from Cambridge University. She is the author of *Providence Island 1630–1641: The Other Puritan Colony* (1993), which won the Beveridge Prize of the American Historical Association. She also authored *Roanoke, The Abandoned Colony* (1984), and *Settling With the Indians: The Meeting of English and Indian Cultures in America, 1580–1640* (1980). Her edited books include *America in European Consciousness* (1995), *Major Problems in American Colonial History* (1993), and *Captain John Smith: A Select Edition of His Writings* (1988). Her essay, "Apathy and Death in Early Jamestown," published in the *Journal of American History* in 1979, won the Binkley Stephenson Award of the Organization of American Historians. She has chaired the Council of the Institute of Early American History and Culture and the editorial board of the *William and Mary Quarterly*.

KENNETH LOCKRIDGE is Professor Emeritus at the University of Michigan. His book *A New England Town: The First Hundred Years* (New York 1970) was voted by the profession one of the significant books in American History in the 1970s. Other works include *Literacy in Colonial New England* (1974), *Settlement and Unsettlement in Early America: The Crisis of Political Legitimacy Before the Revolution* (1981), *The Diary and Life of William Byrd of Virginia 1674–1744* (1987), and *On the Sources of Patriarchal Rage: The Commonplace Books of William Byrd and Thomas Jefferson and the Gendering of Power in the Eighteenth Century* (1992). He has recently appeared on The History Channel with a lecture on "Robert Bolling's Dirty Pictures: Gender and Self-Construction in Jefferson's Virginia."

MELTON MCLAURIN, professor of history at the University of North Carolina at Wilmington, received his Ph.D. from the University of South Carolina. In addition to *Celia: A Slave* (1991), his books on the American South include *Separate Pasts: Growing Up White in the Segregated South* (University of Georgia Press 1987), and *You Wrote My Life, Lyrical Themes in Country Music* (Philadelphia 1992).

STEPHEN NISSENBAUM teaches history at the University of Massachusetts at Amherst. His most recent book is *The Battle for Christmas* (Knopf 1996) He has also written *Salem Possessed: Social Origins of Witchcraft* (with Paul S. Boyer, 1974), *Sex, Diet, and Debility in Jacksonian America* (1980), *The Pursuit of Liberty* (third edition 1996; a multi-authored textbook), and *All Over the Map: Rethinking American Regions* (1996, with Edward L. Ayers, Patricia Nelson Limerick, and Peter Onuf). Active in the public humanities, he has served as member and president of the Massachusetts Foundation for the Humanities. He holds degrees from Harvard College, Columbia University, and the University of Wisconsin.

GREGORY H. NOBLES is Professor of History and Associate Dean for Academic Affairs at Georgia Institute of Technology. His first book, *Divisions Throughout the Whole: Politics and Society in Hampshire County, Massachusetts, 1740–1775,* (New York 1983) dealt with pre-Revolutionary politics in a region that later became the center of Shaysite activity. His most recent work, a book on American Frontiers, will be published by Hill and Wang in 1996. He has held fellowships from the National Endowment for the Humanities and the American Antiquarian Society and has been a Fulbright scholar in New Zealand.

NANCY SHOEMAKER is Assistant Professor of History at the University of Wisconsin at Eau Claire. Her Ph.D. is from the University of Minnesota and she has taught at Texas Christian University and the State University of New York at Plattsburgh. She has published several articles on American Indian gender and family history and is the editor of *Negotiators of Change: Historical Perspectives on Native American Women* (Routledge 1995).

EVERARD H. SMITH is regional coordinator for the North Carolina Information Highway and a part-time faculty member in the Department of History at the University of North Carolina at Wilmington. A specialist in Confederate manuscript sources and on the Valley Campaign of 1864, he was a contributing author to *The Image of War,* published by the National Historical Society, and a consultant to "Civil War: The North Carolina Story," produced by the University of North Carolina Center for Public Television. His articles have appeared in *Civil War Times Illustrated, Civil War Magazine, The North Carolina Historical Review,* and *The American Historical Review,* among others.

PATRICIA J. TRACY is professor of History, American Studies, and Women's Studies at Williams College. She is the author of *Jonathan Edwards, Pastor: Religion and Society and Eighteenth Century Northampton* (New York: Hill and Wang 1980) and articles in the *Journal of Social History,* the *Massachusetts Review* and the forthcoming encyclopedia of *American National Biography.* Having long researched the economic and demographic experiences of New England communities, she is now writing a book on the Anglo-American development of what we now call traditional models of masculinity and feminity in the period 1500–1800 and their place in the culture of capitalism.

ALTINA L. WALLER is professor of history and Chair of the department at the University of Connecticut at Storrs. She received her doctorate from the University of Massachusetts at Amherst and has taught at West Virginia University, Rhodes College in Memphis, Tennessee, and the State University of New York at Plattsburgh. She has held fellowships from the American Council of Learned Societies and the National Endowment for the Humanities. Her books include *Appalachia in the Making: The Southern Mountains in the Nineteenth Century* (co-edited with Mary Beth Pudup and Dwight Billings, 1995), *Reverend Beecher and Mrs. Tilton: Sex and Class in Victorian America* (1982), and *Feud: Hatfields, McCoys and Social Change in Appalachia, 1860–1900* (1988).

PETER J. WAY received his doctorate from the University of Maryland. He is the author of *Common Labour: Workers and the Digging of North American Canals, 1780–1860* which won the Frederick Jackson Turner Prize from the Organization of American Historians and 1994 Phillip Taft Prize awarded by Cornell University's School of Industrial and Labor Relations to the best book published in labor history. His articles have appeared in *Labor History, The British Journal of American Studies,* and *The British Journal of Canadian Studies.* His recent article, "Evil Humors and Ardent Spirits: The Rough Culture of Canal Construction Laborers," won the OAH 1994 Binkley-Stephenson Prize for the best article published in *The Journal of American History* in 1993. He is presently working on a labor history of British regular soldiers in the French and Indian War. Way is a Reader in American History at the University of Sussex in England.

JOHN ALEXANDER WILLIAMS is Professor of History and Director of the Center for Appalachian Studies at Appalachian State University. He holds the doctorate in history from Yale University and has taught at the universities of Notre Dame, Illinois (Chicago) and at West Virginia University. He has served as an administrator in three federal cultural agencies, including the National Endowment for the Humanities. He has published three books on West Virginia (1976–1993) and is the author, with Mark Samels, of the script for *West Virginia: A Film History,* a four-part documentary first broadcast in 1995. His publications also include *Old Ties and New Attachments: Italian-Americans in the West* (1992), co-edited with David Taylor. He is currently working on both print and film versions of the history of the Appalachian region.

Contents

Preface

True Stories is a special kind of reader. It consists of fifteen stories, each thoroughly researched and impeccably crafted by scholars who are authorities in their respective fields. Each story deals with a significant and compelling episode in the history of the United States from the seventeenth century through Reconstruction.

In selecting the stories, we have been moved by the sense that the American past is too rich and varied to be bound and contained by the traditional and comfortable narratives with which most historians are conversant. Nonetheless, some of our stories—the story of starvation and disease during Jamestown's early years, or the account of Benjamin Franklin's intellectual and social transformation from a printer's apprentice to America's foremost Enlightenment figure and "father" of the United States—will be generally familiar to instructors, if not students. Other stories examine familiar historical figures such as William Byrd of Virginia, Andrew Jackson, and Tecumseh from a fresh perspective—in Byrd's case, his domestic troubles and misogyny toward women; in Jackson's case, his resistance to social changes in patriarchy and family life; and in Tecumseh's case, the War of 1812 from the Native American point of view. Still others, including the story of the "Christmas Riots" and the conversion of a Mohawk woman, Kateri Tekakwitha, to Catholicism, concern issues and incidents that are not even mentioned in survey textbooks. We hope readers will appreciate the remarkable diversity of *True Stories*.

Together, the stories cover a wide variety of fields of historical inquiry, many of them new to the study of history in the last two or three decades. These include popular culture; the history of Native Americans; the history of African-Americans; women's history; labor and immigration history; and the social and psychological history of war. Most important, each episode was selected because it promised to make, well, a good *story*.

Why use stories to study and learn history? The idea is not as unusual as it might seem. We live in a culture steeped in stories: the myths of ancient Greece,

Biblical narratives, bedtime stories, fairy tales, newspaper accounts, Hollywood epics, neighborhood rumors, one's personal account of the day's events after a hard day at school or at the office. Even the standard history textbooks are essentially stories—longer, more general, more familiar, and more generally accepted stories than the ones found in this book—but stories, just the same.

The accounts that make up *True Stories* are obviously not myths, or fairy tales, or rumors. They are a certain kind of story that we easily recognize as "history." Indeed, history might be understood as a set of analytical stories about the past whose authors think are "true." When we read an historical account, we expect it to be balanced, to be based on historical research and "fact," and to show respect for the past; by these standards, the stories in *True Stories* certainly qualify as history. But it is not quite the history one finds in a history textbook. *True Stories* features people who live and act in specific places and times and in precise historical circumstances. Its flesh and blood protagonists—some of them resembling mythic heroes or anti-heroes—set out to burn cities, lay siege to forts, challenge superior military forces, build canals, and defy rapists. In short, one function of any story—and one purpose of *True Stories*—is to put people, and people's deeds, back into history.

There is another lesson to be learned from these stories, one that has to do with what a story is. Although the stories presented here often involve individuals acting in specific situations, they have significance that goes far beyond the setting or the actors. The people in *True Stories* (indeed, all of us) inevitably live their lives on the stage of history. The things that they do—even the odd, eccentric, or criminal things—are ultimately historical deeds, carried out within the economic, political, social, and cultural frameworks of a particular historical era. Therefore, a good story provides the insights of the traditional textbook, though in a very different form.

Sometimes it can be difficult to see the connections between a story and history, between the text and its context. When one sees a movie, or watches the 11 o'clock television news, one does not easily or automatically think of these "stories" as part of history; and making the connections between a specific event and the larger past can be more difficult when the event occurred decades ago. To help students make these connections, and to see the need for making them, each episode concludes with an interpretative section that pulls together the themes in the story and links the story proper with some larger and familiar historical context. For example, the seemingly erratic ravings of William Byrd against women and his exaggerated fears of female sexuality emerge from the cultural stresses of colonial status seeking; and the Peggy Eaton scandal was firmly rooted in radically changing definitions of family and women's role in society.

Each episode, then, has two distinct parts. The first part is the narrated story. Our goal was to keep this story section as free as possible from analysis and interpretation, in the hope that students would fashion their own perspectives once freed, if only relatively and momentarily, from the learned authority of the historian. The second part of the episode is a shorter interpretative conclusion, where the authors have been given free rein to bring their considerable analytical skills to bear on the body of the story.

As students and instructors will discover, the attempt to separate narrative and interpretation has been only moderately successful. Even the most rudimentary collections of "facts" and the simplest narratives begin with preconceptions, proceed from moral and ethical premises, and imply interpretive frameworks. So do our "true stories." Despite our efforts to put these elements in the background, they inevitably appear in the stories. Indeed, one purpose of the collection is to draw attention to the inescapable subjectivity of historians. Nonetheless, we also believe that the effort made here to separate narrative and analysis can assist students in generating their own readings of the past and, by doing so, in becoming active participants in the complex process of understanding and creating their own history.

Altina L. Waller
William Graebner

True Stories
from the American Past

Volume I: To 1865

1

THE STARVING TIME AT JAMESTOWN

KAREN ORDAHL KUPPERMAN

The journey of Christopher Columbus in 1492 signaled the beginning of the greatest migration in the history of the world. The Spanish and Portuguese began the great migration with the conquest of the native peoples of Central and South America, building grand cities and extracting the vast gold and silver resources for the benefit of their countries. But it was not long before northern Europeans—the British, Dutch, French, and Scandinavians—emigrated in even greater numbers. By the middle of the seventeenth century, many thousands of people had crossed the ocean from Europe and Africa to the new world, some as hopeful aspirants to a new and better life and many as coerced migrants—criminals, indentured servants, and slaves. All the migrants had to endure the long sea voyage, in which food, water, and exercise were scarce, leading to suffering, disease, and irritable tempers. Upon arrival, even the most privileged were faced with seemingly insurmountable obstacles: food shortages, disease, absence of family and friends, opposition from inhabitants of the land, and sheer exhaustion. Although different groups faced widely varying conditions when they landed in the new world, all had severe adjustments to make as they began to cope with the difficulties of survival in unfamiliar and often threatening conditions.

Karen Kupperman's tale of Jamestown, first settled by the English in 1607, is one of the many stories of the great migration. As inhabitants of the first English settlement to survive on a permanent basis, the migrants to Jamestown had only the Spanish model to emulate, and it soon became apparent that it would not work in the northern hemisphere. There were no gold and silver mines to be exploited and no large populations of Indians to enslave. Lacking these clearly visible sources of potential wealth, financial backers in England had less interest in supporting the attempts of the colonists to stabilize the settlement. Nearby Indians, although at first curious and supportive with gifts of food and advice, were soon alienated by the demanding arrogance of the English and became an ominous and threatening presence. For its first two decades, Jamestown led a tenuous existence as it struggled to survive.

Historians have long striven to comprehend the near disaster at Jamestown, postulating the disease-prone climate, the laziness and greed of the colonists, the exploitation of indentured servants by the wealthy, or the lack of economic incentives such as private property as possible culprits. Kupperman here explores another approach to the problems encountered by early Jamestown migrants. Using documents written at the time by the participants in the settlement effort, particularly those of the irascible and ubiquitous John Smith, she suggests another explanation, one that does not supplant other theories but enriches them by making use of some modern comparisons. What we have learned in the twentieth century suggests that the psychological aspects of such dramatic changes in both the physical and social environment must be taken into account in order to explain the human suffering and callousness toward others apparent in Jamestown.

L ife in Jamestown colony was miserable. By the spring of 1610, three years after the venture's founding, the colonists were desperate, starving, and sick. When reinforcements began to arrive at the end of May and the beginning of June, they found the settlers looking like skeletons and "crying out, 'we are starved, we are starved.' " The newcomers "read a lecture of misery in our people's faces." Of the 500 colonists left there the previous summer, only sixty remained alive. Many had died of dysentery, what the colonists called the "bloody flux," and "burning fevers."

Starvation had driven the men to unheard-of extremes. First they consumed their horses, then they "were glad to make shift with vermin as dogs cats, rats, and mice." When those were gone, the colonists ate their shoes and boots. Finally they began to do things even they described as "incredible." They dug up corpses and ate them, "and some have licked up the blood which hath fallen from their weak fellows." One colonist became addicted to the taste of human flesh and, when he could not be restrained, was executed for it. The "most lamentable" act was committed by a man so desperate that he killed his pregnant wife, threw the unborn child into the river, and chopped up the mother and salted the meat. His crime was not discovered until he had actually eaten some of his cache. The governor quickly had him executed.

Another man, Hugh Pryce, committed an equally distressing act. Pryce, "in a furious distracted mood, came openly into the marketplace Blaspheming, exclaiming and crying out that there was no God" because he thought God would not allow his creatures to suffer so much. When Pryce and a companion ventured into the woods and were killed by Indians, his body was ravaged and disfigured by wolves, but his dead friend was undisturbed. The colonists knew his fate was the judgment of the God he had denied, a punishment delivered as swiftly and surely as the governor's sentence on the cannibals.

Not only did some commit unspeakable crimes, but among the rest there seemed to be no group spirit or sense of mutual respect, none of the "constancy and resolution" leaders expected. Colonists who were able to get into boats tried to sail away to England. Some "unhallowed creatures" actually brought further misery on their "desolate brethren." When sent to trade for corn with the Indians, they disobeyed orders by mistreating the natives whose help the colonists so desperately needed. Then, as soon as their ship was loaded with corn, they conceived the "barbarous project" of deserting Virginia and returning to England. Thus they robbed the settlement of needed corn and turned the natives against it. Then, in order to justify themselves, these "scum of men" spread slanders about the colony back in England.

Colonist Gabriel Archer had warned of the danger almost a year earlier in the summer of 1609, when he returned to Jamestown from a trip to England. He and his companions found the settlers "in such distress" that they were forced to live on what the Indians provided (Archer described them as living on alms like beggars), for an ounce of copper per day. He wrote that the Indians could not possibly have provided more than they did. He blamed earlier visitors who had overpraised the country, describing it as a lush paradise; as a result, backers in England had not seen the need to send sufficient supplies. August, when Archer wrote, should have been a time of plenty when colonists could live off abundant supplies of nuts and berries, game animals, and fish. Instead, they were already in want, and their distress of summer soon turned into the famine of winter. Gabriel Archer would be among the dead of that "starving time" when the winter's toll was counted.

Famine had plagued the colony from the beginning, and it would continue even after the lessons of that terrible winter. Everyone had ideas, and many people spread blame, but no plan seemed able to get the colonists on the right track. The core problem was clear: the colonists were not producing food for themselves. Not only did they not plant and harvest crops, they did not even seem to be able to get food by hunting and fishing. Captain John Smith, who was in the colony from the beginning, wrote of this strange inability: "Now although there be Deer in the woods, Fish in the rivers, and Fowls in abundance in their seasons; yet the woods are so wide, the rivers so broad, and the beasts so wild, and we so unskillful to catch them, we little troubled them nor they us."

Because of their own inability to raise or catch food, the colonists were almost totally reliant on the Indians for sustenance. As the colonists admitted, "had the Savages not fed us, we directly had starved." The Chesapeake-area Algonquians, most of whom owed allegiance to Wahunsonacock, the man the colonists called "the great emperor Powhatan" after the name of his tribe, did have a sophisticated system of food production and storage. Their corn crop, yielding much more food per acre than European farmers could produce, was a marvel to the English. In Jamestown's early days, the Powhatans and their allies were happy to trade food for European manufactured goods that enhanced their own lives. Metal axes and knives, copper cooking pots, and, when they could convince the English to hand them over, muskets were all desirable trade items that could be efficiently integrated into Indian lifestyles.

But as the colony grew and the demands of the settlers became more pressing, Indians grew weary of this continuing reliance, which depleted their own food supplies dramatically. Boats from Jamestown were forced to travel farther and farther around Chesapeake Bay seeking Indians who still might be induced to provide food, and the value of the trade goods became debased. When Indians were reluctant to trade, colonists applied force and threats, which only made matters worse in the long run. Soon a virtual state of war existed, and it became too dangerous to go out to cultivate crops or to hunt because of the fear of snipers who could pick off unwary men without ever even being seen. Thus the crisis of hunger and disease was intensified, and the colonists felt like prisoners in their fort.

The English reading public avidly consumed reports that portrayed the Spanish as ruthless in their treatment of the hapless natives in Latin America, and supporters of English colonization contrasted their peaceful, benevolent intentions with reports of Spanish pillaging. Smith played on that comparison when he dramatically described his own efforts to find Indians willing to trade food for the goods he had to offer: "The Spaniard never more greedily desired gold than he victual." This image was reinforced when Indians, fed up with the colonists' constant pressure, killed a small party of men led by Lieutenant Michael Sicklemore and left the corpses with bread stuffed in their mouths. Colonist George Percy wrote that the Indians thus showed their "contempt and scorn" and signaled "that others might expect the like when they should come to seek for bread and relief amongst them." Percy was reminded of a story he had read of a Spanish general in Chile, who was killed by having molten gold poured down his throat by outraged Indians, who said to him "now glut thyself with gold." That general (Percy thought his name was Baldivia) had "there sought for gold as Sicklemore did here for food."

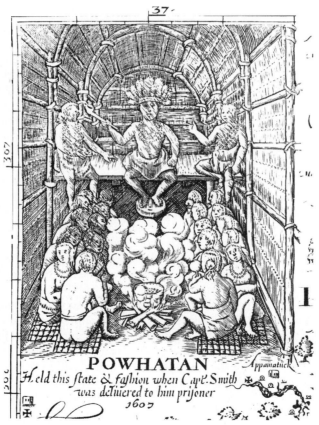

Powhatan holding court. Representations of the eastern woodland Indian life evolved during the early years of contact and settlement. This woodcut, which decorated a map of Virginia in John Smith's history, is adapted from a Roanoke colonists' drawing of a carved wooden deity in a temple. (John Carter Brown Library)

So, the Jamestown colonists had come dangerously close to emulating the example of the despised Spaniards in their dependence on native sources of food. And even by using force and threats, they could not possibly get enough food to keep the colony in health. This brings us back to the main issue: Why did they not take the steps necessary to provide their own food? Everyone who looked at the problem came up with the same disturbing answer: the colonists were lazy and impossible to motivate.

But reports from all kinds of sources agreed that this was not just ordinary laziness; something far more disturbing was at work, a "most strange condition" that no one had seen before. Ralph Hamor later wrote that the colonists, "no more sensible than beasts, would rather starve in idleness (witness their former proceedings) than feast in labor." Colony Secretary William Strachey judged that the suffering at Jamestown was brought on by the settlers' "sloth, riot, and vanity." He described them tearing up their houses for firewood rather than walking a short distance into the woods. Sir Thomas Gates offered an "incredible example" of laziness. He watched colonists eat fish raw "rather than they would go a stone's cast to fetch wood" with which to cook it. Captain John Smith wrote persuasively about Jamestown after his return to England. He described the atmosphere of "malice,

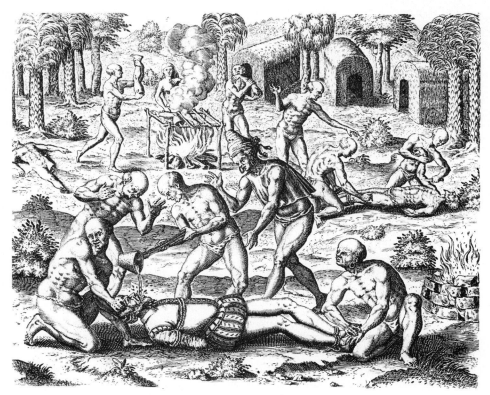

Indians pouring molten gold down a Spaniard's throat. This was a widely circulated legend warning of the dangers of unbridled greed that put more pressure on the Indians than they could tolerate. (John Carter Brown Library)

grudging and muttering" in which the colonists lived. "As at this time were most of our chiefest men either sick or discontented, the rest being in such despair, as they would rather starve and rot with idleness, then be persuaded to do anything for their own relief without constraint."

Even more astonishingly, the colonists did not learn from past suffering. After the starving winter of 1609–1610, they took no steps to plan for the future. Gates wrote that although sturgeon were plentiful in season, the men made no attempt to preserve any fish for later use. Even more incredible was Gates's report that they allowed all fourteen fishing nets to rot so "all help of fishing perished." When interim governor Sir Thomas Dale arrived in May 1611, a full year after the revelation of the colonists' terrible plight, he found that they, "though I sorrow to speak it, were not so provident, though once before bitten with hunger and penury, as to put corn into the ground for their winter's bread." Instead, he found the men "at their daily and usual works, bowling in the streets."

How was this possible? How could starving men spend their time bowling rather than working to produce the food they needed so desperately? Many observers in England feared that Jamestown's experience revealed the degeneration of the nation. Preacher William Crashaw argued that it showed "the pusillanimity, the baseness, the tenderness and effeminateness of our English people, into which our nation is now degenerate, from a strong, valliant, hardy, patient and enduring people, as our forefathers were." Jamestown's experience was a product of "our idleness, laziness and lasciviousness." Crashaw concluded that the English had become "milksops."

Others argued that these reports did not reflect on English society as a whole, because only the poorest-quality people had been sent to America. It became common to sum up the experience as preacher Patrick Copland did in 1622: "(most of them at the first, being the very scum of the land, and great pity it was that no better at that time could be had) they neglected God's worship, lived in idleness, plotted conspiracies, resisted the government of Superiors, and carried themselves dissolutely among the heathens." The epithet "scum" was repeated over and over again. Strachey wrote that the worst of them scarcely seemed human, and he blamed disorders on the "infected minds" sent to Virginia. Ralph Hamor urged sponsors in England to "deter all lazy, impotent, and ill livers from addressing themselves thither" or the colony would not survive. Smith argued along the same lines: "one hundred good labourers [would have been] better than a thousand such Gallants as were sent me, that could do nothing but complaine, curse, and despair, when they saw our miseries, and all things so clean contrary to the report in England." He wrote that "most of them would rather starve than work."

Everyone involved in trying to figure out what had gone wrong assumed there was some defect in the people who were being sent to Virginia. Although it is difficult to know the backgrounds of most colonists for certain, they seem to have divided into roughly three groups. One was the ordinary men, the laborers. Another segment was the skilled men, who were supposed to help the colonists get settled and to produce luxury goods to enrich backers at home. Finally, a very large percentage of the population was gentlemen and their servants. We now know that this was a very poor combination.

It was tempting to blame the laborers, and they were often dismissed as scum because they were from the lower classes in society. Cities sometimes rounded up people from the streets, the "swarming" poor, and shipped them off to Virginia. Poor children, some as young as eight, were shipped out by the city of London in batches of 100. Not only were all these looked down upon, but they were city-bred for the most part and had little knowledge of how one would go about setting up a farm even in England, much less in America. Nobody seemed to care very much what happened to them, although some leaders like Smith appreciated their labor.

The skilled men, who might have provided some leadership, actually created more trouble than profit in the infant society. The Virginia Company in London, made up of investors who bought shares in the expectation of getting a percentage of the profits, based its strategy on glowing propaganda reports that promised rich products from America. The skilled workers were sent at company expense to find and develop these products for the investors, but the work they were supposed to do was ridiculous in a rough settlement. Smith complained that the company cared more about the expected profits than about setting up a truly functional society. The investors had no clear idea of what it would take to get people housed and fed, much less to send home luxury goods. He blamed them for "sending us so many Refiners, Gold-smiths, Jewellers, Lapidaries, Stone-cutters, Tobacco-pipe-makers, Embroiderers, Perfumers, Silkmen" and all their attendants. When gold and jewels were not found and silk could not be produced, the specialists could not be ordered to do other work. Smith wrote that when the colonists thought of the Virginia Company planners at home, they wondered "how it was possible such wise men could so torment themselves and us with such strange absurdities and impossibilities" as the idea that Virginia would be sending home jewels and perfumes right from the beginning. In 1609, two years after the founding, Smith wrote that the skilled workers still included only one experienced carpenter and two blacksmiths.

The worst mistake of all was the English backers' assumption that a person born to high social rank automatically knew how to lead. The investors were mostly gentlemen and aristocrats, and in England high birth meant a great deal. Therefore, the London Virginia Company sent a very large number of gentlemen— about one-third of the total—in the early shipments to Jamestown. These people had no expectation of doing productive work; in fact, they expected to be waited on by servants. Smith complained that even the colonists who were supposed to be workers were mostly footmen and other attendants for the gentlemen "that never did know what a day's work was." Looking back later, even those who supported the company acknowledged it was foolish "to have more to wait and play than work, or more commanders and officers than industrious laborers."

Some gentlemen apparently went because it was an exciting prospect, a lark, and they had no intention of staying. Others went because they lacked other good choices, or because they were escaping debts and problems at home. As Smith wrote, there were "many unruly gallants packed thither by their friends to escape ill destinies" at home. George Percy, for example, was the younger brother of the earl of Northumberland. Like many younger sons, he grew up in the luxury and privilege of a noble house, but then, because under the law the oldest son inherited everything, he became a plain gentleman who had to make his own way. George's oldest brother, the earl, was imprisoned in the Tower of London because he was suspected in the Popish Plot of 1605, a Roman Catholic conspiracy that had planned to bomb the Houses of Parliament and King James. The entire Percy family suffered from the taint of suspicion, and George, who was always sickly, apparently went to Virginia in 1607 as a good way to escape royal wrath and make a career for himself.

Another inheritance-poor younger brother among the first group of colonists was Captain John Martin, a quarrelsome and contentious figure in Virginia, third son of the Lord Mayor of London; his father was also master of the royal mint.

Captain John Smith. Smith deliberately presented himself as a gruff soldier, a man of experience who knew how to get things done. (John Carter Brown Library)

Martin was older than most of the early settlers, forty-five in 1607, and he was "sick and weak" most of the time. He had commanded a ship under Sir Francis Drake twenty years earlier and may have expected to have a greater voice in running things than he did. Another troublesome early leader in Jamestown was a man named John Sicklemore, who sometimes called himself Captain John Ratcliffe. For whatever reason, he disguised his identity so well that even today his origins cannot be traced. One of the original council members was George Kendall, a man who apparently was connected to important families but who, like the younger sons who chose emigration, had been denied an inheritance. He was thrown off the council and later executed, apparently because the other councillors thought he was spying for the Spanish. These men were not prepared to share the burdens of government and work together; each seems to have been seeking advancement for himself that he was denied in England.

Most of the gentlemen in Virginia had no special training for the challenges of confronting people from very different cultures and attempting to re-create English society in a new setting. Edward Maria Wingfield, the first governor at Jamestown, had been a soldier in Ireland and the Netherlands, but he had no talent for getting the men working together toward common goals and no interest in building relationships with the American natives. The rank-and-file colonists suspected that he and his cronies were eating well on secret stores of beef, wine, and eggs, while the colonists were restricted to small amounts of wheat and barley that "contained as many worms as grains." Some thought he was planning to escape secretly with the colony's supplies. When Wingfield was forced out, John Ratcliffe aka Sicklemore became governor.

Other gentleman-colonists were even less well suited by experience. Gabriel Archer, for example, was educated at Cambridge and in Gray's Inn, a law school, and he had participated, along with John Martin, in a voyage to New England in 1602. The New England venture had been led by another of the leading Virginia colonists, Bartholomew Gosnold, so the investors may have thought the men could work well together. Unfortunately, Gosnold died shortly after their arrival in Jamestown. William Strachey, another of the gentlemen, had also been educated at Cambridge and Gray's Inn and was active in London's literary circles when the chance for a Virginia adventure came his way. As the investors learned painfully, high social rank and good academic education did not necessarily prepare Englishmen for the challenges America presented. Leaders in the colony advised against sending too many gentlemen while the settlement was still rough because they, "when they find things not suitable, grow many times so discontented, they forget themselves, and oft become so careless, that a discontented melancholy brings them to much sorrow, and others to much misery."

Very few in any of the three groups—the ordinary laborers, the skilled workers, or the gentlemen—were prepared either by experience or psychologically for the isolated and trying life in Virginia. Smith's report, especially his reference to despair, offers a clue to what was going on. Life in Jamestown was psychologically debilitating, and the planters were apparently falling victim to deep depression. Many reports mention despair or use terms such as Hamor's "infected minds." One newcomer described the colonists as "distracted and forlorn." As George Thorpe later wrote, "more do die here of the disease of their mind than of their body." George Donne, son of the poet John Donne, summed up the Jamestown experience: "He is wretched that believes himself wretched."

Captain John Smith believed he knew what needed to be done. John Smith was unique among the first contingent of settlers. He alone of all the men chosen for the original governing council by the Virginia Company was selected for his knowledge and experience rather than his social status. He was of yeoman background rather than from the gentry. Smith, bored with his apprenticeship to a merchant, had gone as a teenager to fight in the religious wars between Catholics and Protestants in France. He returned to England but was soon back in continental Europe. This time he went out to the eastern frontier in Austria and Hungary, where European armies resisted Turkish forces pushing toward Vienna. Smith wrote an account of this war, highlighting his own exploits. Nonetheless, he was taken prisoner and was for a time a slave in Turkey. He killed his captor and escaped, traveling through much of Europe and even into North Africa before he made it back to England. He was in his mid-twenties, and the Virginia Company was seeking likely people to found the Jamestown colony. Smith was just what they were looking for.

In Virginia he constantly pointed out the deficiencies of the other council members, despite their high birth. They sneered at him as an upstart and tried to freeze him out of the government. During the colony's first year, Smith was away from Jamestown much of the time, leading a small band that explored Chesapeake Bay and traded for food supplies for the colony. He was captured by Powhatan's forces and spent several weeks in captivity. During this time he and Powhatan laid the foundation for a relationship of mutual respect and wariness that bore fruit when Smith finally became governor in September 1608 after all the high-born council members were either dead or too weak to object.

The first winter, during which the frustrated Smith had chafed under what he saw as the mismanagement of those in charge, the population of the colony fell from the original 108 to "about eight and thirty miserable poor and sick creatures." But, as he constantly reiterated in his many books, there was no despair and few deaths during the second winter while he ran the colony.

Along with others, he believed that part of Jamestown's problem was structural: the colony lacked sufficiently good housing and clean water, for example. Reverend Alexander Whitaker wrote that people died from "their own filthiness" but also because of "want of comforts for sick men." George Percy, in describing famine as the main cause of death, also spoke of the "slime and filth" as well as the salty flavor in the river water they drank.

Smith set out to correct these problems, and he wrote vividly of what the men accomplished under his direction: "Jamestown being burned, we rebuilt it and three Forts more. Besides the Church and Storehouse, we had about forty or fifty several houses to keep us warm and dry, environed with a palizado of fourteen or fifteen feet. . . . We dug a fair well of fresh water in the Fort . . . [and] planted one hundred acres of Corn." He also sent parties of colonists farther up the James River and down to its mouth to live off the land and to learn survival techniques from the Indians.

Moreover, he got all the men in Jamestown up and working and thereby cured their apathy and despair. He decreed that the able-bodied must care for the sick and provide food for them. He gathered the colonists together and said, quoting 2 Thessalonians 3:10 in the Bible, "you must obey this for a law, that he that will not work shall not eat." He warned the "drones" not to hope for relief from the Indians, and unlike previous leaders who had considered themselves too important to do manual labor, he set his own labor as the standard: "every one that gathereth not every day as much as I do, the next day shall be set beyond the river, and for ever be banished from the fort, and live there or starve." In Jamestown under Smith's control, even the gentlemen worked, "making it their delight to hear the trees thunder as they fell." Because their "tender fingers" became so blistered and raw, the gentlemen swore with every stroke of their axes, so Smith decreed that at night a mug of cold water would be poured down each man's sleeve for every oath he uttered that day, and swearing was eliminated.

Smith's proof lay in the result: "This order many murmured, was very cruel, but it caused the most part so well bestir themselves, that of 200 men (except they were drowned) there died not past 7 or 8." That was quite a contrast to the death toll of the preceding winter (1607–1608), in which the population dropped from 108 to 38. But Jamestown's misery was not finished. Smith was eased out of the colony by his enemies and sent home in 1609. The worst starving time, in which the population fell from about 500 to 60, came during that next winter, 1609–1610. As Smith put it, "Idleness and carelessness brought all I did in three years in six months to nothing."

C.Smith taketh the King of Pamavnkee prifoner 1608

This woodcut of John Smith capturing the king of Pamaunke foregrounds Smith and his daring against a background of Virginia scenes, many showing conflict, but also illustrating the plants and landscape of Virginia. (John Carter Brown Library)

After that second starving time, reports from the colony were avidly read and analyzed. Jamestown required massive investment to keep it going, and company leaders in London knew that no one would put money into a losing proposition. As John Smith wrote, "the common question is, For all those miseries, where is the wealth they have got, or the Gold or Silver Mines?" Company leaders had to find a solution to Jamestown's problems or give up the venture. Many explanations were suggested by those who wanted to find some hope for the future.

One line of thought suggested that God was testing the English and that therefore to give up would be sacrilege. Writers pointed out that God seemed to intervene on the settlers' behalf just at the point where conditions became unbearable: "Almighty God that had thus far tried the patience of the English, would not suffer them to be tempted above that they were able." When Indians did bring the colonists food, the credit was given to God for moving their hearts to pity. Suffering was also interpreted as "God's rod of mortality," punishing the colonists for their sins. John Rolfe, who earned a place in history through his marriage to Pocahontas, the daughter of Powhatan, wrote in 1616 that God's blessing, though delayed, was now pouring on Virginia. The English, he wrote, in terms usually reserved for the Jews, are "a peculiar [special] people marked and chosen by the finger of God to possess it." Rolfe called those who continued to criticize the venture "incredulous worldlings," and others argued that such critics were persecutors of Christ. Promoters such as William Strachey argued that Virginia should be seen as "a Sanctum Sanctorum, an holy house." England could not just walk away as from an ordinary business venture.

Many observers argued that Jamestown's problems had stemmed mostly from sickness, and they began to analyze the specifics of how immigrants became sick. Those with experience asserted that the ships arrived at the wrong time of year. They came in the early summer, and so "unseasoned" English bodies were confronted by the hot sun of Virginia, to which they were unaccustomed, and a new disease environment all at once. Some reasoned that Jamestown's location, chosen for defensibility, was unhealthy and swampy. Beer was the normal drink for all ages and sexes in England, and many remarked that newcomers were sickened by the switch to drinking water in America. Sir Thomas Gates linked the location and its water, saying that the principal thing that "weakened and endangered" his men was "drinking of the brackish water of James Fort." Some wrote that eating fresh meat when they were more used to salted or dried meat made the newcomers sick.

But many also thought there was a strong psychological component in the way disease struck and that idleness and despair played a role. Whereas Smith ridiculed the "tufftafety humorists" who pined for their featherbeds and taverns, others argued that the gap between expectation and reality was too great for many, who were sickened "by having this country victuals over-praised unto them in England and by not knowing they shall drink water here." Some planters wrote that disease came "either by contagion of sickness or by the mother and cause thereof, ill example of idleness." Ralph Hamor agreed that idleness caused disease and that "few idlers" had escaped "the scurvy disease, with which few, or none once infected, have recovered." Most colonists arrived with scurvy, the result of a lack of vitamin C, because they had no fresh fruit or vegetables on the long sea voyage.

The lethargy produced by scurvy in its early stages was seen as simple laziness, and leaders who saw the disease worsen then concluded that the laziness had caused the disease. Thus, disease grew out of a mental or moral weakness in their interpretation.

If they were to save the venture, like it or not, investors had to pay attention to Captain John Smith and his books explaining what had gone wrong in Virginia. The Virginia Company had no intention of sending Smith back to the colony. His habit of correcting, even ridiculing, his social betters made him unpopular with investors and, they thought, untrustworthy. But they did pay attention to his results.

Many analysts argued that the basic problem in Jamestown was inadequate government. The original plan for the colony had been to send a council appointed in England and to have the council choose the governor. Smith asserted that he was able to be effective only when the other councillors were too sick to interfere, and the Virginia Company accepted the notion that the original government plan had spread authority over too many men. As John Rolfe wrote of the council in 1616, "All would be Keisars [Caesars], none inferior to other . . . and in this government happened all the misery. Afterward a more absolute government was granted Monarchally, wherein it still continueth." When the authority was weak, the colonists degenerated, according to another analysis, into a "headless and unbridled multitude." Sir Thomas Gates, who had arrived to find the scene of des-

Woodcut of Algonquian man and woman eating together. The accompanying legend says that they are eating boiled corn, and in the foreground the artist has illustrated some of the variety of foods available in America. (John Carter Brown Library)

olation in May of 1610, wrote that he had, as an "experiment," instituted a system of strong authority rather like Smith's, and "in a fortnights space [two weeks] he recovered the health of most of them by moderate labor, whose sickness was bred in them by intemperate idleness." His experiment confirmed the conclusion.

So the solution seemed pretty simple: just replicate the order and discipline created by Smith and get all the colonists working again. Purposeful activity would both solve the infrastructure problems and pull the colonists out of depression. Sir Thomas Dale, the governor who arrived to find the colonists bowling in the streets, landed in May 1611 with a set of extremely harsh laws designed to force the colonists to behave responsibly. Unlike the earlier gentlemen, Gates and Dale both had life experience that seemed to suit them to take command of the idle young men in Virginia. Both had been in what some called the "university of war." The two men had served on the Protestant side in the Netherlands, where the Dutch were fighting to free themselves of domination by Catholic Spain, and both had fought against rebels in Ireland. Moreover, Dale's background was similar to Smith's; he, too, had begun as a common soldier and had risen through the ranks to a captaincy. But Dale did not have Smith's talent for creating a sense of common purpose and shared responsibility. Rather, Dale set out to treat the colonists as soldiers under his command. Bowling in the streets was replaced with a regimented day based on military discipline. Every part of life was regulated under the "Laws Divine, Moral and Martial," which stipulated that colonists were to wake up at a drumbeat, go to meals and to work together by the sound of the drum, and go to sleep on orders. Extreme punishments were laid out for even minor infractions.

The laws were controversial even at the time. The planters in the colony wrote home against the "Book of most tyrannical laws written in blood" under which they suffered. They wrote that they

> remained in great want and misery under most severe and Cruel laws sent over in print, and contrary to the express Letter of the King in his most gracious Charter, and as mercilessly executed, often times without trial or judgment. The allowance in those times for a man was only eight ounces of meal and half a pint of peas for a day, the one and the other moldy, rotten, full of cobwebs and maggots, loathsome to man and not fit for beasts, which forced many to flee for relief to the Savage Enemy, who being taken again were put to sundry deaths as by hanging, shooting and breaking upon the wheel and others were forced by famine to filch for their bellies, of whom one for stealing 2 or 3 pints of oatmeal had a bodkin [dagger] thrust though his tongue and was tied with a chain to a tree until he starved. If a man through his sickness had not been able to work, he had no allowance at all, and so consequently perished many through these extremities, being weary of life dug holes in the earth and hid themselves till they famished.

Those who opposed the system could justly point out that the colony held on but did not prosper as long as the martial law administration held.

But the regime also had many defenders. Ralph Hamor wrote that without the severity of these laws, "I see not how the utter subversion and ruin of the Colony should have been prevented." He acknowledged that Dale did carry out severe punishments forbidden in England, especially in executions, where "the manner of their death may some object, hath been cruel, unusual and barbarous, which indeed they have not been, witness France, and other countries for less offences. What if they have been more severe than usual in England, there was just cause for it." And, building on the assumption that the colonists in Jamestown were "scum," he went on to argue that special treatment was necessary to get their attention: "It being true that amongst those people (who for the most part are sensible only of the body's torment) the fear of a cruel, painful and unusual death more restrains them than death itself." The Virginia Company justified their departure from English law, saying martial law was necessary because of the "debased and irregular persons" in the colony. The results were convincing enough for investors, who believed that Sir Thomas Dale had reclaimed "almost miraculously those idle and disordered people and reduced them to labor and an honest fashion of life." But even if the martial law regime held the little outpost together, there was no sign that the settlement was preparing to transform itself into a true colony with planters committed to making whole new lives in Virginia. That transition would require yet a further transformation in the plan.

The planters who survived this period argued that Virginia's problems were not caused by their deficiencies, and they rejected the lable "scum." The selfishness and lack of care had been in London, not in Virginia: "the cause of our factions was bred here in England." As Captain John Smith wrote at the end of his life, the Virginia Company had made "Religion their color, when all their aim was nothing but present profit." The settlers blamed the company leaders for sending ship after ship with too few and too poor quality supplies, with the result that the food they were able to procure was eaten up by newcomers. Dale arrived, they wrote, with food so rotten the hogs refused to eat it. They argued that their working time was spent in a fruitless search for gold to line the pockets of investors or in sawing boards to send home. The company, they said, had threatened simply to forget about their existence and abandon them in America as "banished men" if they did not shape up and start sending home valuable products. They said they were held in a kind of slavery during which they underwent "as hard and servile labor as the basest fellow that was brought out of Newgate" prison. And they were held as virtual prisoners. Their letters home were intercepted and read in London, and any who wrote the truth were punished. None of them were allowed to go home themselves. They scorned the pitiful structures created during that time and wrote that "neither could a blessing from God be hoped for in those buildings which were founded upon the blood of so many Christians."

The colonists were right. No firm foundations were built under the martial law. That regime may have looked on paper like the system instituted by John Smith, but the results were far different. So, the problem remained: Could planners and planters figure out how to create a brand-new society in a distant land in which English men and women could thrive and flourish? Actually, although Virginia continued to look like a mess, and the death rate remained high, particularly for newcomers, the colony was slowly, imperceptibly at first, moving in the right direction as the decade of the 1610s moved on.

Ironically the answer lay not in stricter control but in relinquishing authority to the people who knew what needed to be done, the planters themselves. It should have been obvious how useless it was to expect colonists to work hard to enrich the investors back in London when they stood to gain nothing from that hard work themselves. Instead of holding all the land in company hands, the investors began to divide it up. Big investors could acquire a large estate to develop as they saw fit, but they could have land only if they imported settlers to develop it and gave them the support they needed. Even more important, all immigrants, no matter how humble, were guaranteed land of their own as soon as they had paid off the cost of their passage over by working for the person who imported them. Now people had the incentive to work, and they also had control over what and how they planted. John Rolfe had developed a good marketable strain of tobacco that would sell well in England, and tobacco culture took off in the colony, giving planters a product that they knew they could grow and that consumers would buy. Tobacco production went up dramatically year by year, from 2000 pounds in 1615 to 40,000 pounds five years later. And the upward curve continued so that by 1629, 1,500,000 pounds were sent home. Tobacco, which had been a luxury product for the very rich, became accessible to all in the new craze for "drinking" smoke in England.

Investors also realized that something approaching normal English life was necessary for the colony to move beyond the grim military life of the fort. They took steps to encourage immigration by women, realizing that women were absolutely essential if the colony was to become a true society. As long as normal

English settled life in Virginia. This engraving, published in 1618 as the Virginia colony began to grow rapidly, shows hopes more than reality, as it portrays gentlemen fishing, hunting, and riding through a tamed landscape. (John Carter Brown Library)

family life was absent, colonists would not think of themselves as permanent immigrants. The grant of land was meaningful only when farmers had wives and children to provide for. The Virginia Assembly's first meeting in 1619 transmitted this demand: "In a new plantation, it is not known whether man or woman be more necessary." And the investors understood that this lack of normal life had been a big factor in the strange despair in Jamestown. "By long experience we have found that the Minds of our people in Virginia are much dejected, and their hearts enflamed with a desire to return for England only through the wants of the comforts without which God saw that Man could not live contentedly, no not in Paradise." They now saw that they could not "tie and root the Planters' minds to Virginia" without "the bonds of wives and children."

Although few at the time gave him credit, Captain John Smith had pointed the way to this new understanding of how to create a colony. Once it became clear that the Virginia Company wanted nothing further to do with him, he turned his attention northward. Norembega, as New England was then called, had been considered too cold and unproductive to be interesting for colonization. Smith went to Norembega in 1614 and determined to direct attention there. He coined the name New England to reinforce his point that English men and women would find a familiar setting there in contrast to the hot disease-ridden environment in Virginia, and he began to publicize the region and its rich fishing prospects. To those who hoped in vain for gold, he answered, "The sea is better than the richest mine known."

Smith argued now that the only way to make colonies succeed was to transfer control and incentives to the planters themselves. He was upset that the Puritans who colonized New England—first the Pilgrims at Plymouth in 1620 and then the colonists at Massachusetts Bay in 1630—did not see the need to hire him and instead just followed the advice in his books. But he was pleased to see the family-centered colonies growing up in New England. He died in 1631, just after Massachusetts Bay began, and he endorsed the Puritans' scheme in his last book, *Advertisements for the Unexperienced Planters of New England, or Any Where.* He advised the Massachusetts Bay company "not to stand too much upon the letting, setting, or selling those wild Countries, nor impose too much upon the commonalty . . . for present gain." The way to make the colony a success was to get the colonists committed to it by giving immigrants land for "him and his heirs for ever," and he warned that people would emigrate from England only if they knew they would be better off in the colonies, where, he predicted, "the very name of servitude will breed much ill blood, and become odious to God and man."

Although Smith did not realize it, nor did anyone else at the time, Virginia was moving in the same direction as New England by this time. Although the death rate remained high for newcomers, the colony had begun to settle into a pattern of strong immigration, widespread landowning, and local control by elite planters. The successful pattern had strong elements of similarity in both regions. Smith outlined the attraction of America: "here are not hard Landlords to rack us with high rents, or extorting fines, nor tedious pleas in Law to consume us with their many years' disputation for Justice . . . so freely hath God and his Majesty bestowed those blessings on them will attempt to obtain them, as here every man may be master of his own labor and land . . . and if he have nothing but his hands, he may set up his Trade, and by industry quickly grow rich." These riches were to come not from gold and pearls, as the Virginia Company had sought in vain, but from products raised by English men and women—tobacco in Virginia and fish in New England.

There was a further, and tragic, similarity in the Virginia and New England experiences. In both regions the access to land ownership that made immigration worthwhile for increasing numbers of English men and women created intolerable conditions for the natives. The transition to land ownership and large-scale growth was marked by a major Indian war in both New England and Virginia— the great Powhatan uprising of 1622 in Virginia was followed by ten years of devastating warfare, and the Pequot War in 1636 crippled the leading force in southern New England. Natives in both areas found their traditional ways of life made impossible by European-style farming and the animals—pigs, cows, horses, and chickens—that accompanied it. The great spur to success for the English spelled doom for the natives' way of life.

AN INTERPRETATION

As modern observers have analyzed the reports from Jamestown, diagnoses of the colonists' strange apathy in the early years have moved on several parallel tracks. The men were clearly malnourished. Most probably arrived with scurvy, vitamin C deficiency, from the long ocean voyage. On top of that, a diet consisting largely of corn would have produced pellagra, because corn lacks available niacin. Pellagra's symptoms become more pronounced in warm weather. This disease was common in the American South until supplements were added to cornmeal after World War II, so its symptoms are well known. Victims of these nutritional deficiency diseases look pale and thin, and they develop anorexia, unwillingness to eat. They also become apathetic, exhibiting the despair that so many observers in Jamestown described. As the scurvy and pellagra worsen, the sufferer develops leg cramps and pains in the joints and may have difficulty controlling arms and legs; thus victims may lie down and refuse to get up. Since the first stages of the disease are difficult to diagnose, the symptoms would have appeared to be simple laziness. Then, when the victims became worse, it was easy to conclude that they had brought the entire thing on themselves through their laziness.

Another hypothesis about the debilitation of the Jamestown settlers has to do with the slimy, brackish water they drank. Denying that famine was the principal cause of death, geographer Carville V. Earle has analyzed the flow of water in the James River and concluded that Jamestown was located just at the area where salt ocean water flowed into the fresh river water with each flood tide, creating a circling pool of mixed water when the flow of fresh water was low. Thus in the spring, when runoff and rainfall would make the river flow strong, the water was relatively clean, and the salt ocean water was swept back out to sea. As the summer wore on and the river became low, the salt water would pool up, and stagnant water became breeding grounds for germs. At that season the colonists drank dangerously contaminated water, the "brackish water" that Sir Thomas Gates indicted. The bloody flux and burning fevers that killed so many were probably infectious dysentery and typhoid fever, according to Earle, and the organisms that caused them would have come from the colonists' own wastes. The settlers also suffered from salt poisoning, whose symptoms are swelling, lassitude (the colonists' laziness), and irritability. Thus when Smith and later governors dispersed the settlers to live off the land at other points along the river, they were saving lives by placing settlers in healthier locations. The natives had evolved a way of life that took them away from the river during the summer, and the colonists needed to learn from them.

Both hypotheses—that Jamestown's residents were malnourished and that they were caught in a poisoned environment—certainly contribute part of the answer as to why the colonists appeared to fall into patterns of fatalistic helplessness and died at such an alarming rate. But neither can explain fully why colonists appeared to recover when strong governors forced them to work. There is a link in that some of the work was directed to building good, strong shelters and digging deep wells, as well as planting food. But the results were so dramatic and sudden— if we can trust Gates's account that people began to recover in two weeks—that something else appears to have been at work.

Descriptions of the "most strange condition" of the colonists seem to find an echo in a phenomenon seen in other situations where large numbers of men are crowded into a confined situation, especially a situation from which they see no possibility of rescue. Most recently, this condition, known to psychologists as "fatal withdrawal," was seen among Americans in prison camps during World War II and the Korean War. Such prison camps paralleled life in Jamestown in significant ways. In both settings, the men were confined to the fort, in one by the guards and in the other by fear of the Indians. Within the camp, both sets of men had little meaningful work to do, which was extremely damaging to morale. And both feared that they would never get out alive. In the Korean War, the enemy did not publish the names of prisoners, so prisoners feared they might not be released at war's end. No one knew that captives were still alive, and therefore no one at home could demand their return. And the Virginia Company had threatened more than once simply to abandon the colonists at Jamestown if they continued their unproductive ways. Most must have despaired of ever seeing friends and family again.

Medical doctors were among the prisoners in the twentieth-century examples, and they reported an amazing pattern. All the prisoners of war were malnourished and sick, but doctors and other prisoners agreed that the men who died of fatal withdrawal, or "give-up-itis" as the prisoners called it, were not fatally ill. "Instead what appeared to happen was that some men became so apathetic that they ceased to care about their bodily needs. They retreated further into themselves, refused to get any exercise, and eventually lay down as if waiting to die. The reports were emphatic concerning the lucidity and sanity of these men. They seemed willing to accept the prospect of death rather than to continue fighting a severely frustrating and depriving environment." Thus what may have begun as a nutritional deficiency disease progressed in some prisoners to fatal withdrawal.

There are some striking similarities between the Jamestown case and reports from the Korean War prison camps. Prisoners were said to have been too lethargic to accept guards' offers of a chance to go into nearby forests to collect firewood, and they sometimes refused to eat unfamiliar foods they were offered. Moreover, doctors from the prison camps indicated that "two things seemed to save the man close to 'apathy' death: getting him on his feet doing something, no matter how trivial, and getting him interested in some current or future problem." Like Captain John Smith, doctors in the prison camps learned to force such men to save themselves through activity.

Finally, and most unfairly, in both cases the official response was to blame the victim. Just as William Crashaw thundered that the experience of Jamestown showed the degeneration of the English nation into "milksops," so Army psychiatrists and others used reports from the Korean War prison camps to argue that America had gone soft and was not prepared to confront such focused and dedicated enemies as the Communist nations in the Cold War. Calling the phenomenon of fatal withdrawal "Something New in History," commentators demanded a program of national renewal and character building. Other social scientists pointed out that the phenomenon was not, in fact, new but had been seen in every war in America's history at least back to the Civil War. If this analysis of Jamestown's early years is correct, fatal withdrawal played a role even in America's founding.

Wealthy sponsors of colonies in England slowly came to realize that no system of rules could compel English men and women in America to work solely to enrich investors. The solution was to give incentives, in the form of land, to everyone who emigrated and to give investors land in proportion to their investment on which they could make money by using the estate well. Once this scheme was securely in place, the settlements began to explode over the land. By 1619 there were twenty-three plantations along the James River and two on the Eastern shore. By 1622 there were twenty-three more plantations and plans for others as far north as the Potomac River.

The big losers were the Indians, because their cultivation, gathering, and hunting required large tracts of open land, deliberately kept in various stages of development from meadow to woodland. But as English colonists, realizing the dream of a lifetime, began to establish permanent claims to one piece of land, the Indians' way of life became impossible. As planters took up lands along the rivers, natives were denied access to the traditional water highways. And European animals, allowed to roam free and disturb natives' clam banks and cornfields, completed what fixed cultivation began. In 1622 Powhatan's successor, his brother Opechancanough, planned a simultaneous attack on all the settlements at once. Although about a third of the settlers were killed in this attack, it was too late to stop the increasing flow of settlers from England. The irony is that allowing deprived English men and women to have security they could never have achieved at home robbed Indian men and women of the security on which they had built their lives.

Sources: Primary documents are in Philip L. Barbour, ed., *The Jamestown Voyages under the First Charter, 1606–1609*, 2 vols. (Cambridge, 1969); Susan Myra Kingsbury, ed., *Records of the Virginia Company of London*, 4 vols. (Washington, D.C., 1906–1935); and Karen Ordahl Kupperman, ed., *Captain John Smith: A Select Edition of His Writings* (Chapel Hill, 1988). Histories of early Jamestown are in Edmund S. Morgan, *American Slavery, American Freedom: The Ordeal of Colonial Virginia* (New York, 1975), and Alden Vaughan, *American Genesis: Captain John Smith and the Founding of Virginia* (Boston,

1975). On causes of death, see Carville V. Earle, "Environment, Disease, and Mortality in Early Virginia," in Thad W. Tate and David L. Ammerman, eds., *The Chesapeake in the Seventeenth Century* (Chapel Hill, 1979), pp. 96–125, and Karen Ordahl Kupperman, "Apathy and Death in Early Jamestown," *Journal of American History,* vol. LXVI (1979), pp. 24–40. On Chesapeake Algonquian life, see Helen C. Rountree, *The Powhatan Indians of Virginia: Their Traditional Culture* (Norman, 1989), and *Pocahontas's People: The Powhatan Indians of Virginia through Four Centuries* (Norman, 1990).

2

KATERI TEKAKWITHA: IROQUOIS SAINT

NANCY SHOEMAKER

Kateri Tekakwitha was born about 1656 and grew up in a Mohawk village near present-day Albany, New York. Converted to Catholicism as a young adult, she moved to the Jesuit mission town of Kahnakwe just south of present-day Montreal. Although little is known about the details of her life (just as we know little about the lives of most other seventeenth-century Native Americans), her story reveals the complicated social and cultural issues raised by European conquest. More than a simple story of victimization and defeat, the encounter between Native Americans and Europeans reveals shrewd choices made by Native Americans in their unequal interaction with the conquerors.

On the larger level of economic, diplomatic, and military affairs, the five nations of the Iroquois exerted extraordinary power in the transatlantic power struggle between European nation-states. With their home territory of northern and central New York occupying a key position between the Dutch, the French, and the English, they were in a position to bargain with all these powers not only for trade goods but also for territorial respect. The Iroquois were essential to the Europeans' desire to profit from the fur trade and to control the still unexplored territories to the north and west. The Iroquois League was able to effectively exploit the competition between European powers to preserve their own political and territorial integrity—at least until the middle of the eighteenth century. For over a century, the Iroquois conducted shrewd diplomacy aimed at "playing off" Europeans against each other.

But this integration into the European world system, no matter how successfully negotiated at a diplomatic level, did not prevent European cultural influences from penetrating Iroquois society. By the time Kateri was born in 1656, the Iroquois tribes had been dealing with European traders for almost a century and with Catholic missionaries for a third of a century. The traders and missionaries inevitably had a very personal impact; they came to live and to proselytize in Indian villages. Although the Dutch and English were focused almost exclusively on trade, French traders were accompanied by Jesuit missionaries; all competed for influence and loyalty among the Indians. Indeed, tribes and villages became factionalized by divided loyalties, some favoring the Protestant Dutch and English and others the French, while still others rejected alliances with any Europeans. What is apparent is that

Indians did not yet conceive of themselves, as the Europeans did, as a single group that would need to unify politically if they were to survive the conquest. That would come later in the eighteenth century and early nineteenth century with the leadership of Pontiac and Tecumseh.

When Kateri was a young woman facing difficult relationships with her family and her village, the Jesuit missionaries did not seem like oppressors of Indians and Indian culture but instead offered a choice to Kateri, a choice which seemed to promise a more satisfying and fulfilling life than that available to her within Mohawk culture. As Nancy Shoemaker's story reveals, Kateri did not conceive of this as an abandonment of her Mohawk origins but rather saw the choice as the adoption of practices and beliefs which would enable her to reach the sources of power and strength inherent in her own culture.

At Kahnawake Reserve near the city of Montreal, Canada, lie the remains of Kateri Tekakwitha, a seventeenth-century Mohawk woman converted to Christianity by French Jesuits. After her death in 1680, her tomb became a popular site for pilgrims seeking cures and other divine interventions. The Roman Catholic Church declared Kateri Tekakwitha "venerable" in 1943 and "blessed" in 1980. It is very likely that she will eventually be canonized and thereby recognized as a full-fledged saint. Today, visitors come to Kahnawake to pray at Kateri's shrine, shop for relics in the gift store, and learn her story.

Much of that story comes to us from two priests who knew her when she lived at Kahnawake and who later wrote hagiographies of her life. Hagiographies are biographies of saints and serve to promote an individual's candidacy as a holy person. In their testimonials to Kateri's many virtues, the two Jesuits, Claude Chauchetière and Pierre Cholenec, described in great detail her dedication to virginity, her self-flagellations and other ascetic practices, and her desire to recede from the world and become a nun. They presented her as a devout Christian inspired by God and Jesus Christ to holy extremes. Jesuit accounts, however, also provide historians with ethnographic information on seventeenth-century Iroquois religious beliefs and cultural practices, which suggest that there could be multiple interpretations of Kateri's actions and motivations.

According to Chauchetière and Cholenec, Kateri Tekakwitha was born in 1656 in the Mohawk village of Gandaouage, near what is now Albany, New York. The Mohawks were the easternmost of the five nations making up the Iroquois Confederacy. In the early 1700s, the Tuscaroras joined the Mohawks, Oneidas, Onondagas, Cayugas, and Senecas, adding a sixth nation to the confederacy. The Iroquois Confederacy was an alliance of Iroquois peoples which formed sometime before 1600, perhaps shortly before or after 1492, when Christopher Columbus, sailing for Spain, landed in the Caribbean and initiated further European exploration of this "New World."

Beginning early in the sixteenth century, more than a hundred years before Kateri's birth, a series of French trading companies hired Verrazano, then Jacques Cartier, and finally Samuel de Champlain to sail to North America. Foremost it was hoped that they would find a water route to India, but they were also to collect information on exploitable resources: gold and other minerals, fish, and furs. In 1608,

Champlain established a permanent French settlement at Québec on the St. Lawrence River, and from that point on the colony of New France grew slowly, extending small settlements of French traders, farmers, soldiers, laborers, priests, and nuns along the St. Lawrence. When the "gold" sent from New France to Europe turned out to be "fool's gold," or pyrite, French traders began to concentrate on beaver fur as their most profitable commodity. Hats made from the felted fur of plush Canadian beavers reaped enormous profits for French trading companies and hat manufacturers.

To enhance the fur trade and establish peaceful relations with the native people in the St. Lawrence region—the Montagnais, Algonquin, and Huron nations—Champlain and the French settlers who came after him became entangled in their wars against the Iroquois. The Iroquois inhabited a vast region south of the St. Lawrence River and had developed close trading ties to the Dutch at Fort Orange, now Albany, New York. The Dutch colony, New Netherland, had a history similar to that of New France. Henry Hudson, sponsored by a Dutch trading company, explored the Hudson River in 1609. Then the company established colonies at Fort Orange, on Manhattan Island, and on Long Island. However, few Dutch people saw emigration as a profitable opportunity, and New Netherland remained a small economic backwater, increasingly threatened by the rapid ex-

A 1722 copy of Claude Chauchetière's 1681 painting of Kateri Tekakwitha.
(CATHERINE TEKAWITHA by Daniel Sargent, Longman, Green and Co.)

pansion of the New England colonies, whose beginnings dated to the 1620 founding of Plymouth Colony by a group of Puritan separatists. By 1664, the English colonies far surpassed New Netherland in population and territory, paving the way for the English to conquer the Dutch, quietly, bloodlessly, and with their permission. New Netherland became New York, and the English inherited the Dutch trading connections with the Iroquois.

The French, Dutch, and English all found themselves enmeshed in old wars waged between the Iroquois and the Hurons, Montagnais, and Algonquins, but Europeans also exacerbated the wars between Indian nations by raising the stakes of native warfare. European guns, ammunition, and cloth quickly became necessities in native economies, making Indian nations competitors for the European trade in furs, just as European nations competed with each other for access to the prime fur-bearing regions and for powerful Indian allies in trade and war.

For most of Kateri Tekakwitha's life, the French and Iroquois were at war, and yet this Iroquois woman became the most notable Christian convert of New France. Religion, politics, and economics interacted in complex ways to direct French and Indian relations in Canada. More so than the Dutch or English, the French considered Christian conversion of the native people an essential component of colonization. France had just recently thwarted the Protestant challenge to Catholicism that had swept through Europe, and a resurgence of Catholic fervor known as the Counter-Reformation led to financial and political empowerment for new religious orders such as the Jesuits. Of the several religious orders in New France, the Jesuits were the most active at establishing missions near native communities. The Jesuits first arrived in Québec in 1632 and founded missions among the Montagnais, Algonquins, and Hurons. They were less successful in their several attempts to plant missions among the Iroquois. Still, the French coveted the Iroquois as potential allies in war, partners in the beaver fur trade, and Christian converts.

Kateri was born during a rare moment of peace between the Iroquois and French; more commonly, enmity prevailed. Her own heritage was in part a consequence of wars between the Iroquois and French-allied Indians. She was born into the village of her Mohawk father, but her mother was an Algonquin from Trois Rivières, the site of a Jesuit mission. Kateri's mother had been captured in war and adopted by the Iroquois. It was the custom of all Indian nations in the northeast to adopt war captives, especially women and children, in the place of relatives who had died. As war became more frequent in the 1600s and 1700s, the composition of Iroquois villages came to reflect the loss of native-born Iroquois men in warfare and a rise in the number of adopted Iroquois. These adopted Iroquois shared in the privileges and obligations of Iroquois family life but still may have been perceived of as outsiders. Despite her Mohawk father, people in Kateri's village called her "the Algonquin," suggesting that the Iroquois custom of organizing family descent matrilineally (through the line of the mother) continued to be a powerful influence on one's identity even in the case of adoption.

European settlement of North America shaped Kateri's early life in other ways. When she was four years old, both her parents and a younger brother died from smallpox. Europeans unknowingly brought a host of deadly diseases with them to the Americas. Smallpox was the most devastating, but even diseases like measles and diphtheria, which were children's diseases in Europe, struck native communities with fatal virulence. Lacking immunity to these new diseases, Native Americans succumbed at an alarming rate. Kateri survived the smallpox, but for the rest of her life she bore the pocks, or scars, of the disease and suffered from damage done to her eyes, which could not bear bright light.

Otherwise, Kateri's childhood was much like that of any other Iroquois girl. She worked in the cornfields with the women and children. She helped collect firewood and brought it back to the village. Because of her weak eyes, she sometimes stayed at the longhouse, where she ground corn to make soup and bread, mixed ashes with corn to make a corn mush called *sagamité,* and helped serve food to the rest of the people in her longhouse family. She also learned how to make ribbons from eelskin or tree bark and dye them red with the glue from sturgeons. She was skilled at making baskets, boxes, and buckets for storing food and water and at weaving tree bark into mats.

When she reached puberty, she may have gone on a vision quest, off by herself into the woods, where she would have fasted and waited for a vision from a guardian spirit. If she received a vision, she may have also found a token, perhaps a pebble, feather, or piece of animal bone, connecting her to her guardian spirit and to that larger spiritual power *orenda.* Access to *orenda* through one's own guardian spirit or by soliciting the assistance of a shaman helped the Iroquois learn the location of war parties, determine the future, discern the wisest action, find lost things, and heal people.

Kateri also would have participated in the public, ceremonial life of her village. She would have gorged herself at eat-all feasts, watched and gambled on the ball games against other villages, and witnessed many instances of dream interpretation. Perhaps she herself appealed to shamans to interpret her dreams. The Iroquois believed that during a dream, one's soul left earth and visited "the sky world," the place from which people originated. If someone in the village had a dream, it was considered a message from the sky world, and it was imperative that the dream be acted out. If someone dreamed of a great feast at which a white dog was eaten, shamans interpreting the dream would probably suggest that the village gather for such a white-dog feast. One Iroquois man whom the Jesuits sought as a convert cherished ten knives given to him by others in the village to satisfy his dream, and these ten ordinary knives thus came to be endowed with spiritual power.

Kateri may also have been in attendance at the Condolence Ceremony that elevated her uncle to chiefly office. Very likely it was Kateri's grandmother or great-grandmother who, as clan mother, decided that Kateri's uncle had the ability to represent their clan in council. The Iroquois Confederacy was composed of fifty such chiefly offices, representing the different clans from the five Iroquois nations. Within each Iroquois nation, chiefs for each clan also met in council. When a chief's position became vacant either because of death or because of the "de-horning" of an incompetent chief, a Condolence Ceremony was held. Chiefs' names were passed on within clans, and with the Condolence Ceremony Iroquois communities publicly mourned the death of a chief while bestowing his name on someone else. The new chief was "requickened" as the deceased person: he assumed the name and the responsibilities of that office and was expected to live up to the moral character implicit in that name or title. Other Iroquois could be honored with a new identity and go through are quickening ceremony, but it was an especially important ritual within the Condolence Ceremony, for it legitimated the transmittal of chiefly authority from one person to another.

And finally, despite Chauchetière's and Cholenec's denials that Kateri was ever present during the ritual torture of war captives, she probably was there, for such tortures were important events for the entire village. Like other northeastern Indians, the Iroquois had elaborate rituals surrounding the treatment of war captives. Relatives of recently deceased Iroquois chose to adopt war captives or torture them to death, but in either case they saw this as a way to mourn dead relatives and relieve themselves of their loss. Torturing war captives by burning their skin with hot irons, hot coals, and boiling water or by cutting off fingers or pieces of skin might seem inordinately cruel, but all northeastern Indians understood these rituals. When captured, they knew they had to withstand the tortures and not succumb to cowardly whimpering or crying. Instead, they sang songs to broadcast their bravery. Especially brave captives who died singing were honored by having their flesh eaten, for it was thought that that bravery could be passed on to others.

Several Jesuits captured by the Iroquois were tortured, and those who were killed came to be honored in the Catholic Church as martyrs. The Iroquois twice tortured Isaac Joques. First captured while serving at a mission among the Hurons, he was taken to an Iroquois village, where his captors tore out his fingernails, cut off fingers, and burned him. He, however, lived and several years later accepted a mission among the Mohawks, only to be tortured again, this time to death and in the village of Kateri's birth, Gandaouague. Jesuits came to work in the mission field with a mixture of fear and desire. They feared torture and death but also eagerly looked forward to making such a supreme sacrifice.

Although Kateri's mother had learned of Christianity at Trois Rivières, Kateri herself had little firsthand knowledge of Christians or the French until she was about ten or eleven years old, when three Jesuits, or Black Robes as the Indians called them, visited her village while on a general tour through Iroquois country to propose the establishment of permanent missions. A peace treaty had just been signed between the Iroquois and the French, and the Jesuits were taking advantage of this interlude to make another attempt to bring Christianity to the Iroquois. The Mohawks were cordial to the three missionaries because they were anxious for peace with the French, but they did not trust them.

Most Iroquois despised the Black Robes simply because they were French, but Black Robes were also thought of as dangerous shamans. They possessed mysterious ritual paraphernalia: books, crosses, reliquaries, and chiming clocks. They had their own songs and incantations, and they practiced odd ceremonies. To bring rain, they marched in procession to paintings of the Virgin Mary and Jesus Christ. They tried to heal people by placing crosses on sick stomachs, or they drew blood from the sick person's body. And they refused to marry or engage in any sexual relations. Many Iroquois thought the Black Robes used their power, or *orenda,* for evil purposes. Others questioned whether they had any special access to *orenda* at all. If one appealed to the Black Robes for help in healing or interpreting dreams, they often proved to be ineffective conjurors. The ceremony of "baptism," which the Jesuits delivered most often to people on the verge of death (to ensure them a place in heaven), confirmed Iroquois suspicions that baptism was either a useless curing ceremony or a supernatural means to do harm to those already weakened by disease.

The Jesuits promoted the Indian conception of them as shamans by deliberately competing with Indian shamans for the hearts, minds, and souls of native people. The Jesuits used astronomical knowledge to predict eclipses, they railed against shamans' interpretation of dreams but readily explained the meaning of visions, they sprinkled holy water on cornfields to rid them of ravenous insects and worms, and they fulfilled the primary function of shamans by attempting to heal people who were sick. They challenged native practitioners to show that their gods, prayers, and healing rituals worked better than the Christian equivalents, and they boasted of the power of Christian prayers to change life on earth.

The Jesuits also appeared to be like shamans because Jesuit preachings made few references to the intricacies of Christian theology. The Jesuit philosophy of missionization was to use native languages and cultures as a base for introducing the ideas of Christianity. They relied greatly on painted pictures of hell, the holy family, and incidents in the lives of saints to demonstrate the consequences of leading or straying from a Christian life. The Jesuits also translated prayers, Bible stories, and the lives of the saints into Iroquoian and Algonquin languages, but to do so they had to modify Christian concepts that were beyond translation to fit beliefs and customs that already existed within native communities. Thus, the pains of hell became something akin to but worse than being captured and tortured by one's enemies. Rosaries, strings of beads used for Catholic prayers, resembled belts of wampum, white and purple shell beads which were valued as wealth among northeastern Indians but also had a larger significance when transmitted between parties making political and diplomatic agreements.

In many instances, the Jesuits had to compromise the meaning of their rituals, which meant that the Christianity presented to the Indians was not the same Christianity as practiced in Europe. For instance, the Eucharist, one of the most important rituals within the Catholic tradition, celebrated the sacrifice Jesus made for others. Its main ritual features, sipping red wine and eating bread, were metaphors for drinking the blood and eating the flesh of Jesus. Wary of appearing to sanction cannibalism, the Jesuits told mission Indians that the Eucharist was simply a feast.

When the three Jesuit emissaries came to Mohawk country in the 1660s, they brought with them several decades of experience, built-up assumptions, and techniques for missionizing Native Americans. While at Gandaouage, they stayed in the longhouse of Kateri's lineage because her uncle, as chief, was responsible for hosting them. Kateri therefore probably had some contact with them, but the greater influence on her was the product of their labor, Father Jacques de Lamberville. Lamberville was later assigned to take charge of the mission station near her village. He was the first to instruct Kateri fully in "the mysteries of Christianity." Accounts of her baptism vary. Some say he baptized her when assured of her faith. Others say that she was first baptized because she was sick and seemed on the verge of death. In any case, he baptized her as Katharine, "a name already consecrated by the purity of many holy virgins." Kateri, which the Mohawks pronounce "gadeli," is a Latin variation of Katharine. With baptism, "The spirit of Saint Katharine of Sienna and of other saints of this name, was revived in her."

Saint Catherine of Siena, as her name is commonly spelled today, was a fourteenth-century Italian saint renowned for her extreme self-mortifications, fasting, virginity, and visions. Resisting her parents' intentions to force her into marriage, Saint Catherine of Siena had a vision in which she took Jesus Christ as her spouse, and miraculously a wedding band, visible only to her, appeared on her finger. Recognized as a saint while still living, she went on to advise popes and kings, and upon her death, pilgrims to her tomb sought her intercession with God. In their preachings to the Indians, the Jesuits would have often referred to Saint Catherine of Siena as a model of how to lead a Christian life worthy of imitation.

After her baptism, Kateri recovered from her illness with a new identity, name, and Christian association. Now that she was identified as a Christian, her life in the village became progressively more intolerable. Despite the presence of Jesuit missions among the Iroquois, peace with the French was crumbling, and rising social tensions within Iroquois villages made living there increasingly chaotic and dangerous. The Mohawks detested the Christian converts among them. As Kateri walked through the village, children threw stones at her and said Christians were no better than dogs. Moreover, alcohol acquired in the fur trade heightened violence in Iroquois villages, and Christian Indians and Black Robes were fair game for passions let loose by excessive drinking.

Equally burdensome was Kateri's deteriorating relationship with her family. Her uncle opposed Christianity, and her relatives resented her insistence on maintaining the Sabbath as a day of rest and prayer. And, as Kateri was now about eighteen or nineteen and of marriageable age, her relatives began to urge that she marry. All Iroquois women and men were expected to marry, for the economy of the longhouse depended on a gendered division of labor. Men contributed furs and meat from the hunt and items of European manufacture acquired in the fur trade: guns, ammunition, beads, cloth, and whiskey. Women produced most of the food by growing corn, beans, and squash. Kateri resisted the expectations of her aunts and uncle. When her relatives arranged a marriage, she ran away and hid in the fields to avoid it. Finally, Kateri stole away one day, with some relatives visiting from Kahnawake.

Kahnawake was a community of Christian Indians far to the north, situated opposite the French settlement at Montreal and near the Jesuit Mission of St. Francis Xavier at the Sault. Kahnawake had been founded about fifteen years before by Gandeacteua, a Christian woman of the Erie Nation, and Tonsahoten, her Huron husband. Their relatives soon joined them, and the community grew in population while developing closer ties to the Mission of the Sault. Although the Indian residents of Kahnawake came to see themselves as Christian, their understanding of Christian ritual also reflected continuity with their traditional beliefs. When Gandeacteua fell ill and death seemed imminent, her husband made a speech which greatly pleased the Jesuits, for he seemed to be rejecting paganism. Tonsahoten announced that he "wished to make a feast at which he dispensed with the customs of the infidels. He said, 'Formerly we had feasts in order to cure the sick and in order to follow the customs of our ancestors, but now that we are Christians, we invoke the names of Jesus and Mary and we ask of them the cure of our sickness. That is why I pray you to intercede for my sick wife and to say the rosary for her.' " Both the Iroquois and Jesuits believed there was a power to heal that was accessible to people on earth. Christianity provided Tonsahoten with new ways to access that power. When Gandeacteua died after "eight days of delirium" and many appeals to Jesus and Mary, Tonsahoten may have questioned the efficacy of Christian prayer, but in their accounts the Jesuits refrained from dwelling on their failures and more often reported their successes.

Both Gandeacteua and Tonsahoten had been captured in war and adopted by the Iroquois. Most of the Indian residents who later settled at Kahnawake shared with Gandeacteua and Tonsahoten a dual or marginalized identity as war captives adopted by the Iroquois. Their choice to become Christian removed them further

Chauchetière's drawing of the first chapel built at the Jesuit Mission of the Sault, near the Indian village of Kahnawake. (Drawings by Reverend Claude Chauchetiere, S.J., Archives Department, CAUGHNAWAGA INDIANS by Henri Béchard, S.J., International Publishers' Representatives, (Canada) Ltd. Montreal, 1976)

from their attachment to any of the five Iroquois Nations to the south, and indeed, whenever war erupted between the French and Iroquois, Kahnawake and other Indian "praying towns" in New France usually fought for the French against their former relatives. Huron survivors of the Huron-Iroquois wars had settled at Kahnawake, as had many Christian Mohawks seeking refuge from the rising violence in their own villages, much of which was alcohol-related. The community of Indians at Kahnawake made a pledge against alcohol along with endorsing Christianity.

Despite Kahnawake's identity as a Christian town, the Indians who lived there were politically, economically, and socially much like other Iroquois. They continued to live in longhouses containing several families descended from one elderly woman. In 1677, at about the time of Kateri's arrival there, Cholenec said that the Indian village consisted of twenty-two longhouses. Five years later, his coworker at the Mission of the Sault, Chauchetière, described it as growing rapidly and now consisting of about sixty longhouses, each inhabited by at least two families (by which he meant two nuclear families or subfamilies, descended from one senior woman). The women grew corn, and the men, accompanied by some women, went on annual winter hunts. When she arrived at Kahnawake, Kateri moved into a longhouse headed by a woman named Anastasia. She went on the annual winter hunt her first year there but later chose not to. As at Gandaouage, she spent most of her days working either in the cornfields or in the longhouse.

Life was so much the same as in other Iroquois villages that Kateri soon found herself in the same predicament with her new longhouse family. Anastasia began pressuring Kateri to marry until Kateri begged Father Cholenec to intervene in her favor. As Kateri told him, "she could have no other spouse but Jesus Christ." The Jesuits considered marriage one of the seven sacraments and devoted much of their preachings to trying to convince missionized Indians to avoid divorce and stay in one marriage for a lifetime. However, the Jesuits also greatly admired chastity, and Cholenec began to take her side in the family dispute.

It is not clear why Kateri rejected the traditional expectations for Iroquois women and refused to marry. She was reputed to be shy, always hiding her scarred face and damaged eyes under a blanket. Some acquaintances remarked of her after she died "that God had taken her because men did not want her." Or, she may have claimed Jesus Christ as her spouse in deliberate imitation of Saint Catherine of Siena. If Saint Catherine were her model, it would also partly explain why Kateri devoted her few remaining years at Kahnawake to a brutal regimen of self-denial and self-torture based on the ascetic practices of holy people in the Christian tradition.

Shortly after her arrival at Kahnawake, she and two other women, Marie Therèse Tegaiaguenta and Marie Therèse Skarichions, formed a close friendship in which they encouraged each other to maintain vows of chastity and engage in acts of penance. They originally met in the mission chapel and then continued to meet and sit for hours under the big cross near the chapel, where they discussed how best to lead a Christian life. Marie Therèse Skarichions was from Lorette, which was, like Kahnawake, a community of missionized Indians but located near Québec. While living at Lorette, she had fallen ill and was received in the Hospital at Québec operated by the Sisters de la Hospitalière, an order of French nuns who also had a hospital in Montreal. While there, Marie Therèse Skarichions had learned about how the French nuns lived, and it was she who proposed to Kateri and Marie Thérèse Tegaiaguenta that they adopt the same practices and live together, dress identically, and never marry. The three women determined to leave Kahnawake for nearby Heron Island, where they planned to set up a kind of convent for themselves.

The Jesuits talked them out of such ambitious plans by arguing that Heron Island was too far from Kahnawake and too much in the path of trading traffic heading to and from Montreal. However, the Jesuits may have had another reason for discouraging the nunnery. In theory, they supported the idea of Christian associations and had early in the mission's history established an organization of their own called the Confraternity of the Holy Family, which was intended to bind the most devout converts together. But the Jesuits seem to have been reluctant to sanction any Christian associations that were of Indian invention, perhaps because these organizations risked falling outside the net of Jesuit authority in matters of faith.

Kateri had been a member of the Confraternity of the Holy Family since her arrival at Kahnawake, and she regularly attended mass and other Jesuit-directed ceremonies celebrating Christianity. However, she also pursued a Christian life by following her own initiative. She and her friends conspired to assist each other in secret self-mortifications. Kateri and Marie Thérèse Tegaiaguenta met in the cemetery or sometimes in the woods, where they performed acts of penance. They whipped each other with rods until they drew blood. They put burning embers between their toes, and they used hot irons to burn their legs from their feet to their knees, much in the way Iroquois war captives were tortured. They walked barefoot in snow and ice. They went for long periods of time without food.

Kateri also engaged in penance when alone in the longhouse. She mortified her flesh in new ways after hearing the Jesuits recount the life of a particular saint, and for three days she slept on a bed of thorns, since Saint Louis de Gonzague had done so. She and others acquired instruments of penance from the Jesuits, such as an iron girdle with spikes, which Kateri wore to work in the cornfields. These penances became too much for Kateri's fragile body to withstand, and she became ill. As a lengthy fever brought her closer to death, Fathers Cholenec and Chauchetière came to her cabin to deliver the last rites, a special privilege granted her in recognition of her devoutness. (Other sick "savages" were brought to the chapel on wooden stretchers.) She died in April 1680 at age twenty-four.

Kateri's story does not end with her death, for thenceforth her life as a saint began. Shortly after her death, the Jesuits who knew her began to fashion her into a saint. This involved exaggerating Kateri's holiness to celebrate her as a role model for others. In their successive renditions of Kateri's life and in their histories of the mission enterprise at Kahnawake, they increasingly tried to highlight Kateri's self-mortifications as extreme and therefore unusually holy. In actuality, Kateri was just one of many Indians at Kahnawake to embrace the Christian idea of penance as a source of divine power.

In an early account of this penitential fervor, written while it was still occurring, Chauchetière did not make special note of Kateri and instead suggested that penance had become a community-wide activity.

The use of these [instruments of penance] Daily becomes more general. And, as The men have found that the women use them, they will not Let themselves be outdone, and ask us to permit them to use these every Day; but we will not allow it. The women, to the number of 8 or 10, Began The practice; and The wife of the dogique—that is to say, of him who Leads the Singing and says The prayers—is among the number. She it is who, in her husband's absence, also causes The prayers to be said aloud, and Leads The Singing; and in this capacity she assembles the devout women of whom we have spoken, who call themselves sisters. They tell One another their faults, and deliberate together upon what must be done for The relief of the poor in the Village—whose number is so great that there are almost as many poor as there are Savages [the French word for "Indian" was *sauvage*]. The sort of monastery that they maintain here has its rules. They have promised God never to put on their gala-dress. . . . They assist One another in the fields; They meet together to incite one another to virtue; and one of them has been received as a nun in The hospital of mon[t]real.

In his narrative history of Kahnawake written several years after Kateri's death, Chauchetière blamed the penitential outbreak at Kahnawake on the devil while maintaining that Kateri's excesses had been inspired by God:

The demon, who saw the glorious success of this mission, used another kind of battery. Transfiguring himself as an angel of light, he urged on the devotion of some persons who wished to imitate Catherine, or to do severe penances for their sins. . . . There were Savage women who threw themselves under the ice, in the midst of winter. One had her daughter dipped into it, who was only six years old,—for the purpose, she said, of teaching her penance in good season. The mother stood there on account of her past sins; she kept her innocent daughter there on account of her sins to come, which this child would perhaps commit when grown up. Savages, both men and women, covered themselves with blood by disciplinary stripes with iron, with rods, with thorns, with nettles; they fasted rigorously, passing the entire day without eating,—and what the savages eat during half the year is not sufficient to keep a man alive. These fasting women toiled strenuously all day—in summer, working in the fields; in winter, cutting wood. These austerities were almost continual. They mingled ashes in their portion of Sagamité; they put glowing coals between their toes, where the fire burned a hole in the flesh; they went bare-legged to make a long procession in the snows; they all disfigured themselves by cutting off their hair, in order not to be sought in marriage.

The presence of a saint at Kahnawake would have sanctioned the missionary venture to the Jesuits' financial and political backers in Europe, but the Jesuits also knew that saints were rare and that only one, or at most two, of the Indians at Kahnawake could be put forth as remarkably holy. Kateri became that one.

The penitential fervor that erupted at Kahnawake in the period before and after her death was not entirely a Jesuit fabrication. Clearly, the Indians at Kahnawake, particularly the women, took the initiative in incorporating penance in their daily lives, and from the Jesuit perspective, they carried it to extremes. Penitential practices began at Kahnawake before Kateri's arrival. Anastasia, "the most fervent Christian in the place" according to one Jesuit account, seems to have been the woman most responsible for borrowing the idea of penance from the Christian tradition. As the matrilineal head of the longhouse in which Kateri lived, she was naturally a leading figure in the village and a great influence on other women. Anastasia had instructed Kateri in Christianity by teaching her prayers, recounting the stories of the Virgin Mary and the lives of the saints, and introducing her and other women to the empowering potential of self-mortification.

The Jesuits saw penance as punishment for one's sins. Because "sin" was one of those Jesuit concepts that had no Iroquois parallel, penance probably came to mean something else. The Iroquois word for "penance" was *hotouongannandi*, which the historian David Blanchard has translated to mean "They are making magic." The

The women at Kahnawake formed a holy society. Here, Chauchetière shows one of the women cutting her hair, "in order not to be sought in marriage." (Drawings by Reverend Claude Chauchetiere, S.J., Archives Department, Gironde, France. From THE ORIGINAL CAUGHNAWAGA INDIANS by Henri Béchard, S.J., International Publishers' Representatives (Canada) Ltd. Montreal, 1976.)

Indians at Kahnawake who tortured themselves with spiked iron girdles and burning embers no doubt saw penance as an avenue to *orenda*. The growing popularity of penitential practices at Kahnawake coincided with the occurrence of a minor smallpox outbreak in 1678, which might have meant the practitioners were "making magic" to prevent the spread of smallpox. In this instance, *hotouongannandi* seems to have worked, for this occurrence of smallpox never reached epidemic proportions.

Recognition of Tekakwitha as a saint came only after her death, and thus in her lifetime she never became an adviser to kings and popes as Saint Catherine of Siena had. But with death, her power as an intercessor with God began. In the longhouse where she had died, Father Cholenec, her father confessor, delivered the eulogy, which "caused everyone to regard her body as a precious relic" and to keep "as relics whatever belonged to her." A Frenchman, convinced of her holiness, offered to build a coffin for her remains. Immediately, her reputation for sanctity spread, and her virtues were remembered. Visitors to her tomb attested to the miracles of healing she performed in response to their prayers. Chauchetière was himself the receiver of a miracle, for while in the mission church at Kahnawake he had a vision of Tekakwitha warning him of disaster. He and the other priests quickly left, just as lightning struck the chapel and burned it to the ground.

Chauchetière and Cholenec launched the campaign for her recognition as a holy person within the Catholic Church, but since then others have assumed the burden of promotion. Catholics in the province of Québec and Indian Catholics, many from the western United States, see Kateri Tekakwitha as an important figure in the history of Catholicism in North America. She has also become a model of virtue held up for imitation by Catholic schoolgirls, and so the story of Kateri Tekakwitha's life has become for others what Saint Catherine of Siena's life story was for her.

AN INTERPRETATION

European exploration and settlement of the Americas dramatically changed the lives of Native Americans. These changes often involved choices. Would the French or English make better allies? Who had the most and best trade goods in exchange for the fewest number of beaver pelts? Did Black Robes have a spiritual knowledge that could improve life on earth? As Indians made such determinations, they bound themselves closer to Europeans economically and culturally. They incorporated European technology into their daily lives and gradually became dependent on Europeans for trade goods. Decimated by new diseases, they also lost population to escalating warfare. Alcohol was another kind of plague, disrupting village life with outbreaks of violence. As European contact transformed the material basis of everyday life, Indians may have sought new spiritual answers as well. And yet, it would be a mistake to assume that any of these changes, material or spiritual, entailed a rejection of Indian cultural traditions.

Certainly, the Jesuit missionaries saw Christianity and Indian religions as diametrically opposed. Those who were not Christian were heathen. However, the Jesuits inadvertently provided evidence of similarities between Iroquois and Christian beliefs. To advertise the success of their endeavors, they claimed many traditional Iroquois practices as being signs of Christian devotion. The staple Iroquois food, *sagamité,* was prepared by mixing ashes with corn, but when the Jesuits constructed an image of Kateri as a holy person, the recipe for *sagamité* became an act of self-sacrifice.

Other Christian rituals conformed in meaning with traditional Iroquois practices, making it possible for the Iroquois to adopt the forms of Christianity without radically altering their worldview. The Holy Family, represented by the powerful Virgin Mary and her son Jesus Christ, was much more like the matrilineal Iroquois family than the patriarchal family that structured seventeenth-century

One of the earliest miracles attributed to Tekakwitha after her death was her appearing in a vision to warn the Jesuits of an imminent strike of lightning on the chapel. Chauchetière later recorded the event in this drawing. (Drawings by Reverend Claude Chauchetiere, S.J., Archives Department, Gironde, France. From THE ORIGINAL CAUGHNAWAGA INDIANS by Henri Béchard, S.J., International Publishers' Representatives (Canada) Ltd. Montreal, 1976.)

French society. What the Jesuits saw as Kateri's baptism in the name of Saint Catherine of Siena may have seemed more like a requickening ceremony to the Iroquois. The actual forms of the two rituals differed, but the ultimate objective was the same: with the new name, baptized and requickened individuals gained a new role and status for themselves within the community.

Penance and lifelong chastity were Christian practices that had no exact parallel in Iroquois traditions. Yet asceticism, or the self-denial of physical pleasure, was a source of spiritual empowerment for the Iroquois. It was essential to the vision quest marking an adolescent's transition to adulthood. Moreover, penance had clear parallels to the Iroquois torture of war captives, and the ability to withstand pain was viewed as an inner strength, perhaps even a preventative to torture at the hands of one's enemies or to the pain and death caused by disease. The existence of new diseases in the lives of the Iroquois may have called for new rituals. The Jesuits offered these rituals to Christian converts.

At the most basic level, seventeenth-century Catholic and Iroquois religious beliefs were alike. People could control life on earth by appealing to supernatural forces. Within both cultures, individuals had a variety of means by which to gain access to divine power, or *orenda*. The Iroquois could appeal to guardian spirits, while Catholics prayed to saints and guardian angels. In both religions, a material object served as an intermediary. The Iroquois had tokens connecting them to their guardian spirits. Catholics prayed at the tombs of saints or to other "relics"—saints' bones, pieces of clothing, or hair, anything that had once been part of the saint or been touched by the saint. Catholic stories and ritual were thus added to existing native belief systems.

But were missionized Indians incorporating other aspects of European culture as well? For the Jesuits, being Christian meant more than just believing in Jesus Christ as the Son of God. Christianity was a larger package of beliefs and customs relating to gender roles, family life, social structure, and political order. As part of their mission, Jesuits tried to make Indian gender roles and family life conform to the European model. They expected men to be the leaders of their families and communities and gave men important positions within Christian ceremony by designating them native catechists ("dogiques"). The Jesuits also worried endlessly about the chastity of native women, marriage as a holy sacrament, and the frequency of divorce. In part they saw marriage as a means whereby women became subordinate to male authority. They preached women's subordination but also had traditions that gave women access to authority and status. Holy women, nuns and saints, could be healers, teachers, spiritual advisers, and intermediaries with God. Holy power was available to everyone regardless of gender.

Kateri Tekakwitha and other women at Kahnawake seemed to take to heart this aspect of Jesuit teachings. The Jesuits preached marriage, but some Indian women chose celibacy. The women's work society at Kahnawake also borrowed forms of asceticism from the Jesuits and invented new forms as potentially empowering rituals. And Jesuit accounts of the Virgin Mary and women saints may have even enhanced women's position within Iroquois society, since Christian symbols and stories celebrated the importance of women as mothers and visionaries. The Jesuits intended to recast Indian societies in their own image, but it was the Indians themselves who selected which aspects of Christianity and European culture they would accept.

Sources: French Jesuits wrote most of the primary sources dealing with Tekakwitha and Kahnawake in the seventeenth century. Chauchetière's and Cholenec's hagiographies of Kateri's life have been translated and published in *The Positio of the Historical Section of the Sacred Congregation of Rites on the Introduction of the Cause for Beatification and Canonization and on the Virtues of the Servant of God Katharine Tekakwitha, the Lily of the Mohawks* (1941), edited by Robert E. Holland, the volume of documents presented to the Vatican as proof of Tekakwitha's holiness. The 73-volume collection of *The Jesuit Relations and Allied Documents: Travels and Explorations of the Jesuit Missionaries in New France, 1610–1791* (1896–1901), edited by Reuben Gold Thwaites, is the main source of firsthand accounts of the Jesuit missions in New France. Also an important, contemporary ethnographic resource is Joseph Francois Lafitau's *Customs of the American Indians Compared with the Customs of Primitive Times,* two volumes (1974–1977), edited by William N. Fenton and Elizabeth L. Moore.

Secondary sources are James Axtell's *The Invasion Within* (1985), Daniel K. Richter's *The Ordeal of the Longhouse* (1992), Cornelius Jaenen's *Friend and Foe* (1976), and David Blanchard, ". . . To the Other Side of the Sky: Catholicism at Kahnawake, 1667–1700," *Anthropologica* 24 (1982), 77–102.

3

THE PURITAN CONSCIENCE OF ROBERT KEAYNE

BERNARD BAILYN

Just as the Jamestown colony was recovering from its near disastrous encounter with disease and starvation, New England was settled by Puritans, dissenters from the Church of England. This was a very different story than the one about Jamestown and the Chesapeake Bay. Migrants to New England came in very large numbers from 1630 to 1640, encountering little opposition from a Native American population that had already been decimated by European diseases like smallpox. Although Indians suffered from their lack of immunity to European diseases, the New England colonists found an environment conducive to physical health once they had learned to plant corn and build shelter from the harsh winters. Another key difference was that New England colonists, for the most part, came as families and, in some cases, village groups, a fact which allowed them to reproduce community life and social order much more rapidly than the other colonies. In a healthy environment and with family and community life intact, New Englanders reproduced themselves rapidly with an extremely high birthrate; by the end of the seventeenth century their numbers had quadrupled.

These demographic statistics would seem to indicate that the Massachusetts colonists achieved unprecedented success in the new world. However, the Puritans themselves were not so sanguine; they worried obsessively about the failure of their communities to achieve the harmony and communal sharing which was so fundamental to Puritan theology and social theory. Having escaped persecution and social chaos in England, Puritans were obsessed with building, perhaps even coercing, an orderly and socially homogeneous society in the new world. Recognizing right from the beginning that such ideals would be difficult to preserve, Puritan ministers insisted on tightly knit settlements and close supervision. Indeed, for most of the seventeenth century, they insisted that selfishness, greed, and focus on material goods were causing declension among the colonists. In their view the very mercantile success which indicated that God looked with favor upon these new world communities also tempted their flock to slight or even abandon the ultimate goals of order and harmony. Thus, the ministers and leaders of the colony seemed constantly on the lookout for evidence of selfishness and individualism, which could be punished at its early stages and perhaps kept at bay. Heretics like Roger Williams, Anne Hutchinson, and Quakers were punished and banned from the colony, while the courts kept a close watch on economic heresy.

Bernard Bailyn's story of Robert Keayne reveals some of the complexity of Puritanism in the life of one individual. Keayne was not a minister, but a merchant, and therefore more exposed to the contradictions in Puritan doctrine than ministers or ordinary farmers. The success of trade in Boston presented many opportunities for merchants like Keayne to make unusually high profits. Such profits would indicate success and a favorable attitude from God, but, on the other hand, too much success would indicate an obsession with material possessions and lack of caring about others in the community. It was a fine line for merchants like Keayne to walk. In Bailyn's story about Keayne, he shows the psychological stress and remarkable effort of time and rationalization employed by one individual in order to preserve his Puritan beliefs while at the same time justifying his behavior. The behavior that later would be accepted as success in an individualistic, capitalist society was much more difficult to justify within seventeenth-century Puritanism.

> THOUGH I have undergone many censures since I came hither [wrote Robert Keayne of Boston in 1653] according to mens uncharitable and various apprehentions . . . I have laboured to beare it with patience and to approve my heart and wayes to God that judgeth righteously; yet these things hath made me the more willing to clear myself in all material things in this my last testam[en]t; though it be somewhat contrary to the nature of a will, yet I am willing to leave this upon publique record as a just defense for myself knowing that a will wilbe read and made knowne and may be p[er]used, searched, or coppied out by any when other writings wilbe more hid and obscured.

Three years later Robert Keayne was dead. When his executors came to open this Last Will and Testament, they found not only a complicated allocation of his worldly goods but an outpouring of long-suppressed indignation, a helter-skelter *apologia pro vita sua,* and a reiterated demand that justice be done him even if only in memory. It had taken him five months to write out the document, and when the will was copied into the first volume of the probate records of Suffolk County, it filled no less than 158 pages.

Robert Keayne has been remembered because one Goody Sherman insisted that the unpopular merchant had made off with her sow and because, when the case came before the General Court, the magistrates insisted on retaining a veto against the more numerous deputies, or representatives, who sided with Mrs. Sherman. As a result the legislature of the Bay Colony came to sit in two bodies, an upper and a lower house, and Robert Keayne found a place in American constitutional history.

Yet, though Keayne took pains to publicize his generosity to town and college, it was not his pride in these gifts that kept him adding page after page to his Will, and, of course, he was ignorant of his future place in the history of bicameralism. What lay behind his extraordinary Last Will and Testament was the need to explain a series of episodes in his life that had taken place fourteen years earlier.

The resulting 51,000 words provide an insight into the workings of a seventeenth-century mind. What he had "here writt out of the greife and trouble of my heart" was an appeal to the Puritan conscience of New England to reconsider its "unchristian, uncharitable and unjust reproaches and sland[e]rs" against him, and raised the hope "that such which have taken liberties to load me with divers reproaches and long to lay me under a darke cloude may have cause to see that they have done amisse and now to be sorry for it, though they have not beene so before."

By the time Keayne had finished the Will he had reviewed the main incidents in his life, had rewarded the just and punished the evildoers, and had given to history a picture of the man of business twisting in the confines of Puritan ethics.

I

The man who later boasted that he emerged triumphant from financial losses "sufficient to have broken the backe of any one man in the country" was born the son of a butcher in Windsor, Berkshire County, England, in 1595. He received "no portion from my parents or friends to begin the world withal," and at the age of ten he was apprenticed for eight years to John Heyfield of Birchin Lane, London. Keayne thus spent his formative years in and around that center of commercial activity, the Cornhill district, remaining there until his departure for New England in 1635. In the atmosphere of trade and competition Keayne flourished, and in his twentieth year he was admitted to the freedom of the Merchant Tailors' company. Two years later he married Anne Mansfield. The union was a fortunate one, as it brought Keayne into an established family and linked him with a brother-in-law, the Reverend John Wilson, who was one of the powerful spirits of early Massachusetts. By 1623 he was being called "gentleman," had attained the freedom of the city, and had capped his social activities by being accepted as a member of the Honourable Artillery Company of London. Four children were born to Anne Keayne before 1625, but of these only Benjamin, the eldest, survived infancy.

During the 1620s, Keayne first directed his attention to New England. He was one of the financial backers of the Pilgrims' Plymouth Colony and consequently one of the forty-two men whose economic interest in the colony was bought out by Isaac Allerton's "bargen" of 1626. That Keayne's interest in the movement was not entirely financial may be gathered from a manuscript volume of sermon notes in his hand dated June 1627–August 1628. Two other such volumes, written during his New England years, also attest a contant concern with the church and, if not a deep piety, at least a conscientious attention to what transpired in service and meeting.

By 1634 Keayne had become associated with the Puritans' Massachusetts Bay Company and had probably invested in the venture. In that year the company's General Court appealed to him for further support. He had been consulted in the pricing of certain arms to be sent to the colony, and about the same time shipped to Boston the sizable gift of weapons and goods donated to the Puritans by John Wilson's brother Edmund.

Just why the prosperous merchant chose to emigrate to New England in 1635 is not clear. The questionable supposition that Keayne left wholly for religious reasons is given a certain credence by Governor John Winthrop's remark that Keayne had "come over for conscience' sake, and for the advancement of the gospel here." But it is most unlikely that the man who wrote the Last Will and Testament of 1653 could have left England without carefully calculating his economic opportunities. Certainly Keayne was not indifferent to the fact that God would prosper the righteous and industrious in this promised land.

Whatever the immediate cause for their departure, "Robert Keayne 40: Anne Keayne 38: Ben. Keayne 16" embarked on the *Defence* July 17, 1635, having previously been certified by their ministers and justices as to "their conformitie" and that they owed no taxes. Once in Boston the merchant quickly settled into the little society. He established himself on the southwest corner of Cornhill (now Washington) and King (now State) streets in the heart of the town. His house was separated by one lot from the First Church and faced the central market square. He had brought over with him "two or 3000 lb in good estate of my owne." A few months after his arrival he was listed by the Boston Town Meeting as having contributed £5 toward building a strong battlement on Fort Hill, and in March of the following year he was officially accepted by the community when he was received into the brotherhood of the First Church.

A reputation for sharp dealing and heartlessness in business had preceded him to the New World. In 1639 Winthrop wrote that the "corrupt practice of this man . . . was the more observable, because he was wealthy and sold dearer than most other tradesmen, and for that he was of ill report for the like covetous practice in England that incensed the deputies very much against him." Until his death in 1656, however, despite unpopularity and repeated controversies with his fellow citizens, Robert Keayne continued to fill responsible public positions. He held his earliest public office in 1636, when the Boston Town Meeting elected him to a committee charged with the ordering of all land allotments and other business. In the years that followed he was reelected selectman four times, chosen as a representative to the General Court at least seven times, and served in innumerable lesser functions such as surveyor of the highways.

Keayne's first activities in New England were colorless enough, but in November 1639, only three years after his arrival, both church and state struck down the ambitious merchant. This blow to his pride and reputation he felt throughout his life. In drawing up his Will he returned again and again to the events of 1639 as if to ease the pain of that "deepe and sharpe censure that was layd upon me in the country and carryed on with so much bitterness and indignation of some, contrary both to law or any foregoing president [precedent] if I mistake not, and I am sure contrary or beyond the quality and desert of the complaynts that came against me." Keayne had been charged with "taking above six-pence in the shilling profit; in some above eight-pence; and, in some small things, above two for one." The General Court took the charge, and the surrounding circumstances, most seriously. It noted, first, that "the cry of the country was so great against oppression" and then that "some of the elders and magistrates had [already] declared such detestation of the corrupt practice of this man." What made it all worse was that Keayne was "an ancient professor of the gospel" and "a man of eminent parts," that he was wealthy and so clearly did not need the money, that he had "come over for conscience' sake and for the advancement of the gospel here," that he had been warned earlier and had promised to reform, and finally that what happened in New England was under the "curious observation of all churches and civil states in the world." In view of all this, the court fined Keayne £200, though the following May it was reduced to £80.

The church then took up the matter. The elders studied "how farr I was guilty of all those claymors and rumors that then I lay under," and after an "exquisite search" into Keayne's defense, they dismissed him with a severe admonition. He was condemned "in the name of the Church for selling his wares at excessive rates, to the dishonor of God's name, the offence of the Generall Cort, and the publique scandall of the cuntry." Keayne lived under this ban until the seventh of May following, when, after acknowledging "with tears . . . his covetous and corrupt heart," and "upon his penentiall acknowledgment thereof this day and pr[o]mise of further satisfaction to any that have just offence against him," he was officially reconciled to the Church.

The merchant protested in his Will, however, that this account, written into the records of state and church and accepted by the community as true, was a fabric of malicious falsehoods. Instead of a sharp-dealing sinner, Keayne saw himself as an honest tradesman who had been savagely libeled by his personal enemies.

> It was the greife of my soule (and I desire it may ever so be in a greater measure) that any act of mine (though not justly but by misconstruction) should be an occasion of scandall to the Gospell and p[ro]fession of the Lord Jesus or that my selfe should be looked at as one that had brought any just dishonor to God (which I have endeavored long and according to my weake abilitie desired to pr[e]vent) though God hath beene pleased for causes best knowne to himselfe to deny me such a blessing, and if it had beene in my owne power I should rather have chosen to have p[e]rished in my cradle than to have lived to such a time.

The truth of the matter, Keayne insisted, was that he had sold a bag of sixpenny nails at the moderate markup of two pence, by no means a "haynous sine" or even an unusual practice. But the purchaser (who becomes the devil of this tale) found the nails too small for his use and exchanged them for some of the eightpenny variety. The merchant charged him ten pence a pound and changed the "8" in his account book to "10." For a period of years Keayne continually requested his payment, but finally, when the buyer could "for shame keepe the money no longer," he brought Keayne into court on the "quarreling exception and unrighteous complaint" that he had bought only six-penny nails and that Keayne had "corrupted my booke in adding more to the prize than I had set down for them at first delivery."

The buyer was almost successful in sustaining this charge until the messenger who had delivered the second bag of nails testified on Keayne's behalf. But by this time, other busy people were at work, and charges for overpricing a bridle, "great gold buttons," and a skein of thread were also leveled against him. Keayne wrote that all these accusations were as false as the first one, but the chief malcontent had won over enough of the court to convict him. The censure was passed, however, "against the desire and judgment of allmost the greatest number of the chiefest and wisest of the Magistrates and Deputies." As for the church conviction, "lesse they could not doe, without some offence, considering what had passed before against me. . . ."

To Keayne's apparent amazement, the accuser next claimed that his father in England had sent him £200 by Keayne which he had never received. The merchant protested the statement as an outright lie: he had returned the sum long before leaving England. But how was one to find proof for this ancient transaction, "it being soe long agoe and things much out of minde and many things passing through my hands in so great a remoovall from on[e] Country to another"? But when it became clear that the fellow intended not only to have him severely punished for something he had not done but also "to make me pay that 200 lb twise over," Keayne applied himself with increased zeal in searching and at last found a full and clear receipt for the money. Backed by this evidence, the long-suffering tradesman turned on his accuser and demanded indemnity for slander and injuries.

Captain Thomas Smith. Self-portrait. Smith (d. 1691), a Boston mariner and merchant, was an ambitious amateur potraitist who must have studied art on his travels, probably in Holland. (Courtesy, Worcester Art Museum, Worcester, Massachusetts.)

But the Reverend Mr. Cotton advised him to forbear because of his recent troubles and await a more seasonable time for the countersuit.

A meeting of some of the most honored citizens was later held at the house of Keayne's friend Captain William Tyng, and Governor Winthrop indicated that he would move the General Court to revoke the original conviction. But since death kept Winthrop from fulfilling his promise, Keayne admonished the overseers of the Will to see that justice was done.

In 1642 the unpopular merchant was again haled through the courts in the famous "sow case." The charges against him were weak, but the controversy over whether or not Keayne had robbed Mrs. Sherman of her sow was soon dwarfed by the refusal of the deputies to abide the "negative voice" of the magistrates. The separation of the houses, hence the origins of bicameralism, came about when Keayne's countersuit for slander, successful before an inferior tribunal, was appealed to the General Court.

Keayne's public activities in the five years following this episode seem to have reached their zenith. As selectman and representative, he served on innumerable committees, was active in several large land deals, became involved in the Lynn iron works, sat in judgment on several petitions, and throughout the period carried on his mercantile interests. His son became one of his London agents, and his trade with the West Indies continued.

Yet misfortune continued to nag after him. In the May court of 1646 he was fined for being absent at the appointed time. To this indignity the merchant replied, according to the court's record, that "he would pay five pounds as soone as 6d, for which affront he was fined twenty shillings." It was only "upon his acknowledgment of his miscarriage therein" that the court remitted this second fine. Keayne's son finally went back to England after the "evill carriages" of his wife Sarah Dudley that resulted in her banishment from the church. Her offense, recorded in the church minutes for October 1647, was not only "irregular prophecying" but also "falling into odious, lewd, and scandalous uncleane behavior with one Nicholas Hart an excommunicate p[er]son of Taunton."

It was in 1652 that Keayne came into final and definitive disgrace. The previous year the fifty-six-year-old tradesman had been elevated to his most important public post. Considering the "great concourse of people and increase of trade" that clogged the Suffolk County court, the colony had created an inferior tribunal to try civil cases within the town of Boston that amounted to less than £10. Keayne was one of the seven men appointed to this judicial position. But shortly thereafter shocking reports reached the ears of the magistrates. By June of 1652 the situation was bad enough to warrant an official inquiry, and the damning evidence was heard before a clerk of the General Court. Two of Keayne's former servants said that they had seen their employer staggering home from Charlestown in the company of one Thomas Lake. They swore that "we saw Captaine Kayne . . . to be full of beere or wyne." The two men, they continued, "led one another for they both fell downe together; and [though] the weather was frost and snow . . . wee apprehend that hee was full of drink till wee be otherwise satisfied." Joseph Armitage had a similar tale to tell. The testimony of Johana Joy must have been even more convincing. She recalled an evening in a neighbor's house when she saw Keayne "to be much overcome with drink for as he went towards the fyre to take a cole to light a pipe of tobacco he reeled with his head soe forward that she was afraid he would have falne into the fyre." When he finally got the coal, "he assayed to take his tobacoe soe unseemly that did plainly declare him to be much in drink." Her husband and a friend concurred in this opinion and added that "they saw him butt his head against the james of the chimney as he sate by it and in lighting his pipe he slavered in a beastly or unseemly manner." And, they continued, when Keayne went outside, "as he stood upp against the pale he stood nodding his head against the said pales as not being able to stand upp-right."

The case against the unhappy Keayne was complete, and the Puritan Commonwealth wasted no time in showing him the cost of such miserable "carriages." On May 31, 1652, the General Court pronounced the following sentence:

> Whereas Capt Robt Keayne beinge acused to this Court for drunkenes, the evidences having been perused, and findinge that he is proved to have been three times drunke and to have drunke to excesse two times, for which offenses the Court doth fine him thirty six shillings and eyght pence.

To this was added the fifty-five shillings two pence which the Court had paid in expenses to the witnesses. This time the merchant made no effort to challenge the legislative authority. Instead, he petitioned to resign his place on the Boston tribunal. The members promptly agreed, "as judging him not meet to contynue therein."

II

Keayne's Will would be of interest if it only contained the strange version of the 1639 trial for price-gouging and covetousness. But it is a document of considerable historical value for the picture it supplies of the mind of a Puritan merchant.

The word that expresses best the most basic activity of Keayne's mind is *calculation*. The veil through which he saw the world was not so much colored as calibrated. It was *quantity* that engaged his imagination. The Will shows numerous instances of Keayne's mind working in abstractions or normative judgments and slipping unconsciously into quantitative measurements. After requesting his executors to petition the General Court for a reconsideration of his case, he wrote: "and were it possible for me to know it [his vindication] certainly before I dye (though it be not for love of the money, nor for addition to my estate by it, though it was a considerable sume about eighty pounds as I remember) it would much ease and refresh my spirit in respect of the equity of it."

Consider the system, the calculations, implicit in Keayne's "gift to the poore":

> Now for this 120 lb. before mentioned I am bound to acknowledge and to leave this testimony behinde me concerning it and how I came by it, for I doe not account it properly my owne nor simply my gift to the poore now but theire due and debt as that which, for these many years, long before I came out of Old England, I began to gather and devote to God . . . which stocke I have gathered and from weake to weake layd apart by taking one penny out of every shilling

> which I have gotten by my trade . . . so that when I gayned much in a weeke there hath beene the more layd aside for any good use, and when trayding hath beene dead and the gaines lesse there hath beene the lesse layd a syde for this stocke and use . . . by which meanes I have had comonly lyeing by me 50 lb. 60 lb. or 80 lb. ready money, especially in old England, and some pretty quantity here, till more lately since hath beene so scarce amongst us whereby I have been fayne to borrow out of that stock my selfe for my owne necessary use and occasions when I have wanted money of my owne, and a good comfortable helpe it hath beene to me that way in many pinches but doe still keepe a carefull account what at any time I take out and pay it in againe as money comes to hand.

Besides the sums he gave away, he lent money from this fund to "any poore godly Christian or Minister in neede." Sometimes he had adventured part of it to sea, "that the benefitt of it might redound to the stocke for the poores use."

Consider also the account books he described to his executors. They were first told of an "inventory booke . . . in which particulars of my whole estate from yeare to yeare, with all that I owe and all debts that are owing to me is breifly set downe under my own hand." Then there was a "receipt booke of moneyes that I have payd fro time to time," in which he had located the missing receipt of 1639; a "day booke of what I buy or sell"; a "pocket booke . . . of my dayly or weekely expences and charges for dyett, apparell, housekeeping which is sumed up every weeke from yeare to yeare and what ev'y weekes charges amounts to . . . what is payd to bakers, butchers shops, carting of wood, rates and divers such charges." The overseers of the Will were also to note "2 other bookes bound up in vellam in my closet at Boston which I call number bookes which were of use when I kept shop in London and here." Also of importance were his debt books, "of which there is cheifly three in use, namely one bound in browne vellam . . . , the other . . . I call the new debt booke, the third . . . is called my booke of creditor and debitor." At his farm the executors would find "a long paper booke bound in parchment . . . which I keepe locked up for my owne use, which is the p[ar]tic-ulrs of the charges and profitts that I make of my ffarme ev'y yeare." And since he had had at one time the supervision of rents from certain holdings of his London relatives, he described a rent book in his possession, as well as various out-dated account files, a variety of boxes stuffed with bills and papers, and two cash containers with enumerated contents.

In this absorption with figuring and cataloging, Keayne was little different from most other successful businessmen of his time. The calculating trait was not restricted to business, however, but found ample expression in his religious life:

> happy yea more happy would it have beene for me if I had beene as carefull and as exact in keeping an account of my sinnes and the debts that I owe to God and of that spirituall estate betweene God and my owne soule [as he has been in keeping his business accounts] that I could as easily have made it appeare to others or to my selfe when I gained or when I lost and to have taken as much paines this way as in the other, which though I cannot truly say I have altogether neglected or omitted, yet comparatively I may justly say I have beene greatly deficient in that one thing necessary.

At one point he declared that his whole life had been recorded in one or another of his accounts "since I was a prentice . . . [and] now wilbe exposed to the view of others and there censure, when they wilbe p[er]used after my death." The implication was that righteousness can be measured, cataloged; it took only simple arithmetic to separate the saints from the sinners.

Next to calculation, the attitude most characteristic of Keayne was his timidity before public opinion. Fear of unpopularity is obvious on almost every page of the Will, which, it will be recalled, was written to rescue his reputation from the darkness into which it had been cast by the trials of 1639. Keayne examined every possibility of being held in public disrepute. He charged his executors to administer his will most carefully, that there may be no "report that I have given away more than my estate will beare and that I have made a great show of charite, and have nothing or not enough to perform it with." When he left £300 for a water conduit and a town house, he anticipated a charge that he did so to increase the value of his own property. As he listed his bequests to the poor, he explained why he had not made these gifts before. He finally declared his intention to make no great show of charities, "least some should approach me with an affectation and vaine glory."

Keayne's mind was tenacious and unforgiving. He recalled injuries done him in the past which he had never repaid. For her scandalous behavior, his ex-daughter-in-law, Sarah Dudley, was left no inheritance and forbidden to share in her own daughter's portion. His brother-in-law, John Mansfield, he left not a farthing, because that ungrateful relative had plagued him constantly despite all Keayne's generosity. Among the many minor gifts is the following:

> Item I give unto our Brother Renolds shoomaker senior twenty shillings as a token of my respects to him if he be liveing two yeares after my decease, not forgetting a word that he spake publiquely and seasonably in the time of my distresse and other mens vehement opposition against me.

Keayne's religion did not desert him in his justification of this hardness of heart toward his antagonists. In no less a person than Jesus he found sufficient precedent. "Our Savior remembers his disciples unkind forsaking of him and flying from him in so great a tyme of need," Keayne reminded his readers. Likewise, Jesus "keeps in memory and records the unkind usage of many citties and townes and the injuryes that he received of his unthankfull countrymen to his dying day." In fact, "the Scriptures are full of example[s]."

After "renowncing all manner of knowne errors, all Popish and prelaticall superstitions, all anabaptisticall inthusiasms and familisticall delusions, with all other fayned devises, and all old and new upstart opinions, unsound and blasphemous errors, and other high imaginations," Keayne expressed his personal creed—an unsophisticated statement of certain aspects of Calvinist doctrine. He desired

> from my heart to renownce all confidence and expectation of merritt or desert in any of the best duties or services that ever I shall or can be able to p[e]rform, acknowledging that all my righteousness, sanctific[ati]on and close walking with God, if it were or had bin a thousand times more exact than ever I attayned too, is all polluted and corrupt and falls short of comending me to God in point of my justification.

Though he deserved nothing at God's hand "but hell and condemnation," he believed his "wayes of holynesse . . . may not be neglected . . . without great sinne," for they were "ordained of God for me to walke in them carefully" and were to be considered as "good fruites and evidences of justification." His conclusion was, "therefore renowncing though not the acts yet all confidence in those acts of holynesse and workes of sanctification performed by me, I look for my acceptance with God and the salvation of my soule only from the merritts of righteousness of the Lord Jesus Christ, and from the free bountifull and undeserved grace and love of God in him."

Such humility before an omnipotent God was, however, difficult for the merchant to maintain. On the next page in the Will he spoke of the hereafter, where he should "receive according to the works that I have done in this life according as they have beene good or evill in the sight of God" as well as be rewarded from the "full grace and merits of the Lord Jesus Christ." Protesting his innocence, he expanded on the idea of earthly rewards for holy mortals.

> I have and shall still committ my cause and cry to him [God] for right and I have many testemonyes in my spirit that he hath righted me therein, not only in the hearts and judgments of many men that knew and heard of those proceedings, but also in my very outward estate that thought [though?] some intended it for my great hurt, yet God hath beene pleased to turne it to my good so that I have not since fared the worse nor lost by it but hath since carryed me through many and great engagem[en]ts with comfort.

The merchant saw that God meted out reward or punishment according to His unfathomable intentions, but in the particular case of Robert Keayne, God had clearly made known his pleasure. Despite the opinion of the community, the merchant had been provided with sound evidence of his sanctification. Keayne explained how God had helped him through a period of severe reverses. "I begin but now to breathe as it were and through the great mercy and unexpected support and assistance of my good God to stand upon my owne leggs and doe but now as it were learne to goe alone." This was no God of terror and inscrutable purposes but one obviously interested in furthering the welfare of Robert Keayne, seeing to it that those who undervalued the righteous merchant were given proper punishment.

> Let such know that if they grow proud and high minded and scorne the kindnes and endeavors of othrs [read: Keayne] that desire to doe more good then themselves, God can and it may be will bring such high spiritts into a lower frame and putt them into such a condition that they may stand in need of the helpe of as meane and as much dispised p[er]sons as my selfe before they dye.

Toward the leaders of the church Keayne showed the highest respect, even insisting on space in his proposed town house for "a gallery or some other handsome roome for the Elders to meete in." And he provided a fund made up of the income from "some of my shops in Boston" to supply the elders with refreshments and occasional meals at their meetings. But let the reverend ministers, men of God though they be, tread warily where they had no business. Note the case of Reverend John Eliot: after the merchant had gone to the trouble and expense of surveying and bounding new land which he had bought, and after the General Court had confirmed him in his ownership, the famous missionary had endeavored to reclaim the land for the Indians. Indeed, "he would not be taken off nor p[er]suaded by any, nay by none that spake with him about it, to surcease his prosecution or endeavor to plucke it out of our hands againe for the Indians." The result of this "unsavory and offencive" conduct was that Keayne reconsidered his original bequest to aid the missionary work and left it to "larger and fuller purses to carry on this great and good worke amongst the Indians."

It was at this point that Keayne made clear the boundary between the things of the spirit and those of the world.

> Therefore I would make it my request to the Reverend Eld[e]rs of this country not to be too stiffe and resolute in accomplishing theire owne wills and wayes but to

Major Thomas Savage. Attributed to Thomas Smith, 1679. Savage (1606-82), like Keayne, arrived in Boston in 1635 and became a member of the Ancient and Honorable Artillery Company and a successful merchant. Note the lace finery and the coat of arms, suggesting wealth and pride in status - a "vain show" which Keayne said he denied himself. (Bequest of Henry Lee Shattuck in Memory of the late Gray, 1983)

harken to the advice and counsell of there brethren and to be as easily p[er]swaded to yeeld in civill and earthly respects and things as they expect to pr[e]vayl with any of us, when they have a request to make to us for one thing or another, least, by too much stiffnes to have their owne wills and ways, they hinder many good workes that may be p[ro]fitable to themselves and to the whole Country.

Though the subtleties of predestination translated themselves for the merchant into a conviction of election, though Christ became remarkably like Keayne in his relentless revenging of old injuries, and though Eliot's efforts to preserve a plot of land for the Indians was seen as at best an "unkinde carriage," nevertheless religion exerted a discipline on Keayne's mind and consequently on his actions. He felt the obligations of the stewardship of wealth, and the public donations in the Will testify that this was not mere verbiage. There was no question in his mind that the accumulation of wealth solely for personal use was sinful; neither, however, must one deny himself to effect the betterment of others. A nice balance should be reached wherein one strove for success in his calling, provided himself and family with a comfortable estate, yet discharged a standing obligation for the good of others.

In several unintentionally humorous sections of the Will Keayne displayed what may justly be called a guilty conscience concerning his money. He frankly set out to dispose of all possible objections to his righteousness that might arise from considerable success in trade. Where had his money come from? "First if I value my estate to be worth 4000 lb or thereabouts, how could I get such an estate with a good conscience or without oppression in my calling, seeing it is knowne to some that I had no portion from my parents?" He answered that he had "had good creditt and good esteeme and respect" wherever he had lived; that he had been "industrious and provident" and had not trusted "chapmen" or given "creditts"; that he had had between two and three thousand pounds when he landed in America; and lastly that he had not, after all, made such a vast fortune as to warrant a suspicion of corruption. "I have not cleared neare 100 lb a yeare above my expenses since I came hither which is not 5 lb. p cent cleare gaines."

Although Keayne said that he was worth £4000, he had a tax rating of only £1000, "or sometimes lesse." An explanation of this inconsistency caused Keayne considerable difficulty. He claimed that one need not declare one's whole estate and be taxed to the limit if one "can honestly pr[e]vent it," and he drew examples from common English practice to prove his point. He would injure himself unnecessarily if he declared all, because he would have to include much real estate, cattle, and "household stuffe" which "are never valued to the uttermost worth to no man" and because much of the £4000 was in outstanding debts and goods still at sea, "which none can reckon as a sure and safe estate till God brings backe the returnes, as wee finde by sad experience and losse."

The world to Keayne was a battlefield where wills were pitted against each other: good against evil, malice against innocence, creditor against debtor. The weak and easily distracted fell to one side as the vigilant triumphed. Good intentions were not sufficient armament for life's battles. The weapon absolutely required for both worldly and spiritual success was effort, constant striving. What was most important for successful living was the grim persistence that refused to relent in the face of adversity. A relaxed enjoyment of life was suspect, and Keayne thus remarked that his many account books would testifye to the world on my behalfe that I have not lived an idle, lazie, or dronish life nor spent my time wantonly, fruitlessly, or in company keeping as some have beene too ready to asperse me, or that I have had in my whole time either in Old England or New, many spare houres to spend unprofitably away or to refresh myselfe with recreations, except reading and writing hath beene a recreation to me which sometimes is mixt with paine and labor enough, but have rather studyed and endeavored to redeeme my time as a thing most deare and precyous to me, and have often denyed myself in such refreshings that otherwise I might lawfully have made use of.

AN INTERPRETATION

If Keayne had been born a century and a half earlier his career might have been one of those studied by Sylvia Thrupp in her *Merchant Class of Medieval London.* Certain of the traits we find in the Boston merchant were exhibited by his occupational ancestors in London. These medieval businessmen trained their children in the exercise of prudence, and they grew up in an atmosphere of calculation. No less does calculation characterize the teachings of a fifteenth-century Florentine, Leon Battista Alberti. Most successful men of business, whether Renaissance figures or Andrew Carnegies, have had minds that were rooted to external reality, preeminently practical and empirical. Yet there is an important difference between the minds of the medieval and Renaissance merchants and that of Keayne. Thrupp writes, "Although thoughts thus tended to gravitate to the making of money the medieval merchant class does not seem to have generated a gospel of hard work. It was probably the practice to keep the apprentices well occupied in waiting upon customers and carrying messages, but there was no great pressure of office work to harass them, nor were they enjoined to spend all their days on earth at labor."

One of the elements that had been added to the merchant's creed in the course of the sixteenth century was the supernatural sanction that rigorized and steeled the personality traits originally engendered by the bourgeois occupations. The prudence that had once been accepted for its utility and stiffened by habit and custom was now further reinforced by revelation. The virtues that Keayne displayed to a hostile community would not have displeased a medieval merchant, but his ancestor might have been surprised at the conviction and self-righteousness with which he buttressed his actions. Moreover, in the cities of the Old World the superior prestige values of gentility and nobility had tended to dilute the attractiveness of purely economic success, but in the New England soil hereditary aristocracy, with its disdain for trade and the shopkeeper's acquisitiveness, found transplantation difficult if not impossible. Thus when we view Keayne's life in a larger perspective, we find that the milieu of his society doubly intensified his business drive: by the support of its religion and by its weakening of the superior social values of gentility.

On the other hand, Keayne may also be distinguished from the medieval merchants by his intensified concern with the proper uses of wealth and with the religious limitations of his economic life. English Puritanism was a movement of organized idealism. The same body of religious precepts that had systematized the virtues making for business success checked their free play in behalf of the community good and the avoidance of the sins of self-indulgence and sensuality. It was to Keayne's intense chagrin that the community reminded him of his moral weakness and went on to lay out the "rules for trading" that merchants were expected to follow:

> 1. A man may not sell above the current price, i.e., such a price as is usual in the time and place, and as another (who knows the worth of the commodity) would give for it, if he had occasion to use it. . . .

> 2. When a man loseth in his commodity for want of skill, etc., he must look at it as his own fault or cross, and therefore must not lay it upon another.

> 3. Where a man loseth by casualty of sea, or, etc., it is a loss cast upon himself by providence, and he may not ease himself of it by casting it upon another; for so a man should seem to provide against all providences, etc., that he should never lose; but where there is a scarcity of the commodity, there men may raise their price; for now it is a hand of God upon the commodity, and not the person.

What was demanded of the Puritan merchants, at least as represented in Keayne's career, was character strong enough to maintain its integrity in the face of this simultaneous stimulation and regulation. In a series of incidents, from the trials of 1639 to the disgrace of 1652, Keayne showed his inability to keep these burdens in balance. As the possibilities of economic exploitation in the New World became apparent and the religious intensity slackened, the environment of northern society tended to magnify one aspect of the Puritan personality and minimize the other.

It might have been in the very year that Keayne wrote his Last Will and Testament that the pious Pilgrim William Bradford, thumbing through the pages of his *Plymouth Plantation,* fell to musing on the disappointments of his life. When he came to his account of the year 1617 he read again the pledge of the Pilgrims to continue on as they were, "knite together as a body in a most stricte and sacred bond and covenant of the Lord . . . straitly tied to all care of each others good, and of the whole by every one and so mutually." On the back of the page the old Pilgrim wrote an epitaph to those noble hopes:

> But (alas) that subtill serpente hath slylie wound in himselfe under faire pretences of necessitie and the like, to untwiste these sacred bonds and tyes, and as it were insensibly by degrees to dissolve, or in a great measure to weaken, the same. I have been happy, in my first times, to see, and with much comforts to injoye, the blessed fruites of this sweet communion, but it is now a parte of my miserie in old age, to find and feele the decay and want thereof (in a great measure), and with greefe and sorrow of hart to lamente and bewaile the same.

The society Bradford had striven for did not condemn the life of business but placed it within the structure of a community in which all were devoted to the general good and one person's passion for private gain was not allowed "to untwiste these sacred bonds and tyes." Looking back from an age that celebrates possessive individualism and the triumphs of entrepreneurial skills free of religious scru-

ples, one is apt to find in Robert Keayne if not "that subtill serpente" at least one
of the forces that pointed to the future.

Sources: The entire text of Keayne's 50,000-word Will was published by Bernard Bailyn in *The Apolo-gia of Robert Keayne: The Self-Portrait of a Puritan Merchant* (Harper & Row, 1965). An earlier, fully annotated version of the essay on Keayne was published in *The William and Mary Quarterly,* ser. 3, vol. VII (1950), pp. 568–587. Bailyn discussed Keayne and the pressures of Puritan culture on the life of trade in *The New England Merchants in the Seventeenth Century* (Cambridge, Mass., 1955).

4

THE DOMESTIC BATTLES OF WILLIAM BYRD

KENNETH LOCKRIDGE

William Byrd has long been legendary in American history as an example of the cavalier culture and society that, by the eighteenth century, had come to dominate the Chesapeake colonies. After a very rocky start at Jamestown, followed by the struggle to find an economic base for success within the Atlantic economy, the planters of the Chesapeake discovered tobacco. This new crop was in great demand in England and could be easily grown in the southern colonies by unskilled workers. Tobacco quickly became the foundation for the plantation society that was to replace the earlier pattern of small farms. As plantation owners became wealthier, they engrossed more and more land, pushing small farmers with fewer resources west into the mountain regions. By the end of the seventeenth century plantation owners had begun to import large numbers of African slaves to grow the tobacco and to sustain the aristocratic lifestyle desired by the owners. It was this aristocratic lifestyle that produced the great dynasties which in turn produced the "founding" generation of the United States.

While many historians have long been uncomfortable with the irrefutable fact that these "fathers" of our democratic society emerged from a society and culture built on the enslavement of human beings, that has not significantly dimmed their legendary fame as bearers of a "genteel" and civilized tradition. Nor has overwhelming evidence of the arrogance and brutal violence with which the plantation system was preserved tarnished the reputation of the Virginia gentry. Until recently, however, historians have not paid much attention to another dimension of the plantation gentry's lifestyle—their relationship to and attitudes toward the women in their own families. True, women's historians have begun to reveal the patterns of family life and the attitudes of women within the plantation household, but few political historians have considered the question of masculinity and gender relations as pertinent to the evolution of Chesapeake Bay society.

Thus, although many scholars and students are familiar with the secret diary kept by the subject of this essay, William Byrd, most have not quite known what to make of Byrd's entries regarding his wife—anger, arrogance, paternalism, humor, even cruelty all seemed mixed together in his descriptions of their lovemaking as well as their fights. It was easy for readers to be titillated but ultimately to laugh off these references to women and sexuality as irrelevant to serious history. However, as this story by Kenneth Lockridge shows, Byrd's relationship to and feelings about his wife and other women in his life were not peripheral but absolutely central to his conception of himself as a man, a master, and a political figure. Because they were so central to his self-image, they bore important implications for his interactions with other men in the arena of politics and the economy. Lockridge reminds us that it is only from our modern-day perspective that the Chesapeake planters were secure in their aristocratic status; from their own perspective and, indeed, from the perspective of the British gentry, the colonials were little better than the savage Indians they had replaced. Only someone of low status who could not "make it" in England would emigrate to the wilderness of the new world. This kind of attitude prevailed right up until the American Revolution; we have ample evidence that George Washington's goal as a young man was to prove his worthiness to become a British officer, to throw off the stigma that he knew was attached to him as a boorish "colonial."

Byrd's commonplace books and diaries reveal just how severe this sense of inferiority was and how he attempted to cope with it. Lockridge's story of Byrd's struggle with masculinity and gender then reveals more than just domestic habits and customs; it helps us to comprehend a political world which produced George Washington, Thomas Jefferson, James Madison—the founding fathers of the United States.

William Byrd was a magnificient man. Educated with his Cavalier cousins in England, he was the owner of 100,000 acres in Virginia and of hundreds of slaves; the possessor of the largest library in colonial America; the host at Westover, a Palladian brick pile emblazoned along the shore of the James estuary; and a member of His Majesty's Council for the Royal Colony of Virginia. More, he was the first great mythmaker of his class, the newly self-confident Virginia gentry.

Even his mythmaking was gracious. In 1728, when he was fifty-four, he was invited by the royal governor to lead a dangerous mission far into the wilderness, to establish the boundary between Virginia and North Carolina. On his return he turned the tale of his expedition into a lighthearted, ironic essay on the virtues of an American aristocracy. "Well," he seemed to say, in his *History of the Dividing Line,* written around 1735, "North Carolina is full of backcountry clowns, and the laziness, disrespect and disorder of the frontier threatens to undermine all social coherence in both colonies. But a steady gentleman like myself can lead these frontiersman in the difficult task of drawing the border between North Carolina and Virginia, and in so doing can clarify for them the figurative line between social chaos and social order." At about the same time this modest representative of a hierarchical social order criticized slavery for its destructive effects on slaves and masters alike. In this blend of magnificence, modesty, and benevolence, William Byrd II was trying to sketch out an image of a uniquely flexible, and in these ways superior, American aristocracy. In so doing he created a myth which Thomas Jefferson would expand into the image of an aristocracy of merit, fit to lead a democratic nation.

Yet great images can grow out of strange historical soil. We begin with a simple fact: only a few years before, William Byrd II, the first apostle of a benevolent aristocratic order in America, had not even been able to create order in his own family. In 1715 Byrd had left his Virginia plantation for England, abandoning his pregnant wife and children. Before he fled, Byrd had explained the domestic turmoil which was the main impetus for his departure in a letter to an invented friend. Several years before, his wife Lucy had invited a woman friend to live in their house, but in time, according to Byrd, she had conspired with the guest to usurp control of the servants. Byrd referred to these actions on the part of his wife and her friend as a rebellion which "must necessarily root out all confidence between me and my wife." "This heavenly confidence," he concluded, "is the only tie of affection, and when that is broken, farewell love, farewell peace, farewell happiness. Tis impossible to love those we can't trust, and therefore the most absurd thing in nature for a wife to sacrifice that sacred fidelity, not only to her husband's bed, but also to his interest, to any friend or flatterer in the world." After he fled, his first family was never again reunited.

A domestic crisis does not necessarily disqualify a man as a mythmaker or render his visions invalid. In this case, however, to go back in time and to seek out the roots of this explosive separation is to uncover whole new meanings for William Byrd, for the situation of the Virginia colonial elite, and for the mythmaking he wove around it.

I

Our William Byrd's very origins were troubled. His father, William Byrd I, had been born in 1652, the mere younger son of a London goldsmith. His chief claim to be a gentleman was his combined interest in land, money, and power. That he had to come to the miserable little colony of Virginia in 1670 to prosecute his desire for these prerequisites of gentility reveals that he had very little chance of inheriting them in England. In Virginia he became his uncle's protégé and soon inherited from him a small empire, based chiefly on trade with the Indians, on the fringes of the maturing tobacco boom. A hard-headed man given to blunt language, the first William Byrd soon turned this small empire into a larger one. He joined his traders in probing the interior for beaver pelts, for deerskins, and for anything else desirable that could be extracted from the tribes there in exchange for muskets, powder, and blankets. His realm came to be centered on a simple, wooden house west of the main tobacco regions, halfway from the sea to the falls of the James River.

From this first "Westover" William Byrd I studied the sources of power in the Virginia colony's royal government. He cultivated the king's governor, Sir William Berkeley, and obtained a share in a monopoly of the Indian trade from Berkeley and his minions on the Royal Council and in the House of Burgesses. Access to those in power also guaranteed the first Byrd generous grants of the king's good lands in Virginia and appointment to profitable offices in the government. By 1676, William Byrd I, only twenty-four years old, was doing very well indeed.

In 1676 the first Byrd met his first crisis and emerged from it at the very center of power in the colony. In that year the Burgesses and Council canceled the monopoly of the Indian trade which Byrd had shared with the well-connected newcomer, Nathaniel Bacon. Incensed over the loss of the monopoly and impatient with Governor Berkeley's inability to maintain order among the warring Indians on the frontier, the wildly ambitious Bacon raised a punitive expedition against what he saw as the guilty Indians. They slaughtered innocent tribes. With this victory for "order" under their belts, Bacon's ragtag "army" soon followed him into open rebellion against the government. Their goals were many and included control of the Indian trade, free land, and a foreign trade free of English control. It is a measure of William Byrd I's blind ambition that he momentarily joined his partner Bacon and his crew of impoverished former indentured laborers in this bloody challenge to established authority.

Or perhaps joining Bacon's rebellion was a measure of Byrd's cleverness, for in the midst of the rebellion this particular rebel evidently used his outlaw status to strike a quick bargain with Sir William Berkeley and emerged on the governor's winning side, abandoning Bacon and his cohorts to a feverish death in the swamps or to execution. From that day on William Byrd I's access to the Indian trade, to huge grants of good tobacco land, and to such profitable offices as membership on the Royal Council for Virginia and simultaneous receiver and auditor of the royal revenues in Virginia was never in doubt.

Yet there had been a lesson in the horrors created when Bacon's rabble wandered the countryside slaughtering Indians and burning down the houses of Berkeley's favorite planters while mocking their pretensions to gentility. The lesson was that neither connections with Governor Berkeley nor new wealth had guaranteed even the top Virginia planters secure status as gentlemen and so legitimized their leadership. As Bacon himself had said, Berkeley and his clique of local favorites lacked education and social credentials:

> Let us trace these men in authority and favor to those hands the dispensation of the country's wealth has been committed; let us observe the sudden rise of their estates compared with the quality in which they first entered this country; or the reputation they have held here amongst wise and discerning men. And let us see whether their extractions and education have not been vile, and by what pretense of learning and virtue they could [come] so soon into employments of so great trust and consequence. Let us also consider whether any public work for our safety and defence or for the advancement and propagation of trade, liberal arts or sciences is here extant in any [way] adequate to our vast charge. Now let us compare these things together and see what sponges have sucked up the public treasure and whether it has not been privately contrived away by unworthy favorites and juggling parasites whose tottering fortunes have been repaired and supported at the public charge. Now if it be so, judge what greater guilt can [there] be than to offer to pry into these and to unriddle the mysterious wiles of a powerful cabal.

By the time Bacon had uttered these devastating words, William Byrd I had joined Governor Berkeley's side and had once again become one of those public "sponges" to whom Bacon had referred shortly before he went down into death and darkness. Furthermore, many of Bacon's lesser followers had subsequently slipped away and survived or even been pardoned, so the rebels' corrosive hatred of the Virginia elite endured, fed with contempt for the nouveau-riche favorites who had rallied around the victorious Berkeley and who now more than ever claimed to be the ruling class of colonial Virginia. William Byrd I still lived in a dangerously exposed situation. In the years before and after 1676 he and others like him had failed to establish a stable claim to education, experience, and social gentility, which would put their economic and political leadership beyond such dangerous challenges.

Even before Bacon's Rebellion the first William Byrd had already reached for the gentility which legitimized power by marrying Mary Horsmanden Filmer. She was the daughter of English Cavalier gentry and the widow of Samuel Filmer, a successful Virginia planter. Samuel Filmer had been the son of Sir Robert Filmer, an English gentleman and philosopher and the great propagandist for patriarchal absolutism in the family and in the royal state in England. William Byrd I had acquired this distinguished royalist former-father-in-law by his marriage to the widow Mary Horsmanden Filmer. He called Sir Robert Filmer "father" as if to appropriate some of the Great Royalist's social cachet. But Byrd knew, as Bacon and his followers had known, that such second- and third-hand gentility acquired by marriage was only a smoke screen. Like most of the first successful planters, William Byrd I was still a newcomer of essentially middle-class or very minor gentry origins and little fortune who had inherited and scrambled his way to money, land, and power in Virginia. A decent marriage alone could not establish his claim to gentility, protect his family from future rebellions from beneath, or earn the genuine respect of their English overlords.

Five years after Bacon's Rebellion, William Byrd I moved to create true gentility for his family by sending his seven-year-old son, William Byrd II, to England for a gentleman's education. He sent his son to Felsted, the school where Mary Horsmanden Filmer Byrd's Cavalier relatives had sent their sons. As a second-generation Virginian liberally educated at Felsted and introduced into ruling circles in England, the younger Byrd could safely return one day as one of the first generation of legitimate Virginia gentlemen. He could manage his ambitious father's 100,000 acres, tobacco plantations, slaves, Indian trade, and high offices in full confidence that neither the lewd Virginia rabble nor haughty royal governors could challenge this Byrd's proud possessions. Nor could they take lightly his credentials to rule.

II

This was the historical burden placed upon the shoulders of a seven-year-old boy as he embarked in 1681 on a voyage to relatives, to a school, and to a country he had never seen. He would see his father alive only twice more in his life and his mother only once.

William Byrd II would do his best, but it was never an easy task either to awe the fluid society of colonial Virginia or to impress the condescending coteries of the English metropolis. In 1704 he emerged from over twenty years of education in England, at the age of thirty, to all appearances an English gentleman and one with stylistic pretensions to high aristocracy. His first portrait, painted in the studio of the society painter Sir Geoffrey Kneller, leaves little doubt about the surfaces of his achievement. But beneath the aristocratic veneer lay a series of failures which left in doubt the success of the mission on which his father had sent him. On the other hand, he did not wish to leave the charmed circles of aristocratic London life, so he might never fulfill his father's plan for him to return and rule securely in Virginia. Yet on the other hand, his efforts finally to be accepted into high London circles had been failures, so he could not surpass his father's dreams by becoming a true English gentleman either. Thus, young Byrd had failed to obtain a position in the Imperial bureaucracy because in English eyes he was still a mere colonial. Some English gentry and merchants of the time still expressed surprise that colonials, whom they rarely encountered, were white and could speak English. Surely they were all dusky, mostly slaves or savages? Who, after all, but slaves and savages inhabited colonies? Probably for similar reasons, young William Byrd had also been humiliatingly rejected in a series of courtships of wealthy English ladies far above him in station. Given his Felsted education, their money and connections would have established his genteel status irrevocably, but most of the young ladies involved scarcely noticed that he was courting

William Byrd II, probably painted in London before his return to Virginia in 1705. (Colonial Williamsburg)

them. Similar rejections would recur throughout his life whenever he was in England.

After his father's death in 1704 a frustrated younger Byrd returned to Virginia to take up the inheritance his father had so ferociously gathered for him. He would try to guard it with all the style and education the old man had lacked. It was not a migration the young man wanted to make; he later referred to being in Virginia as "being buried alive." But London had as yet nothing to offer the excessively ambitious, slightly supercilious, and sarcastic colonial. In Virginia his English patina and second-generation wealth guaranteed he would take over most of his father's offices, as well as his estates, and would possess a certain social cachet which would impress the lower orders. He soon married the willful Lucy Parke, a woman of little fortune but daughter of Daniel Parke, who was then the only Virginian to be made governor of a royal colony (albeit of Antigua), and so the only Virginian yet to establish unquestioned status as an English gentleman. Like his father, Byrd had married as much distinction as he could. Like his father, he would find it not enough. He sought to combine his father's ambitions and his own by being made Royal Governor of Virginia—thereby becoming an unimpeachable English gentleman yet continuing the family line in Virginia—but in 1710 was crushingly rejected because he was a colonial.

By 1712, Alexander Spotswood, an English war hero and the new governor of Virginia—the very office Byrd himself had sought—had begun to challenge

Westover, William Byrd II's mansion on the James River, possibly begun by him in the 1720s and possibly completed by his son, William Byrd III, around 1750. (Colonial Williamsburg)

Byrd's possession of his father's old office of receiver of the royal revenues. By implication Spotswood was accusing Byrd of being a corrupt and greedy colonial. Even at home in Virginia, his entire political career was at risk, and it was his colonist's sarcasm toward royal government as much as his performance as receiver which had put it in jeopardy. Further doom impended when Lucy's inheritance from her father Daniel, whose estate Byrd had insisted on managing, proved to be a series of crippling debts which they as heirs must now pay. As the younger Byrd's political and financial worlds began to fall apart around him, in the years from 1712 to 1715, he discovered he could not even control his wife or his household.

Byrd's relationship with Lucy had always been complex. He tended to be a brittle, self-conscious man, arranging every day around a set of rigid routines— reading, devotions, exercise, business, more readings, and evening reflection. He seemed to think rituals would make him a true gentleman. Lucy had to persuade him to make time for the walks in the garden which meant so much to her, to give her access to his library, or, in one case, to lie abed with her: "January 6, 1712. I rose about 8 o'clock [instead of the regulation 6 or 7 o'clock] because my wife made me lie in bed and I rogered her." The words "rogered my wife" or "gave my wife a flourish," which Byrd used to describe intercourse with his wife, did not always imply the arrogant superiority they seem to. On this occasion Byrd was responding as best he could to Lucy's need for intimacy. The same could be seen in September of 1711, after Lucy had cared for Byrd "with a great deal of tenderness" while he had a bout of malaria. Perhaps in gratitude, he walked frequently with her later in the month and, on September 24, "rogered" his wife, then on the 26th "rogered my wife in the billiard room." The language he used was self-centered and graceless, but that September was a time of real intimacy between Lucy and William.

Yet Byrd's obsession with control of his feelings, his schedule, his wife, his servants, and his plantation was usually predominant. "Rogering" or "flourishing" Lucy often did imply an act by which the master performed one of the many roles of mastery expected of him, and such acts were used on occasion explicitly to establish his control of his wife. In the most notable instance, on July 30, 1710, "In the afternoon my wife and I had a little quarrel which I reconciled with a flourish. . . . It is to be observed that the flourish was performed on the billiard table." Smug and self-satisfied, this Byrd was offering his wife only control. He railed at her for excessive purchases, some of which he sent back, forbade her to use his library, and refused to let her pluck her eyebrows. In the end such control led Lucy to "mad" fits of anger.

Sadly, the servants and inferiors became the battleground on whose bodies Lucy's struggle for a share of power, and Byrd's for complete dominance, were inscribed. Byrd, who had servants whipped frequently, drew the line when "my wife against my will caused little Jenny to be burned with a hot iron, for which I quarreled with her." It was, alas, as much his wife's seizure of his authority as her methods which outraged Byrd on such occasions, as witness May 22, 1712, when he and Lucy disagreed over which of two black servants to punish: "My wife caused Prue to be whipped violently notwithstanding I desired not, which provoked me to have Anaka whipped likewise who had deserved it much more, on which my wife flew into such a passion that she hoped she would be revenged of me. . . . I said my prayers and was reconciled to my wife and gave her a flourish in token of it." Control, violence, passion, and sex were a frequent mixture in this household.

It was in this cumulative context of ambition, failure, and a need for control that, by 1715, William Byrd finally lost control of his household and shattered his family.

III

It happened like this: In 1711 Byrd's friend Parson Dunn had left his wife, a friend of Lucy's named Mary Jeffreys Dunn. Lucy had then brought Mrs. Dunn to live in the Byrd household. The ensuing struggle for control between Byrd on the one hand and Lucy and Mrs. Dunn [identified as "Incendia"] on the other is documented in a long letter Byrd wrote sometime after 1713 to a fictive female friend he named "Dunella." He evidently intended to leave the letter on his desk where Lucy and Mrs. Dunn would see it. Byrd begins with a sketch of "Incendia" herself, the viper he has taken to his bosom.

> "Dunella"   [ca. 1711–15?]
>
> I have never writ to you since you left this melancholly corner of the world, nevertheless I hope you have not forgot the freindship settled between us. I us'd to unbosome all my greifs to you, and you must bear with me for doing so. I have no other freind I can trust with a secret of importance.
>
> You may have heard that there is a gentlewoman in my house call'd Incendia. She was forsaken some time ago by her husband: but she told so fair a story in her own favor, that her freinds cast all the blame upon the man. I cou'd not forbear pittying the matron. The truth is, she had tolerable good sence, and I thought for that reason she might be an agreable companion for my wife.
>
> On this consideration I invited her to my house & treated her with all the civility due to a gentlewoman in distress. But she had not been with us long before I was convinced that her husband might have had some provocation to treat her as he did. For besides a certain impurity she had upon her almost continually, which was enough to make her loathsome, she had also a rash way of reparté, which a husband jealous of his authority might think intolerable. It is dangerous to admit a woman into your house, who had liv'd very uneasily with her own spouse, for she won't fail to infect any other wife she converses with, with her own [discontented and rebellious] humours, and like the Devil, will endeavour to bring her to be as unhappy as herself. If Incendia tarry with us much longer my wife and I, who us'd to be envy'd for a happy couple, shall very probably come to extremitys.

"Incendia"'s primary evil, then, is that she preaches rebellion to wives. Specifically, she has persuaded Lucy to usurp Byrd's authority over finances:

> And tis remarkable that every family this woman has liv'd in without her spouse, (who us'd to keep her in some order) hath been unfortunate. What with seasonable flattery, and humouring all my wives foibles, and easeing of some of her domestique troubles, she has gain'd so intire a power over her that she draws her into her interests even against mine. She has also preacht up a very dangerous doctrine,

that in case a husband dont allow his wife mony enough, she may pick his pocket or plunder his desk to do her self justice, of which she is to be her own judge.

Losing control of the finances has plainly made Byrd furious. He confirms that he and Lucy are now quarreling and once again seems to imply that he may go to "extremities," this time called "consequences."

I leave it to you Madam whether this be doctrine very conducive to the peace of familys, and whether those that propagate it don't deserve to be expell'd from all well-govern'd societys in the universe? The following these seditious rules, and the barefac'd espouseing Incendias practices against me, have bred very unpleasant controversys betwixt me & my wife, and if some effectual remedy be not taken in time, I cannot promise for the consequences.

Gradually Incendia/Mrs. Dunn and Lucy have also taken control of the material resources of the household and of the house servants, ordering them to make fine clothes for Mrs. Dunn, directly against Byrd's will:

You must know this gentlewoman carrys on a separate interest in my family, to keep her self in fine clothes, to which she has a vast and very unbecomeing inclination. She is homely, middleag'd, & a parsons cast off wife, and has nothing but what she gets by the opportunity she meets with in my family, and yet she loves to make an appearance as she prettily calls it, and to adorn a person which by too much gaity only becomes more remarkably disagreable. I consented to her bringing a maid into the family to assist her in making her clothes that she might not employ my servants which I was promis'd she shoud not do. But she has ever since employ'd clandestinely severall of my servants to the neglect of my business. And if any of my people dar'd to neglect her affairs, tho it was to do what I had set them about, she chastis'd and threatend after a shamefull manner, & said that if they told me, they shou'd have their tongues cut out.

My wife has notwithstanding adher'd to her friends interest against her husband. Incendia perswaded my wife to threaten all the servants with whips and scorpions, if they ever told me one syllable, tho I shoud be never so inquisitive about it. And some were in earnest beaten for answering the truth to some questions I put to them.

When the two women finally moved to gain control of one of the plantation's master artisans, a weaver, a boundary had been crossed which must not be violated:

You may guess what wars and domestique disputes [these previous episodes] created in the family and yet my patience and love of peace stil forgave it. But behold what a man gets by giveing way. I have a weaver in the house, which I keep to weave course cloaths for my servants, and I charg'd him strictly to weave for nobody without my express orders. However when I was gon abroad Incendia took upon her to command the weaver to take my cloath out of the loom and put in a piece of hers.

The weaver told her plainly he durst not do it. She call'd him a sawcy rascal for disputeing her commands, and assur'd him she had a great mind to break his head. This did not discharge all her gall, but she came instantly and exasperated my wife against the fellow, notwithstand[ing] my wife's [pregnant] condition made her utterly unfit for such a ruffle. In short for presumeing to obey his masters orders, this unhappy servant was not only menaced after a very rugged manner, but had some of his cloths taken from him.

The weaver lookt so scared when I came home, that I wonder'd what ail'd him. I askt him several times, as I did the other servants, what had betided him: but not one syllable cou'd I get out of any of 'em, so well they had been threatened to secrecy. Upon this I began to suspect some hard usage. I therefore brandisht a good cudgel over the weavers head protesting I wou'd break his bones, if he did not disclose what disturb'd him. He fell down upon his knees, and told me how he had been used. The man might well appear terrifyd in so wretched a circumstance. For he was in danger of a beating by me if he did not follow my orders, and in a fair way of haveing his bones broke by Incendia if he did.

But because my wife was pregnant, and too apt to fly into intolerable passions in favour of her freind Incendia, I concluded the best way woud be cooly to let her parasite friend know I was informd of the whole matter. I told her that in case she offerd to discompose my wife with what I told her, or in case the weaver had any hard word, blow, or other ill usage directly or indirectly on her account, I would put it out of her power to disturb the peace of my family any more.

Yet despite further transgressions, "Incendia" remains in the household as the letter is written, and Byrd's only recourse seems to consist of pleading, nominally to his invented friend "Dunella" but really to Lucy and Mrs. Dunn, whom he hopes will see this letter, to restore his manly authority:

Now dear Madam you must judge whether I am fairly treated in these matters. Is it a handsome return in Incendia for the civility I show her, to sow discord & confusion in my family? or if she hath no regard to me? Is it gratitude to my wife, to put her upon such [rebellious] methods, as must with a husband of spirit and understanding make my wife wretched? I am very unwilling to come to extremitys: but [Lucy] may depend upon it, I will be master of my family in spight of all the weak politiques practic'd to abuse my good nature.

Is it not introduceing confusion (the greatest of domestique misfortunes) into a family, to perswade the mistress to command a servant under severe menaces to do what his master had forbid him to do just before?

In the end a desperate Byrd implies that Lucy must choose between her friendship with Mrs. Dunn and her duty to her husband and to his ultimate control of the plantation.

The last words of the letter imply that Byrd and Lucy are already sexually estranged, perhaps that Lucy and Mrs. Dunn are sexually entangled, and certainly that separation or divorce will ensue if Mrs. Dunn's hold over Lucy is not broken:

Tell me my dear friend ought a person with such unsociable qualitys, to be sufferd in the family of any man that loves peace and order, and will assert the soveraignty of his household? I have given you this tedious trouble that you may not be alarmd, if you hear of any vigorous measures that I may happen to take if these proceedings be not alterd. I should stil be content to continue my civilitys to Incendia, provided she discontinue those methods that must of necessity root out all confidence betwixt me and my wife. This heavenly confidence is the only tye of affection, and when that is broken farewell love, farewell peace, farewell happiness. T'is impossible to love those we can't trust, and therefore t'is the most absurd thing in nature for a wife to sacrifice that sacred fidelity, not only to her husbands bed, but also to his interest, to any freind or flatterer in the world.

William Byrd kept his ultimate threat. Shortly after writing the letter, he fled to England.

Byrd had had reason enough to go abroad already by 1711, when Mrs. Dunn arrived in his household, for by then his political and financial affairs were in a disarray which could only be righted in London. Governor Spotswood was out to seize his offices, and the Parke debts, many owed in England, were mounting steadily. Byrd needed whatever influence and credit he could muster in London to rescue his career and his estate. But he did not ask official permission to leave until late in 1713, by which time "Incendia"—Mrs. Dunn—had begun playing fast and loose with his domestic authority. From the long history of building tensions it portrays, the "Dunella" letter was written after 1713, probably sometime in 1714. Moreover, it refers to his wife as "breeding." Since no miscarriages are recorded for Lucy in 1713 or 1714, it is possible that "breeding" refers to her pregnancy with their daughter Wilhelmina, which could have begun as early as February 1715 and which terminated in a successful delivery on November 6, 1715. If the reference was to the pregnancy with Wilhelmina, then Byrd's "Dunella" letter of complaint was written as late as 1715, and it was indeed a last, desperate plea for his wife to restore his authority, for it was followed immediately by his departure for England early in that year. His arrival is not clearly documented, but he was sending letters from London to friends in Virginia by the middle of 1715. The conclusion is inescapable that it was "Incendia"'s dominance of his wife and household which finally forced Byrd to go to London.

William Byrd II's first family was never again reunited. Lucy left their two daughters in Virginia and joined Byrd in London in 1716, where they were reconciled. But that very autumn, in the height of the social season, she caught the smallpox and died. Having first lost control of his household and fled, William Byrd II had now lost his wife forever. The only thing he had not lost was his ambition and a growing fury at women. It is this fury, in turn, which will illuminate his mythmaking.

IV

In 1717 Byrd was still in London, still hoping to be made governor of Virginia and borrowing to pay off the Parke debts when, less than a year after Lucy's death, he began to pursue the beautiful young daughter of the Commissioner of the Excise. Here was wealth and influence in abundance! With her resources, he might yet become governor of Virginia. And perhaps this rich young woman might bear him the son he still lacked, in this way keeping the family's nascent dynasty alive. The story is long and painful, but the courtship ended in 1718 in a rejection as utterly emasculating as a middle-aged (he was by now forty-three) colonial would-be patriarch and gentleman could possibly experience. By his own account, Byrd broke down in tears and felt close to insanity. This crisis was followed promptly by his political neutering by a Board of Trade thoroughly fed up with his relentless assertion of what they felt was his inappropriate political ambition to become

Virginia's governor. By 1720 he was ordered home to Virginia to apologize to Alexander Spotswood for his subversive ambitions. Thereafter, a chastened Byrd returned to London to seek a wealthy wife, only to be rejected by at least two more well-placed young English ladies, "Minionet" and, at last, "Charmante." In 1724 he settled for a maiden lady, Maria Taylor, with much sense but little dowry. At this point in his life, after his years of vain struggle for domestic and public power and status, Byrd vented his frustration in furious outpourings against women in his "commonplace book."

Commonplace books are more cryptic than letters. They are copybooks which contain excerpts from a schoolboy's or a gentleman's readings and in which the writer was supposed to recast selected past wisdom and wit from his readings partially in his own words. In this way he would appropriate for himself both moral and practical knowledge and could practice the rhetorical flourishes with which such epigrammatic knowledge was to be presented. These books of rephrased excerpts varied considerably in what they included, but all followed two implicit rules: variety and detachment. A true gentleman never entered in his commonplace book a long series of excerpts on a single subject, and certainly never on an emotionally laden subject. Even in the pages of a private notebook, such synthesized tirades were inappropriate to eighteenth-century gentility. Yet at this moment in his life, with his political, financial, family, and marital ambitions vastly reduced in scale, William Byrd entered a highly emotional sequence of rephrased excerpts on women, reproduction, sexuality, and power in his "genteel" commonplace book.

Most of the excerpts Byrd used were taken from widely spaced locations in an encyclopedic "medical" book of information and tales on marriage, sex, and reproduction, *L'Amour Conjugal*. This chatty collection had originally been assembled by a late-seventeenth-century French physician, Nicholas Venette,* and was translated into English in repeated editions early in the eighteenth century. As a whole, Venette's work was seldom obviously misogynistic. Indeed, Venette was something of a poet of the sexual act and a great advocate of marriage. To him sexual pleasure, if placed within a marriage of mutual esteem and restraint, was nature's great gift to humankind. William Byrd's version of *L'Amour Conjugal* in his commonplace book was something else. He cut deeply into Venette's encyclopedic work, taking and resequencing isolated excerpts at long intervals, appropriating only about two percent of the Frenchman's huge compilation. Through ruthless selection, underlining his fury with his own added words and with still more pointed excerpts from other published books, Byrd extracted from Venette what can only be called the war of the sexes.

War it was. Byrd's personal conclusion both outside marriage and within it was that the sexes were in a perpetual state of reproductive, sexual, moral, and political warfare, a war in which men were almost inevitably the losers. Personal and social oblivion awaited the male victims of this eternal struggle. Thinly disguised in a veneer of implied but strained wit, this conclusion was never directly uttered, but it lurked between the lines of nearly every excerpt and in the spaces

*Kevin Berland, Department of English, Pennsylvania State University, had found this source, and he, Jan Gilliam, and I will soon publish our edition of Byrd's commonplace book.

between excerpts across the seven full pages in Byrd's commonplace devoted to this subject. His final point was that for men the only way to avoid being consumed by women is to take limited doses of the deadly hemlock, in a desperate effort to contain their desire for women. This idea can be found in Venette's encyclopedic collection, but placed at the end of Byrd's version of the war of the sexes, without Venette's variety of views, personal detachment, or warm praise of conjugal love, it is a shocking conclusion.

Byrd begins at the heart of the matter; male inadequacy:

> T'is a Common thing for Rams to tup 50 to 60 Sheep in one night which denotes a prodigious natural Vigor especially when we consider that they Seldome miss to impregnate the Female every leap they make. how short do poor men fall of these Feats!

The mirror image of this male inadequacy is, of course, female lasciviousness. So uncontrollable is female lust, indeed, that women can suppress it only by drinking blood of the object of their desire or by annihilating him.

> Faustina the Daughter of Antoninus Pius was desperately in Love with a Gladiator. She was sensible of the absurdity of so low a passion, & tryd all the Remedys of Prudence as well as abstinence against it. But alas all her Endeavours were vain, & had the effect that oil would have towards extinguishing a flame. At length she consulted the oracle which told her, nothing woud calm her concupiscence but drinking the bloud of her Beloved. This she did, & afterwards hated him to that degree that she causd him to be put to death. A very cruel Remedy against Love invented *to be sure* by the Devil himself.

With women's insatiable lust delineated, the commonplace pauses to echo Byrd's own experience with his wife's "rebellion":

> A man & his Wife were one morning in high dispute which shoud wear the Breeches. In the midst of the Fray somebody knockt at the Door, & wanted to speak with the Master of the house. Pray friend said the good man, tarry a moment, til that matter is decided & you shall have an answer. Then he returnd to the charge, & haveing subdued His Spouse with . . . arguments that convinced her *only* of his superiority, he went back to *ye* Stranger, & gave him audience to his satisfaction.

We are left by these initial passages with the impression that what a man must fear is female lust in particular but also an overweening female desire to dominate men. This line of thought is taken up again several pages later, when Byrd enters a tale in which a "philosopher" (the very term he is now using to describe himself) observes that sex is not just a pastime, because sexual intercourse and the progency it produces are a man's only path to immortality. Men *have* to have women.

> It was the hard Fate of a grave Philosopher to fall in love with a Damsel, with whome he desird to have an affair; he determind to put it to Her, but instead of makeing love in the language of other Mortals, when he got the girle alone, come my Dear said he, let you & I go this moment and make our Selves immortal; & since we must dye ourselves let us get a child that may represent us, & he another and so into all generations. This is the only way left for Man to live for ever in this world, & that way let us resolve to take.

This is harmlessly enough phrased, but in the context of the preceding entries, what Byrd seems to be saying here is that not only desire but the need to reproduce and so to be immortal lead feeble man into woman's clutches. And the ensuing entries confirm this conclusion. Over the next few hours or days or weeks—it is not certain what time was involved—he appears to have ransacked Venette, yes, but also his memory and formidable library for related quotations, as the next seven pages and thirty-five entries surge down the mental avenues opened by the thought, implicit in this passage, that even philosophers need to have intercourse with women—those lustful, powerful, dangerous beings—in order to become immortal. These thirty-five entries represent a set of appropriated and implicitly linked reflections on male and female sexual anatomy, sexuality, and reproductive power which extends far longer than any other set of entries on any subject or set of linked subjects in the entire book.

The cumulative picture implied, as such entries unfold, is one of women sexually and reproductively stronger than men, indeed reproductively virtually independent of men, nearly capable of parthenogenesis. Yet somehow women demand men's sexual attentions: "The Spartans had so much Regard for Marriag[e] that they enacted a Law by which they condemnd all old Bachelors above the age of 24 to be whipt publickly by women upon a certain Festival, and the Women were sure to lay it on very heartily, for shewing so great a disregard to their charming Sex." And men, who, whatever sexual desire they may or may not feel, wish to be immortal, dare not refuse. Is it an accident that the following entry depicts a kind of gendered genocide in the womb? "Where there are twins of different sex tis observd that the Female Seldome lives because the Male takes from it too much the natural *nourishment* & starves it in its Mothers Belly." With this entry the contest between men and women assumes the dimensions of a life-or-death struggle between two similar yet profoundly different races, who in theory need one another to reproduce, though in fact women scarcely need men, and who otherwise in their desires threaten, torture, and consume one another. But most often, women consume men.

Yet it is not lust alone but women's cleverness as well which threatens men, and in the end in the combination of female lust and cleverness is a pure and deadly power that women wield over feeble men. Men's best efforts cannot avail to save themselves from this combination. Drawn to women by a desire for sex and by their need to reproduce themselves, men are consumed and discarded by the stronger sex. Thus,

> Semiramis was very strongly inclind to the passion of Love: but at the same time so great a Prude that she constantly took care to order every Man, with whome she had an affair, to be instantly bury'd alive that he might not either thro' vanity or levity, discover her Secret. Tis pity she had not respited their punishment til they had boasted of her Favors, and then I think they would have had their Reward. But she took it for granted all men were Traytors to the Fair & therefore woud not wait for their Treason, but orderd their punishment before hand to make sure work of it.

The entire outburst ends with a series of recipes for controlling male desire, presumably in order to save men from being consumed by such females as Semiramis. In some earlier anecdotes cited here, philosophers and aged and feeble men had seemed especially vulnerable to women's lust; but now it is all men who are at risk, and the problem is not so much male age or feebleness as male desire, which draws men into a contest they cannot win. A leaden girdle upon the loins, sour lemons, and an abundance of cooling lettuce can be used. "Others have applied a Plaister of white Lillys to the Small of their backs and taken them inwardly to dry up their Seed, and Stiffle their disorderly Inclinations." And there it is, at last. Female desire is an invitation to disorder as well as, with Semiramis, to death. All male power and order, like life itself, dissolves in the female-dominated vortex of desire. Men must stifle their seed, their very chance to reproduce and to become immortal, in the hope of avoiding the deadly disorder of that vortex. Perhaps they must nearly stifle life itself: "A deccoction of Hemlock *moderately taken* will have the same Effect." Placed here at the end of the outburst, this suggestion borrowed out of context from Venette implies that men should imitate Socrates and take the hemlock, half dying in order to suppress their own feebler desires, suppressing in the process their chances of self-reproduction, in order to maintain their ordering of the world, which is their true life.

At this point, as suddenly as it began, Byrd's tirade on women is ended by the insertion in the manuscript commonplace book of a series of love letters cut from his own letterbook. These letters were written to the last of a long series of elegant English ladies who had refused to marry him. This lady is identified only as "Charmante," and she had turned him down in the last months of 1722, at most three or four years before the preceding passages were inscribed in the commonplace. What was different about "Charmante," the letters show, was that Byrd had disclosed himself to her by sending her an artificial but deeply revealing self-portrait which he had written some years before. He had sent her himself, and she had refused him. In fact, she had not even answered his letters. The inserted letters are followed in turn—still in the pages of the commonplace book—by a long reflection by Byrd on his failure to win Charmante. He makes it clear that she was desirable but promiscuous, with "more charms than honor." She had permitted him "many a close hugg and tender squeeze," not to mention "other familiarities," and then turned him down for a younger man, an Englishman of good family, renowned for his wit. At this point the letter launches into a long warning on the dangers of wit, as if this were the sole criterion on which he had been rejected.

But surely we are entitled to ask here if, by inserting these letters at this point in the commonplace, just after his long, agonized reflection on male weakness and female power, in a kind of aside without precedent in his many books-of-himself, William Byrd is not also telling us the real source of the hostility toward women which has run rampant in the immediately preceding pages of his commonplace book. By inserting these letters to break off his tirade against women, he seems to be saying that in his own mind he fears it was in fact his many weaknesses—his very maleness, his age, his reproductive and sexual inadequacy, perhaps even his colonial status—and not simply his lack of wit which had forced him to endure this last bitter rejection by "Charmante." And by inserting these letters he seems in some sense to be justifying to himself the long, impassioned tirade against women with which he has just violated the rules of that very gentility he so craved, here in the preceding pages of his commonplace book. He seems to be telling us that as a feeble man, he had been defeated, by Charmante, yes, and by Lucy, by

Incendia, and by all the women who had through the years refused the proposals of this ambitious colonial and/or denied him the control and resources he sought, and if so he is telling us that he has a right to be angry at women.

V

Byrd's fury at women had not quite spent itself. In 1725, just as the psychosexual tirade in the commonplace had ended and been excused with the tale of "Charmante"'s rejection of him, Byrd wrote an essay called "The Female Creed" in which he seems to be attacking women's minds instead of their bodies. Only women, he is saying, are still superstitious, still believe in ghosts, prophecies, dreams, and suchlike, whereas men are more enlightened and more rational. But one or two brief excerpts from Byrd's creation will show that the physically uncontrolled female still looms as large in his mind here as in the outburst in the commonplace. Really it is the lack not just of mental rationality but also of basic bodily self-control that he is projecting into "superstitious woman" in this essay. Speaking nominally in "woman's" voice, hence clad in a kind of linguistic drag, he proceeds to degrade women for their very physicality and finally, once again, for their lust:

> Hence it comes to pass that so many [superstitious] Females in all countrys can scarce hold their precious water, haveing been terrify'd in the Nursery with Bulbeggars and Apparitions. This is the case of the unfortunate Dripabunda, who when She fancy'd She saw the Ghost of her deceast Husband. From that fatal moment she lost her Retentive faculty, beyond the Relief of Pills, nor can even a Dr. intirely stop the Leak, but stil whenever she laughs beyond a Simper or a Broad Smile, the liveing Salalmoniac flows from her.

> But then alas if the fatal Point of the [fortune-telling] Pin lye towards a poor Girle, every thing that day will fall out wrong, she cannot stoop but she'l squeeze out a f . . . t, or laugh but she'll be-piss her self.

> Recommend me to discreet Fartamira, who never pretends to wipe her Backside on Such a [omen-filled] day as this, for fear of bedaubing her taper Fingers.

> It was in one of these morning-slumbers that the agreable Decora fancey'd [in a prophetic dream] she saw count Gimcrack rideing Bare-backt upon a colt which galloping up directly to her, cast his feeble Rider plumb into her lap.

> I believe when a young Gentlewoman's Elbow itches, [it is an omen that] she will shortly steal out of bed from her Sister, like Miss Fondlefellow & notwithstanding her pretended fear of Spirits, go in quest of a more Significant Bedfellow.

VI

After these misogynistic outbursts, William Byrd settled down to become what some have called "The Great American Gentleman." Just before he was to scribble his frantic projections of lust, chaos, credulity, and incontinence into women in his commonplace book and in "The Female Creed," he had taken up life with his second wife, Maria Taylor. Maria was an educated, calm spinster who brought Byrd no great dowry or distinction but provided him with a socially acceptable marriage and would later bear him his only surviving son. Though their relationship would be somewhat distant, it would continue until Byrd's death without either the passions or the obvious furies which had marked his marriage to Lucy Parke. In 1726 Byrd took Maria with him back to Virginia. England had once again refused to offer him any avenue to the wealth and influence which would have enabled him to stay on as an English gentleman of unimpeachable credentials, and his revenues in Virginia—that "melancholy corner"—badly needed his attention. He never returned to England.

Remarkably, in the years before his death in 1744, William Byrd would mature into a solid Virginia gentleman, which is probably all his father had ever intended him to be. The governorship of Virginia would never be his, but he would keep his seat on the Council and would hold other offices, ending shortly before his death in 1744 as President of the Council, the next highest official after the governor. He would also seek, in essays he never published, to create for the first time that myth of a unique *Virginia* gentility. This latter is the world of William Byrd we know best, a world of vast patriarchal estates presided over by rational, wise masters who hate slavery and ameliorate its harshness, giving occupation to all in an Edenic paradise free from the corruptions of Europe. This is a world in which a modest, persistent Virginia gentry leads lesser men through patience to draw the lines between chaos on the one hand and Virginia's hierarchical yet mutual social order on the other. Imposing yet gracious, energetic yet considerate, Byrd's Virginia gentlemen earn the respect of their inferiors, stand as reproof to the arrogance of European aristocrats, and melt our hearts with longing.

William Byrd's life poses a problem for us, however, because of the suspicion that his misogyny and his later mythmaking were somehow connected, and that a fear and hatred of women were somehow part and parcel of the agonizing process by which he reached for, and finally achieved, a stable American identity. It is precisely this argument which now needs to be drawn out of these raw materials of his life.

AN INTERPRETATION

By 1725 William Byrd II had moved from the failure of his first marriage and from the subsequent failure of his ambition to be an aristocratic English gentleman to an intensely expressed fear of and disgust for women. He passed through this brief misogynistic transition en route to a later life as a great *Virginia* gentleman and as the creator of a gorgeous myth of the Virginia gentry. How could such a creative man have been a raging misogynist? The answer is that these two prominent features of Byrd's life, his misogyny and his mythmaking, were intimately connected. They sprang from the same source, a colonial's doomed struggle to achieve distinction in the eyes of a competitive and hostile European world. This struggle gave rise both to fury at women and to a myth of American distinctiveness.

The pressures at work on William Byrd II that first made him a misogynist and then a mythmaker for his class were powerful and transitory and created a paradigm of colonial frustration. In the seventeenth and eighteenth centuries, European men's struggle to become genteel was far more demanding than a modern sensibility can recognize. Aristocratic elites controlled the centralizing monarchical states of the time. In their eyes, to fail to become a gentleman was to be consigned to the realm of the ordinary, where servants, women, and slaves dwelt. Gentility, on the other hand, conferred an unquestionable masculinity, provided acceptance everywhere in European society, and gave access to wealth, power, and influence. The competition for this status was correspondingly intense. No aspect of self-control, no detail of learning, no article of manners, and no display of taste and style could safely be neglected in the eternal crafting of the genteel self as a tool which would gain access to the elite and to the resources of its state.

Yet in this struggle aspiring men found that the financial resources they needed for genteel display, as well as the contacts they needed in order to achieve social acceptance and lucrative state contracts or offices, were frequently in the hands of women. There was no faster way to the aspects of gentility which money would buy—education, dress, fine houses, dinners, coaches, servants, bribes, the purchase of office—than marrying a woman with a large dowry or inheritance. There was no faster way to be seen in the inner circles of the resurgent aristocracy who ran the councils of state than by marrying a woman whose family was already received in these circles. For a man with minimal qualifications but few other avenues of success, marriage to the right woman could bring the full rewards of gentility overnight. But marrying a wealthy woman was not easy, and most suiters were refused.

Once a man married well, the struggle to maintain gentility, reputation, influence, and power was never over. The minimum performance expected of a gentleman, whether or not his marriage was the royal road to success he had hoped, was that he be the patriarchal master of his household. He must rule his wife, children, and servants with unquestioned authority. Without this local mastery, a gentleman lost all wider credibility. Within his family, too, then, women stood athwart the path to power, and women's power was growing. Increasingly, women's fathers protected their daughters' dowries from a new husband's control. The state itself began to limit his legal power over his wife and daughters. Simultaneously, a new ideology of benevolence urged the genteel husband to control his household through fatherly love rather than patriarchal power. By 1725, in England, gentlemen were no longer allowed to be the controlling patriarchs they were once told they had to be. To be fashionable, they had to be graceful about this loss of power; but to be too accommodating was to risk losing control, and to lose control, above all over the women in one's household, was to be no gentleman at all. Loss of control over his women could throw a would-be gentleman in a hurry badly off schedule.

In the American colonies, the handicaps on would-be gentlemen trying to master the role (and women) were vastly greater because no one could be of more doubtful gentility than a colonial. In the minds of otherwise well-informed English men and women, even as late as 1725, colonials were conceived of as black persons incapable of speaking the metropolitan tongue. To such minds colonial status automatically implied racial otherness, and so time and again Englishmen were astonished to meet *white* colonials actually speaking *English*. Curiously, those

Englishmen who knew better denigrated Virginia planters for a precisely opposite reason, not because they were "black" but because they held slaves. Slavery was increasingly out of place in an age which prided itself on its benevolence toward others. "Who are these drivers of slaves," asked Dr. Samuel Johnson when the Americans finally declared independence in 1776, "to speak thus of liberty?" To Johnson, "drivers of slaves" could not *be* gentlemen and so could claim no liberty.

These and a thousand other condemnations rained down on the heads of colonial "gentlemen" in general and often wounded Virginians in particular. Colonial gentry were labeled mere "bourgeois" who traded in rum or tobacco or were mere pettifogging lawyers, not truly genteel. At the bottom of all these accusations lay the metropolitan suspicion and the colonial fear that colonial men were little more than women, feminized by their subordinate political status and by the withering cultural contempt that accompanied that subordination. Often thwarted by women who would not marry them or submit to their control, aspiring colonial gentlemen were in English eyes themselves women, subordinate and lustful. Soon metropolitan contempt would be echoed by an evangelized agrarian populace within the colonies themselves, and hints of a corrosive American skepticism about the social claims of all would-be colonial gentlemen could already be felt in the southern back country by William Byrd II's time.

Although William Byrd II finally found a constructive way out of this dilemma by creating the myth of a modest but effective *Virginia* gentility, before he found it he would—as we have seen—work some destruction on himself and on others. Most notably, he would resent the women who stood in his way by denying him resources and control, and he would attack women in general, into whom he displaced his own feminization, his own subordinate status, and his uncontrollable lust to escape it. Byrd was in these respects very much like other men in later generations in Virginia, most notably Thomas Jefferson and his relative and ally Robert Bolling in the 1760s. All showed to an unusual degree the strains of trying to become unimpeachably genteel, and masculine, in the face of their dubious colonial status. Their particular dilemma was that the harder they tried, the more obviously colonial they were, and so the more English contempt they would earn. The result was a kind of fury in all three men, a kind of self-colonization by metropolitan standards in which the contempt of the mother culture for their colonial strivings after gentility became a self-contempt aimed at their own degrading inability to keep from striving ever harder after a European model of gentility they knew they could never reach.

All three men showed two very marked reactions to their maddening colonial situation. At one time or another all became furious with the propertied women who stood in their way, usually prospective brides who might reject them but in Jefferson's case also his mother, who controlled his inheritance. Such women repeatedly refused their overtures and so denied them the resources which they imagined would give them the gentility they craved. In the colonies, indeed, far more than in England, inheriting women were very nearly the *only* rapid source of money and connections. Clusters of ambitious men surrounded every eligible woman, elbowing one another politely in a competition Bolling was to portray as essentially unworthy and as destructive of male friendships. In any given case women used their moment of power to choose as well as they could, while most men were rejected and so lost another vital opportunity to establish their gentility—and their masculinity. When they tried for British brides, these rejections became metonymies of their larger cultural rejection by the mother country. Misogyny, fury at women, followed by a cold distancing from women, marked all three men's lives and erupted in their writings as well. And all three men condemned all women for being what they so clearly feared they themselves were: "feminine," that is, inferior, ridden by desire, and out of control.

Byrd's, Jefferson's, and Bolling's other reaction to the situation of their respective generations of Virginia men was to become local mythmakers. They became the great mythologizers of the Virginia gentry, spinning out in essays, speeches, and poetry the defensive dream of a responsible, meritorious *Virginia* gentility which put the artificial corruption of aristocratic Europe to shame. This is the myth which Jefferson and other founding fathers temporarily wrote across the face of a new independent American nation in 1776. A spartan, manly, *American* gentry, which did not need great expenditures or displays and could not be purchased by offices or honors, would lead ordinary Americans to a republic of virtue, thereby earning deference, gratitude and fame. Revolutions, it seems, are even better devices for establishing gentility than marriages. So the deadly cycle of striving, self-hatred, and extreme misogyny was finally broken by the realization of an American myth of leadership in the Revolution.

William Byrd II's fury at women, then, in the "Dunella" letter, in his commonplace book, and in "The Female Creed" must be seen in this larger context of a colonial striving to be truly genteel. It expresses the great power of the wealthy women who seemed to stand between ambitious colonial gentlemen and the full masculinity, acceptance, and power to which they aspired. The misogyny of these ambitious colonials expressed their sense of powerlessness and displaced their fear of their own lusts, failure, and potential feminization onto the very women who seemed to stand in the way of their success. While they failed to control the women who rejected them, they did renew a cultural trope under which women could be degraded, threatened, and controlled. Women, it seems, were greedy, lustful, uncontrolled, and unreliable—everything these colonial men feared they themselves were.

Under this trope men also sought meek as well as wealthy wives in order to control at least the miniature domestic universes they must rule absolutely. In this respect Byrd had once made a mistake with Lucy Parke, whose household power he had fled en route to his still more disastrous failures in England. But when he came home again to build the myth of a satisfactory Virginia gentility, he brought with him from England a less overtly challenging wife, Maria Taylor. By 1726 he had found at last two worlds, Virginia and Maria, he could master. He did so, as both mythmaker and politician, until his death in 1744. What Byrd's women thought of him, we cannot know, save that Lucy fought him tooth and nail, and many others rejected him. For the most part their letters have not been saved, nor have their commonplace books or diaries. We know only that Maria outlived him and that she also outlived their son, who committed suicide in 1777, to become mistress of Westover.

That our myths—these myths, anyway, Byrd's and Jefferson's—are grounded in such troubled soil does not make the myths less beautiful. It means that history hangs always between pain and myth, and in the space between, we make our lives, men and women alike, wisely or at least wittingly.

Sources: Most of the surviving historical documents on William Byrd's life, above all most of his own writings and letters, are readily available in published editions. The "Dunella" letter is in *The Correspondence of the Three William Byrds of Westover, Virginia, 1684–1776,* edited by Marion Tinling, published in two volumes for the Virginia Historical Society by the University Press of Virginia (Charlottesville, 1977), vol. I, p. 275. "The Female Creed" is in *Another Secret Diary of William Byrd of Westover,* edited by Maude H. Woodfin and Marion Tinling (Richmond, 1942), pp. 449–475. Byrd's sole surviving commonplace book, dating roughly from 1721 to 1726, is in the Virginia Historical Society in Richmond; with the society's permission it is being edited for 1997 publication by the Institute of Early American History and Culture and the University of North Carolina Press. The remaining published sources—above all Byrd's other two diaries—and the details of Byrd's life are recounted in Kenneth A. Lockridge, *The Diary, and Life, of William Byrd II of Virginia* (Chapel Hill, 1987), in Lockridge, *On the Sources of Patriarchal Rage: The Commonplace Books of William Byrd and Thomas Jefferson and the Gendering of Power in the Eighteenth Century* (New York, 1992), and in the introduction by Kevin Berland, Jan Gilliam, and Kenneth Lockridge to the forthcoming edition of the Byrd commonplace book referred to above. For recent and well-considered looks at Byrd at his magnificent, and mature, peak, see Margaret Beck Pritchard and Virginia Lascara Sites, *William Byrd II and His Lost History* (Williamsburg, 1993), and Susan Manning, "Industry and Idleness in Colonial Virginia: A New Approach to William Byrd II," *Journal of American Studies,* vol. 28, no. 2 (1994), pp. 169–190.

5

THE GREAT NEGRO PLOT IN NEW YORK

THOMAS J. DAVIS

Before the American Revolution the institution of slavery was deeply embedded in every colony in North America. Although it was the southern colonies that found the greatest economic use for African slaves, northerners were actively engaged in the slave trade as well as the ownership of slaves. Before the English conquered New Netherland in 1664, Dutch merchants in New Amsterdam (later New York City) were the most active slave traders, and their colony held the greatest percentage of African slaves outside of the South. When the English crown captured New Netherland and defeated the great seagoing empire of the Dutch, it also took over the leading role in the slave trade and continued the tradition of slavery in New York City.

Some historians have assumed that conditions of slavery in New Netherland and New York were much more benign than in the plantation South, that slaves were allowed more freedom and given better care. But as T. J. Davis's story reveals, that assumption is erroneous; slaves were just as likely, if not more likely, to revolt in New York than in the South. In 1712 there was an uprising of slaves which was met with a bloodbath of retaliation on the part of frightened whites. New restrictions were imposed on the movement of Africans, and punishments were increased for violations of the regulations. A generation later, in 1741, Africans once again protested their treatment in ways that whites chose to interpret as a "conspiracy." This time the retaliation was swift and even more brutal than it had been following the 1712 revolt; seventeen African men were hanged and thirteen were burned at the stake. Thirteen men burned at the stake! In the century of the Enlightenment, this fact requires us to pause and reflect on what was at stake for the white population.

Davis's essay, however, is not so much concerned with white fears and reactions to Africans as with the experiences of Africans themselves. In traditional historical sources the lives of powerless and frequently illiterate men and women are almost impossible to recover, but an unusual or dramatic event can generate documents (trial transcripts, for example) that illuminate the lives of ordinary people. Thus, Davis wants not so much to relate to us the events of the "revolt," as dramatic and compelling as they were, but to reveal the human reactions of African men and women caught in the institution we abstractly know as slavery. Davis has focused on one of

*the men eventually tried, convicted, and burned at the stake for his part in the
"conspiracy," allowing us a glimpse of what it is like for human beings forced to exist
in a completely inhumane system. Davis's principal character, Quack, clearly longed
for freedom from the slave system and shared many tirades with his friends about such
a possibility, but it was the personal level, about such things as being allowed to see
his wife, that led to Quack's deepest frustration and prompted him to take action
directly against her owner. It was not a consciously political protest or an organized
conspiracy, but it was certainly a personal act of resistance that was ultimately
political.*

*In the wake of the 1741 "revolt," New Yorkers did not even consider abolishing
slavery; they simply took more measures to confine and restrict African freedom. Not
until the American Revolution did New Yorkers legislate the gradual abolition of
slavery—there were slaves in the state of New York until 1827, a full half century
after the Declaration of Independence.*

I

Quack went to visit his wife on a late winter night in 1741. She lived at Fort
George, on the west side of Manhattan Island's southern tip. Later residents
of New York City called the area Battery Park. The seat of government for Great
Britain's colonial Province of New York occupied the site in 1741, for the fort—
named successively after the reigning monarch, who then was George II (who
reigned from 1727 to 1760)—was the colony's administrative center. It housed
the Assembly, the province's legislative body, and the provincial records office. It
held an arsenal and barracks for the royal army garrison. Its guns guarded New
York harbor, commanding approaches along the East River and along what contemporaries called the North River, later known as the Hudson. The fort also held
the official residence of the colonial governor. It was there that Quack went.

Making his way against the chill in the gloomy shadows on the frost-hardened
dirt cow path called Broadway, Quack strode with doubtless delight and dismay.
For while thoughts of being with his wife perhaps warmed him, having to make
the trek at all had to gnaw at him.

Quack's journey was one of a sort that New York City's citizenry forced him
and most other African-American men to take if they cared to share a few mo-
ments' intimacy with their spouses or their children on an occasional night or on
a day other than that declared day of supposed rest which was the Lord's Day and
simultaneously the enslaved's day—the day custom lightened their usual burden.

Quack hardly stood alone in chafing at the one-day-in-seven interval of temporary relief from enforced separation. Restrictions slaveholders personally, and
the ruling community collectively, placed on visitations were common themes of
complaints among blacks. In word and deed, Quack and other black men complained and challenged the common and long-established practice in colonial
New York City of holding enslaved spouses in separate residences.

The configuration of separation that prevailed in the colonial eighteenth-
century English city existed long before Quack's outing. As early as 1703, less than
half of all the African-American males fourteen years or older in Manhattan—

which constituted all of colonial New York City—lived in a household with an African-American female fourteen years or older. Only ninety-five black males resided in a household where a black female also lived. They were 40.4 percent of the 235 black males in the city.

The household distribution of enslaved blacks by gender in 1703 illustrated the character of the separation. There were 303 households reported as containing enslaved African-Americans. Most of these (139 in number; 45.4 in percent) had only one black resident—a black female in 91 households and a black male in 48. Seventy-nine residences had two blacks: in 46 the blacks were both male; in 22 they were both female; and in 11 there were one black male and one black female. The other 85 households held three or more African-Americans, 84 of whom were males and 251 of whom were females.

Separate residences, then, were a fact of life for the majority of enslaved blacks in New York City at the beginning of the 1700s. It was so for Quack and his wife and other blacks among the nearly 2000 on Manhattan in 1741. And it would continue to be so. Yet a significant difference marked the gender configurations among the city's total population of 11,000 in 1741, for while white women outnumbered white men by 100 to 91, the ratio of black men to black women stood near its historic high: there were more than 120 black men for every 100 black women.

The ratios reflected a relatively high number of black men in the city in 1741, for about 1 in 4 of all the city's males aged sixteen to sixty years then was black. The high ratio strained social control and produced some anxiety because black men—particularly those like Quack between sixteen and thirty years of age—often proved troublesome in the eyes of many. They were the ones who usually packed illegal drinking houses and had their hands in burglaries and other non-petty crimes. And they were the ones who were generally what whites called "insolent." The sheriff, constables, nightwatch, and other officials of the city and of the colony complained repeatedly about black men's violating what the law deemed good order, peace, and quiet.

Being on his way to see his wife that winter night, Quack was breaking the law. He was on the street in violation of statutes and ordinances that required him and all other slaves to be within their own holders' households after dark unless accompanied by the holder or the holder's designated agent, or unless on the holder's business and with the holder's written permission and illuminated by a handheld lamp.

Quack carried no lamp to illuminate himself. He was not accompanied by his holder, the prominent house painter John Roosevelt—a distant forebear of Presidents of the later United States. Nor did Quack have his holder's express written permission. Nor was he with any designated agent. He was about his own business—as he often was.

That night Quack was off to see his wife. On another night he might have been off to Hughson's. The constables tagged the place down toward the riverside off Broadway, not far from Trinity Church at Wall Street, a "disorderly" public house.

Hughson's was one of at least a dozen pubs where blacks gathered to get away, to drink, to party, or just to relax. All that was, of course, illegal, as statutes and ordinances sought to confine blacks to work and tried to restrict their personal expression, individually and collectively. But blacks almost routinely ignored the law and carved out their own space. And they were not alone.

Whites found lucrative profit in catering to blacks' needs and desires. The illegal traffic was a boon to John Hughson and his wife Sarah and to other whites who owned and operated spots blacks frequented. Other whites frequented the tippling houses too. Sailors, soldiers, and workingmen—the lower sort, in some eyes—rubbed elbows and shared complaints with blacks about the whites who ran New York to suit themselves. Blacks called the ruling whites "Backarara" or "buckra" and talked about being "rich like the Backarara." Whites like the sailor Christopher Wilson of the *Flamborough*, the soldier William Kane of the Fort George garrison, and the hat-maker David Johnson frolicked with the blacks and along with them cursed the Backarara.

The public authorities loathed places such as Hughson's and the mixing that occurred there. Justice Frederick Philipse of the Supreme Court of Judicature, New York's highest colonial bench, decried the pubs and "all such persons who sell rum, and other strong liquor to Negroes" as "notorious" and "wicked." "It must be obvious to every one," the judge declared, "that there are too many of them in this city who, under pretence of selling what they call a penny dram to a Negro, will sell to him as many quarts or gallons of rum, as he can steal money or goods to pay for."

Constables raided pubs to deter the gatherings. They hit Hughson's more than once. City Constables Joseph North and Peter Lynch recalled one raid in April 1740 when about fourteen lawmen fell on the place and cleared it out.

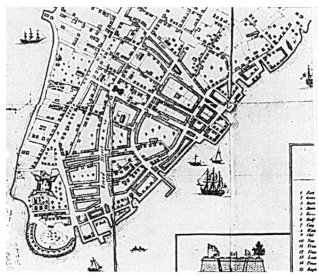

New York and environs, 1742-1744, with Fort George. (*Valentine's Manual,* 1854)

"When we came there, we went into the room where the Negroes were round a table, eating and drinking, for there was meat on the table, and knives and forks; and the Negroes were calling for what they wanted," the two constables declared with apparent dismay at blacks' dining well with proper utensils and being waited on by whites—particularly by fair, young white women. North made his sore displeasure plain: He "laid his cane about them, and soon cleared the room of them," Lynch reported of how the blacks were dispatched.

The constables had other worries about places like Hughson's, for stolen goods were trafficked there to pay for liquor and other liberties, lawmen claimed. In fact, one of Hughson's frequent customers and a drinking companion of Quack's was reputed among authorities to be one of the city's major traffickers. His name was Caesar—at least that is what his holder, the baker Jacobus Vaarck, called him. Word was he preferred to call himself John Gwin. Word also was that he headed a theft ring labeled the Geneva Club. It had been operating since at least 1736, when Caesar and another black named Prince were caught and publicly whipped for stealing some Holland gin named Geneva from Baker's Tavern.

No evidence indicated that Quack had a hand in illegal, heavy lifting. He apparently left such larceny to Caesar, Prince, and others in the city's underworld. Nevertheless, he clearly shared in the organized crime environment created largely by oppressive regulations that sought to isolate and impoverish not merely enslaved blacks but others also. He joined with his fellow blacks such as Caesar and Prince and Will and Cuffee and with whites such as the sailor Christopher Wilson, and the soldier William Kane, and the hat-maker David Johnson to curse the upper-crust for leaving only crumbs for the less fortunate and to re-claim what they saw as necessary for ordinary living.

Like the others, Quack also uttered more personal grievances. He shared particularly with Will complaints about how his wife's holder treated him. Held by the clock-maker Alexander Ward, Will was a relatively recent arrival in New York City. He had come in 1736 from Antigua, shortly after the West Indian island suffered a major black uprising. Slaveholders there had been quick to ship out likely troublemakers, and Will was on the list to go. In Manhattan he settled in to his trade and found a wife. She was a slave held by Abraham Van Horne, a member of the governor's council. The elderly Van Horne may have been a friend of the governor's, but he won no favor with Will. "Van Horne won't allow me to come to my wife," Will griped. "But before long I'll show him a trick," he threatened and added, "the Negroes here are cowards. They've no hearts as those in Antigua."

Quack commiserated with Will in his anger at controls on conjugal visits. Such restrictions clearly cut to the core of the lack of self-determination enslavement imposed. But the limits on liberty were everywhere, and the complaints flowed freely. At Hughson's and elsewhere, blacks like Quack and Will complained about their circumstances and condition. They cursed holders too cheap to supply them with more than shabby clothing or shoddy goods or meager meals. Many supplemented their lot by taking what they needed or wanted. But nipping at the edges fell short of the central reality, and they talked about changing that too. They talked openly about overthrowing slavery and agreed that would be a change worth killing for and perhaps worth dying for.

One group was especially vocal in cursing their enslavement in the winter of 1741. Known collectively as the Spanish Negroes, the group was made up of shipmates captured aboard the sloop *La Soledad*. Privateer Captain John Lush seized it at sea as a prize in the war with Spain that had begun in 1739 and become known as King George's War. *La Soledad*'s fair-skinned, European-featured crewmen were handled as prisoners of war, but counting African features as a presumption of slave status, the admiralty court condemned nineteen dark-skinned crewmen to slavery and sold them as bondsmen. Their English was halting, but they made themselves understood as they refused to submit quietly. "If the captain [Lush] won't send us back to our own country, we'll ruin all the city, and the first house we'll burn will be his," they declared. "Damn that son-of-a-bitch. We'll make a devil of him."

Quack and others respected the Spanish Negroes' bold talk, but Quack understood the need for more than talk. And so he was off that night to his wife.

II

Quack's wife lived in the governor's residence. She was the governor's cook. The extant records have noted her not by name but only by her intimacy with Quack and her employment by the widower George Clarke, who in 1741 was acting governor of New York. She was a woman entered in the public record, like most of her gender regardless of race, not in her own terms but in terms of her relations to men. Among men acquainted with Quack, she was called merely "Quack's wife" in a form of address that differed not so much from that which referred to Mrs. George Clarke or the governor's wife, for example.

The marital relationship between Quack and his wife was not a matter of law. The law denied their capacity to form any contract, including the agreement to marry. It denied them the status of being one in law, united as a man and woman owing each other and the community the legal duty to discharge each other's obligations. The law further denied them the act of a ceremonial marriage that followed all statutory requirements.

The law lacked the power, however, to deny the fact of the two's consensual, ceremonial marriage. Quack and his wife, like Will and his wife and other men and women similarly situated, exercised their own personal power individually and collectively to exchange commitments with each other, to consummate their commitment to each other, and to have their commitment solemnized by social recognition. The exchange at times was favored among the Dutch predecessors of the British in colonial New York both with religious rite, complete with a minister presiding, and with recording in a church registry. So, the impediments that denied Quack and his wife legal recognition as spouses failed to block the essential fact of their union as husband and wife.

Like the fact of Quack's presence on the streets that winter night, the fact of his and his wife's union embodied the tension between the theory instituted in law and the practice established in fact in the lives of African-Americans in colonial New York. In law the institution of slavery defined the status of African-Americans. But their standing before the law and their actual living of everyday life were not one and the same.

The law defined relations of an individual or a group of individuals to others in the community. It recognized capacities, incapacities, and duties. The law stood, however, as a more or less systematic statement of principles. It elaborated a mental plan that represented an idea of what relations should be in prescription. What the law imagined did not necessarily correspond with what actually occurred.

New York law—like that of other American colonies and later states that maintained slavery—created fictions in an effort to distinguish, establish, and protect a bundle of legally enforceable claims called property rights. The law deemed slaves property, not people: that was a patent fiction. And to enforce the law, to make the legal relations appear as actual relations, demanded immediate and threatened brute force aimed at preventing the natural development and expression of personality among the enslaved.

Legal and social repression, however severe or strict, failed to so subdue enslaved African-Americans as to deny the fact of their personality. Quack and his wife were natural persons, regardless of what the law decreed. No force could extinguish their personality, even if it snuffed out their lives. In exercising and expressing their personality in relation to each other and the wider society day in and day out, enslaved blacks like Quack and his wife acted out the most profound defiance and opposition to slavery. They simply refused to be controlled.

The law said Quack and others like him were not to be out after dark unescorted and without permission. Nor were they to seek or succeed in gratifying basic human urges for companionship and diversion by gathering together, by taking time to relax and play and laugh, by feeling unfettered and acting freely as a person for at least an hour or two or more. All that was prohibited to Quack and his wife by law. All of it was criminal for them and others like them.

The class of crime consisted not in what lawyers would describe technically as *malum en se* (evil in itself). The activity was not necessarily evil in itself. Nor was the character of the activity as proscribed what determined the crime. It was the specified character, the personal condition, of the doer that determined the crime. Thus, specified activity became a crime for a slave not because the activity was evil in itself or a crime for anyone else; the activity was a crime because the person was a slave.

As a class, the activity was status crime. It was a crime for the enslaved because they were enslaved. The society's law enforcement minions sought to compel compliance. But Quack and his wife and others like them denied their authority and defied their control, for the law's repressive regulations were unrealistic and thus ultimately unenforceable.

No means existed to check the slaves' every move, every moment of the day, every day. Supervision, whether at home or at work, was often casual and sometimes perfunctory. Indeed, holders usually showed themselves more interested in services than in systematic supervision. Most interested themselves in what their slaves did in relation to them, their families, and their business. Holders usually left public officers to maintain public order.

Recognizing the futility of trying to enforce every element of the legal and social regulation of the slave status, law enforcers necessarily concentrated on preventing slaves from disturbing the peace in any major way. Insurrection was the gravest fear among the citizenry. In fact, slave insurrection was a constant fear. It was the dread spectacle. All else paled in comparison in the popular white imagination. All else was not insignificant, but against the less spectacular—the common, cumulative, and continuous—resistance to enslavement, the authorities only occasionally cracked down because the behavior was so difficult for them to control. When they did punish, however, the city's official guardians believed in making examples.

Because the authorities usually winked at common infractions such as breaking curfew, Quack walked to his wife's in no great danger of the regular forces of repression.

But Quack was headed for trouble.

III

Like other slaveholders, Governor George Clarke was jealous of his slaves' services. Sentiment like his showed itself in New York City especially among holders of enslaved females used for domestic service, as Quack's wife was. Holders continually complained about domestic interruptions. They complained about enslaved women's childbearing and childrearing. For example, one holder placed an ad in a city newspaper offering for sale a female cook, like Quack's wife, with the complaint that "she breeds too fast for her owner to put up with such inconveniences."

Clarke and others like him were not agreeable to domestics' not being accessible or at hand on demand. Such holders resented any interruption or intrusion within their households, and for that reason they often frowned on and at times forbade their domestics' receiving visitors—particularly female domestics' receiving black male visitors, especially at night.

The prospect of having to face down in the dark of night a black man who was perhaps unfamiliar, unknown, or unruly troubled many slaveholders. They had no direct control over such men. Female visitors at night were seldom a concern. Men might go out after dark, but women ventured outside at night on only a few occasions in the New York City of that time. And if they did go out, it was unlikely they went either unescorted or uninvited. Night visits from women were not a problem. Night visits from men were a problem.

Black men were a most troublesome presence. They accounted for the bulk of crime among slaves. More than three-fourths (77.1 percent) of all crimes by enslaved persons that reached court throughout the Province of New York from 1691 to 1776 involved a charge against black men. When black women appeared in colonial New York courts for an offense, it usually was for petty theft. The disorderly conduct that officials termed "illegal relations" and crimes of violence that so worried citizens invariably involved black men. They were the ones who evaded curfew, as Quack was doing that late winter night in 1741. They were the ones who crowded "disorderly houses" such as Hughson's. They were the ones whose furtive knock at the kitchen door caused fright and trouble.

Holders who had experienced some disorder or who were apprehensive of some disturbance from black men's visiting their household often issued instructions to stop the visitations. They forbade the men from coming and the women from receiving them. Ordering such a cessation and enforcing it were not the same thing, and both created obvious tensions. Keeping husbands from visiting their wives was a prescription for resentment and confrontation.

IV

When Quack arrived at Fort George that March night in 1741, he found that the sentry at the gate was Private James McDonald. Quack knew the soldier, and the soldier knew Quack at least from Quack's frequent visits to see his wife. McDonald also knew that Quack's appearing that night spelled trouble because Governor Clarke had issued orders forbidding Quack's entry into the fort to visit his wife. Simply put, Clarke had tired of Quack's being in his house at night or at any other time. But there Quack was, seeking entry. And that was McDonald's problem.

As governor, Clarke had the privilege of an armed guard to compel obedience to his personal edict denying Quack's visitation to his wife. Without the garrison sentry, Clarke would likely have had to face Quack himself and enforce his own rule.

Private McDonald later testified to the difficulty of his task.

"I knew that the governor had some time before forbid Quack coming to the fort," McDonald explained. "I opposed his entrance within the gate. But Quack was resolute and pushed forward."

"Whether you will or not, I'm coming in," Quack said.

McDonald refused to yield, and Quack refused to retreat.

A scuffle ensued.

McDonald clubbed Quack to the ground, using his rifle. But Quack did not stay down. He rose, collared McDonald, and gaining an opening dashed into the fort and then into the governor's kitchen, demonstrating a fierce determination to do what he set out to do—at least see his wife.

If victory it was, it was short-lived.

The officer of the guard heard both the bustle and McDonald's report. Leading a detail of sufficient force to the governor's kitchen, he located Quack.

McDonald summarized the result succinctly. "We went and fetched him and turned him out of the fort."

The rough handling was more than Quack would bear. He vented his indignation at Hughson's, joining others in angry talk of returning injuries for the wrongs done them. Talking of revenge, nodding and agreeing with one another, however, was like so much else in the after-hours world created at Hughson's and other such places: it was legally criminal. In this case the talk and agreement created essential elements of the crime of conspiracy.

In speaking of doing harm and agreeing to it, Quack and his companions such as Caesar, Prince, and Cuffee agreed to act illegally. They had dared not merely to think forbidden thoughts; they dared to give voice to such thoughts and then to agree one with another on the doing of such thoughts. It was talk, but because the talk was agreeing to an unlawful purpose, the talk itself constituted the basis of crime. The only essential evidence needed to convict was proof of the talk and the agreement.

Quack did more than talk, however.

V

Quack returned to the fort in mid-March, but not to visit his wife.

He gained entry without a bustle. He then did what he had talked of.

"I took a firebrand out of the servants' hall and carried it up into the garret on the seventeenth at night, St. Patrick's [Day]," Quack confessed. He intended to set the place afire.

"I thought the fort would've been on fire [that] night. . . . [W]hen I came up the next morning into the garret, I found the brand alight, and then went away again," he explained.

If Quack was disappointed by the timing, he had no need to be disappointed by the result.

Near noon on March 18, 1741, flames leaped from George Clarke's roof. The fire not only caught the governor's official residence but also felled the entire fort. The chapel, the provincial secretary's office, the barracks, the armory—the whole structure surrendered.

The blaze leveled the fort and threatened to burst beyond. Flames licked at houses bordering the fort on Stone Street, on Broad Street, and on Broadway. Most of New York City—which then occupied a mere six square miles on Manhattan's southern tip—lay within the fire's reach. As the sparks flew to the first rows of homes, fear spread of a conflagration like the five-day great fire that destroyed much of London, England, in September 1666.

A rain shower citizens called providential dampened the flames and saved the city, although Fort George was laid waste and its rubble long smoldered. Among the city's cluster of 11,000 residents a collective sigh at escaping greater destruction mingled with mutterings about the fort's devastation. In almost the same breath as the sigh, people asked how the fire had started.

Time for reflection proved brief, for exactly one week after the blaze at the fort, fire struck again as the home of the colonial chief justice's brother-in-law went ablaze. And in the next thirteen days fire struck eight more times, igniting profound fears.

When fire struck houses on either side of a home where a Spanish Negro named Juan lived as a slave, angry townsmen interrogated him. Not liking his answers and thinking he was "behaving himself insolently," in one observer's words, citizens dragged Juan to jail and raised a hue and cry to "Take up the Spanish Negroes."

Reports of another black's being overheard whooping "Fire, Fire, Scorch, Scorch, A LITTLE, damn it, BY-AND-BY" added consternation among citizens.

On Monday, April 6, 1741, when four fires struck the city and Quack's companion Cuffee was caught fleeing the scene of one of the worst fires, citizens began to scream, "The Negroes are rising!"

White mobs snatched black men everywhere in the city and hustled nearly two hundred into the cells at City Hall. A six-month-long investigation and prosecution ensued. It fixed on a sensational vision of many whites' worst fears—a coordinated, armed insurrection of slaves.

The war with Spain deepened the dread. No combat had yet reached New York's soil, but the colony's ships and men were in combat in the Atlantic and the Caribbean. Whether the fighting would reach New York was a repeated question; and the suggestion of some concerted action between blacks and the Spanish, particularly in light of the presence and demeanor of the Spanish Negroes, sounded credible to many.

History heightened the prospect of attack, for New York City had suffered successive invasion and capture. The English themselves laid claim in 1664 by forcing what then was called Nieu Amsterdam to surrender. The Dutch returned the favor in 1673, capturing the city during the Third Anglo-Dutch War and only restoring it to the English as a result of the Treaty of Westminster in 1674. In 1740 and 1741 Spanish warships were frequently reported off the Carolinas coast, and Spanish merchant ships like *La Soledad* taken as prizes of war already sat at Manhattan's docks. So the enemy did not appear distant.

Not merely the prospect of an armada unnerved many New Yorkers. In their minds they faced not simply an antagonistic empire in Spain but a diabolical ideological foe—the Roman Catholic religion. They viewed Spain as the primary proponent of an Antichrist, the Pope. They feared then not just the Spanish at arms but Catholics in any guise, for they viewed them as spies plotting to destroy Protestants everywhere. No machination was too large or too small for some New Yorkers to envision as part of an ongoing Catholic conspiracy seeking worldwide papal dominion. Thus, a slave-Spanish plot stood starkly in many minds.

Even while many citizens conjured up images of being beset by foreign enemies, most closely at hand and most suspicious to most were the city's 2000 blacks. Almost all enslaved, the blacks proved perennially troublesome. They often appeared intractable, sometimes disorderly and even rowdy. Their public disobedience worried many whites, who constantly doubted blacks' allegiance. Common distrust, then, made blacks popular targets when the community felt imperiled, as it did amid the fires from March 18 to April 6.

Nothing akin to the slaughter of whites during the black uprising in the city during 1712 had occurred. The events then had begun with fire, as in 1741. Just after midnight on the April day in 1712, a group of at least twenty-five African-Americans pounced on whites in the city's east ward. They bludgeoned, hacked, stabbed, and shot nearly two dozen whites.

Nineteen blacks paid the ultimate price in public executions for that ultimate impudence. Fourteen hanged immediately. A pregnant woman named Sarah was the fifteenth set to hang, but she was reprieved until her baby's birth. One burned at the stake. Another roasted to death from eight to ten hours suspended over a slow fire. One was hung in chains and left to starve to death. The last was broken on the wheel.

The price paid in 1741 was similarly horrific. The prosecution began in April and ended in August. Pressing an underlying charge of conspiracy, it used the events to sweep through New York City. As a result, thirty black men were executed, seventeen by hanging and thirteen by burning at the stake. Four whites were also hanged: John Hughson and his wife, Sarah; one of their lodgers, Margaret Kerry, who was reputed to be intimate with Geneva Club chief Caesar; and John Ury, a schoolmaster accused of being a combination of Roman Catholic priest, Spanish spy, and mastermind and instigator of a slave uprising.

The first blacks to die were Caesar and his Geneva Club mate Prince. They were hanged on May 11.

Quack was one of the first two burned. He died May 30. His companion at the stake was Cuffee. He had once declared, "A great many people have too much and others too little." His arrest after fleeing a warehouse blaze on April 6 had touched off the final mobbing of blacks. The clock-maker Will also was burned at the stake; he was executed on July 4. Juan and four others among those called the Spanish Negroes were among seventy-two black men banished from New York as punishment for what came to be called the New York Conspiracy, or "the Great Negro Plot."

AN INTERPRETATION

The fateful episode immortalized as the New York Conspiracy, or "the Great Negro Plot," has received relatively little attention. Indeed, for long it was an obscure curiosity, with even less recognition than the fact that New York City ranked second only to Charleston, South Carolina, as an urban center of slavery in colonial British North America. When the episode has received attention, it usually has been approached by way of a dichotomy that asked if there was a conspiracy and then wrote off all the events as a tragic error on the part of a prosecution unleashed by popular hysteria.

Only rarely has the episode received attention for its intrinsic detail. In that regard it has been treated very differently than the Salem witchcraft episode of 1692, where the historical question has not been simply whether there really were witches. The question in Salem has been, How was it that nineteen persons were hanged and one crushed to death? Similarly, what happened in 1741 to move New York to execute thirty-four persons deserves attention for what the answers reveal about the nature of colonial New York.

The episode fully exposed the prevailing racial attitudes and the troubling black presence in colonial New York. It exposed, however, not merely frightful tensions of race but also hateful strains of class, national origin, and religion. It revealed a world not merely of black-white suspicions but one where consuming suspicions of difference set group against group on the basis of color, creed, ethnicity, and wealth.

The episode had many stories and perspectives. The one emphasized here was the individual, intimate, private, and personal interaction in the life of a slave in colonial New York City. The fire Quack set sparked a conflagration. Yet it was no cataclysm. It signaled nothing of the too often storied ultimate black rebellion to end all enslavement and oppression. What it did signal was perhaps more formidable, for it was not merely fantasy. It altered reality.

Day in and day out Quack and others like him resisted the essence of the repression that aimed at denying their humanity. They refused to succumb. They forced adjustment. They made accommodation two-sided, pushing slaveholders and their society perforce to recognize and respect, however reluctantly, blacks' needs and desires or pay a price for the refusal. Therein lay the most meaningful and powerful resistance to enslavement, for it was what altered the streaming substance that from moment to moment made up African-American life.

Quack and those like him did not go gently into the night or to their death. They defied and denied their enslavement. Theirs was not the arms-in-hand fight to the death of the uprising in New York City in 1712, the Stono Rebellion in South Carolina in 1739, or Nat Turner's renowned insurrection in Southampton, Virginia, in 1831. Such occasional explosions have too often seized all vision and imagination and blinded viewers to the persistent, powerful, and less spectacular struggle not for overall control of the society or the slave system but over the choices of daily life—such as to be or not be with one's spouse.

Sources: This story is extracted largely from T. J. Davis, *A Rumor of Revolt: The 'Great Negro Plot' in Colonial New York* (New York: Free Press, 1985; pb. ed. Amherst: University of Massachusetts Press, 1990). The book contains full documentation. The main primary sources are available in Thomas J. Davis, ed., *The New York Conspiracy* (Boston: Beacon Press, 1971).

6

BENJAMIN FRANKLIN'S NEW WORLD

PATRICIA J. TRACY

In 1771 Benjamin Franklin—already famous as a journalist, popular philosopher, and scientist, becoming known as a statesman—began to write his autobiography. Since its first publication in English in 1817, this text has usually been read as representing the inevitable political radicalization of an intelligent British colonist as well as the conscious creation of an "American" personality. Patricia Tracy's essay calls our attention to problems with these common impressions of Franklin's Autobiography, *as well as to the intriguing layers of craft with which this calculating narrator seeks to shape his factually true but ideologically "packaged" story. That craft and its resulting ambiguities are as revealing about the culture of eighteenth-century America as is the basic story of a "self-made" man.*

The Autobiography *actually ends with events in 1757, long before anyone imagined American political and cultural independence, and even as he began writing in 1771, Franklin was trying to mediate between the King and his rebellious colonies. The last section of the narrative, written in 1784 and just before his death in 1790, never tells the reader directly how this "citizen of the world" came to reject his British identity. This* Autobiography *is, on the surface, in fact, the story of Franklin the loyal Briton! The hard-working, ascetic personality that Franklin cultivated so deliberately from his childhood was designed to ensure a successful career—as a businessman and an intellectual—by catching up with the cutting edge of cultural change in Europe. The spread of capitalism and Enlightenment philosophy revised forever the rules of being a citizen in Europe and its colonies, and Franklin tells us how he rose from poverty and ignorance to comfort and public renown. As the political implications of the new commercial and intellectual behavior came to be recognized, however, this remodeled self became more characteristic of America than Britain, because the ideas of "self-government"—in personal and community terms—that were first developed in Europe could be put into practice more easily in the New World.*

In this new culture, men such as Benjamin Franklin could also revise an old form of instructive literature—the biography or autobiography of men who mastered great events in war, politics, or religious life (a genre that traces back to ancient Greece)—and offer an everyday self-education in the details of an ordinary businessman's life as a model for other citizens. In contrast to the forthright religious preaching of the didactic literature on which he had been raised, Franklin the professional journalist used a "folksy" style to promulgate a newly secularized common-sense morality that was learnable in easy steps. Undoubtedly aware that his narrative would be published, he poked gentle fun at his own "errata" that taught sound lessons, and he couldn't resist a printer's joke that he would live his wonderful life over again if he could have an author's chance at "correcting in a second edition some faults of the first." In the interest of morality or personal privacy, however, he chose not to reveal more serious sins such as the illegitimate birth of his son William, who became governor of New Jersey in 1763 despite his humble beginnings.

In the new American republic, Franklin suggested that opportunities for success awaited anyone who was hard-working and self-disciplined. But although Franklin has always been hailed as the American "Everyman," we shouldn't leave our encounter with his Autobiography *without questioning whether his life and his political program really lived up to the claims about representativeness that he made for himself and that have been made for him as a "model" American.*

S tarting off in life in 1706 as the fourteenth of seventeen children of a poor soap-maker in Boston did not predict great economic success, let alone international acclaim as a journalist, scientist, and diplomat. But Benjamin Franklin remade himself into one of the leading citizens of the world by the time of his death in 1790. It took hard work, skill in thinking and writing, a talent for sensing the political wind, and an even greater talent for self-advertisement. All of these traits are revealed in his *Autobiography*, begun in his sixty-fifth year, when he could look back with tender amusement at the scruffy and ignorant but clever boy who had become a great man.

Ben's father, Josiah Franklin, was an English immigrant whose two wives gave birth to seventeen children, of whom thirteen lived into adulthood. About double the average size in New England, this family was more typical in its migration for religious and economic opportunity, with mixed results. Josiah, a silk-dyer in England, scraped by in Massachusetts as a soap- and candle-maker. He was free to practice his Presbyterian faith, but his dream of sending Ben, his youngest son, into the ministry foundered when he could afford to give him only two years of formal education. Ben then fretfully helped in his father's workshop and was patiently trotted around the city to observe all sorts of tradesmen: apprenticeship was the only way to learn a skilled craft, and neither father nor son was apparently tempted by the farming life.

But the boy refused to show interest in any craft and kept threatening to run off to sea. Historians know so little about the experience of children in this era—they rarely recorded their own views of things—that we can't tell if Ben was an unusually difficult child for his parents to guide toward adulthood. When he reminisced with affectionate nostalgia in his old age, he saw his childhood resistance to authority not as the sin of disobedience (undoubtedly his parents' view) but as the seed of a positive virtue in adulthood. In the *Autobiography* he used a characteristic mock-apologetic voice to recount his "scrapes" with the neighborhood boys, including organizing his playmates to steal a huge pile of stones from a house-construction site to make a fishing wharf. These pranks exasperated his father but also demonstrated "an early projecting public spirit, tho' not then justly conducted." He would learn in time to expend his organizing talents on socially useful projects.

Josiah Franklin finally apprenticed his wayward boy to another son, James, a printer, and Ben liked that trade mostly because he was "passionately fond of reading." Since the idea of a public library had not yet been invented, Ben made friends with gentlemen with private libraries who would lend books to a boy so hungry for education that he would sit up all night to finish them. Any money that came his way went for books: his first purchase was a multivolume set of the works of John Bunyan, whose *Pilgrim's Progress* was a best-seller in the colonies as well as England, read by children and adults who appreciated the dramatized struggles of Christian

Painted by Charles Willson Peale, one of America's premier artists, in 1785, this image was part of a series of likenesses of the heroes of the American Revolution intended for the museum that Peale was establishing in Philadelphia. Peale's style is the most realistic of all the American painters of his generation, although this may be a flattering view of the face of Franklin at almost eighty years old, and the plain ordinary-human quality of the characterization (no wig, no velvet coat, no accessories to indicate his scientific or diplomatic accomplishments) had a definite political meaning in the new American republic. (Courtesy of The Museum of American Art of The Pennsylvania Academy of Fine Arts, Philadelphia. Bequest of Mrs. Sarah Harrison [The Joseph Harrison, Jr. Collection])

against a succession of vividly embodied challenges to his faith. Among Ben's early favorites were Plutarch's *Lives of the Noble Grecians and Romans* and books of moral instruction by the Englishman Daniel Defoe and Boston's own Reverend Dr. Cotton Mather. (The influence of these latter two is strongly evident when Franklin's *Autobiography* turns to its own explicit lessons in morality.) By his mid-teens, Ben was reading the most serious new philosophy from Europe—Locke's *On Human Understanding* and translations of French Cartesian treatises—as well as classical texts. He taught himself to write by studying the popular new English magazine called *The Spectator,* an innovative mix of serious political ideas and bawdy entertainment. His appetite for all of this was insatiable—and despite his lack of formal academic training, he thought deeply about the meaning of what he read.

He was receiving mixed messages about the conduct of life, because this was the era of a deep shift in European culture. Bunyan, articulating a now traditional Reformed Christian philosophy, prescribed a model of ethics that replaced the classical emphasis on fate with a definition of goodness as implanted directly by God's grace. Sin was very obvious, and so with right thinking, the correct path would be chosen. (There was so little room for disagreement about what was sinful, in colonial Massachusetts at least, that a man who committed an offense was often punished for "disobeying his own conscience," which could not refuse God's instructions.) One of the secrets to a righteous life was the acceptance of one's place in the social order God had designed. Virtues were precise but situational, with the rich man required to be charitable, a poorer man obligated to be gratefully respectful to his betters. Good Protestant preachers always exhorted their flocks to behave virtuously, because God would punish sin in the here and now as well as in the afterlife, but the Anglo-American Calvinist tradition which was dominant both in Boston and in Ben's English reading insisted that only God's arbitrarily given grace, not good works, earned salvation.

This ethical system was the backbone of the Puritanism that was the official religion of seventeenth-century New England but was fading from dominance during Ben Franklin's youth. It was a European ideology, not a product of the frontier experience, and its nostalgia for communities where every person did indeed know his place was a complex response to the anxieties about social ethics that accompanied the dynamic economic growth and social fragmentation of early modern Europe. By the late seventeenth century, some philosophers were starting to articulate a more optimistic ethical model, one which embraced the changes that were pervading the transatlantic world. Wealth was coming to be seen not as the winner's loot in a zero-sum system of economic relationships (one man's wealth equaling the impoverishment of many) but as the morally neutral product of hard work and clever risk-taking. A new metaphor for economic growth was the rising tide that lifted all boats. (No one seemed to worry about a complementary low tide elsewhere.) The new philosophy called the Enlightenment put a great deal of trust in the ability of ordinary men to make correct decisions. The special contribution of John Locke's treatise on human psychology, of which Franklin was apparently one of the earliest American readers, was to locate the concept of goodness in the material world, not the supernatural: men received impressions through their natural senses, and the brain somehow would weigh the facts and balance personal desires with a sense of social justice. Each man could therefore be trusted to pursue his own ambitions without guilt that every worldly goal was sinful, every urge to individualism an injury to his neighbors. The opportunity to exercise such choices was most obvious in the cities of Europe and its colonies, such as Boston.

Ben Franklin, the quintessential urban boy and then man, seems to have embraced the new ideas with great zest from a young age, and every piece of his writing that survives testifies to his commitment to the modern ethic. His brother James began *The New England Courant,* the second newspaper in America, and at fourteen Ben was submitting anonymous essays on current affairs. His tone was always mockery of old-fashioned authority, especially the eminent local minister Cotton Mather, whose ploddingly didactic *Essay Upon the Good* exhorted personal and community reformation within the traditional ethic suited to a controlled economy and tightfisted rule by a hereditary elite, rather than an open and expanding market society. Young Franklin was thrilled to find his humorous stories about "Silence Dogood" (a fictional vulgar countrywoman whose philosophy was a satire of Mather's) praised for their "learning and ingenuity" by the gentlemen authors who used the printshop as their club. (Looking back on his boyish arrogance, he later decided that he had been "rather lucky in my judges . . . perhaps they were not really so very good as I then believed them to be.") Only Ben's brother withheld praise; insightful or just jealous, he felt that such praise puffed up his little brother's vanity.

Ben developed his personal commitment to resisting authority not just through book-learning but also through his experiences as an apprentice. Thinking himself clever and knowledgeable enough to be independent (he was, after all, reading books well beyond the capacities of most adults), Ben resisted the discipline of his brother/master and hated being legally bound to his supervision day and night for eight "tedious" years. When James was jailed temporarily in 1722 for criticizing the government, Ben became acting editor and tried to trick his brother into canceling his apprenticeship. Though he approved Ben's editorials, which "made bold to give our rulers some rubs" about their infringement of colonists' rights during the recent war with France and caused the colony's conservative elite "to consider me in an unfavourable light as a young genius that had a turn for libelling and satire," James returned home to his role as master. Quarreling with his apprentice resumed, as did the customary "blows his passion too often urged him to bestow upon me, though he was otherwise not an ill-natured man. Perhaps I was too saucy and provoking." So Ben concluded, in old age.

Fired up by philosophical theories and personal grievances about liberty, in 1723 at age seventeen Ben ran away to New York, the nearest place where there would be work for a printer. In his *Autobiography,* he blames his desperation on his brother's tyranny, but he might also have noted that Boston offered only a gloomy future. There was a welcome temporary peace after a series of Anglo-French wars since 1689, but peace ironically brought depression to the seaport. By the early 1720s, it was clear that the thin New England soils would never produce enough agricultural commodities to support much export trade or a broad market for imported goods. The transatlantic and Caribbean commerce that had been the engine of Boston's growth was migrating to New York and Philadelphia, each of which had a rich agricultural hinterland and ample capital undepleted by the war.

These were not the only reasons for Ben to quit Boston. His political writings had put him on the governor's list of subversives, and some "indiscreet disputations about religion" he had authored (probably his "Silence Dogood" satires) "began to make me pointed at with horror by good people as an infidel or atheist." He was neither but increasingly committed to the creed called Deism, to which he claimed to be converted by reading Calvinist tracts against it. Deists believed that God worked through secondary causes, without intervening directly in the ongoing process He had designed for Creation. Nature, including human nature, was designed to be harmonious and beautiful, and man had been given his rational faculties and sociable dispositions in order to create good communities in the temporal world. Scripture provided basic rules that human beings were expected to adapt to changing circumstances. Although many respectable people would hold to such beliefs by mid-century, this was heresy in Boston in the 1720s.

Rejecting Boston and its ethos and his brother's printshop in one grand gesture of self-liberation, Ben sold some books to pay his passage on a boat to New York and then to Philadelphia (one of many instances in his memoirs in which books were the agency of his development). During his voyage, remarkably much like the hero, Christian, in the copy of *Pilgrim's Progress* carried by a fellow traveler (and carefully noted in the text so that readers would see the parallels), Ben faced many temptations to the kinds of sin that represented short-term pleasure but long-term dangers to a young man's career. The common eighteenth-century sins were borrowing money, giving in to weariness, and being enticed by loose women, and Ben avoided the second category completely. He admitted to misusing a friend's money—"one of the first great errata of my life"—and flirting with "strumpets" with a frankness, characteristic of the eighteenth century, that would be edited out of the *Autobiography* in the more prudish nineteenth. So far, his rational good sense had kept him from sins more serious than he could afford to label half-jokingly as "errata," a printer's term for typographic errors.

Philadelphia, though itself suffering a temporary depression, was the best place a young man could go to make his fortune. Forty years old, the Quaker-founded city was about to boom as transatlantic trade flourished in its harbor and thousands of European immigrants poured through the city on their way to the rich interior farmland called "the best poor man's country" in the world. Except for the gentle Quaker pressure for the successful to be charitable stewards of God's blessings, the Philadelphia economy was much freer of restraint than was Boston's.

A striking self-portrait from the *Autobiography* enables us to imagine young Ben just after his arrival, tired and dirty, his pockets bulging with extra shirts and stockings, walking through central Philadelphia munching on the big puffy rolls that were all the food he could afford. With one roll in hand, another under each arm, he passed a young woman standing in her doorway who "thought I made— as I certainly did—a most awkward, ridiculous appearance." This observer was Deborah Read, who would, after a long series of difficulties, become Ben's wife.

He boarded with her family for his first few years in Philadelphia and eventually received some financial help from them in setting up his own printshop. Ben

The South East Prospect of The City of Philadelphia was painted by Peter Cooper about 1720, perhaps under commission from the Penn family (whose arms appear in the upper left, paired by the arms of the city in the upper right). The idealized orderliness of the city, including some invented church steeples to dramatize the skyline and suggest sophisticated architectural development, may have been intended to advertise the city's growing wealth to prospective settlers. (Library Company of Philadelphia)

and Deborah developed "great respect and affection" for each other, he later wrote, but were considered too young to marry (and he too poor and unreliable) at age eighteen. So they were forced to wait, and during the interval from 1724 to 1726, when he went off to London and wrote only one letter to her to tell her he would not return soon, Deborah married a man named Rogers, who turned out to be a rumored bigamist, treated her badly, and ran off to the West Indies—from which rumors but not proof of his death left her alone but not free to remarry. When Ben returned to Philadelphia, he spent some time looking in vain for a wife with a large dowry to capitalize his business before rekindling his romance with Deborah. If his treatment of her seems callous by modern standards, we must note that the candor with which Franklin admits in his *Autobiography* to his search to marry for money suggests that this was considered appropriate behavior for a young tradesman. When sustenance depended on a man's owning a farm or having a well-developed set of craft skills, rather than just "getting a job," and on a woman's ability to produce food and clothing from scratch, it was a reckless adolescent who indulged passion over careful calculation in choosing a mate. In this context sexual attraction and mistakes—like Ben Franklin's fathering his illegitimate son William—seemed less important than they would come to be in later eras. Though he did not, after all, mention this problematic birth in the *Autobiography,* he was also candid in admitting that before he decided to marry Deborah, "that hard-to-be-governed passion of youth had hurried me frequently into intrigues with low women that fell in my way, which were attended with some expense and great inconvenience, besides a continual risk to my health" from venereal disease. Ben and Deborah were never legally married because of her uncertain status as Rogers' wife—Ben wrote that he "took her to wife September 1, 1730"—but the customary acceptance of "common-law" unions granted them respectability. William was born about this time, to an unknown mother, and soon came to join his father's household. Another son, Franky, died at age four from smallpox; a daughter, Sally, became her father's caretaker in his old age, and her husband, Richard Bache, took over Franklin's printshop.

Ben and Deborah thereafter lived a most respectable life, quite typical of the successful urban tradesman's family. He later testified succinctly to his happiness with his spouse: "she proved a good and faithful helpmate . . . we throve together and ever mutually endeavoured to make each other happy. Thus I corrected that great erratum [of having earlier abandoned her] as well as I could." He praised her for her work in helping in the printshop, especially as the salesperson for his products and as manager of what became essentially a general store of useful household goods. She never, however, learned arithmetic or spelling well enough to escape his cranky criticism of her account books and letters when he was off in Europe for so long (1756 to 1762 and 1764 to 1776). History, in fact, knows the most about Deborah Franklin through those letters, and her imaginative concern for Ben's welfare: she sent him warm nightshirts and mince pies when he was out on the Pennsylvania frontier, clothes and even good American apples when he was in England. (He, in turn, bought her presents of special cooking pots and a large-type Bible so she could read in church without her spectacles.) We know little else about her, or about their family life in Philadelphia, because the facts just listed here are almost all that Franklin says in the *Autobiography* about his private life.

If his narrative is to be taken as a record of what was important to him, Franklin gave little attention to the demands of domesticity.

As an ambitious young tradesman, starting with very little but his wits, Ben had to devote a lot of energy to looking for people to help him, and one of his major challenges was to learn to read the character of men who offered patronage. There were many: his self-making was supported by a number of gentlemen, as well as his wife and her kin. Franklin's interest in books often attracted the favor of educated men. Among them was Sir William Keith, governor of Pennsylvania, who invited the bookish lad to dinner and promised him a letter of credit in England to buy modern printing equipment to set up his own shop in Philadelphia. But great men were sometimes frauds. Keith never wrote the letter of credit, because he knew no one would trust him to pay his debts (colonial governors were often Englishmen escaping financial problems at home): "what shall we think of a Governor playing such pitiful tricks and imposing so grossly on a poor ignorant boy! It was a habit he had acquired. He wished to please everybody; and having little to give, he gave expectations." Other men's promises turned out to be equally hollow. So Ben had to learn to be cynical about the traditional system of patronage as an avenue of upward mobility.

Settled in Philadelphia for a time, Ben took his father's advice to work hard and stay out of political controversies like the ones that had tarnished his reputation in Boston. Two parables from the memoirs of these years use stories about food to convey, with his distinctive wit, the principles of reasonableness and self-discipline by which young Franklin was learning to live. While working for his brother, he had become a vegetarian (to save money for books and avoid mental sluggishness, but also out of a reverence for living things), but Ben found himself desperately tempted by the smell of frying codfish when he was on his first voyage to Philadelphia. "I balanced some time between principle and inclination till I recollected that when the fish were opened, I saw smaller fish taken out of their stomachs. 'Then,' thought I, 'if you eat one another, I don't see why we mayn't eat you.' " He thereafter ate in moderation whatever was available. Writing in 1771, he used his characteristic tone of humorous ambiguity to underline the moral lesson: "So convenient a thing it is to be a *reasonable creature,* since it enables one to find or make a reason for everything one has a mind to do." One had to rely on logic and the self-discipline to experiment carefully with what was right or wrong— but Reason itself was too human to be an infallible guide to goodness.

Franklin's other food parable focused on his first employer, the German printer Keimer, who appears in the *Autobiography* as slow-witted and authoritarian, the convenient butt of his apprentice's tricks. Franklin eventually persuaded Keimer to join him in a vegetarian diet: "He was usually a great glutton, and I wished to give myself some diversion in half-starving him." Franklin liked this regime, "but poor Keimer suffered grievously, tired of the project, longed for the flesh pots of Egypt, and ordered a roast pig. He invited me and two women friends to dine with him, but . . . he could not resist the temptation and ate it all up before we came." This is a story about more than what we might call a "pig-out": readers used to Franklin's humorous didacticism by this point could predict that Keimer's lack of self-discipline would lead to business failure.

Keimer's problem was that he hadn't adopted the new measures of achievement. He wasted his money and energy on gluttony, just as he foolishly wouldn't learn to operate the new printing press he bought, and he alienated customers with his unpredictable temper. Simply "getting by" was no longer the ideal, and Keimer's young apprentice was in tune with the new cultural standards of capitalism (he cared little for wealth in order to buy luxuries, but he would reinvest his profits in tools for higher productivity, including a constant enhancement of his own skills). This was no longer a world with a limited number of skilled craftsmen, in which customers had little choice of whose services to buy. Even farmers now had to experiment to determine the best crops for their land and the desires of consumers nearby or far away, as well as to calculate their costs precisely to earn a profit when they sold their commodities. Economic development, as well as remarkable population growth in places such as Philadelphia, brought increased competition: while Keimer was feasting (and undoubtedly napping thereafter on a full stomach), some other printer was offering his customers more efficient service.

At eighteen, Franklin did go to England with a friend, and even without Governor Keith's promised letter of introduction, he managed to find work and have a wonderful time seeing the sights of the great city (and flirting with its ladies). Always the organizer of self-improvement projects, Ben tried to persuade his mates in his English printshop—as he attempted everywhere he worked in America—to give up their custom of drinking beer every few hours and instead eat porridge and bread, which provided better nutrition at far less cost. But he also loaned them beer money at interest, and he made a tidy profit on their incorrigible self-indulgence. He even found that avoiding "St. Monday" (the customary holiday of hung-over laborers, a notorious cause of inefficiency) and his "uncommon quickness" at setting type earned him higher pay.

Such good habits continued as he earned his passage home by apprenticing to a merchant who taught him the science of keeping account books. When this patron died eighteen months later, Ben failed to find a similar position. Returning reluctantly to Keimer's disorderly shop, he taught the apprentices better working habits, learned to cast metal type so that they wouldn't have to wait for replacements from England, made the ink, organized the warehouse, and learned the general management of the printing business. (Keimer himself was still hopeless.) Along the way, because Keimer kept a Saturday Sabbath but allowed his employees the customary Sunday rest, Ben—who never went to church—had two whole days free for reading each week.

At twenty-one Franklin was able to set up his own printing house and stationer's shop, and within a very few years he had paid off his debts and established a sound reputation. He was given most of the Pennsylvania Assembly's business, including the printing of the laws and a new issue of paper money (which he had advocated in an influential pamphlet). He took over an amateurish newssheet and made it into the sophisticated *Pennsylvania Gazette,* and in 1733 he began writing and distributing the widely popular *Poor Richard's Almanac.* Besides offering the customary astronomical and geographic information, the fictional "Richard Saunders" shared his accumulated wisdom in quotable proverbs: "he's a fool that makes his doctor his heir"; "fish and visitors stink in three days"; "he that drinks fast, pays slow." Many of his aphorisms outlined the habits of a sound, independent businessman: "all things are easy to Industry, all things are difficult to Sloth"; "he that waits upon Fortune, is never sure of a dinner"; and "early to bed and early to rise, makes a man healthy wealthy and wise." Practical education, hard work, and efficiency were not really *new* principles: they would not have "worked" in this popular advice literature if they hadn't been familiar truths. But Franklin was advocating them in a newly focused way and with the humor that made the lessons easier to swallow than the old-fashioned, dead-serious preaching of previous moral guides such as Cotton Mather, who was still being satirized gently by "Poor Richard," as he had been savaged by "Silence Dogood" back in Boston. Franklin's comic touches are an ingratiating voice that says, in effect, "It's safe to take me seriously, reader, because I'm not too superior to you—I have noble ideals, but I slip up, so I will draw a moral path for you that can be followed in reasonably easy steps." Beneath the humor, however, was sound advice: this self-disciplined behavior was the road to success. Highly successful tradesmen and merchants had always followed such rules, as had the most progressive sectors of English capitalism. But now these tricks of the trade were "democratized" in America as appropriate for every craftsman and even for farmers hoping for more than mere subsistence. In an expanding society with few regulations, discipline brought reward.

Franklin took this practical attitude toward life home with him: he described in the *Autobiography* his early-adulthood undertaking of "the bold and arduous project of arriving at moral perfection." He deduced twelve key virtues from Christian doctrine and the wisdom of the Classical authors: temperance, silence, order, resolution, frugality, industry, sincerity, justice, moderation, cleanliness, tranquillity, and chastity. Little parables illustrated his good practices: he took care to be seen to cart his own paper to the shop in a wheelbarrow and to let his neighbors observe, through unshuttered windows, that he worked late by candlelight. This was not hypocrisy, because he was, in fact, working very hard, but simply a strategic advertisement that here was a responsible tradesman. He "dressed plain and was seen at no places of idle diversion"; the only distraction from work he allowed himself was reading (including teaching himself French, Italian, Spanish, and some Latin). "In order to secure my credit and character as a tradesman, I took care not only to be in *reality* industrious and frugal, but to avoid all *appearances* of the contrary." He recognized the power of reputation in an expanding market society where strangers were potential customers.

To train himself in the habits of self-discipline, Ben of course devised a mechanism—a chart to help him focus on one virtue each week but record the "errata" he made. Soon the tick marks got so dense that erasing made holes in the paper, so he inscribed his charts on sheets of ivory sewn into a little packet. (It kept a good record—but also erased easily with soap and water! He still had this with him, in fact, in his old age in France.) Then someone suggested to him that his confidence of achieving virtue smelled of pride, a cardinal Christian sin, so he added a thirteenth virtuous habit, humility, and its method: "Imitate Jesus and Socrates."

It is difficult not to hear a sly comic voice in Franklin's advice to himself—to attempt being like these great men even in their humility was rather a stretch for a young ink-stained printer. Franklin's conclusion to the narrative of his moral reforms confirms suspicions of a tongue-in-cheek tone: he confesses that not only did he never achieve anything close to perfection in any category, but he came to worry that "a perfect character might be attended with the inconvenience of being envied and hated." He concluded that "a benevolent man should allow a few faults in himself, to keep his friends in countenance." Then he confessed, in the same sly voice, that if he had overcome the sin of pride, "I should probably be proud of my humility."

No one would have doubted that Franklin's goals were virtues, despite his ironic tone in their narration, though cultural conservatives would have objected to their substitution of humanistic standards for the old scriptural injunctions. Most innovative, however, was the suggestion that these moral habits be inculcated *scientifically,* as though one's very character could be an experimental object. This was the application of the Enlightenment notions of determining truth by observing nature and inferring its rules of order, with the assumption that God intended his creatures to live in personal freedom and neighborly harmony based on the strict control of selfishness. Abandoning the medieval notion that mercantile

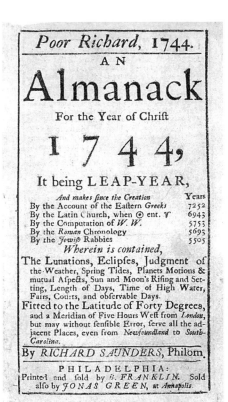

Franklin's *Poor Richard's Almanac,* first published in 1732 and continued by his partners after he left for England in 1757, competed quite successfully with other examples of this popular genre. Useful facts for predicting weather, remembering holidays, and estimating distances between towns on established roads were mixed in with practical advice in entertaining formats, such as proverbs and jokes. Franklin offered nuggets of wisdom in the voice of "Richard Saunders," who—like his creator—learned his lessons usually through mistakes. Almanacs were often the only books in colonial homes except for bibles, and in a culture where paper was expensive and therefore rare, the blank spaces around the printing provided space for personal notations or handwriting practice. (Library Company of Philadelphia)

profit had to be usury (that is, a form of stealing from the defenseless customer or borrower of credit), rationalist ethics insisted that making money and enjoying the pleasures of the flesh were not innately sinful, if kept within moderation and pursued without exploiting others. Business profits, for example, should be reinvested in enterprises that provided honest employment. Sexuality, another area of traditional taboo, was part of God-given human nature and not innately sinful if enjoyed within socially acceptable boundaries (specifically, marriage). Food and wine and holiday celebrations were acceptable recreations, as long as they didn't interfere with regular hours of work.

Good character needed a supportive community, but for this purpose Franklin rejected the old model of a religious congregation: like other declared deists and indeed many of the intellectuals of his time, Franklin disparaged organized religion as more likely to divide than unite a community. (Franklin criticized severely the heated competition among denominations during the "Great Awakening" of religion in the 1740s, though he was not immune to the emotional appeal of a good evangelical preacher.) Neighborly cooperation was to be organized through sustained discussion groups. Shortly after settling in Philadelphia, Franklin gathered together a club of young tradesmen like himself, the "Junto," to pool their resources for a lending library and meet to discuss ideas and critique each other's essays on current affairs. This group—and a network of similar clubs—became the sounding board for Franklin's writings on political issues and provided him with information about the impact of government policies on the small-scale merchants and skilled tradesmen who were a significant sector of the

Franklin took over a crude local newsheet in 1729 and made it into one of the premier newspapers in the colonies. (Library Company of Philadelphia)

colonial economy but underrepresented politically. Making customary talk among neighbors or coworkers into a formal institution with political consciousness was an important innovation, especially in its relative democracy.

This model was then extrapolated into more direct civic projects: from the 1730s to the mid-1750s, Franklin gathered his neighbors together to promote public education (especially an academy emphasizing studies in English and mathematics, rather than the classics), a public hospital, street lighting and cleaning services, fire brigades, and a volunteer militia to defend the colony in the renewed Anglo-French wars. (The latter adopted the radical New England system of democratically elected officers.) Fifty years before the concept became a familiar slogan, "the greatest good for the greatest number" was the criterion for successful social organization, and the "good" was calculated in material terms. The most critical change from historic notions of the public good was the process of defining it by the personal participation of all citizens, even those without great wealth or much formal education. Enlightenment thinkers had been developing a theory of the "social contract," in which men voluntarily gave up some of their autonomy in order to promote everyone's prosperity through peace—but that scenario only explained the "original" organization of society in the prehistoric past. Benjamin Franklin's Junto was, in fact, a model for putting the theory into practice: men who had even modest property (or the vocational skills that were the equivalent of capital) would gather together and decide what public policies would foster their common welfare. The next step was organizing a party of citizens to vote for these procedures. Linking the principles of individualistic political rights to the responsibilities of a self-disciplined householder and businessman, Franklin helped to translate the grandest theories of republican (as opposed to monarchical) government into a practical system of self-governance.

Franklin involved himself in electoral politics primarily as the representative of ordinary citizens and the Assembly against the Proprietors of Pennsylvania, the descendants of William Penn (no longer Quaker) and heirs to the king's grant of the whole colony. Franklin served as Assembly delegate for ten years and as their clerk; then he took up their constant battle against the Proprietors' appointed governor by traveling to London to lobby the Crown to take the colony under direct royal control. (Franklin was pursuing this effort in 1765 when the Stamp Act demonstrations back in America, in which colonial leaders attacked the Crown for its allegedly exploitive new policies, made a joke of Pennsylvania's claims to *want* royal control.) When the Assembly itself proved unwilling to listen to the views of ordinary citizens, Franklin took to grass-roots organizing, including some of the earliest known campaigns for "slates" of candidates, based on publicly debated positions.

It was this combination of the colonists' growing understanding that they had, in fact, been enjoying self-government in America, along with the development of a theoretical justification, and new methods for actually organizing the opinions of ordinary citizens that brought the American colonies to a readiness for rebellion in the 1770s. Much of the early protest against new British imperial regulations in the 1760s had been led by colonial elites—New England merchants and southern tobacco planters, whose personal economic situations were endangered by the new system of control—but before the American colonies were ready for a war for independence, ordinary citizens had to be mobilized to cast their votes and put their lives on the line for the principles they had come to espouse. Through such modest-sounding mechanisms as the political discussion group, the volunteer militia that elected its own officers, and the canvassing of votes among the ordinary men of crowded city neighborhoods, Ben Franklin ultimately promoted a revolution—though until the 1770s, he thought he was only promoting the more efficient functioning of the British Empire.

Efficiency was always his criterion, even for international affairs. In 1754, at an intercolonial defense conference at Albany, New York, Franklin drafted a plan of union to wage war, collect taxes, and even adjust colony boundaries. But this "Albany Plan" was rejected by both the English (as too much colonial self-government) and the respective colony legislatures (as too threatening to their independence from each other). The Empire was starting to break down—but it would take twenty years for the colonists to see that they could work collectively for a common good. Among the most direct commentaries on what was wrong with the imperial administration to occur in Franklin's *Autobiography* before it breaks off in 1757 were two stories about British military commanders such as Lord Loudon (who kept Franklin aboard a ship for weeks waiting to sail while he dithered about sending letters to London) and General Edward Braddock (famous for the ambush of his "thin red line" at Fort Duquesne in 1755), whose arrogance and inefficiency made the Americans doubt that English "protection" was worth the price. Franklin joined the collective judgment of "not worth it" only in 1774, after decades of trying to mediate the fractures in the transatlantic intellectual world he loved.

If we had been able to ask Benjamin Franklin, as he sat writing his memoirs, which accomplishments he was most proud of, he would surely have said not his political activities but his scientific experiments. It was for these that he was most well known in the Euro-American world in his own time. As soon as his printing business was well established, and even before he was able to retire from that trade in 1748 at age forty-two, he began to be interested in what was then called "natural philosophy"—the analysis of nature. He cultivated friendships with all the serious scientists in the colonies and was fascinated by electrical experiments. Demonstrations of electrical properties were all the rage—glass rods were rubbed to attract lint, and Leyden jars gave off sparks from the static electricity they stored. Such entertaining parlor tricks were also the serious experimental physics of the age. This was the Enlightenment in practice—the use of human rationality to observe, experiment, and measure. Franklin himself was widely regarded as an eminent scientist: the amusing classic image of the portly gentleman with the kite and the key in the rain disguises the fact that such simple procedures, coupled with a lot of hard thinking, were the cutting edge of physical science. One of the first to recognize that electric charges moved from negative to positive poles, Franklin also established that electricity was not generated by the equipment but already pervaded the atmosphere and that lightning was electricity. A few weeks earlier, Franklin had almost killed himself while trying to electrocute a turkey with the charge moving between two large Leyden jars! This was not, however, one of the "errata" to which he admitted in the *Autobiography*.

Though Franklin was kept from deeper involvement in the most sophisticated theorizing of his era by his weak Latin and mathematics, he helped found the American Philosophical Society in 1743 (America's first scientific society), corresponded with the great scientists of Europe, and won renown as an experimentalist, especially as the inventor of lightning rods, which saved many houses and public buildings from destruction. (He had earlier invented an efficient little stove that was invaluable to ordinary householders. As with all his other inventions, he spread information as widely as possible rather than keeping the design secret for personal profit. He would always rather make friends than make money.) Franklin's writings were published in England and France, and in 1753 the Royal Society awarded him its prestigious Copley Medal, the equivalent of the modern Nobel Prize. Most of the great American and European universities granted him honorary doctorates.

It was this international reputation as a scientist that moved Franklin the politician from the local concerns of Philadelphia into the arena of international diplomacy. The intermediate stage was his involvement with Pennsylvania politics, and it was as a paid emissary from the Pennsylvania Assembly that Franklin first got to visit Europe and confer with the philosophers who made up his intellectual community. Subsequent trips were financed by representing Pennsylvania and other colonies, up to the crisis of 1774; then, his role in making public old private letters in which Governor Thomas Hutchinson of Massachusetts had advised his London superiors to take a hard line with the childlike colonies caused Franklin to be summarily dismissed from his role as colonial postmaster and from any credibility in negotiating with the king's ministers. For the moment, he was a man without a country: "while I have been thought here to be too much of an American, I have in America been deem'd too much of an Englishman." The pain with which he wrote about these events suggests that the boy who had once run away from traditional Anglo-American life into the new culture of individualism and rationalism and optimism about social progress now felt orphaned. The Empire had run away from him—from its role as benevolent parent to a willful tyranny. His only son, Governor William Franklin of New Jersey, added to Ben's pain by choosing loyalty to the mother country over an alliance with his natural father.

Benjamin Franklin, embracing the inevitable (once he recognized it) with characteristic energy that shamed men decades his junior, returned to Philadelphia to take part in the Second Continental Congress and the founding events of the new nation. Many men of Franklin's class still had qualms about independence; many of the best-educated and most economically successful colonists still lived their lives in a European tradition of learning and social models. One of the key elements of readiness for independence, for the elite and for ordinary citizens, was learning to see that the relative primitivism in which the colonists had lived, and their sometimes crude experiments in self-government, had in fact been a successful beginning of a legitimate new system. So ironically, we can look to the *Autobiography* of Benjamin Franklin, the almost-Loyalist, for a rather representative narrative of American cultural independence that didn't recognize itself until it achieved the perspective of hindsight.

The thirteen separate colonies had to learn that they had more in common with each other than each had with England, that they had a collective identity that was "American." On a personal level, there had to be a process of men much like Franklin redefining their identities as citizens. From the sixteenth to the mid-eighteenth century, it was common for political thinkers to use a familial metaphor for the organization of nations: the king was a benevolent father, and his subjects were well-disciplined children. In the late eighteenth century, reflecting deeper cultural changes that would condition the movement for American independence and then the French Revolution, the center of gravity in the metaphor shifted, and attention was directed to the role of children—to their *rights* to have proper nurturance, even from stingy parents, and to the inevitability of their growing up to adulthood, to a new identity. All they had to do, finally, was to be self-disciplined enough to take the risk of independence.

AN INTERPRETATION

When we follow Benjamin Franklin's intentions and read his *Autobiography* as a series of experiments in character building and the pursuit of success, we confront some interesting ambiguities about the self-making of the British colonist in North America. European culture, like the imperial governance system, was there in the background, but it generally left the playing field of ordinary life open for individual initiative in an environment that would bring material security for hard work, as Franklin always claimed in praise of his homeland. But as the ambitious man became successful, he reached toward the imperial system. Enterprising farmers might desire Caribbean or European markets, aggressive merchants would crave international customers, local political leaders might dream of a royal appointment as governor, men of learning would yearn to participate in the European debates about religion and science and social theory. In some ways, the successful men of America came to be more tied to Europe than their emigrant ancestors would have imagined possible.

Franklin was, at the height of his achievements as a scientist and a diplomat, torn between the Old World culture and that of the New. Europe offered sophisticated thought and conversation and elegant parties (Franklin *loved* the parties). It was, more importantly, the place where the affairs of the western half of the globe were managed. It was logical, though ironic, that almost immediately after voting in Philadelphia for independence, he was on his way back to Europe—this time to solicit French help in the war, later to negotiate a peace settlement with the British. But the other side of the character of Franklin the scientist and politician revealed different implications for the future. The eighteenth-century scientist was a rationalist committed to experimentation rather than complacency, change rather than tradition, and the democratization of education, the economy, and society. If the universe was orderly and observable and understandable, so was the human character, and so was the organization of society: the last two could be improved. Politics was the art of social engineering.

There was an unbreakable connection between the virtuous individual and the good society, and Franklin wrote his *Autobiography* as a modest (or perhaps not so modest) blueprint. Modern readers are entitled to interpret the text as a conscious political parable for a variety of reasons. We know that Franklin was a professional journalist, and his audience was used to reading didactic literature that couched moral lessons in the form of parables and allegories. He offers us passages, such as the following, that beg for explicit political readings: "I fancy [my brother's] harsh and tyrannical treatment of me might be a means of impressing me with that aversion to arbitrary power that has stuck to me through my whole life." And it is clear that his scathing exposure of the inefficiencies of British military and civil officers was meant to be a telling contrast to the hardworking virtue of the colonists. Though there is not a word about independence in the text, it lays out the inevitability of that result.

The "virtuous" behavior that Franklin prescribed, the ethical system he outlined, is not one he invented single-handedly, but it was the forward edge of cultural change in his times. Through *Poor Richard's Almanac* and other writings, he was the great popularizer of the new mode of self-controlled, industrious, and profit-minded behavior that did indeed earn a decent living for many men like himself. This code of conduct is sometimes referred to as the "Protestant ethic" (or "Puritan ethic," when Puritanism is misunderstood as endorsing wealth as a measure of holiness), but it is actually a "capitalist" ethic. It was a logical and optimistic response to the expansion of economic opportunity in colonial cities such as eighteenth-century Philadelphia. As the ideology of liberalism, it would eventually transform even Puritan Boston, although the development of theory seemed to lag behind the new behavior that it explained. The world of Cotton Mather gave way to the world of Ben Franklin—but that was not yet democracy. It would take many more generations before the promise, so elegantly phrased by Thomas Jefferson, that "all men" were "endowed by their Creator" with "inalienable rights" to "life, liberty, and the pursuit of happiness" became a realistic description of actual political practice in the United States.

Franklin's political-economic model seemed optimistically radical by the standards of the eighteenth century. The good society was the Junto writ large: hard-working, productive, educated men were trustworthy with power because they disciplined themselves to be good neighbors even in an openly competitive society; then they gathered together to determine the greatest good for the greatest number, in theory and in practice. This was an enormous advance in empowerment for men like Franklin, and the pride in their achievements shows through all the writings of the generation who made an American revolution in political culture.

But Franklin's *Autobiography* also should provoke its readers to notice who is in the Junto and who is not there. In fact, if we read that text as an artifact, we might notice that the nonparticipants in the Junto are also "not there" in the text in certain ways. He sincerely didn't notice that when he gathered together "men like himself" to constitute the social compact, persons who weren't men like himself were left out—and were *so* inappropriate for inclusion that their absence didn't have to be explained, either in Franklin's text or in the documents that founded the new American republic.

Native Americans and African-Americans appear in the writings of Franklin and most other Euro-Americans as either clowns or demons: there was no way they counted as potential members of a community of self-educating capitalist tradesmen and professionals. (Most Native Americans never adopted Euro-

American cultural practices, but after slavery was ended in the north, many African-American communities demonstrated "Franklinian" economic and political behavior. Franklin's last public act, it is gratifying to note, was petitioning Congress to end slavery and the slave trade.) Even the German immigrants who confused colonial-Pennsylvania politics because they insisted on keeping their own language and were loyal to the Proprietor (who had provided them refuge from persecution in Europe) were disparaged as culturally beyond the pale—even incurring a racist label as "swarthy" in Franklin's *Autobiography.*

And, of course, when Franklin gathered together a group of men like himself to form the new social compact, there were no women present. (Perhaps they were in the room, but only serving refreshments.) As with men of nonwhite races, the absence of women from participation in the republican order—from the Junto to the voters included in Pennsylvania's remarkably democratic constitution as a new state—was taken so much for granted that it did not have to be stated. Silence marks their place in Franklin's *Autobiography* and in the new state. The exclusion of women presents a different kind of problem than that of racism or linguistic-cultural differences. Women, after all, were people whom these men allowed into the most intimate recesses of their homes and into their hearts, whom they trusted to raise their children as well-disciplined citizens of the republic. Why were they not part of the Junto?

Here again, we can read attitudes in the statements and the silences in Franklin's *Autobiography.* Even if we believe he loved his own wife deeply, despite the restrained rhetoric in his public writings (a convention of the times), it is worth noting that his highest praise for her was as a "help-mate." She raised his children (even his illegitimate son), tended his shop, and kept him fed and clothed and healthy, but he did not think of her as a person who could hold political opinions. We have evidence that only a few men of Franklin's class did so: John Adams's high regard for the sagacity of his well-educated wife Abigail is the most well-known example. There were, in fact, a number of women like Abigail in the colonies—and some of them wrote public demands for increased rights for women. But those rights were largely imagined simply as education, with the goal of making women better mothers and household managers. Ultimately, they wanted more respect for those roles, which were increasingly significant in a republican culture where virtue needed to be enshrined in domestic life and taught to the rising generation. (This was primarily the mother's responsibility, since men of the middling and upper classes in modern capitalist culture usually worked in shops or offices separate from home.) But no one argued that even the best-educated woman deserved the vote that was given to illiterate (white) men.

A woman must have female versions of all the Franklinian virtues, except that her hard work and self-discipline did not lead to self-determination: legally and socially, she was the ward, equivalent to a child, of her father and then her husband. A good woman was not allowed a few "errata," because she did not write the script of her own life and had no "second edition" in which to erase the mistakes. She was not among the "all men" endowed by their Creator with the rights to define a "pursuit of happiness" that put her in the political debating circle, rather than feeding and nursing the citizens of the republic. This was so obvious to everyone that Franklin didn't have to explain it, though *we* have to wonder what Deborah Franklin thought of all this—and regret the fact that no one bothered to record her opinions.

Because he would insist, we should let her husband have the last word. In *Poor Richard's Almanac* of 1738, he wrote a little poem that sums up his own life, and Deborah's hidden life, and the new American definition of citizenship, and the function of his *Autobiography* as a cultural artifact:

> If you wou'd not be forgotten
> As soon as you are dead and rotten,
> Either write things worth reading,
> Or do things worth the writing.

Sources:: There exist dozens of biographical studies of Benjamin Franklin: as the quintessential modern man he becomes a tempting screen on which scholars can project their favorite theories about the origins of liberal political economy in America and the culture of individualism. The best place for a reader to begin is with Franklin's own *Autobiography,* which is available in many editions. Franklin's papers are being published in a multivolume set by Yale University Press, and a very useful compilation of his works was edited by J. A. Leo Lemay and published by the Library of America in 1987. The personal side of his life is insightfully explored by Claude-Anne Lopez and Eugenia W. Herbert in *The Private Franklin: The Man and His Family* (New York: Norton, 1975). One of the most interesting recent studies of the politics of the 1760s through the 1780s is Sheila L. Skemp's *Benjamin and William Franklin: Father and Son, Patriot and Loyalist* (Boston and New York: Bedford Books, 1994).

7

ETHAN ALLEN AND THE FALL OF FORT TICONDEROGA

MICHAEL A. BELLESILES

Ethan Allen became the leader of a group known as the Green Mountain Boys long before most English colonists ever thought of a military challenge to Great Britain or contemplated independence. Allen and his followers were simply trying to compete in the struggle for landed resources so essential to survival in an agrarian society. Allen and his family, like thousands of others, had been forced to leave the more densely populated New England states like Massachusetts and Connecticut when it became apparent that the amount of land available would no longer support a burgeoning population. Avenues to the west were, before the American Revolution, largely blocked by the resistance of the powerful Iroquois League of Nations and the huge land claims held by the king's favorites in New York. At first it seemed that northern New England—today's New Hampshire, Maine, and Vermont—was a promising place to find land for the large numbers of children being produced by New England families. But as Michael Bellesiles tells us in the following essay, the Allens and their cohorts migrated to the Green Mountains east of Lake Champlain only to find the land on which they had built their homes the subject of a jurisdictional dispute between New Hampshire and New York. Refusing to be intimidated by the great landlords of New York, long one of the most aristocratic of the English colonies, Allen gathered together a group of like-minded settlers to protest in the long-standing English tradition of "regulation." Regulators were men who saw themselves as upholding the law and their rights as Englishmen to a landed freehold.

Allen's resistance was necessitated by the chronic conflict that existed between New York and New Hampshire over territorial possessions, and it points out the reality that such conflicts existed between many of the English colonies, so much so that they found it difficult to unite in opposition to the alliance of Indians and French which had for so long challenged British hegemony. At the beginning of the movement for independence, which took place largely among the merchant elite of Boston and Philadelphia and the wealthy planter dynasties of the Chesapeake, these geographic divisions threatened to impede the protest against the hated British regulation of commerce and trade. Fortunately for the independence movement, the British acted with such an arrogance and contempt for the colonies, especially their leaders, that it became easier for them to unite in common cause against their oppressors.

There was another division, however, which is cogently reflected in the evolution of Ethan Allen's struggle from an internal class conflict which pitted wealthy colonial elites against ordinary farmers into a political revolution against the British Empire. Although Ethan Allen was an unusually loud and forceful man, his situation was not very different from that of the thousands of small farmers and craftsmen who had been feeling the pressures of economic decline in the eighteenth century. Class conflict had been increasing, although usually not on such a dramatic level as that between the Green Mountain Boys and the New York elite. At first, most of these small farmers did not support the protests against the British, associating such protest with the wealthy landholders who stood in the way of more widespread distribution of land; Bellesiles's essay clearly reveals Ethan Allen's hatred of the New York aristocracy. Yet as the independence movement gained strength, Allen came to believe that it represented an avenue to the kind of equality he had been fighting for. That transition, on the part of thousands of "ordinary men" like Allen, was to make the American Revolution possible.

In May 1775 the most famous outlaw in America became a revolutionary hero. Ethan Allen was any government's worst nightmare. Over the previous five years he had succeeded in stealing New York's northeastern frontier—all of it. Not content to break the law, Allen rejected it entirely. According to the government of His Majesty's province of New York, Allen was a thug leading a motley collection of bandits, a loudmouthed terrorist, and an atheist for whose head they offered the princely sum of £100.

A master of guerrilla warfare and political theater, Ethan Allen stood out in every way. A huge man who delighted in displays of strength and florid oratory, Allen was a revolution unto himself. He defied every traditional authority, political and social. In an age which employed "democratick" as a pejorative, Allen was the complete democrat. He treated everyone, even New York's royal governors, as his equal. Allen mocked every inherited standard, insisting that the land belonged to those who worked it, that communities should elect their own leaders, that slavery was evil, and, most intolerable of all, that the Bible was not the revealed word of God. Allen had never attended school, but he claimed a native understanding of the universe and proudly called himself a "clodhopper philosopher." Members of the colonial elite agreed with the clodhopper part, observing that this uneducated bumpkin had been kicked out of two New England towns for his big mouth and religious opinions. But what moved New York's legislature to place a reward on Allen's head was the way he took advantage of the confusion of the British Empire.

The problem, a recurrent one in American history, emerged from the one commodity which North America had in abundance, from a European perspective: land. Lots of land. So long as one felt not the slightest qualm in taking it from its rightful owners, the American Indians, that land seemed free to whomever claimed it first. And there was the rub. Barely an acre of British North America lay unencumbered by competing claims. Some of the resulting conflicts were minor; surveying techniques in the eighteenth century were notoriously inept and ignored such mathematical standards as two parallel lines not meeting. Other conflicts had an enormous impact, embroiling several governments in disputes which ranged over decades. Every British colony claimed significant chunks of its neighbors. Several behaved like cats and assumed that everything they saw was theirs, up to and including the Pacific Ocean.

In 1749, New Hampshire's ethically challenged governor, Benning Wentworth, saw his chances in the marvelously vague wording of his province's charter. By his reading, nearly all of northern New York belonged to him; and he meant it in the personal sense. He began modestly, issuing a patent for the town of Bennington, just 40 miles east of Albany. Over the next fifteen years, Wentworth carved up the region between the Connecticut River and Lake Champlain into 129 townships; he sold the land cheap to close friends, family, and political allies, always reserving a large piece for himself. These initial purchasers hired agents to sell the nonexistent townships to groups of New Englanders, who invested the bulk of their capital in the land titles and then had the poor judgment to move with their families to the Green Mountain frontier.

Wentworth did nothing exceptional in granting land titles on vague claims. Most colonial governors, including New York's, enriched themselves by manipulating the inefficiency of the British Empire. Wentworth just outdid all his colleagues in ambition and audacity, creating more townships than any other colonial governor. In 1764 the king's Privy Council finally cut through the red tape and confusion, declaring all New Hampshire titles in the Green Mountains void, validating New York's sole authority over all lands up to the west bank of the Connecticut River. Untroubled by this decision, Wentworth passed the governorship on to his nephew and retired to enjoy his loot. Over the next decade, New York's governors also increased their personal wealth by granting titles to 2,300,000 acres in the area.

Less fortunate were the three thousand people already settled in the Green Mountains. Their land titles, issued by a royal governor in the king's name, had less value than the usual British treaty with the Indians. They suddenly discovered that the land they had bought and improved in good faith belonged to one of the great New York landlords. If there was one fate they all sought to avoid, it was being reduced to tenancy, which was all New York offered them. New York's tenant farmers were a notoriously miserable bunch, consigned to a life of poverty without hope of ever owning their own land.

But among the large New England families settling the region was the Allens. Ethan Allen and his many brothers and sisters, cousins, and nieces and nephews were not given to lives of quiet desperation. For four generations the Allens had struggled on the frontier edges of New England to attain a "respectable mediocrity"; they had never risen any higher than that. Ethan Allen's father, Joseph, had been of the "middling sort," a yeoman farmer in a rugged Connecticut hill town working to acquire enough land to settle all his children in the area. As a youth, Ethan had shown a precocious promise of intellectual ability which convinced his father to make the sacrifices necessary to send Ethan on to Yale College. But just as seventeen-year-old Ethan was preparing to apply to Yale, Joseph Allen died, and responsibility for the family fell on Ethan. After fifteen years of downward mobility, Ethan made the decision to try his luck, and that of his family, in the Green Mountains.

The Allen family purchased hundreds of acres under New Hampshire deeds. When the Privy Council voided these titles, Ethan Allen tried to work within the system, even hiring the prominent Connecticut attorney Jared Ingersoll to represent the settlers in New York's courts in early 1770. Given that the judge was Robert Livingston, Jr., himself a large landowner in the area, the court's perfunctory judgment that no New Hampshire title could enjoy any standing in a New York court should not have been too surprising. But Ethan Allen seemed authentically stunned by the injustice of the court's finding. The plaintiffs, Allen wrote, had enjoyed every advantage, arriving "in great state and magnificence." In contrast, the defendants, "appearing but in ordinary fashion having been greatly fatigued by hard labor," made an impression matching their poverty. The poor farmers lost before the trial began, for "interest, conviction and grandeur being all on one side, easily turned the scale against the honest defendants." The decision, Allen concluded, served the greed of a small "junto of land thieves."

Within days the whole direction of Allen's life took a dramatic change as this former outcast became a political insurgent seeking the politicization of his neighbors. Allen returned from Albany and organized his fellow settlers into the Green Mountain Boys, an extra-legal militia intent on preserving their landholdings and keeping New York out of what Allen called the New Hampshire Grants.

Over the next five years Allen perfected a largely nonviolent form of guerrilla warfare which relied on intimidation, posturing, and rumor. New York's officials and supporters never knew when and how Allen and the Green Mountain Boys would strike; and Allen actively encouraged the circulation of stories describing his savagery and brutality. In one instance he convinced two Albany sheriffs that he had just hanged the other, allowing them each to escape and spread their rumors of his brutality. On another occasion Allen was confronted by Dr. Samuel Adams, a supporter of New York, armed with a pair of pistols. Allen knocked the guns to the ground, tied the hapless Yorker in a chair, and suspended him from the catamount sign outside the tavern where the Green Mountain Boys met. The poor doctor sat up there for some hours facing the remorseless stare of the stuffed catamount while a crowd jeered below. Allen sought not to hurt or kill his opponents but to neutralize them. And Dr. Adams went home an apolitical man.

Allen consistently avoided acts of extreme violence, intending to impress or intimidate the undecided with his resolve and frighten off the officials and supporters of New York. Allen and his Green Mountain Boys set up "Judgment seats" and tried those who acted in New York's name. Ignoring the niceties of legal form, as had New York, Allen acted, in both meanings of the word, as prosecutor and judge. The "guilty" verdict predominated in Judge Allen's court.

Benjamin Spencer, one of the few New York justices of the peace bold enough to live in the Green Mountains, experienced Allen's extralegal court first-hand. Allen the prosecutor accused Spencer of owning a New York land grant and speculating in more, of holding a commission as justice of the peace from New York, of trying to convince his neighbors to obey New York's laws, and of "cudling with the Land Jobbers." Cuddling aside, Spencer was guilty of all these charges, as Judge Allen determined. The jury favored a serious whipping, but Allen overruled them with a more "lenient and just" punishment. Since Spencer's house stood on land lacking a New Hampshire title, it constituted a public nuisance and should be burned. The excited jury agreed and set the roof ablaze. Spencer's plead-ing so touched Allen that he ordered the burning roof knocked off, saving the house—though it was rather exposed to the elements.

What is worth noting in this story is that Spencer's neighbors understood the meaning of this tale, and those without New Hampshire titles acted quickly to buy them. Allen was then able to further enhance his authority, while denigrating New York's, by ensuring that these deeds went for a fair market price, one well below New York's. As Spencer reported, only four of the town's 250 inhabitants remained loyal to New York; the rest turned to the outlaw Allen for protection.

Meanwhile New York's government did little except issue angry proclama-tions and frustrated appeals for British Regulars. They found it difficult to culti-vate supporters. As early as 1771 loyal New Yorkers were refusing to act in sup-port of their province, writing in terror that "Allen was in the woods with another party blacked and dressed like Indians," with plans to kill all Yorkers. New York's government officials failed to act, even to protect their few adherents, largely be-cause they did not see why they should. As the properly constituted authorities, they should be obeyed by the lower orders—and these frontier farmers were about as low as one could sink. Anne Grant, the niece of Philip Schuyler, described the region as "a refuge for the vagabonds and banditti of the continent." Repeatedly, New York's government issued broadsides reminding the Green Mountain set-tlers that the king had declared their titles void. Allen simply turned the equation around, using these statements to demonstrate that the king was as bad as his of-ficials in New York.

Combining traditional Old Testament bombast with the new republican ver-nacular, Allen issued a stream of articles and pamphlets defending the settlers' right to their land, moving to ever more radical positions in the face of New York's in-transigence. Allen drew upon a rich New England heritage of communal rights and resistance in insisting on the primacy of local rights over legal forms, but he expanded the reach of community to include an entire region. It was the govern-ment, Allen argued, which usurped property rights and under "the handle of ju-risdiction" destroyed "faith in communities." Allen also transformed the New Eng-land tradition of communal action by invoking the language of class conflict. External authority was in the wrong not simply for violating local norms but also as it served the specific interests of an oppressor class. The government of New York, though claiming to be the "great advocate for law, order, and good govt," lost its legitimacy by serving the economic needs of an elite, making war upon "the numerous families settled upon the land." The Green Mountain settlers did no more than protect their families and property from a band of well-organized thieves who used "what they call the law" to try to steal the value that others had created with their labor. "We mean no more by that which is called the Mob," Allen wrote in defense of the Green Mountain Boys, "but to defend our just Rights and Properties."

The government of New York had a simple response: obey proper author-ity. Any complaints must proceed through channels, and if, as in the court case in Albany, the result meant losing one's property and livelihood, well those were the breaks. This position backfired badly on New York, as Allen identified this call for order with disorder. As early as 1772, Allen lumped the government of

New York and the British Empire into the same feudal corruption and called for the termination of both. "There seems to be a generation arisen" in New York, "extravagent in their loyalty to the king," which "talk[s] much of implicit obedience to government. This seems to be the first and greatest article of their creed, mighty sticklers for loyalty and submissiveness to government." New York offered the "peasants" of the Green Mountains the opportunity to give up the property "made valuable by extream labor and fatigue to these loyalists" and either become tenant farmers or try their luck in some other wilderness. Allen allowed that political order had its value, but when a demand for order destroys a stable community, it "terminates in the destruction of that very society which it was designed to protect." Allen found the British Empire corrupt and inefficient but hoped that he could use its ponderous mechanisms against the New York elite.

The irony in early 1775 was that the leadership of New York largely opposed the British government, though they kept demanding Regulars to put down these annoying frontier outlaws as they had their tenant rioters a decade earlier. When it came to land speculation, political theory vanished for New York's patriots.

Colonial America witnessed many uprisings by frontier settlers. The Carolinas, Maine, Pennsylvania, New Jersey, and New York all experienced these expressions of dissatisfaction by poor farmers against the economic and political clout of a few wealthy landholders and speculators. Upstate New York's rebellions were particularly bitter, as the settlers did not own their land but rented it from a small number of powerful families without any opportunity to ever purchase these farms for themselves. These tenant farmers rose on several occasions in the 1760s and 1770s against what they saw as the feudal power of the great New York landlords, a group that included some of the very same people, such as the Livingstons, who led the fight for American autonomy within the British Empire. But the patriot leaders consistently put aside their differences with the British government in order to crush their tenants with the full force of the state. The only area in which they had never enjoyed any success lay to the east of Lake Champlain, where the local farmers simply ignored New York's authority and had even gone so far as to organize their own government. It seemed obvious to the patriot leadership in Albany and New York that no reliance could be placed on these "vile wicked animals," as Robert Livingston, Jr., called them, to even take the same side in the emerging struggle with Britain.

Ethan Allen and his Green Mountain Boys had never really concerned themselves much with the larger questions of imperial policy. They were dissatisfied with the way the Empire kept siding with the New York elite, but the vast majority of Allen's neighbors did not share his radical impulses, and they were certainly far from revolutionaries in early 1775. They had no desire to change their local relations; the primacy of family, religion, and community remained beyond question. Nor had they ever indicated any dissatisfaction with the British Empire to which they belonged. Yet they certainly desired an end to the political and economic power of New York's wealthiest families, which threatened those very values which would have otherwise fostered more conservative attitudes. In the last week of April 1775, everything changed.

Lexington and Concord galvanized America. Though few people had any sense of where their actions might lead, thousands of Americans rushed to arms in open opposition to British rule. Up in the New Hampshire Grants, Ethan Allen called together his Green Mountain Boys. Allen felt that quick action would finish elite dominance everywhere in America. Here was the chance of a lifetime; a complete break with Britain would terminate the legitimacy of traditional authority and elevate the common man to sovereignty. The Green Mountain Boys hesitated, for, as Allen pointed out, if "they should take an active part with their country, and . . . an accomodation should take place, and the Colonies return to their former allegiance, what would become of them?" Familiar with the duplicity and greed of the New York elite, many of Allen's neighbors feared that the British might buy off the patriot leadership, leaving the poor farmers at their mercy. In fact, Allen had been informed by allies in New York that the great landlords of that province had requested British troops to put down the Green Mountain Boys. What Allen did not know was that on the very day of Lexington, General Gage, the military governor of Massachusetts, wrote General Guy Carleton in Montreal requesting that the 7th Regiment be sent into the Green Mountains to squash the insurrection there.

Despite their reasonable doubts about the commitment of the New York elite to the cause of America, the Green Mountain Boys agreed with Allen that much could be gained by joining "the cause of their injured country." With only a single dissent, the Green Mountain Boys voted to join the struggle against Britain. Transforming their rebellion against New York into a rebellion against Britain would present an opportunity to create their own state. Besides, Allen stated, there was little difference between resisting either authority. "I was called by the Yorkers an outlaw, and afterwards, by the British, was called a rebel; and I humbly conceive, that there was as much propriety in the one name as in the other." To prove that commitment, Allen determined to take the biggest prize of all, Fort Ticonderoga.

Fort Ticonderoga loomed over the landscape, gigantic and threatening. In the imagination of the inhabitants of Britain's northern colonies, it had stood for two decades as, first, the embodiment of the French menace and then as the symbol of British power.

The French built the fortress they called Carillon in 1755 on a steep bluff overlooking the confluence of Lake George and Lake Champlain. These lakes had long served as routes for trade and war between the Hudson River and Canada. It was here in 1758 that Montcalm had won his stunning victory over Abercrombie's massive army of 15,000 men. The 1763 Peace of Paris handed the fortress, renamed Ticonderoga, over to the British. Surrounded by water on three sides, Ticonderoga's star-shaped outer walls rose one hundred feet above the lakes, maintaining a clear line of sight, and shot, on all water-borne movements. To the south, swamps prevented any quick assault on its battlements. Bristling with cannon, Fort Ticonderoga commanded the lakes and stood as the pivot of British authority on the frontier between its older colonies and its new acquisitions to the north and west. A powerful fortress defensible by a small force, Ticonderoga earned its reputation as the key to control of the northern colonies.

In the centers of rebel resistance, Philadelphia and Albany, Hartford and Cambridge, it was understood that Fort Ticonderoga not only controlled the invasion route to and from Canada but also had what the Americans desperately needed: arms. By the end of April 1775, thousands of colonists encircled Boston, laying siege to the British troops who still occupied the city. But contrary to current mythology, the Americans were mostly unarmed or poorly armed. There were no gun manufacturers in North America. And worst of all, the ragtag army lacked the one weapon they most needed if they were going to expel the British from Boston: cannon.

This need for artillery and munitions was evident even before Washington arrived. The patriot leaders looked to Fort Ticonderoga. Behind its high walls stood more than one hundred cannon. But the fortress's garrison was not just going to hand over the weapons. The Americans would have to take Ticonderoga by force. Doing so required an offensive operation. The Continental Congress agonized over this necessity, for many members of Congress hoped to resolve this latest crisis with Britain, and they united in telling the world that the Americans acted only in self-defense. The British were the aggressors; British regulars attacked loyal subjects at Concord and in New York City, as they would later shell an unresisting Falmouth, Maine. The innocent Americans simply responded to the latest outrage. Attacking Fort Ticonderoga would clearly violate that spirit and probably destroy any chance for a quick negotiated settlement with the British government.

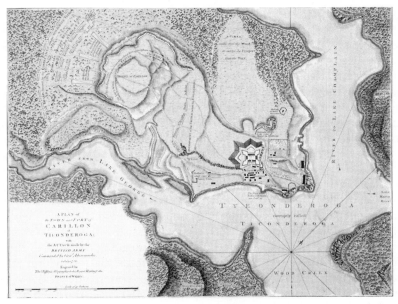

Map of Fort Carillon In 1755, just a year before the beginning of the Seven Years' War, the French built a massive fortress on Lake Champlain near where it met Lake George. They intended Fort Carillon to act as a barrier to further English expansion north. It was here that Louis Joseph de Montcalm defeated the numerically superior Anglo-American force of General Abercrombie in 1758. The battle plan is pictured in this map, drawn by Britain's leading cartographer, Thomas Jeffreys. In 1763 the fortress, given the "corrupted" name of Ticonderoga, passed into British hands. (Fort Ticonderoga Museum)

On the other hand, the Americans could not just let such a powerful bastion sit on their northern flank, a constant threat to future operations by the Americans.

There was a larger problem: Just who would act? The jurisdictional complications alone froze the wheels of the new revolutionary councils. Massachusetts's Committee of Safety hesitated to order an attack because Ticonderoga stood within the territory of New York. On April 29, the committee wrote a polite inquiry to New York's Provincial Congress setting out the difficulties: "It has been proposed to us to take possession of the Fortress at Ticonderoga. We have a just sense of the importance of that fortification, and the usefulness of those fine cannon, . . . but we would not, even upon this emergency, infringe upon the rights of our sister Colony, New York." It took a week for the letter to reach its destination, effectively precluding action from Massachusetts.

But even if they had the will to do so, the Americans could not bring any force to bear swiftly enough to attack Ticonderoga before British reinforcements arrived. The Americans did not really have an army yet or even a unified command, and Ticonderoga stood amidst the wilds of the northern frontier, in a region populated by only a few scattered farmers who appeared equally wild. And here was the final complication: the area around Fort Ticonderoga had been in open rebellion for the previous seven years. No one could be certain which side the Green Mountain Boys would take.

While the colonial leaders hesitated, a few New England radicals conspired. In Pittsfield, Cambridge, and Hartford, local Committees of Safety moved swiftly to block all the roads leading toward Ticonderoga in hopes of keeping news of the war from reaching the fort. They also scrambled to organize some sort of force to march on Ticonderoga. Down in New Haven, one man thought he saw the chance to finally attain the prominence he so richly deserved. Hurrying up to Cambridge, Captain Benedict Arnold of the Hartford militia convinced the Committee of Safety to grant him a colonel's commission to conduct "a secret service" of raising four hundred men in western Massachusetts for an assault on Ticonderoga. Arnold decided to forgo the recruiting aspect of his instructions and rushed north with his entire force, one servant, to launch his attack on Fort Ticonderoga. He assumed he would just take command of whatever militia forces he found on the way.

What Arnold discovered when he arrived on the shores of Lake Champlain with his single follower surprised him enormously. There, in the dark night of May 9, on a little bay directly opposite Fort Ticonderoga shielded by a thick screen of trees, was a force of more than two hundred men calling themselves the Green Mountain Boys—and it was their intention to attack the fort within the hour. Arnold was stunned by the resolve of these simple farmers; they showed none of the irresolution so common among the patriot leadership. And then he met the leader of the Green Mountain Boys.

Ethan Allen and Benedict Arnold did not exactly hit it off. In fact, Arnold rarely loathed anyone quite so much as he did Ethan Allen. He hated everything about Allen, from his easy familiarity with whomever he met to the way he walked. Arnold decided to put this frontier buffoon in his place immediately and demanded the command of the Green Mountain Boys.

But Arnold had not collected these troops; Ethan Allen had. And Allen knew something that few others did: that the British had allowed Fort Ticonderoga to fall into disrepair. Ethan Allen knew exactly how unprepared the British were for this war. He had sent a number of spies into the fort on various pretexts, and they all reported back that the fifty-man garrison enjoyed a relaxed duty and that their commander, Captain William Delaplace, was making no preparations for the coming conflict.

It seemed that the British were the only ones not to appreciate the strategic importance of Fort Ticonderoga. Allen stationed guards on all the roads leading to the fort and sent one last spy inside. In the early evening of May 9 that spy reported that, incredibly, the British still had no idea that they were at war. Tonight, Allen told his troops, they would seize Ticonderoga.

But here stood Benedict Arnold, resplendent in his scarlet officer's coat and bearing an official commission. Should Allen, the elected choice of his soldiers, give way to his seemingly legitimate claim to command? As Arnold angrily reported to the Cambridge Committee of Safety, Allen resolved the question in a most unorthodox manner: he asked the troops. The Green Mountain Boys voted unanimously that they would serve under no one but their own officers and that Ethan Allen was their commanding colonel. "We were shockingly suprized," one Massachusetts militia officer who was present wrote, "when Colonel Arnold presumed to contend for the command of those forces we had raised." Arnold's interference almost "frustrated our whole design," so thoroughly did he alienate the assembled volunteers. When Arnold insisted that the opinion of the common soldiers was irrelevant to military command, "our men were for clubbing their firelocks and marching home." Only Allen's impassioned plea prevented the attack on Ticonderoga from collapsing before it had even begun. In an effort to soothe any hard feelings, Allen offered Arnold a place at the head of the column, which position he grumblingly took.

Allen had only two boats, which held eighty-five men between them. It was a moonless night, so Allen felt certain that he would have time to ferry his complete force across Lake Champlain without being detected by the British. But the business with Arnold delayed their departure, and the packed boats moved more slowly than Allen expected. Arriving at the opposite shore and looking up at the bulk of Fort Ticonderoga towering above him, Allen realized that even the fort's small garrison could present an effective and bloody defense. So he decided to proceed with just a third of his troops and hoped to catch the British off guard. Allen later recalled giving an inspiring speech before the assault, complimenting his soldiers as "a scourge and terror to arbitrary power." But others remembered a more likely whispered "Let's go."

At about 3 A.M. on May 10, 1775, the Green Mountain Boys started their climb up the narrow path leading from the beach to Fort Ticonderoga. At the head of the column, stepping quickly side by side, marched Ethan Allen and Benedict Arnold. When they came within sight of the narrow covered entrance to the fort with its low gate, the two officers broke into an undignified trot, each determined to gain the honor of pressing the attack first. Allen won the race.

The Green Mountain Boys ran along the walls of the fortress, encountering no resistance. It seemed as though the fort was abandoned, "a ghostly threat guarded by but two drouzy Regulars," as one American put it. Bursting into the barracks, the Americans discovered the British soldiers mostly still asleep. A few of the Regulars were just getting out of bed, wondering what all the noise was about. But the British could offer no resistance. Their weapons were stacked neatly, and the Americans, though armed mostly with axes rather than muskets, stood between the soldiers and their guns. The Green Mountain Boys quickly roused the confused Regulars from their beds and herded them outside.

Meanwhile, back in the courtyard, Allen was running up the stairs to the commandant's room, shouting, "Come out of there, you damned British rat!" The second in command, Lieutenant Jocelyn Feltham, "was awaken'd by numbers of shrieks, & the words no quarter, no quarter." Jumping out of bed, he ran to the door carrying his pants to confront "a number of arm'd rabble." The leader of this mob, a huge ruffian named Allen, called upon Feltham to surrender the fort. Feltham asked by what authority Allen could make such a ridiculous demand. Allen responded with his usual Old Testament fervor, "In the name of the great Jehovah and the Continental Congress." Neither authority meant much to Feltham, who was Church of England.

Awakened by all the noise, Captain Delaplace, who took the time to dress appropriately, confronted Allen with an angry demand to know the meaning of this disruption. Getting to the point, Allen threatened to kill everyone if Delaplace did not surrender immediately. If there "was a single gun fired in the fort," Allen warned, "neither man woman or child should be left alive." Trying to tone down the rhetoric, "Mr Arnold begg'd it [surrender] in a genteel manner."

Delaplace did not have a clue what was going on. For some reason which Delaplace never understood, Governor Guy Carleton in Canada had made no effort to inform him about the war. Still, no matter who these lunatics might be, the British commander could see no alternative and handed Allen his sword. He then turned and ordered his soldiers to lay down their arms. But, as Feltham reported to General Gage, that order was largely irrelevant, as "when I did see our men, they were drawn up without arms," already prisoners of the Americans.

From Delaplace's and Feltham's perspective, chaos reigned. While about ninety Americans had participated in the assault, more kept arriving "to join in the plunder." By ten o'clock there were over three hundred of the "rabble" milling about the fort, shouting and drinking and seizing whatever they could, "whether belonging to his majesty or private property." The British officers acknowledged in their report to General Gage that Allen "acted with cunning through this affair," but they felt that in doing so he had violated the rules of war, winning by trickery rather than courage and strength. To the British, this sudden assault on His Majesty's fortress violated the very order of society and contradicted all reason.

To Ethan Allen, it was a perfect, bloodless victory. The Americans had taken the most formidable fortress in British North America by complete surprise. The "sun seemed to rise that morning with a superior lustre," Allen wrote, "and Ticonderoga and its dependencies smiled on its conquerers, who tossed about the flowing bowl, and wished success to Congress, and the liberty and freedom of America."

After securing his prisoners—fifty-five soldiers and thirty-four women and children—Allen sat down to inform America of his stunning success. Sending the captured flag to the Second Continental Congress, which had just begun its first meeting that very morning, Allen wrote, "Gentlemen, I have to inform you with pleasure unfelt before, that on break of day of the tenth of May 1775 . . . [we] took the fortress of Ticonderoga by storm." It was a miraculous victory, which came close to indicating divine intervention. But being a deist, Allen gave all the credit to his men. "The Soldiery behaved with such resistless fury, that they so Terrified the King's Troop that they durst not fire on their assailants, and our soldiery was agreeably disappointed."

Allen also wrote to the Albany Committee of Correspondence, hoping that the Green Mountain Boys' brilliant triumph would win over their most bitter opponents. As Allen told his followers, the time had come to "annihilate the old quarrel with the government of New-York by swallowing it up in the general conflict for liberty."

Acting quickly to consolidate their victory, Allen sent detachments of Green Mountain Boys and hastily arriving New England militia units to seize Crown Point and the other British bases in the region. Within four days a crudely armed and organized group of farmers had captured, without loss of life, every British post and ship on Lake Champlain. The inadequacy of British communications and defenses defied belief but emboldened the Americans to ever grander visions. It seemed to many, Allen included, that Canada lay open to invasion, and he encouraged Congress to act immediately. Allen also thought to draw the local Indians into his scheme, inviting them to join in fighting the British, who "stumble

Based on the classic Vauban star shape, Fort Ticonderoga crouched on its high bluffs dominating Lake Champlain in all directions. Viewed from below, it was a most formidable fortress. It is, however, in far better repair today than it was in 1775 when Ethan Allen and the Green Mountain Boys decided to begin the American Revolution in earnest. (Fort Ticonderoga Museum)

along close together rank and file," while the Green Mountain Boys "fight as Indians do. . . . Your Warriors [can] join with me and my Warriors, like brothers, and ambush the Regulars." The Indians wisely determined to wait and see how affairs developed.

Meanwhile, the captured British soldiers tried to figure out what had happened. The whole world seemed disordered. Lieutenant Feltham wrote General Gage that the absolute refuse of society had taken possession of His Majesty's fortress. The British officers had no idea what was going on as they witnessed one bizarre spectacle after another. Captain Delaplace wrote the Connecticut Assembly to inquire what they had done to deserve this treatment. "Being ignorant of any crime" which they had committed, Delaplace asked that his troops be returned "to the post from whence they were taken." If they "are considered in the light of prisoners of war, your Honours would be pleased to signify the same to them, and by whom they are detained." But Delaplace received no satisfactory answer and reported to General Gage that "I have resentment sufficient to prompt me to any revenge ordered by you on account of my king, country, & your Excelly all of which I have been obliged to hear most villainously traduced." He told Gage that he was surrounded by barbarians. Even the minister, Samuel Allen, "utters from the pulpit words shocking to hear, and commits or gets effected actions almost as base as his words." Far worse was "this person Ethan Allen" and his cousin Seth Warner, who "are as great villains as anyone on earth." Only one of the Americans, Captain Benedict Arnold, struck Delaplace as a true gentleman, spending time with the British prisoners, complaining about the poor conduct of his fellows, and promising the British that their arms would be returned to them.

Encouraged by Delaplace, Arnold again claimed the command. He even asserted that he had been in command when the fort was taken, and so any effort to deny him that authority was mutiny. Arnold insisted that Allen give way, as he could not maintain proper military discipline, even allowing the Green Mountain Boys to expropriate Delaplace's rum supply. The American soldiers "paraded, and declared they would go right home, for they would not be commanded by Arnold." A Council of War was formed to consider Arnold's charge that Allen might be the "proper man to head his own wild people" but was "entirely unacquainted with military service" and maintained his command only because of his democratic principles. Besides, Arnold, not Allen, had a commission. The council resolved the dispute by issuing Allen a colonel's commission and confirming his command. Arnold wrote angry letters to various officials, complaining about his mistreatment, which extended to Green Mountain Boys taking potshots at him.

While Arnold sulked, America exulted. Newspapers throughout the colonies gloated over their string of victories on Lake Champlain. The *Worcester Spy* wrote of the "battle" of Fort Ticonderoga that "the possession of this place affords us a key to all Canada. . . . What think ye of the Yankees now?" So thrilling were the victories that a rather undignified scramble for credit ensued. Allen, angry now with Arnold, shared the glory widely but stopped mentioning Arnold. Arnold and Colonel Easton of Massachusetts wrote letters to various officials and the newspapers, each stating that he had been in command and implying that hardly anyone else had been present for the capture of Ticonderoga. Colonel Samuel Parsons, who had arrived from Connecticut to try to straighten out the confusion, wrote that " 'Tis a matter of diversion to me to see the various competitors for the honor of concerting and carrying this matter into execution, contending so strenuously about a matter, in the execution of which all concerned deserve applause. But some cannot bear an equal, and none a superior." As Parsons understood, none of this desire for individual glory really mattered beside the enormous implication of the seizure of Britain's premier fortress by a group of American farmers. Allen wrote the New York Provincial Congress that the capture of Ticonderoga had brought America to a point where "A vast continent must now sink to slavery and poverty, bondage and horror, or rise to unconquerable freedom, immense wealth, inexpressible felicity, and immortal fame." Joseph Warren put it more succinctly: "Thus a War has begun."

Congress, however, proved less confident of the meaning of these military victories. First they had to face a number of jurisdictional headaches. The Green Mountain Boys, while acting in America's name, were also in rebellion against New York. Since the fortress was within New York's boundaries, that state should have command of further operations there, but nearly all the soldiers on hand came from New England. And then there was Benedict Arnold. Arnold ordered the Council of War at Fort Ticonderoga to disperse, as he was "at present the only legal Commanding Officer." When every other officer present voted to leave command with Ethan Allen, Arnold declared a mutiny, arrested several officers, and assaulted Major Samuel Elmore—as Arnold wrote, "I tooke the liberty of breaking his head." Faced with this quandary, Congress awarded authority to New York, which then asked Connecticut to deal with it, which in turn decided to leave military decisions in the hands of the officers on the ground, who again voted Ethan Allen in full command.

Further complicating matters, the capture of Fort Ticonderoga violated Congress's policy of defensive actions only. The Green Mountain Boys had committed the first offensive act of the war, confronting Congress with the need to declare itself. Congress refused, setting a precedent of sorts, and sought an imagined middle course. The Continental Congress apologized to the people of Canada for the attack on Fort Ticonderoga and promised that no invasion of their soil would follow. Congress also ordered Allen to move all the cannon and military stores to the end of Lake George so that they could be returned to the British.

Congress, Allen thought, had evidently lost its collective mind. Declaring himself surprised that he would have to point out something so obvious, Allen reminded Congress that they were at war. Reconciliation was quite simply impossible, and "it is bad policy to fear the retribution of an enemy." Not content with writing Congress, Allen and Seth Warner rode to Philadelphia so that they could personally plead for a reversal of this decision and for the pursuit of more aggressive actions. They must have made quite an impression, for not only did Congress vote to organize the Green Mountain Boys into a Continental regiment to be commanded by officers of their own choosing, but John Hancock also wrote New York's Provincial Congress to request their cooperation with Allen. Even more surprising, Congress reversed itself and ordered the new commander of the northern department, Philip Schuyler, to invade Canada, if "it will not be disagreeable to the Canadians."

The capture of Fort Ticonderoga set the American colonies on an irreversible course toward independence. The British government and Parliament proved very unforgiving over this aggressive act and refused to consider any substantive negotiation. Not that the Americans would have been ready to negotiate after such splendid and decisive victories. Complete success appeared within their grasp. As Allen wrote, America had reached a "critical juncture" in its conflict with "a tyrannical ministry." If it seized the opportunity, America "might rise on eagles wings and mount up to glory, freedom and immortal honour."

Standing in their conquered fortress above Lake Champlain, the Green Mountain Boys, as Allen put it, "attempted to explore futurity, but it was found to be unfathomable." None of them could imagine the direction of events now that their local uprising had become part of a much larger, national revolution. The possibilities appeared endless and as likely to produce disaster as triumphs.

Still, as Allen later admitted, "happy it was for me . . . that the then future pages of the book of fate . . . was hid from my view." Through a monumental miscalculation, Allen was captured by the British and became the most famous prisoner of war in the Revolution. Treated with remarkable severity by the British, Allen retaliated by writing a narrative of his captivity which became second in popularity only to Tom Paine's *Common Sense*. Published in 1779, in the Revolution's darkest hour, *A Narrative of Colonel Ethan Allen's Captivity* reanimated the popular commitment to the American cause by demonizing the British. Making the American prisoners of war heroes in a fight to the death against tyranny, Allen found the route to victory in their perseverance. Allen's *Narrative* stands with Paine's *Crisis Papers* as one of the great evocations of America's superior virtue and endurance and as an effective call for continued struggle at the very moment when America's military fortunes nearly hit bottom.

A romanticized nineteenth-century portrait of Ethan Allen based on written descriptions. Allen, a frontier settler, was almost certainly never so well dressed and clean-shaven. Contemporaries described him as a huge man of enormous strength and rugged appearance, possessing a rough demeanor and aggressive style capable of frightening his enemies and commanding the respect and loyalty of his followers. (Fort Ticonderoga Museum)

The settlers of the northern frontier had the opportunity to make use of this lesson of perseverance. Allen certainly would have rejected in 1775 as completely unreasonable the suggestion that the conflict between the Green Mountain settlers and the government of New York would last twice as long as the Revolution. Allen never could understand the almost fanatic insistence of the New York elite that the Green Mountains belonged to them; but then he failed to appreciate that the very wealthy are never rich enough. Despite the Revolution and the services of the Green Mountain Boys, despite the creation of the state of Vermont in 1777 and the personal intervention of George Washington, and despite the end of the war, offers of restitution, and every trick Ethan Allen could think of, the New York elite just refused to give up their claim to the region. The disagreement nearly disrupted the American union; New York threatened on several occasions to withdraw from the war effort and the union, and Ethan Allen spent years in a very public negotiation with the British in an effort to scare Congress into recognizing Vermont.

And Congress was generally scared. Ethan Allen emerged from the Revolution even more dangerous to established authority. Not only could he now draw upon a widely accepted rhetoric of revolutionary action and shared self-sacrifice, but he also had a living example of the democratic ideal. In 1777, while Allen was an uninvited guest of the British, a convention of the Green Mountain settlers led by Ira Allen and Thomas Chittenden wrote the most democratic constitution of its age. In a position to write any document they pleased, the Vermonters did not hesitate to base their government on democratic values. Vermont's constitution guaranteed the validity of land titles which had been based on nothing more than Allen's intellectual argument, that the land belonged to those who gave it value through their labor. All adult males were granted the right to vote, and slavery was terminated without qualification. But most important, the constitution institutionalized one of the most radical ideas of its age: the people as constituent power. The Vermonters did not look to any ancient traditions or inherited legal fictions for their legitimacy; their right to exist as a state was founded solely on the will of its citizenry. In Vermont, democracy had turned from a synonym for chaos into the fundamental basis for good government. In approving their constitution, Vermont's voters revolutionized American politics.

In the ensuing years Vermont's constitution became a model and ideal for radical movements elsewhere in America—and a terror to the established leadership. Even Thomas Jefferson, who thought a little revolution now and then a good thing, shuddered before what he called "the Vermont doctrine"—the right of the people to create their own states. If this principle gained general currency, no state was secure in its borders and no elite in its speculative land titles. Or as Henry Knox wrote Lafayette, "The maxim that all power is derived from the people" could too easily be "perverted by a certain proportion of the people" into a dangerous social democracy.

But it took another rebellion, this one led by a man named Daniel Shays in western Massachusetts, to finally persuade the New York leadership to make a deal with Vermont. The Shaysites, as good republicans, felt that they had been pushed to rebellion by a hostile government. The Shaysites perceived themselves as protecting their property from an avaricious elite which used the government of Massachusetts Bay for their own ends in a conspiracy "to crush the power of the people."

At first, in late 1787, the Shaysites enjoyed some success. Unable to rely on the militia, the state government organized a private army under General Benjamin Lincoln which set about crushing the uprising. In early 1788 Shays appealed to Ethan Allen and the Green Mountain Boys for aid. But Allen told Alexander Hamilton that he would withhold that support if New York recognized Vermont. Hamilton and John Jay, among others in New York's government, understood that too much was at stake to risk the expansion of Shays's Rebellion, and so they led the legislature into finally acknowledging that the time had come to cut their losses and negotiate. Allen did not turn Shays over to Massachusetts, as that state demanded, but he flatly refused to allow any Green Mountain Boys, who were now the official militia of the independent state of Vermont, to join in the rebellion.

The uprising collapsed, but Vermont finally gained recognition. It took a few more years to work out the details, but in 1791 Vermont became the first new state to join the United States under the Constitution—two years after Ethan Allen died and sixteen years after that glorious dawn of freedom at Fort Ticonderoga.

AN INTERPRETATION

Historians have long debated the degree to which the Revolution was revolutionary. From one perspective, very little changed. The basic social arrangements remained unaltered, cultural values retained their cohesion, and local elites maintained their authority. Yet the surprising victory at Fort Ticonderoga unleashed forces no one could hope to contain, though many tried. The political leadership of the several states and of the Continental Congress hoped to attain American independence with a minimum of disturbance to other social institutions. Thus, when Abigail Adams called on her husband John Adams to "Remember the Ladies" when the Continental Congress was writing new law codes, John bluntly retorted that "I cannot but laugh" at her suggestion. "We have been told that our Struggle has loosened the bands of Government every where," John complained. "Children and Apprentices were disobedient," and even "Negroes grow insolent to their Masters." And now it seemed that women expected equality; it was just too much, and John Adams promised his wife that the revolutionary leadership would throw aside their conflict with Britain rather than abandon their traditional social arrangements.

But certain class tensions could not be contained. Men like Ethan Allen— "levelers," as they were generally called in the eighteenth century—rose to positions of authority on a rhetoric of social equality and class conflict. Even the Continental Army found it difficult to institute standard military values of deference and obedience. In 1775 General Montgomery wrote George Washington that he would "use my best endeavors to establish order and discipline in the troops under my command." But he sincerely doubted that he would succeed, for "it is extremely difficult to introduce a proper subordination amongst a people where so little distinction is kept up." Montgomery complained bitterly of the "levelling spirit" of his soldiers, "who carry the spirit of freedom into the field, and think for themselves." Even these young soldiers felt that their world had undergone a fundamental change and that they were entitled to a respect long denied them.

But the Revolution's most dramatic transformations were confined to the local level. The Revolution made the Green Mountain Boys, a group of frontier outlaws, into patriotic heroes. The fluidity and uncertainty of revolutionary America gave these poor farmers the chance to legitimate their long struggle against an entrenched elite intent on taking away their land. And therein lay the very limitation of the Revolution's more radical impulses: its localism. Radicals throughout America united in a faith that those who worked the land gave it value. Few issues disrupted early America to the same degree as disputed land titles. Common farmers could unite to protect one another's perceived property rights from outsiders who sought to seize their land because of weak titles or unpaid debts, the product of weaknesses in the larger political and economic systems well beyond the control of the poor yeoman. But what happened once the farmers won? The Shaysites, for instance, just like the Green Mountain Boys, focused on local and limited issues revolving specifically around the security of the land. But once the Vermonters secured their property, they saw their political conflicts as ended and made no connection between their continued economic plight and that of the Massachusetts insurgents, most especially as their local governments in Vermont responded to their needs. So once the New York legislature voted to recognize the legitimacy of Vermont, the struggle in the Green Mountains was over, and the Shaysites were on their own. Class conflict, even for Ethan Allen, gave way before geographic constraints and the primacy of local politics.

Agrarian radicals may not have made the connection between their various uprisings, but other Americans did. George Washington wrote to Madison that "We are fast verging to anarchy and confusion," finding the crisis in Massachusetts but a local variant of a national problem requiring a federal solution. Most of the new nation's would-be leaders found the Shaysites and their ilk dangerous levelers who could easily link up with other supporters of excessive democracy. Secretary of War Henry Knox perceived the specter of class conflict in the defeated Shaysites and the successful Vermonters, telling Washington that their "creed is, that the property of the United States, has been protected from confiscation of Britain by the joint exertions of *all,* and therefore ought to be *the common property* of all." Washington suspected that the Shaysites had "real grievances" which the government of Massachusetts did not address. Nonetheless, he agreed with Knox that the states must act quickly to defend their interests or witness the dissolution of government in the United States. The answer seemed apparent: a more vigorous national government.

The Constitution which Washington and his colleagues wrote in Philadelphia in 1787 sought to put a cap on the radicalism set loose by the Revolution. The war had been a national effort which affected every community in America. Men like Ethan Allen, who would never have come near the levers of power under the British Empire, found themselves commanding large forces and influencing the destiny of a new nation. A wide diversity of social conflicts came to the fore in the Revolutionary years, such as that between frontier settlers and seaboard elites. Every social institution came under scrutiny, and to many Americans it seemed as though the Revolution might run away from them and end in social chaos. The Constitution would bring order and meaning to the long struggle for national independence. After the wrenching changes of the 1770s and 1780s, America needed a time for consolidation and peace, and the energies of men like Ethan Allen needed to be directed into more acceptable channels. In short, those who wrote the Constitution felt that it was time for the Revolution to end.

For many, the Revolution remains a frustrating story of unfulfilled promise. Certainly on the national level, this reading holds true, as slavery and the legal subjugation of women remained unchallenged. Yet for those individuals and groups who could enjoy their newly won freedoms—religious, social, cultural, and political—the Revolution shined in their memories as a transforming moment. Perhaps there is no better reflection of that reality than the state of Vermont. In 1777, in a time of near crushing uncertainty, the frontier settlers in Vermont placed their faith in democracy, writing the first constitution to institute universal manhood suffrage and the first to outlaw slavery. The Revolution remains unfinished; but it got a fair start on the shores of Lake Champlain.

Sources: Documents concerning these events can be found in Allen French, *The Taking of Ticonderoga in 1775: The British Story* (Cambridge, Mass., 1928); Lucius E. Chittenden, *The Capture of Ticonderoga* (Rutland, Vt., 1872); Peter Force, ed., *American Archives* (9 vols., Washington, D.C., 1837–1853), vol. 1; and *Collections of the Connecticut Historical Society,* vol. 1 (Hartford, Conn., 1860). For Benedict Arnold's version, see "Benedict Arnold's Regimental Memorandum Book," in *The Pennsylvania Magazine of History and Biography,* vol. 8 (1884). For Ethan Allen's version, see his *Narrative of Colonel Ethan Allen's Captivity* (Philadelphia, 1779), which is still in print.

8

REBELLION IN THE NEW REPUBLIC: MASSACHUSETTS 1786–1787

GREGORY H. NOBLES

When the military struggle for independence had been won, the new nation still faced enormous economic and political problems. Operating under the Articles of Confederation, the first constitution of the United States, the fledgling national government had managed to fight a successful war and hold thirteen very independently minded colonies together, but it had not fared so well in the economic arena. The costs of the war were formidable, and debt piled up everywhere—on the national and state governments, on large-scale merchants and country storekeepers, and on common people both in the cities and in the countryside. The Continental Congress had printed large amounts of paper money, which only made matters worse, creating a crisis of confidence in which currency fell so rapidly in value that it almost ceased to have meaning as a medium of exchange. The phrase "not worth a Continental" became a widespread expression of worthlessness.

This economic crisis revived a political debate which many thought had been solved by the adoption and ratification of the Articles of Confederation. The Articles represented the triumph of those (probably a majority of Americans) who favored a loosely organized federation of states in which the national government would have very little power. Their opponents, led by Alexander Hamilton, had consistently fought for a stronger central government but in the end had retired from Congress in defeat. After the surrender of the British at Yorktown in 1781, however, the economic situation did not improve but rather worsened, allowing the nationalists to blame (convincingly) the Articles of Confederation. In 1785 Hamilton had issued a call for a meeting of leaders from every state to convene at Annapolis, Maryland, in the summer of 1786 to discuss revisions to the Articles. However, so few people bothered to show up that the assembly was canceled. Not to be deterred, the nationalists rescheduled the meeting for the next summer in Philadelphia, giving themselves time to lobby state leaders and persuade them to attend. It was a matter of convincing those who had supported the decentralized government of the Articles that their economic problems could be alleviated by the institution of a more powerful centralized national state.

Inadvertently, the proponents of centralization received some help from the social unrest that was occurring in many of the colonies because of the worsening economic conditions. Rural farmers, on whom the "chain of debt" fell disproportionately, began petitioning their state governments for relief. They argued that while they were in a "distressed" condition, the merchants and lawyers "riot in grandeur and luxury." The solution, they suggested, should be a new emission of paper money, which would increase the currency supply and make it easier for debtors to pay their bills and a tender law which would allow farmers to pay their debts with farm products as they had been accustomed to doing previously. In addition, these petitioners attacked the court system, which, they claimed, acted arrogantly and without compassion in confiscating farms just because their owners could not pay debts in specie (gold).

To the large landholders, merchants, and lawyers who occupied the political offices in most states, this seemed a radical solution because it threatened their own economic interests. However, before Shays's Rebellion in western Massachusetts in the fall of 1786, it was only the words that were radical; when Shays and his men actually took up arms against the government of Massachusetts, the threat became much more serious. Now the nationalists could argue that a stronger central government was needed not only to regulate the economy but also to prevent and put down radical threats to the social order. The story of Shays's Rebellion as revealed by Gregory Nobles in this essay was not really the threat the nationalists claimed, but it certainly influenced the fifty-five men who wrote the Constitution when they convened in Philadelphia in the summer of 1787.

Late in the afternoon of January 25, 1787, a small army of over a thousand men trudged through the snow into Springfield, Massachusetts. Converging in two columns from the north and northeast, the troops marched toward the lowering winter sun until they came within three hundred yards of their objective— a United States government arsenal that held several hundred tons of arms and ammunition. The supplies inside the arsenal would give the attackers the additional firepower they would need to march on Boston, where, some said, they intended to overthrow the government of Massachusetts.

Defending the arsenal was a force almost as large as their own, around a thousand Massachusetts militiamen under the command of Major General William Shepard, who had the advantage of being behind fortified walls and supported by artillery pieces. As the attackers assembled into battle formation in front of the arsenal, General Shepard shouted that if they did not retreat, he would open fire on them with his cannon. The men outside the arsenal met Shepard's threat with derision and defiance, and the leader of one of the columns, Daniel Shays, ordered them to press the attack. As the closely massed force marched forward, warning shots from two cannons in the arsenal sent shells whistling harmlessly over their heads, causing a few men to duck but no one to stop. But the next shells came in low and on target. Over a dozen rounds of grapeshot tore through the ranks of the attackers, leaving four dead and twenty wounded and sending the rest into a confused retreat. Within a matter of minutes, the attack was over, and General Shepard had saved the arsenal. He might well have saved the state.

In doing so, though, he had shed the blood of his fellow countrymen. The men who marched on Springfield were not an invading foreign force but citizens of the United States, most of them farmers and artisans from rural communities in Massachusetts. Some of them, in fact, had taken exactly the same sort of action before in defense of Massachusetts. Not quite a dozen years earlier, in 1775, another small army of farmers and artisans from all over Massachusetts had likewise risen up in arms against government troops. In that case, however, the government in question was British, and the troops had been sent across the sea to control the colonists in North America. When the Massachusetts minutemen first faced the British soldiers at Lexington on April 19, 1775, the "shot heard round the world" set off a widespread rebellion that would soon engulf the colonies and ultimately end in revolutionary victory in 1783, making the United States an independent nation.

Now, however, the government under attack in 1787 was the Commonwealth of Massachusetts, one of the new states of the new nation. Its leaders were not appointed by the British crown but elected by the voters of Massachusetts; its troops were not imported mercenaries but local militiamen who came largely from rural communities in the surrounding countryside—just like the men who marched against them. The confrontation at Springfield pitted citizens of the state against each other in an armed struggle and raised the unmistakable specter of civil war. Coming so soon after the end of the American Revolution, it also raised disturbing questions about what the new experience of independence and self-government would mean for Massachusetts—and maybe for the United States as a whole.

The man who ordered this rebel army to attack, Daniel Shays, had reason to question results of the Revolution himself. Shays was a respected veteran of that struggle; he had been wounded at the Battle of Bunker Hill in 1775, and he had stayed in the fight for five more years, rising to the rank of captain by the time he left the army in 1780. There is a story that Shays was such a good soldier, in fact, that he was given a ceremonial sword by the Marquis de Lafayette when the French general recognized able American officers after the Saratoga campaign in 1777. But realizing that the new sword would be worth more in barter than in battle, Shays apparently sold it or traded it away. Many of his fellow officers were outraged at this obvious insult, but Daniel Shays was a practical Yankee, and he needed to get what he could for it.

Whether true or not, the story makes an important point: Daniel Shays was not a professional soldier but a common yeoman. After leaving the army, he moved into the town of Pelham, a small community of just under a thousand inhabitants nestled in the hills above the Connecticut River valley about thirty miles north of Springfield. Like many of his neighbors in Pelham and people in other rural communities, Shays eked out a hardscrabble existence as a farmer, usually growing enough food to feed his family but also borrowing money and buying on credit and, on at least two occasions, falling far enough behind that he wound up in court as the defendant in a debt case—a widely shared situation in the 1780s.

Daniel Shays was by no means the only person in postwar Massachusetts facing financial trouble, and for many people like Shays, it appeared that the economic situation would get worse before it got better. American merchants, eager to expand their business after years of being commercially cut off from Great Britain, quickly resumed trade relations with British merchant houses, importing large amounts of manufactured goods in exchange for agricultural products, fish, and timber. Unfortunately, the value of imports far exceeded that of American exports, and the United States, not to mention many individual merchants, ran up a significant trade deficit with the former parent country. Moreover, when British merchants demanded payment in specie—that is, hard money in the form of gold and silver—American merchants had little to give them. In New England, where the rush to resume transatlantic commerce had been especially energetic, the problem of suddenly securing specie for payment became acute. Large wholesalers, who owed debts directly to mercantile firms in Great Britain, turned to their customers, the retail merchants in the cities and countryside, and increasingly insisted on payment in specie. Retail merchants in turn pressured their local customers to pay their debts in hard money. In general, the postwar credit crisis created what one historian has called a "chain of debt," in which common people at

This map of western Massachusetts shows some of the significant sites of Shays's Rebellion, including Springfield, the location of the federal arsenal (designated "East Springfield," in the lower central part of the map), and Petersham, the scene of the last major engagement between militia troops and insurgents (above the "E" in "HAMPSHIRE"). (From a map by J. Reid, 1796)

the lower end of the chain, like Daniel Shays, bore the ultimate burden of coming up with hard cash.

That burden fell especially hard on people in rural regions, who had been accustomed to covering their store debts through various forms of noncash payment—farm produce, homemade goods, labor, and the like. When local storekeepers began to refuse such payments and insist on specie, many rural people found themselves in an unsettling situation: the customs of the local economy seemed to have changed rather suddenly, and debtors had no real ability to bargain for better terms before cash-hungry creditors dragged them into court. In some rural regions of New England, particularly the western parts of Massachusetts, the number of debt cases rose dramatically in the early postwar era. At best, debtors might be able to use the court proceedings to stall while they scraped together the means of payment or negotiated a settlement with their creditors. At worst, though, many of them faced the prospect of having their property seized by the sheriff and sold at auction to meet the creditors' demands. In some cases, they might even be thrown into jail for debt, losing their liberty as well as their property. Thus the chain of debt could weigh heavily, indeed.

To make matters even worse, the state government only added to the economic pressures on common people. In a sense, the government was in much the same position as the merchants, trying to establish its credit by paying off its debts in good order. More to the point, the government was heavily influenced, if not dominated, by representatives of the state's mercantile interests, who saw stable state credit as beneficial to business. Accordingly, in the early 1780s the Massachusetts state legislature, or General Court, undertook a policy of paying off the state's debt; to do so, it raised taxes and, equally important, required that taxes be paid in specie. If taxpayers could not come up with proper payment, they might face the seizure and sale of their property. Thus the hard-money policies of the government, following on (and reflecting) those of the merchants, made a difficult situation seem potentially unendurable.

Beset by both creditors and tax collectors, common people began to complain. In 1784, the inhabitants of Conway, a small farming community in western Massachusetts, petitioned the state government about "the great difficulty we labor under in regard to paying our taxes" because of "the great scarcity of a circulating medium" in their rural region. Given the possible penalties for failure to pay their debts and taxes in specie, they especially dreaded the prospect that they might lose their property in debt proceedings. To people who owned their own land—"purchased with our money, and converted from howling wilderness, into fruitful fields, by the sweat of our brow"—the thought of becoming "tenants to landlords" seemed "truly shocking." Over the course of the next two years, similar petitions poured in from dozens of other Massachusetts farm towns, all of them seeking relief from the burdens of taxation and debt. Petitioners from Dracut complained that it was becoming impossible "to Extricate themselves from the Labyrinth of Debt into which they are fallen" because hard money "seems to have taken its flight to some other Country." In addition to asking for an increased supply of paper money, they proposed another solution: a tender law that would allow people to pay their debts with farm products, as they had been accustomed to doing for years.

In addition to writing petitions, many of these towns also sent delegates to special county conventions, called for the purpose of voicing a common plea for reform. The conventions not only echoed the appeals for making debts payable in paper currency and farm produce but also articulated even broader attacks on the very system of law and government in the state. In August 1786, for instance, delegates from fifty towns in Hampshire County, in the western part of the state where Shays lived, issued a long list of grievances that included complaints about the costs and cumbersome nature of the court system (and, almost as an aside, about the lawyers who made their livings in those courts); about the unfair imbalance of the tax system in favor of the "mercantile interests" at the expense of farmers; and even about the location of the government in Boston, which was not only at the far eastern end of the state but, more important, in the center of mercantile activity and interest.

To an uneasy merchant or member of the government, this outpouring of petitions from farming regions may have looked like a truly radical threat. In fact, both the actions and words of the rural people remained very much within the traditions of Massachusetts politics. Individual towns had petitioned the government from the earliest days of Massachusetts's history, and county conventions had been an important part of the pre-Revolutionary protest that had made Massachusetts the most vocal colony in the 1760s and 1770s. Indeed, the Massachusetts state constitution of 1780 had enshrined such outspoken protest in law, declaring that "the people have a right, in an orderly and peaceful manner, to assemble and consult upon the common good . . . and to request of the legislative body . . . redress of wrongs done them, and of the grievances they suffer." Moreover, even though some of the petitions questioned the apparent bias of the political and legal systems in favor of the "mercantile interests," they did not call for a radical restructuring of either: after all, complaining about the government's being in Boston only implied a desire to move it, not overthrow it. In general, these first petitions used dramatic, sometimes overdrawn, rhetoric to make their appeals, but in the end they always respectfully asked for reform, not revolution.

Unfortunately for the petitioners—and perhaps for the state as a whole—their appeals did not meet with much sympathy or support. The majority of merchants, lawyers, and members of government dismissed the reform appeals of rural people as unwise, even unpatriotic and immoral, policies that could ruin an already unstable economy. Merchants certainly felt they had little to gain and much to lose if the requested reforms became reality. As they had learned during the Revolution, paper money could collapse in value almost overnight. By the same token, taking crops or other farm goods to cover store debts meant taking a chance on not being able to dispose of them for a good price. In general, having recently seen the possible consequences of accepting paper currency and crops, merchants had little inclination for loosening the laws to make life better for debtors. Like many other prosperous people in both the past and the present, members of the mercantile elite offered a simple solution to the problems of poverty: "Industry, economy, and honest principles," as one writer put it. If poor people would only be more frugal and save their money instead of spending it on alcohol and luxury items, so the standard argument went, they would soon be able to get themselves out of debt—and become better people in the bargain.

Perhaps not surprisingly, the government agreed with the merchants' position. The strong influence of representatives from the larger commercial centers, especially in the eastern part of the state, doomed the reform measures to failure. In 1785, the Massachusetts General Court rejected a proposal for paper money by an overwhelming margin, 93 to 23, and then turned down a bill for a tender law by almost the same vote; a few months later, in May 1786, similar proposals met a similar fate. Some towns and county conventions still submitted plaintive petitions after the negative votes, but the prospects for debt relief seemed destined to die a lingering legislative death.

The movement for reform did not die out in the rural regions, however, but took on new life and, more important, new tactics. At town meetings and county conventions, as frustrated farmers and artisans voiced their anger at the attitude of the government and the economic elite, they reinforced their resolve not to accept rejection quietly. A growing number of people decided that the time had come to take direct action. In the late summer and early fall of 1786, mobs began to move against the government.

The first acts of physical protest began in late August and continued through September 1786. In two of the largest rural counties—Hampshire and Worcester—mobs numbering in the hundreds converged on the county seats, coming from the surrounding communities to make sure the courts did no business. People surrounded the courthouses in an organized, quasi-military manner, some marching to the music of drums and fifes; almost everyone was armed, some with clubs and sticks, others with guns and bayonets. To the justices assembling for court, this display of militant spirit was a perplexing, distressing sight. Knowing they had no chance of holding court as usual, the justices had no choice but to give up. During September, threats of similar action swirled through Berkshire, Middlesex, and Bristol counties. Suddenly it seemed as though the whole legal system in Massachusetts was about to be undermined by mob action.

Clearly, the government had to do something to enforce—or restore—its authority, and Governor James Bowdoin hastily assembled a group of advisers to help him deal with the crisis. They were in an uneasy and certainly unenviable situation. Although they had the right to issue proclamations against riotous behavior and to call out the militia to confront mobs—both of which they did—Bowdoin and his advisers still had to tread carefully. They found themselves in the potentially unpopular position of opposing a movement of the people, trying to stop the sorts of actions that had helped make Massachusetts an independent state in the first place. Indeed, closing the courts was one of the first and most effective methods of challenging British rule in the early Revolutionary era. Now, twelve years later, Governor Bowdoin was confronting a situation in which hundreds, eventually thousands, of citizens were adopting the political practices of the past, identifying themselves with the heroic actions and patriotic traditions of the Revolutionary era. No matter what power he had under the law, he could not act in a heavy-handed manner. The British had tried that, and everyone in Massachusetts knew the result.

The dilemma of dealing with court closings came to a head at the end of September 1786, when rumors began to spread that a mob would descend on Springfield to block the Supreme Judicial Court. Springfield was not just the location of the court's sitting but also the site of the federal arsenal, with its huge stores of weapons and supplies. Bowdoin, who had been opposed to bloodshed from the beginning, had to be especially careful not to create a violent confrontation that might escalate and, quite literally, blow up. In close consultation with Secretary of War Henry Knox—a prominent Revolutionary War general from Massachusetts whose federal position now included oversight of the arsenal—Bowdoin ordered Major General William Shepard of the Hampshire County militia to keep order.

Unfortunately for Shepard, neither Governor Bowdoin nor Secretary Knox could assure him that either the state or the national treasury would be able to pay to keep his militiamen in the field. Moreover, Shepard had reason to suspect that many of the 900 or so men under his command were less than eager to stand against the insurgents, who were, after all, their fellow citizens and who, perhaps more important, were rumored to number anywhere from a thousand to two thousand. Thus the position of the government was not just worrisome but weak.

Despite the fears of Bowdoin, Shepard, and the militiamen, the insurgents were equally intent on avoiding bloodshed in the first encounter at Springfield. As had been the case in the other court closings earlier in the month, the mob marched on Springfield in a rather ragtag military manner, somewhat sloppy in appearance but still in generally good order. This time, though, it seemed clear that the people from the various towns had one man who assumed command over the movement that would later bear his name—Daniel Shays. (The term "Shays's Rebellion" did not become common until the 1790s, after the insurrection was over. During the events of the 1780s, the insurgents tended to call themselves "Regulators," hearkening back to earlier rural resistance movements in the Carolinas in the 1760s. Still, some of their opponents began to refer to "Shays & Co." or "Shaysmen" by late 1786.)

Shays always denied being the instigator of the insurrection, and to a large degree he was right. In the early stages of protest, direct action was largely a local affair, a loosely organized coming together of community bands for the immediate purpose of closing a court. In most counties, one or two men, usually Revolutionary War veterans, might assume a commanding role. In addition to Daniel Shays, Luke Day became a leading figure in Hampshire County, and Adam Wheeler of Worcester County and Job Shattuck of Middlesex County also assumed positions of leadership in their respective counties. Although Shays had been an effective officer during the Revolutionary War, nothing in his postwar career seemed likely to propel him to the front rank of an insurgent movement; indeed, Shays had been only a comparatively minor official in Pelham in the early 1780s, probably because he was still a comparative newcomer to the community. Yet by the fall of 1786, he found himself pushed to the forefront of a widespread insurgent movement, probably because of his military experience and personal qualities of leadership. Although Shays consistently insisted that he never sought the position, suddenly he was the main strategist and spokesman for an armed mob that had come to town to shut down the court.

By September 26, Shays's men numbered around a thousand, about the same size as the militia force, and they occupied a campsite about a mile away from Shepard's government troops; for the next three days, the two forces went through their maneuvers and waited to see what the other would do. The situation quickly turned into a stalemate. Protected by Shepard's militiamen, the justices of the court took their places in the courthouse, but when most of the jury members failed to show up, the court could not do any serious business. Outside the courthouse, the two forces paraded around town, each trying to prove its strength to the other while still being careful not to provoke a violent attack. Just to be sure that everyone knew who was who, the insurgents stuck sprigs of hemlock in their hats, and the militiamen and their supporters put pieces of white paper in theirs. Finally, after Shepard entered into negotiations with Shays and a committee of insurgent leaders, the two sides worked out a compromise to end the confrontation: the court would adjourn on September 28, and both the insurgent and the militia forces would leave town. As a last gesture to end the three-day drama, "the Committees agreed that the Militia [should] march to the Labratory Hill & there disband, that Capt. Shays might march thro' the Town . . . & then dismiss them . . . [and] that they [would] each Throw off the Badges a white paper in ye Militia Hats, Green Bush in ye Mobb, & go Home friendly."

This peaceful, almost polite closing ceremony seemed to underscore the positions of both sides. With the help of the militia, the justices had been able to keep the court open, even though they accomplished nothing before adjourning; in the face of the militia, the insurgents had been able to demonstrate the legitimacy, if not the legality, of their role in local politics. Then, once both sides had played

This woodcut, printed in an anti-Shaysite almanac at the time of the insurrection, depicts Daniel Shays and Job Shattuck as military leaders and mockingly gives them inflated military rank. Shays was sometimes called the "generalissimo" of the movement that came to bear his name. (National Portrait Gallery, Smithsonian Institution/Art Resource, NY)

their respective parts in this political pageant, everyone could indeed "go Home friendly."

The situation did not stay friendly for long, however. In response to the court closings in August and September, the government of Massachusetts took a two-pronged approach, placating the insurgents on a few issues while, at the same time, pressuring them to give up their protest. For instance, the General Court streamlined debt proceedings and temporarily suspended the requirement that debts and taxes be paid in specie. Although it did not consider increasing the money supply by issuing paper money, it did provide for minting copper coins. Finally, it appointed a committee to study the question of moving the state capitol out of Boston—but then adjourned before the committee could report.

At the same time, the legislature adopted strong measures to discourage extralegal political protest. It passed a riot act, which imposed severe penalties on anyone convicted of participating in mob activity, and gave the governor authority to suspend the right of habeas corpus for anyone even suspected of seditious behavior. To soften the political impact of such harsh laws, the legislature allowed people who had already engaged in antigovernment activity to be pardoned if they signed an oath of loyalty.

While taking these legislative steps to deal with the rural insurgency, the government also tried to shore up its military strength. In response to a request from Secretary of War Knox and the Continental Congress, the Massachusetts government increased its commitment of manpower to the federal army; the ostensible purpose of this military expansion was to prepare for an Indian war brewing in the Ohio territory, but many people in Massachusetts suspected that the real reason behind Knox's request for mobilizing Massachusetts troops was the trouble in his home state. (In fact, as later revelations of the federal government's true intentions would make clear, those suspicions were correct.) But when neither the state nor the federal government proved able to raise and pay for an adequate fighting force, merchants in Boston and other commercial communities contributed funds to support a special force of over 4000 militiamen to deal with the insurrection. Moreover, to fill the ranks, the merchants recruited their sons and servants; there was even a separate unit composed of Harvard students.

In the minds of government leaders and the merchant elite, the uprising had to be suppressed at almost any cost. They feared not only the disruption of the legal system but, in their worst nightmares, the possible overthrow of the government, a radical restructuring of the economic system, and a descent into anarchy and barbarism. To many fearful men with much to lose, the dictatorship of Daniel Shays did not seem at all far-fetched. Neither did a malicious British conspiracy, in which Tory agents might use the unrest in Massachusetts to undermine American stability and perhaps eventually restore the authority of the Crown in the United States. In this rather excited scenario, local protest was only the first step toward national catastrophe.

The fears of the insurgents were equally great. The recent actions of the government—the passage of the riot act, the suspension of habeas corpus, the mobilization of the merchant-funded militia—convinced many disaffected farmers that their lives and liberties were in extreme danger. One rural writer warned his fellow farmers about the "bloodshed and prisoners made by tyrants who are afighting for promotion to advance their own interest which will destroy the good people of this land." The specter of tyranny suddenly seemed as real in 1786 as it had in 1776.

Therefore, in the fall of 1786, Shays began to organize a more effective military force to oppose the government troops. In October, he issued a circular letter to towns in western Massachusetts asking them to "assemble your men together, to see that they are well armed and equipped . . . and be ready to turn out at a minute's warning." Shays's reference to being ready "at a minute's warning" was no accident but a conscious association designed to awaken the patriotic memory of the earlier "minutemen" of Massachusetts, who rose up to confront the British at Lexington and Concord in 1775.

For many of the men who responded to the call, however, that was a childhood memory. Unlike Shays and some of the other leading men in the rebel movement, the vast majority of the insurgents were not actual veterans of the Revolution, primarily because they had been too young to serve at the time, especially in the early years of the war, when the military action had been closer to their homes in New England. In 1786 and 1787, at the time of the insurrection, they were comparatively young men, in their late twenties or early thirties, in the early stages of establishing farms and families. Still, if they had not personally felt the pressure of debt proceedings, they nonetheless understood the threat: seeing one's neighbor or kinsman become the victim of the economic and legal system could make a young man feel vulnerable, fearful of what the future might bring. That vulnerability became one important reason for their response to the call to rebellion.

By January of 1787, Shays and other local leaders had drilled enough discipline into their followers to have a formidable fighting force in the field. Their first real test would be a second march on Springfield, but this time not just to make a military parade around the courthouse, as they had done in September. Now they were coming to attack the arsenal and take its guns.

As three columns of rebel forces under the command of Shays, Luke Day, and Eli Parsons converged on Springfield, a nervous General Shepard realized that he and his militiamen were surrounded, outnumbered, and cut off from reinforcements. He wrote the commanding officer of the Massachusetts militia, General Benjamin Lincoln, a letter of alarm on January 24:

> Shays and Day with their forces have stopped every avenue by which supplies and recruits can be brought to this post. The provisions designed for the support of the troops under my command are now converted to the use of the Insurgents. . . . If you cannot grant me any reinforcement, or relief, I shall try to work out my own salvation before it is too late. Shays' and Day's forces are about two thousand strong. Before tomorrow morning I expect the trial will be made to force me from this post. It is no time for delay, and operations must be quick and spirited, or they will answer no purpose. *That mans* party is increasing fast.

As it turned out, Shepard received no relief from General Lincoln, but he got a bit of inadvertent assistance from rebel leader Luke Day. On January 25, the morning of the planned attack, Day sent Shepard and the militia troops defending the arsenal an ultimatum offering them twenty-four hours to lay down their guns and go home. He also sent a copy of the message to Shays and Parsons to notify them of his plan to delay the attack until January 26, but the messages apparently never arrived. This military miscommunication may have proved fatal: while Day held his men in check, the other two leaders launched the attack late in the afternoon of January 25. Coming forward with just over half the insurgent force, they had neither the manpower nor the firepower to frighten Shepard into submission. Instead, Shepard's artillery broke their ranks and, in doing so, broke up the insurgent army altogether. The blood of the dead and wounded on the snowy ground was a sure sign that as the autumn of 1786 changed to the winter of 1787, the fortunes of the rebel forces had changed as well.

After the defeat at Springfield, some of the rebels were able to regroup, and Shays led a sizable force northward to the small hilltown of Petersham, closer to the center of insurgent strength in western Massachusetts. There Shays hoped to assemble more men and make a stand against the state troops. But the commander of the militia force, General Lincoln, was equally determined to defeat the rebel army once and for all, and he came after them in dogged pursuit in the dead of winter. On the cold, snowy morning of February 4, 1787, Lincoln launched a surprise attack against the insurgent camp and threw Shays's men into confusion and flight. Shays, Day, and other leaders fled Massachusetts for shelter in neighboring states, as did many of their followers. Some rebels held out and continued the fight in Massachusetts, staging occasional attacks against local lawyers and merchants. For most, though, this second defeat proved to be the crucial blow. After the brief battle at Petersham, the rebels never regained their unity, and the movement began to collapse.

While General Lincoln was attacking the Shaysites with guns, the government was attacking them with more laws. On February 4, not yet knowing that Lincoln had scattered the Shaysites at Petersham that morning, the Massachusetts General Court back in Boston declared that *"a horrid and unnatural* REBELLION *and* WAR, has been openly and traiterously raised and levied against this Commonwealth." That declaration made clear the government's commitment to resolve the political crisis on its own terms and not to accommodate the demands of the rebels. During the next few weeks, the General Court passed legislation to offer pardon to the rebels, but only if they took an oath of allegiance, gave up their guns, and paid a small fine; those who did so would still be denied the right to vote, hold office, and serve on juries for three years, after which they would have their rights restored, subject to good behavior. But there would be no immediate pardon for Daniel Shays and the other men identified as ringleaders of the rebellion; they were indicted for treason *in absentia*. Some Massachusetts officials desperately wanted to get their hands on them and hang them.

No one was more eager to resolve the problems with a rope than Samuel Adams—the pre-Revolutionary radical activist who had himself been high on the British government's list for hanging in 1775. Adams had no trouble disposing of the apparent contradiction between his own radical activity then and that of the Shaysites now. The Revolution, he insisted, had changed the rules of repression: "In monarchies, the crime of treason and rebellion may admit of being pardoned or lightly punished; but the man who dares to rebel against the laws of a republic ought to suffer death." In order for a new republic to be credible and survive, it had to make painfully clear that any violent challenge to a freely elected government would be met with superior violence. If people chose to go outside the bounds of law that they had (theoretically) created for themselves, they should expect no mercy.

Fortunately for the condemned Shaysites, Samuel Adams did not have ultimate authority for punishing political offenses against the state. Governor Bowdoin and, later, John Hancock—who succeeded Bowdoin in the governor's chair after statewide elections in the spring of 1787—leaned toward leniency. They were (or became) astute enough to realize that executions would only add to the antagonism of an already uneasy populace. A lesser punishment would be a gesture of conciliation that would help win back the disaffected communities. In the end, only two condemned Shaysites, both of whom were found guilty of theft in addition to their political activity, went to the gallows.

Still, no political leader, either in Massachusetts or anywhere else in the new nation, could easily take the recent rebellion lightly. Citizens of other parts of New England—Vermont, New Hampshire, and Connecticut—also engaged in acts of local protest in the 1780s, as did rural people in New Jersey, Pennsylvania, Virginia, and South Carolina. Clearly, Shays's Rebellion was only the most extreme expression of agrarian discontent that ran throughout the new nation.

Political leaders at both the state and the national levels understood the implications of such widespread unrest. If insurrection could make one state unstable, it could do the same in all of them—and perhaps in the nation as a whole. With such a threat hanging over the future of the fragile federal union, a growing number of leaders began to argue that the infant republic needed a stronger degree of central authority than had been provided in the Articles of Confederation. In the fall of 1786, when the events in Massachusetts were moving toward violence, Washington wrote his fellow Virginian James Madison about the dangers of social unrest:

> What stronger evidence can be given of the want of energy in our governments than these disorders? If there exists not a power to check them, what security has a man for life, liberty, or property? . . . [T]he consequences of a lax, or inefficient government, are too obvious to be dwelt on.

The problems apparently seemed equally obvious to many of Washington's political peers, especially those who made their way to Philadelphia in the spring of 1787 to begin work on a new constitution for the United States. At the time, Shays's Rebellion had essentially run its course, but it was still on the minds of the delegates to the constitutional convention. To be sure, the events in Massachusetts did not create the call for a new constitution; like Washington, many other political leaders had already determined that the nation needed a stronger central government, and plans for designing a new framework had been developing since 1785. Still, Shays's Rebellion contributed to the context of constitution-making in 1787 and, later, to the ratification debates in 1788.

The most famous of the *Federalist Papers,* James Madison's Number 10, clearly raised the specter of the recent insurrection with a reference to the "rage for paper money, for an abolition of debt, for an equal division of property, or for any other improper or wicked project." The "abolition of debt" and "equal division of property" were exaggerations, of course; the Massachusetts Regulators

THE

HISTORY

OF THE

INSURRECTIONS,

IN

MASSACHUSETTS,

In the YEAR MDCCLXXXVI,

AND THE

REBELLION

CONSEQUENT THEREON.

BY GEORGE RICHARDS MINOT, A. M.

PRINTED AT *WORCESTER,* MASSACHUSETTS,
BY ISAIAH THOMAS, MDCCLXXXVIII.

1788

George Roberts Minot's *History of the Insurrections* **(1788)** took a strongly progovernment stance toward the events in Massachusetts. Subsequent studies in the twentieth century would be more sympathetic toward the insurgents' situation. (American Antiquarian Society) never called for such extreme leveling. Still, Madison's evocation of the recent rebellion helped make a compelling polemical point. In the minds of many fearful federalists, the Massachusetts insurrection had already become a symbol of the excesses of democracy.

On the other hand, some people saw in this rising of rural people the best expression of democracy. Thomas Jefferson, who had been out of the country serving as American minister to France since 1785, missed most of the furor surrounding the Massachusetts insurrection. He thought, in fact, that the furor had been a bit overblown. At the end of 1786, before the attack on the Springfield arsenal, Jefferson wrote Ezra Stiles, the president of Yale College, that he saw "nothing threatening" in the "commotions" in Massachusetts. "If the happiness of the mass of the people can be secured at the expense of a little tempest now and then, or even of a little blood, it will be a precious purchase." Writing to Madison a month later, he expressed the same sentiment in one of his most well-known sentences: "I hold that a little rebellion now and then is a good thing, & as necessary in the political world as storms in the physical." For a former revolutionary like Jefferson, political protest clearly had a place at the center of self-government.

For a former revolutionary and rebel like Daniel Shays, however, the recent actions of his government meant that he had no place in Massachusetts. Although he eventually received a pardon, he never came back to live permanently in his home state. He settled for a while in Vermont, and after a brief return to Pelham, he moved to western New York sometime around the turn of the century. In 1818, he was living in "reduced Circumstances" in Livingston County and applying for a Revolutionary War pension. There is a story that a young man named Millard Fillmore—who would one day be a member of the New York state legislature, a member of the U.S. House of Representatives, and then President of the United States—used to visit with Daniel Shays in the last years of the former rebel's life. No doubt they talked politics, both past and present. When Fillmore entered the state legislature in 1829, one of the first issues he put before his fellow lawmakers was a bill for debt relief. It came too late for Daniel Shays: he died in 1825, a relic of the Revolutionary era who spent his last years in poverty and obscurity.

AN INTERPRETATION

Although it was short-lived and unsuccessful, Shays's Rebellion sent a shock through Massachusetts and, indeed, through the rest of the United States. It revealed the depths of the economic and political crisis that gripped the nation, especially New England, in the immediate postwar era. Moreover, it also revealed that although the war was over, in some respects the Revolution was not: the process of political change was still not altogether complete, and the proper relationship between the people and their government had certainly not been settled.

As had been the case in 1775, the people who took up arms in 1786 did so because they felt their government took little note of their needs. Having thrown off what they considered oppression at the hands of the British government, some people still felt they suffered oppression at the hands of their own. Feeling that the political system still did not provide equitable taxation and equal representation, people were by no means reluctant to protest. At first, they followed the proper procedures in a republican government, petitioning their elected leaders for a remedy to, or at least recognition of, their problems. But when they found their leaders treating their entreaties with apparent indifference, they resorted to old forms of political protest—closing courts and eventually taking up arms—that had served them well in the protests against Great Britain just over a decade before. In that sense, the uprising of the 1780s indicated that some people in the post-Revolutionary era still reserved the right to revolt.

Exactly who exercised that right, and why, is a question that has engaged historians since the days of the insurrection itself. The first chronicler of the rebellion, George Richards Minot, wrote in his *History of the Insurrections in Massachusetts* (1788) that the rebellious farmers were "malcontents" who had been "deluded" by demagogues—especially Daniel Shays. Throughout the nineteenth century, other historians and antiquarians held to much the same view, often becoming even harsher in their condemnation of the insurgents as unprincipled people who would undermine legitimate government for the sake of their own petty complaints. Similarly, some historians have argued, taking their cue from Samuel Adams, that anyone who rebelled against an elected, republican government had no claim to a tenable political position. Such judgments are in the minority these days, but they still have a place in historical debate.

More recently, most historians have been inclined to set aside explanations based on delusion and demagoguery and take both the insurgents and their grievances more seriously. Clearly, attacking an established government was not something people would do, as Thomas Jefferson had put it in the Declaration of Independence, "for light and transient causes." Collective action stems from common problems; no mere demagogue can convince people to risk their lives and property without some compelling sense of crisis. Thus the analysis of the post-war economic situation in rural society—and, equally important, the government's apparent inability or unwillingness to address it—continues to engage scholars.

Still, the outbreak of insurrection in post-Revolutionary Massachusetts does not lend itself to some simple analysis based solely on obvious factors like economic antagonism between creditors and debtors, for instance, or geographic antagonism between east and west. If nothing else, the fact that many of the militiamen who faced the rebels at Springfield came from much the same social background within the same region suggests that the actual pattern of protest is neither predictable nor precise. Historians are now beginning to look more closely at various factors of communal cohesion—especially a community's long-term religious and political background, its patterns of leadership and behavior in the generation preceding the insurrection—to help explain why people in one town may have supported one side while their neighbors supported the other. In the end, the exact explanation for communal or personal involvement may be one of the (many) things that historians can never fully know for certain.

What historians can say for certain, however, is that the Massachusetts insurrection was not a unique event, either in its own time or in times since. In the years since Shays's Rebellion, American history has recorded numerous cases of what Jefferson called "a little rebellion now and then"—from the Whiskey Rebellion of the 1790s to the slave rebellions of the antebellum era to a long string of demonstrations and protests mobilized by the labor movement, the civil rights movement, the women's movement, the antiwar movement, and a host of other movements. Whether these "tempests" have always been "a good thing" is, of course, a matter of some debate among historians, not to mention political leaders and common citizens. But as Daniel Shays and his followers made dramatically clear in the years immediately after the American Revolution, the birth of the American republic did not mean the end of the struggle to define such basic issues as freedom, justice, and equality. As thousands of Americans have made equally clear in more recent times, that struggle still remains very much alive, repeatedly being reborn as people of each generation seek to fulfill even further the promise of the Revolution.

Sources: The most extensive collection of primary documents on Shays's Rebellion is in the Massachusetts Archives in Boston. The Robert Treat Paine Papers at the Massachusetts Historical Society, also in Boston, likewise contain valuable materials. The first published study of the rebellion—George Richards Minot, *The History of the Insurrections in Massachusetts in the Year Seventeen Hundred and Eighty Six and the Rebellion Consequent Thereon* (Boston, 1788)—has a strong anti-Shaysite bias but is still a useful source. More recent secondary works include Robert J. Taylor, *Western Massachusetts in the Revolution* (Providence, R.I., 1954), especially Chapters 5–8; Robert A. Feer, "Shays's Rebellion," Ph.D. thesis, Harvard University (1958), which has now been published by Garland Publishing Company (New York and London, 1988); Stephen Patterson, *Political Parties in Revolutionary Massachusetts* (Madison, Wis., 1973); David P. Szatmary, *Shays's Rebellion: The Making of an Agrarian Insurrection* (Amherst, Mass., 1980); and Robert A. Gross, ed., *In Debt to Shays: The Bicentennial of an Agrarian Rebellion* (Charlottesville, Va., 1993).

9

"THE GATES WERE SHUT AGAINST US": TECUMSEH AND THE WAR OF 1812

R. DAVID EDMUNDS

Throughout the colonial period Native Americans often held the balance of power between European nations which were contesting for the control of North America. In the northeast, the Iroquois Confederacy and several of the Algonquian tribes walked a diplomatic tightrope between the British and the French, using their military power or strategic location to obtain political and economic concessions from both sides. Since neither the British nor the French could be assured of the Native Americans' continued loyalty, Indian leaders shrewdly utilized the European uncertainty and need for Native American allies to forge positions of relative independence in which the tribes were courted by both sides but retained much of their sovereignty.

With the British victory in the Seven Years War, Native Americans lost the French counterbalance to British hegemony, and in 1763, when the British refused to honor the old patterns of political and economic concessions, Native Americans throughout the Great Lakes region erupted in Pontiac's Rebellion. Although the uprising eventually failed, it took a heavy toll of British lives and resources. In the rebellion's aftermath the British reevaluated their Indian policies, introducing new measures designed to limit colonial settlement in the Indian country and to minimize conflicts between settlers and Native Americans. Ironically, some of these policies (the Proclamation of 1763 and restrictions upon the colonial Indian trade) so angered the colonists that they were contributing factors to the American Revolution.

In the Revolution the Indians again had the option of choosing between two sides, but by 1776 the Shawnees, the subject of R. David Edmunds's essay, were so angered by American settlement in Kentucky, a region they claimed as a hunting area, that they cast their lot with the British. It was American settlers, not British officials, who threatened the Shawnee homeland. Well supplied by British officials at Detroit, the Shawnees and their allies carried the war to Kentucky, raiding at will across the bluegrass region and creating havoc among the settlements. The Indians believed that they had won the Revolutionary War, and the British capitulation at the Treaty of Paris caught them by surprise. Yet continued British military support and the inflated

146

promises of British Indian agents did much to assuage Native American suspicions, and they followed their old policies of supporting the European power who posed the least threat and offered the most concessions. In return, British officials in Canada encouraged the tribesmen to resist American settlement north of the Ohio, envisioning the region as a Native American buffer zone which limited American expansion and protected Canada.

The War of 1812 proved to be the final showdown between the Americans and the British. Although that war was begun by the Americans, ostensibly to protect their ships on the high seas, many westerners saw it as a chance to expand the boundaries of the United States north into Canada and west into British-controlled territory. Once again, Indians were caught in the middle. This time, however, as R. David Edmunds shows in this essay, a charismatic leader called Tecumseh and his Shawnee followers attempted to take advantage of the outbreak of war to protect their homeland from the voracious land appetite of American settlers. Clearly, their interests would be best served by an alliance with the British. But as shrewd and determined as he was, Tecumseh and his Indian allies were continually frustrated by the fact that they could not win the battle with the Americans on their own, and when British objectives diverged from Indian goals, there was little hope for the Indians. This is the story of a determined and courageous defense of a nation in the face of insurmountable odds.

O n September 18, 1813, the Shawnee war chief Tecumseh met in council with the commander of His Majesty's armed forces in Upper Canada. Holding a belt of wampum to signify the importance of his comments, Tecumseh stood before an assemblage of warriors and British officers and delivered a scathing denunciation of the British decision to abandon their post to the Americans and retreat toward Niagara. Comparing the actions of the British commander to those of an Indian camp dog "that carries its tail upon its back, but when affrightened, he drops it between his legs and runs off," Tecumseh disdainfully accused his allies of betrayal and bad faith:

> The War before this [the American Revolution], our British father gave the hatchet to his red children. . . . In that war, our father was thrown on his back by the Americans, and our father took them by the hand without our knowledge. . . .

Then, referring to the Battle of Fallen Timbers, which had taken place in 1794, the Shawnee pointed out that "when we retreated to our father's fort at that place, the gates were shut against us. . . . We are afraid that our father will do so again at this time."

Tecumseh concluded his speech with a plea that summarized the Indians' frustration with British military policies during the War of 1812. He added, "You always told us that you would never draw your foot off British ground; but now we see you drawing back, and we are sorry to see our father doing so without seeing the enemy." According to the Shawnee, if the British wanted to flee, they were welcome to do so, but they should give their arms and ammunition to the Indians, for:

> Our lives are in the hands of the Great Spirit. We are determined to defend our lands, and if it be his will, we wish to leave our bones upon them.

Although Tecumseh's speech was delivered during the War of 1812, the roots of his bitterness stretched back to the closing years of the American Revolution. West of the Appalachians, but especially in Kentucky and the Old Northwest, the American Revolution had been fought between American frontiersmen and British-allied Native Americans. Much of the conflict had taken place along the Ohio and Wabash valleys. Tecumseh had been born in 1768 and was too young to participate in the fighting during the early years of the war, but older Shawnee, Wyandot, and other warriors had repeatedly crossed the Ohio River to strike at frontier settlements in Kentucky. Yet in the final three years of the war, Tecumseh, an adolescent warrior of fourteen, participated in the skirmishes. In 1782 he joined a small party of warriors who fired upon an expedition of Kentuckians which burned a Shawnee village in Ohio, and one year later he assisted in the successful capture of an American flatboat on the Ohio.

Throughout the war, Native Americans in the Ohio Valley inflicted more damage than they received. When the American Revolution ended, those Kentuckians who had not fled back across the Appalachians to Virginia existed under a state of siege. American settlement still was generally restricted to lands south of the Ohio River, and although the Americans coveted the rich bottomlands of southern Ohio, Native American resistance prevented any significant white settlement in the region. Indeed, from Tecumseh's and the Shawnees' perspective, they were the winners, not the losers, in the American Revolution.

Yet as Tecumseh later reminded the British, "Our father [the British] took them [the Americans] by the hand without our knowledge." What the Indians had won on the battlefield they lost at the conference table. Short of funds and eager for at least a temporary peace, in 1783 the British signed the Treaty of Paris with-

Historians consider this portrait of Tecumseh to be the most accurate. It is based upon a sketch drawn by Pierre Le Dru, a trader at Vincennes, and was included in B. J. Lossing's *Pictorial Field-Book of the War of 1812*. (From TECUMSEH AND THE QUEST FOR LEADERSHIP, by R. David Edmunds, Little Brown, 1984)

out consulting their Native American allies. In the treaty the British relinquished their claims to all lands south of the Great Lakes and north of the Ohio River, but British officials misrepresented the Crown's capitulation to the bewildered Indians. Although they no longer claimed sovereignty over the lands in the Ohio Valley, British officials assured the tribespeople that their government had not relinquished proprietary rights to the region, since the lands still were "owned" by the Indians. They assured the Shawnees that they had every right to defend their homeland, and they encouraged the tribes of Indiana, Ohio, and Michigan to band together in a general confederacy to protect tribal lands in the region. British officials also provided the tribespeople with seemingly genuine, if generally ill-defined, assurances of British military assistance.

It was these final promises that were less than honest. Although young Shawnee warriors such as Tecumseh assumed that the British would provide troops, the Crown's commitment was more ambiguous. British officials were less interested in the Shawnees' welfare than in the fur trade, and they were eager to keep the Native Americans trading at British posts at Detroit, Michilimackinac, and Green Bay, sites the Crown continued to occupy in violation of the Treaty of Paris. Although these posts were on American territory, the British refused to evacuate them until American merchants paid debts to British creditors which had been incurred prior to the Revolution. The American army in the postwar years was so small, it could not force the British to withdraw, but the British believed that a well-armed, pro-British Indian confederacy would provide additional protection for the retention of the posts in Michigan and Wisconsin. Consequently, British officials encouraged the creation of a pro-British, anti-American tribal confederacy which would defend British interests but which would not overtly attack the United States. If such a confederacy could repel American attempts to occupy Ohio, so much the better, but British officials had no intention of sending troops to support the Indians. Tecumseh and other Shawnees interpreted the British commitment from a different perspective. Since the Shawnees and other tribes still occupied the region north of the Ohio River, they were determined to defend it against American settlements. Moreover, they believed that the British commitment was more substantial. Evidence suggests that British Indian agents who lived among the Shawnees and other tribes probably overstated the British commitment. In retrospect, these agents, many of whom were married to Indian women and who exercised considerable influence within the Indian communities, held many grievances against the Americans, and they actively encouraged the Native American resistance.

While the Indians and the British were forging their ill-defined alliance, the Americans made plans to occupy Shawnee lands north of the Ohio. In 1785 Congress passed the Northwest Ordinance, which provided systematic guidelines for integrating the region into the new United States. Section 3 of the ordinance stated that since the Indians had supported the British during the Revolution, they had forfeited all rights to their homelands, and proprietary control now belonged to the government. Yet government officials hoped to forestall warfare with the tribes and instructed American Indian agents to inform the Indians that "through motives of compassion," the United States would "draw a veil over what is passed." A less generous people, they asserted, might force the Indians "to retire beyond the [Great] lakes," but the Americans were "disposed to be kind to them" and would permit the Shawnees to occupy small portions of their former territory.

Tecumseh and the other Shawnees were dumbfounded. They still envisioned themselves as the victors, not the vanquished, in the American Revolution, and they rejected the government's proposals. When settlers attempted to establish farms north of the Ohio, the Shawnees burned their cabins and stole their livestock. Other Americans were ambushed in the forest or fired upon as they ventured down the Ohio on flatboats. A few small settlements formed beachheads north of the Ohio, but they remained fortified camps, and their future seemed uncertain.

In response, the government attempted to negotiate with individual tribes, hoping to split the Native American ranks. Between 1784 and 1786 officials signed three treaties with Indians from several tribes, but Tecumseh and most other Native Americans in Ohio, Indiana, and Michigan considered the agreements to be spurious and refused to abide by them. Shawnee attacks upon the settlements increased, so in 1789 Governor Arthur St. Clair of the Northwest Territories met with a few Shawnees and members of other tribes at Fort Harmar, near Marietta, Ohio, but the resulting Treaty of Fort Harmar was a fiasco. The Indians present grudgingly agreed to the American demands, but according to missionary John Heckewelder, no prominent Native American leader was present, and "only the most inconsiderable clan of the Delawares were in attendance" along with a few friendly Shawnees, Ottawas, and Potawatomis. American attempts to secure a Native American agreement to the settlement of Ohio had ended in failure.

In contrast, British influence among the tribes increased. In addition to supplying the warriors with arms and ammunition, in 1786 British officials sponsored a multitribal conference at Detroit. Although the Shawnees and other tribes in attendance disagreed over the proper response to American aggression, the emerging Native American confederacy sent a message to the United States warning officials that the lands north of the Ohio River must neither be surveyed nor settled. Moreover, the warriors were encouraged when British Indian agents assured them that the Crown's continued occupation of Detroit and other American posts was indicative of British support and fidelity.

Since negotiations had failed and Indian resistance continued, the new federal government decided to conduct a military campaign against the tribes. In September 1790, General Josiah Harmar marched from Fort Washington (modern Cincinnati) intending to attack Shawnee, Miami, and Wyandot villages along the Maumee. But Harmar's army was ambushed twice by large parties of warriors, and he lost almost half his soldiers. With this victory morale soared and the warriors boasted that they planned to force all settlement back across the Ohio River into Kentucky. But Governor Arthur St. Clair immediately planned another campaign against Native American villages in Ohio. If Harmar's expedition encountered defeat, St. Clair's march ended in disaster. In the autumn of 1791, St. Clair led an expedition north from Fort Washington (modern Cincinnati) toward the Maumee, but shortly after dawn on November 4 he was surprised by a well-equipped Indian army of over one thousand warriors. The ensuing battle was another great victory for the Shawnees which only reinforced their ties to the British. Reveling in the American defeats, during 1792 British officials suggested to the

United States that it withdraw its claims to the region north and west of the Ohio so that the territory could secede and reemerge as an independent Native American political state which would serve as a barrier between the United States and Canada. With the construction of a new British fort near modern Toledo, it seemed that war with the United States was imminent.

Although the renewed British militancy encouraged the Indians, it infuriated the new United States. Yet following St. Clair's defeat, the American military position was so weak that federal officials possessed neither the manpower nor other resources to mount another campaign. In 1793 they met again with the Shawnees and their allies and announced that the federal government now was willing to admit that the Treaty of Paris had not transferred the proprietorial ownership of lands north of the Ohio to the United States and that the region still was owned by the Indians. The commissioners offered to relinquish claims to all lands in Ohio except for those territories already sold to private individuals or land companies. In addition, they promised to evacuate Fort Washington and Fort Harmar and offered the tribespeople cash gifts and annuities.

The Native Americans rejected the American concessions. Instead, they suggested that the federal government use money it had offered to the Indians to compensate those settlers who now would have to abandon their farms north of the Ohio, for according to the tribesmen:

> We know these settlers are poor, or they would never have ventured to live in a country which has been in continued trouble. . . . Divide, therefore, this large sum

Sir Isaac Brock, by J. W. L. Forster. Brock commanded the British and Indian army that captured Detroit in 1812. Much admired by Tecumseh, Brock was killed at the Battle of Queenstown, in New York, in October 1812. (C-7760 Public Archives Canada)

you say you have offered us, among these people. . . . If you add, also the great sum you must expend in raising and paying armies with a view to force us to yield [to] your our own country, you will certainly have more than sufficient for re-paying these settlers.

The Native American rejection, followed by the construction of a new British military post on American soil, convinced Secretary of War Henry Knox that only a military solution would assure American interests in the region. Following St. Clair's defeat, Knox had appointed General Anthony Wayne as the commander of American forces in the west, and Wayne spent two years enlisting and training a highly disciplined new force, which he named the "American Legion." By the summer of 1794 he had assembled almost 1500 men at Fort Washington, and he constructed a series of small posts stretching as far north as Fort Recovery, built near the site of St. Clair's disaster. In 1794, when Knox ordered Wayne to lead his army against the Indians, these small posts already were garrisoned and well supplied. Moreover, "Mad Anthony" and his legion were well equipped and eager for action.

Staunchly opposed to any land cessions, Tecumseh had refused to even participate in the negotiations with American officials, but he and other Shawnees were aware of Wayne's plans. During the summer of 1794 they joined with warriors from other tribes to form a large multitribal force which assembled in the Native American villages along the Maumee. In late June Tecumseh accompanied a large war party which attacked an American supply train as it left Fort Recovery. They captured several dozen horses, but in the aftermath of the battle an intertribal quarrel emerged over the distribution of the animals. In consequence, many of the Potawatomis, Ottawas, and Chippewas angrily abandoned the Indian cause and returned to their villages.

When his army arrived on the Maumee River in mid-August, Wayne found the Native American ranks much diminished. He also found that the remainder of the Indian forces had occupied a defensive position at "Fallen Timbers," a tangle of storm-felled trees on the northern bank of the Maumee, about five miles upstream from the new British post at Fort Miamis. Leading a small party of Shawnee warriors, Tecumseh concealed his men in a thicket, in front of the Indian lines, and as the Americans advanced, the Shawnees fired from ambush, momentarily halting the American troops. Yet Wayne's troops were well equipped and highly disciplined, and the Indian ranks had been depleted by the withdrawal of the northern tribes. The Americans re-formed and stormed through the Shawnee position, and after a brief but hard-fought battle, Tecumseh and the other Indians retreated to Fort Miamis, where they assumed that the British commander would give them both refuge and assistance. Yet when they reached the post, they were refused admission into the fort. The Shawnees found that "the gates were shut against us." Discouraged, the Indians scattered through the forest. Wayne did not attack the British fort, but he spent several days burning deserted Indian villages and destroying Indian cornfields.

Three months later, in November 1794, British and American emissaries signed Jay's Treaty, in which the British promised to evacuate Detroit and the other western posts. Abandoned by their British allies, in August 1795 leaders from the former Native American confederacy met with Anthony Wayne and signed the

Treaty of Greenville. Tecumseh refused to attend the proceedings, but other Shawnees and their allies agreed to the cession of all Native American lands in Ohio south and east of a new "treaty line" stretching from just west of modern Cincinnati to Greenville, then east to the Tuscarora River and north to modern Cleveland. In addition, they were forced to relinquish small plots for new federal posts at Fort Wayne, Chicago, and other strategic locations. The Redcoats again had betrayed them. The Shawnee homeland was opened to the Long Knives.

The decade following the treaty was particularly difficult for Tecumseh, the Shawnees, and their neighbors. Although American settlement supposedly was limited to the region south and east of the Greenville treaty line, white farmers spilled over onto Indian territory, particularly in southern Indiana and western Ohio. Meanwhile, American hunting parties from Ohio and Kentucky repeatedly trespassed upon Native American hunting lands, and William Henry Harrison, the governor of Indiana Territory, admitted that white frontiersmen "make a constant practice of crossing over onto the Indian lands . . . to kill deer, bear, and buffaloe—the latter from being in great abundance a few years ago is now scarcely to be met with. . . . One white hunter will destroy more game than five of the common Indians." The fur trade declined accordingly, and the Shawnees were hard-pressed to support their families.

They also were unable to obtain any equitable justice. Indians accused of crimes against whites were tried before white juries, which systematically found them guilty, while whites committing crimes against Native Americans (who also were tried before juries of frontiersmen) rarely were convicted. Harrison reported that many white settlers "consider the murdering of the Indians in the highest degree meritorious" and that the tribes of the Wabash Valley bore "these injuries with astonishing patience." Meanwhile, the Shawnees and other tribes fell prey to the white man's diseases and his whiskey. By 1805, many of the villages were in chaos, as depression and alcoholism permeated tribal society, while the network of kinship and extended families, the very warp of tribal community, began to fray, beset by circumstances over which the Shawnees had little control.

During these years Tecumseh and a small village of followers moved from Ohio into eastern Indiana, where they established themselves on the upper White River, near modern Anderson. Rejecting federal programs which urged Native Americans to become small yeoman farmers, Tecumseh and his people still followed traditional ways. Men hunted, trapped, and traded for necessities, while women raised crops of corn, beans, and other vegetables. Yet like the other Native Americans who lived in the region, Tecumseh's followers suffered from a shrinking economic base, and their village also was vexed with some of the problems that plagued their neighbors.

In April 1805 the lives of Tecumseh and his followers changed forever. Among the residents in Tecumseh's village was his younger brother, Lalawethika ("the Noisemaker"), a ne'er-do-well alcoholic seven years younger than the Shawnee chief. During April Lalawethika experienced a vision so profound that his family at first thought that he had died. When Lalawethika returned to consciousness, he claimed that he had been chosen by the Creator of Life to lead his people along a new path to righteousness. Lalawethika urged the Shawnees to reject the Americans, who were the children of the Great Serpent, the evil power in the universe. He also denounced American technology and instructed the Shawnees to return to the ways of their fathers. Firearms could be used for protection, but game should be taken only with traditional Native American methods. Alcohol was forbidden, and those who drank it were condemned to a fiery hell resembling that of the Christians.

Transformed by his vision, Lalawethika took a new name, Tenskwatawa, or "The Open Door," and began to spread his doctrine among the Shawnees and the Delawares. In 1806, after he denounced several acculturated Christian Delawares as witches, their kinsmen burned these hapless victims. Angered, Harrison wrote to the Delawares, denouncing "the Shawnee Prophet" as a charlatan. According to Harrison, if Tenskwatawa was "really a prophet," the Delawares should "ask of him to cause the sun to stand still—the moon to alter its course— or the dead to rise from their graves. . . . If he does these things, you may then believe that he has been sent from God." In response, in June 1806 Tenskwatawa predicted a full eclipse of the sun, and his fame spread like wildfire. By 1807 so many Indians were journeying to a new village which the Prophet and Tecumseh established near Greenville, Ohio, that the Shawnee brothers and their immediate followers could not feed the throng. In response, early in 1808 they established a new village, Prophetstown, at the juncture of the Tippecanoe and Wabash rivers in western Indiana. There, further removed from American influence, they could raise sufficient corn to support the many tribespeople who now journeyed to their

Tenskwatawa, the Shawnee Prophet. This portrait of Tenskwatawa was included in the McKenny Hall portfolio, a collection of paintings compiled in the 1830s, but was based on an earlier portrait completed by James O. Lewis, at Detroit in 1824. (Library of Congress)

camp. Moreover, at Prophetstown Tecumseh labored to transform his brother's religious movement into a political and military confederacy.

The emergence of the Shawnee Prophet caught both the Americans and the British by surprise. American officials refused to admit that Tenskwatawa and Tecumseh led an indigenous movement that had emerged in response to American injustice and Native American deprivation. Instead, they envisioned a British conspiracy, and in 1807, when the United States and Britain almost went to war over the Chesapeake Affair, a naval confrontation in the Atlantic, American officials suspected that the British had secretly sponsored the Prophet. Tecumseh's efforts to build a pan-Indian confederacy and his stance against the further cession of Indian lands only seemed to confirm their suspicions, and they accused the Crown of again "meddling" with the tribes in a pattern reminiscent of the Revolutionary War and the intertribal confederacy of the 1790s.

Ironically, the British were just as surprised at Tenskwatawa's emergence as the Americans. Also unable to comprehend that the Prophet's religious revitalization movement resulted from deep-seated Native American frustration, British officials at first suspected that "that rascal, the Prophet" was "a French agent," and when both Tenskwatawa and Tecumseh initially refused invitations to meet with him in Canada, the deputy superintendent of Indian affairs reported that the Shawnees and their motives remained a "mystery."

Aware that the tribesmen lacked the technology and economic base to support a large, centrally organized confederacy, Tecumseh eventually was once again forced to turn to the British for military aid. In June 1808 he journeyed to the British post at Amherstburg, where British officials still remained so ignorant of the Shawnee chief and his movement that they referred to him only as "the Prophet's brother." Tecumseh informed the British Indian agent that he and the Prophet had established Prophetstown as a center for Native American resistance and that he planned to recruit followers from all the tribes of the Great Lakes region. The Shawnee brothers wished to live in peace with the Americans, but they were determined that no more Native American land should be ceded to the United States. He also told the British agents that he wanted no part of their quarrels with the United States, but he would accept British logistical support and would join with the British if such an alliance was in the Native American interest.

Despite Tecumseh's efforts to unite the Indians, in 1809 the United States purchased over three million acres of land in Indiana from friendly Potawatomis, Delawares, and Miamis. In response, Tecumseh warned the Americans that they should not attempt to settle on the lands or pay those tribesmen who had agreed to the purchase. In turn, Tecumseh was reminded that the government already had provided several of the tribes with "annuities" (payments in cash or goods) for the ceded lands, but the Shawnee leader replied:

> Brother, when you speak to me of annuities I look at the land and I pity the women and children. I am authorized to say that they will not receive them. Brother, they want to save that piece of land. We do not wish you to take it. . . .

Determined to unite all Indians, Tecumseh met once again with British agents, insisting that his movement had already spread through the Great Lakes tribes and that he would soon go south to solicit the support of the Creeks,

Choctawas, and Chickasaws. He assured the British that the Indians did not want to incite a war between the British and the Americans, but he did want the British "to push forwards toward us what may be necessary to supply our needs." In response, the British Indian agent furnished Tecumseh and his party with ample supplies of clothing and ammunition and promised that additional trade goods would be sent to Prophetstown.

During the following summer, as Tecumseh journeyed down the Wabash en route to the southern tribes, he passed through Vincennes and met again with Harrison. Attempting to prevent the governor from taking any action while he was in the south, Tecumseh did his best to assure Harrison of his peaceful intentions. He did not deny that he hoped to unite all the tribes, but he stated that his political movement was modeled after the organization of the United States, which

William Henry Harrison. This portrait of Tecumseh's foremost American opponent was completed in 1814 and depicts Harrison in an American military uniform from the War of 1812. (Courtesy of Indiana Historical Society Library)

had set him the example of forming a strict union amongst all the fires that compose their confederacy . . . the Indians did not complain of it—nor should his white brothers complain of him doing the same with regard to the Indian tribes . . . they really meant nothing but peace.

When Harrison suggested that the Shawnee should travel to Washington and meet with President Madison, Tecumseh agreed. He informed the governor that after he returned from the south, he would "go and see the President and settle everything with him." Convinced that Harrison would take no action until he returned, Tecumseh departed from Vincennes in August 1811. Yet while Tecumseh was in the south, Harrison marched against Prophetstown. On November 8, 1811, following the Battle of the Tippecanoe, he forced Tenskwatawa and his followers to abandon the village; then he burned Prophetstown, including large quantities of food, ammunition, and clothing which the Shawnees had stockpiled in the village. When Tecumseh returned to Indiana in January 1812, he found his followers scattered and his village in ashes. He also found his brother living in disgrace. Prior to the Battle of Tippecanoe, Tenskwatawa had assured his followers that they would be immune to American bullets, but since many warriors had fallen in the encounter, the Prophet's influence was much diminished.

Tecumseh immediately began to rebuild his confederacy. Throughout the spring of 1812 he again recruited warriors, while the British sent food, arms, and ammunition to a new village established by Tecumseh at the site of the ruined Prophetstown. In May 1812 Tecumseh attended an American-sponsored multitribal conference on the Mississinewa River in Indiana, where he attempted to temporarily placate U.S. officials, but at the conference he met secretly with a messenger sent by the British, who informed him that Britain and the United States were on the brink of war and that if he would come to Canada, the British would furnish him with additional stores of arms and ammunition. Tecumseh returned to the Tippecanoe in June, where he instructed the Prophet to keep his followers at peace until he could return with the British supplies; then he left for Canada.

Tecumseh arrived on July 1, and within the next few days he learned that war had been declared between the British and the Americans. Instead of returning to Prophetstown, Tecumseh stayed to assist British Indian agents in securing the support of the Wyandots, a nearby tribe which held a key position along British supply lines. These efforts seemed to pay off, for the war turned in the British and Indians' favor. Tecumseh led the Native Americans who joined with British forces to block supply routes to Ohio. When the Americans sent troops to reopen the road, the British and the Indians ambushed them, humiliating American troops, and they turned back another American column four days later. Tecumseh was wounded in the second encounter, when he was hit in the leg by an American buckshot. Yet he took heart from the fact that the morale of American troops was collapsing and the British seemed ready to pursue a vigorous campaign against the Americans. The British even used the widespread fear of Indians as "savages" to advantage, warning the American commander that if a battle ensued, the British would not be able to control the Indians. The threat was completely untrue, but the shadow of Indian warfare so frightened the Americans that they capitulated. Shortly before noon on August 16, they surrendered.

Mid-August 1812 marked the high point of Indian and British success. Tecumseh and the British had triumphed, but unfortunately, the triumph was short-lived. In a series of military reverses, the Americans gained control of the war. Never one to give up easily, Tecumseh spent the winter of 1812–1813 recruiting additional warriors in Indiana and Illinois, but when he returned to Canada in late March, he learned that the Americans already had advanced down the Maumee Valley and had built a new fort. Tecumseh was eager to attack the new American outpost, and after some deliberation, his British allies agreed. Late in April 1813 they led a combined British and Indian army of over 2000 men up the Maumee Valley, where they besieged the fort, but they were unable to dislodge the Americans. On May 5, however, the Indians surprised and defeated approximately 600 Kentuckians who had descended the Maumee to reinforce the fort. In the aftermath of this American defeat, some of the warriors began to kill the captured Kentuckians, but Tecumseh intervened to save most of the prisoners. Yet the warriors captured so much American equipment that they abandoned the siege and returned to their villages. On May 9 the British abandoned their Indian allies and returned to Canada.

During June Tecumseh desperately urged the British to renew their campaign against the Americans, without success. The British argued that since American naval raiders on Lake Erie had disrupted their supply lines, the army need to focus its attention there. Discouraged, Tecumseh reminded them that Native Americans had joined with the British not to defend Canada but to secure permanent tenancy of Indian lands in Ohio, Indiana, and Illinois. As long as the British remained in Canada, the Americans were free to strengthen their control over the Shawnee homeland. Unlike the British, the Indians were in a life-and-death struggle over their homeland. Tecumseh needed a series of decisive victories if he was to wring major concessions from the Americans.

In early July 1813, Tecumseh and other Native American leaders persuaded the British to make another assault upon an American post located in the Native American heartland. Despite this commitment, the British were less than enthusi-

Colonel Henry Procter, by J. C. H. Forster. Procter, who commanded British forces on the Detroit Frontier during 1813 was not popular with the Indians. His disregard of Indian interests was indicative of British policy during this period. (Courtesy Fort Malden)

astic. Late in July approximately 1000 British and Indians crossed Lake Erie to again surround the American post, but they found that the outpost had been reinforced and strengthened. The Indians and British unsuccessfully besieged the fort for seven days and then attacked, but they failed in their efforts. Dejected, on August 2 the Indians and British boarded British barges and gunboats and sailed back to Canada.

The lack of military success caused a further deterioration of the Indian-British alliance. Many of the Sacs, Foxes, Chippewas, and Menominees—Native Americans from Wisconsin and northern Illinois—now abandoned Tecumseh's cause and returned to their villages. In addition, since the Americans seemed to be gaining the upper hand, the Wyandots met secretly with American enjoys and assured them that if the Americans recaptured Detroit or invaded Canada, they would join with them. More significant, however, were the defeats suffered by the British on Lake Erie. As a result, the British began to load military supplies, records, and personal possessions on wagons in preparation for a full-scale retreat. Tecumseh was furious. He confronted the British commander, accusing him of cowardice, and demanded arms and ammunition so the Indians could continue to fight. Yet his pleas had little effect. Because their ability to fight depended on British support, the Indians were forced to accompany the retreat along the Thames Valley.

On the morning of October 5, 1813, the British and Indians finally prepared to make their stand on the road along the north bank of the Thames River. Opposite the road was a swampy thicket in which Tecumseh and the warriors took their position. The British arranged themselves in two lines across the road to block the American advance. In mid-afternoon, as the Americans approached, Tecumseh rode on horseback along the Indian lines, rallying his followers. He then met with the British commander for the last time, reassuring the nervous officer: "Father, tell your men to be firm, and all will be well." But nothing went well. The British lines collapsed almost immediately, and the British artillerymen fled so abruptly that they forgot to fire their cannons. The infantry fired two or three volleys and then followed the artillerymen. The total British resistance, from start to finish, lasted no more than five minutes.

In the thickets, Tecumseh and the warriors fought on. Angered by the British flight, they still were determined to fight for their homeland. But with the British in retreat, the Americans now turned the full force of their army against the Indians. The warriors fought valiantly, repulsing several American attacks, but in the midst of the battle, Tecumseh fell, mortally wounded by a gunshot to his chest. Demoralized, his followers continued to fight for another thirty minutes and then abandoned the field and melted into the forest. The Battle of the Thames was over. Tecumseh was dead. The promise of a unified Native American resistance had ended.

In the aftermath of the battle, American officials searched for the fallen chief's body, but they were unsuccessful. Immediately after the fighting ended, the Kentucky militia swarmed across the Native American position, skinning and mutilating the corpses of the fallen warriors so badly that many could not be identified. The bodies eventually were buried in an unmarked, mass grave on the battlefield. The remains of Tecumseh still rest there, surrounded by his comrades.

AN INTERPRETATION

The "closed gates" at Fort Miamis, following the Battle of Fallen Timbers, ushered in a new reality for Tecumseh and his Shawnee followers. British officials had continued to furnish arms and moral support, but the British obviously were unwilling to risk their troops (or political interests) to support the Native Americans, and many Indian leaders now faced the prospect that the Americans, indeed, were going to occupy their homeland. While some village chiefs sought an accommodation with the Americans, others such as Tecumseh withdrew, clinging to the hope that the old ways could be retained and that they might continue to live in the lands of their fathers.

Yet in the decade following the Treaty of Greenville, the tribespeople were overwhelmed. White settlers flooded into Ohio, Indiana, and Illinois, and the Shawnees and their Indian neighbors found themselves outnumbered. Moreover, their traditional economic base dwindled, and they were subjected to the injustice of a frontier judicial system. In addition, they fell victim to alcoholism and disease. The social cohesion of the tribal villages disintegrated, creating a fear that there was no solution for their problems. But the very desperation of their circumstances also gave rise to Tenskwatawa, whose promises of a religious deliverance seemed logical within the framework of tribal cultures. The Prophet's faith was a syncretic religious movement (it incorporated certain beliefs, such as a fiery hell, from Christianity), yet it certainly was Indian in its origin. During times of considerable duress, Native Americans often have sought a religious deliverance, and Tenskwatawa was part of an ongoing tradition of revitalization that manifested itself in leaders such as Neolin of the Delawares (1763), Handsome Lake of the Senecas (1800), Kennekuk of the Kickapoos (1830s), and Wovoka and the Ghost Dance (1890). Ironically, neither Tenskwatawa nor any of these other religious leaders were understood or appreciated by their European or American contemporaries.

An adept and resourceful leader, Tecumseh added a political and military component to his brother's teachings and transformed the religious movement into a political alliance. Unlike the British-Indian alliance of the American Revolution or the multitribal confederacy prior to Fallen Timbers, the Shawnee Prophet's and Tecumseh's movement was entirely of Native American origin. Tecumseh had been present at Fallen Timbers and had been embittered by the closed gates at Fort Miamis. In contrast to many Shawnees and members of other tribes, Tecumseh had avoided contact with the British in the decade that followed the Treaty of Greenville, but as his movement began to coalesce, he realized that Native Americans possessed neither the military technology nor the logistical base to arm his followers and support the population at Prophetstown. He obviously had no great admiration for the Redcoats, but he was forced to turn to the British. He had no choice.

By 1812 the British desperately needed the Indians. They were outnumbered by the Americans, who had every intention of invading Canada and adding it to the United States. In contrast, British officials held no illusions of seizing Michigan or Ohio and attaching it to Canada. Their strategy at the western end of Lake Erie was entirely defensive, although they were willing to invade Detroit or the

Maumee Valley to destroy American posts (Fort Meigs) that might be used as a base for an invasion of Canada. They also were willing to arm Tecumseh and his followers and to use them against the Americans, but there is little evidence to suggest that they ever envisioned committing troops to fight for Native American homelands within the United States. The British commander's reluctance to take the initiative, while despicable to Tecumseh, generally reflected British policy.

Tragically, for Tecumseh and his followers, most Native Americans were unwilling to transcend their local or tribal ties and refused to join a political movement that required an allegiance to a centralized political structure. In 1810 Tecumseh boasted to Harrison that "I am alone the acknowledged head of all the Indians," and his efforts to centralize political control over the tribes seemed logical to Harrison and other white observers, but these endeavors reflected European concepts of political organization more than those of Native Americans. In reality, many of the village chiefs were jealous or suspicious of Tecumseh, and instead of cooperating with the Shawnee leader, they either remained aloof from his confederacy or assisted the Americans.

And finally, the period when Native American people had any chance of achieving a permanent, political independence from the United States already was past. It may have ended with the fall of New France, but most certainly the British surrender of the trans-Applachian west following the American Revolution was the death knell for Native American sovereignty in the region. For all his valor, the heroic Tecumseh probably was doomed to failure. By 1812 the Shawnee chief and his followers were outnumbered by their enemies. They did not possess the technology or the logistical base to sustain an extended military campaign, and their British allies, never faithful, again deserted them.

Sources: Colin Calloway has written extensively on British-Indian relations in the Revolutionary period, and his *The American Revolution in Indian Country: Crisis and Diversity in Native American Communities* (1995) presents a good survey of Native American participation in the contest. Arranged topically, Calloway's *Crown and Calumet: British Indian Relations, 1783–1815* (1987) provides an excellent analysis of the relationship between the two sides in the post-Revolutionary decades. Reginald Horsman's *Matthew Elliott, British Indian Agent* (1964) illustrates the major role that British Indian agents played during this period, while Wiley Sword's *President Washington's Indian War: The Struggle for the Old Northwest, 1790–1795* (1985) presents a very detailed discussion of the diplomacy and warfare between the tribes and the United States in the five years preceding the Treaty of Greenville. R. David Edmunds' *The Shawnee Prophet* (1983) analyzes why Tenskwatawa's religious teachings were so readily accepted among Native Americans, while Edmunds's *Tecumseh and the Quest for Indian Leadership* (1984) presents a balanced biography of the Shawnee chief and does much to separate the man from the myth. John Sugden's *Tecumseh's Last Stand* (1985) features an in-depth discussion and analysis of the retreat from Amherstburg and Tecumseh's death near Moraviantown. More recently, Gregory Dowd's *Spirited Resistance: The North American Indian Struggle for Unity, 1745–1815* (1992) argues that Tecumseh's ill-fated confederacy was similar to previous Native American efforts to combine religious and political movements and that these movements failed because of intratribal or intracommunity dissension rather than rivalry between the different tribes.

10

PEGGY EATON AND ANDREW JACKSON: A PRESIDENTIAL SCANDAL

ALTINA L. WALLER

The election of Andrew Jackson in 1828 as President of the United States inaugurated a new era in political history—the "era of the common man," as it has been dubbed by historians. Jacksonian democracy was perceived at the time, and has been perceived ever since, as a period when the promise of democracy embodied in the American Revolution and the Constitution finally came to fruition. By the time Jackson came to office, most states had revised their constitutions, providing for universal manhood suffrage; that is, the property qualifications for voting were removed so that all white men, regardless of wealth or property, could vote. Many of these men, hardscrabble farmers on the frontier or members of the new working classes in the cities, closed ranks behind Andrew Jackson as the candidate who would champion their interests in Washington.

Indeed, Jackson himself seemed to embody all the hopes and aspirations of these ordinary men. He had been born in poverty on the North Carolina frontier, moved to Tennessee, fought Indians, and devoted himself to the economic development of western Tennessee. Along the way he became a military commander in the War of 1812, gaining fame and recognition for his victory in the battle of New Orleans. When the frontier had been secured from the Indians and the British, Jackson pursued his own fortune in western Tennessee as a lawyer, merchant, and land speculator. He took every opportunity to achieve wealth and social status. Even his marriage to Rachel Donelson Robards, as controversial as it was, brought with it the resources of the large and politically powerful Donelson family. By the time Jackson ran for President, he had achieved what many young men only dreamed about; he was famous for his military exploits, he had acquired a large plantation in Nashville complete with slaves, and he was politically powerful in his home state.

Although such rags-to-riches stories have become a staple of American political history, when Jackson was elected, it was the first time that a President did not have a background that placed him in the wealthy elite from either New England or Virginia. He was the first President who began life in poverty and the first from the western frontier. As the initiator of a new pattern of political history and of American

162

democracy, Jackson has received much attention from historians. Some have applauded the changes his administration brought, while others have shown that the actual changes instituted by Jackson were not nearly as dramatic as he and his supporters claimed. Yet in all the debate and argument about Jackson himself and his administration, historians have ignored the scandal that plagued the first two years of his administration—the scandal that revolved around Peggy Eaton.

Altina Waller's essay about the Peggy Eaton affair reveals that important changes were taking place in social and domestic life as well as in politics. Peggy herself seemed to take the rhetoric about democracy seriously; although she never argued that women ought to have the right to vote (nor did other women make this argument in the antebellum era), she did seem to assume that her status as a tavern keeper's daughter would not prevent her from achieving status as a "lady" in Washington society. And Jackson did not understand why Peggy, as the wife of his best friend and officer of the Cabinet, could not rise to high social status. What neither realized was the opposition that would be mounted by the society "ladies" of Washington and then exacerbated by Jackson's political opponents. Altina Waller's story shows why Peggy Eaton became the subject of a scandal and why Andrew Jackson, in his attempt to defend her honor, escalated the scandal and jeopardized his own administration.

On March 18, 1829, the Reverend Ezra Stiles Ely, an influential Presbyterian leader, sat down to write a letter to Andrew Jackson. The clergyman had only a few days before returned from Washington, where he attended the inauguration of the new President. Despite the well-known fact that Andrew Jackson was more noted for military battles, dueling, Indian fighting, and hard drinking than for religious piety, the two men had been casual friends for thirty years. Jackson's wife Rachel, always more religious than her husband, had encouraged the friendship. Ely prefaced his long letter by explaining why he was compelled to write rather than speak to the President personally. He had intended, he said, to initiate a personal conversation on this important matter but was prevented from doing so by the crowds and excitement which surrounded the President at the inaugural festivities. This explanation was entirely believable, especially since Andrew Jackson's inauguration was considerably more boisterous, rowdy, chaotic—and democratic—than previous ones. Although a wealthy plantation owner himself, Jackson claimed to represent the interests of the "common man," and indeed, his inauguration was notable for the crowds of country folk and poor people who showed up to celebrate his triumph in Washington. Others were not so sanguine. One longtime Washingtonian described the scene with more than a little apprehension:

> The Majesty of the People had disappeared, and a rabble, a mob, of boys, negroes, women, children, scrambling, fighting, romping. What a pity what a pity! . . . Cut glass and china to the amount of several thousand dollars had been broken in the struggle to get the refreshments, punch and other articles had been carried out in tubs and buckets, but had it been in hogsheads it would have been insufficient. . . . Ladies fainted, men were seen with bloody noses and such a scene of confusion took place as is impossible to describe,—those who got in could not get out by the door again, but had to scramble out of windows. . . . The noisy and disorderly

rabble in the President's House brought to my mind descriptions I had read, of the mobs in the Tuileries and at Versailles . . .

Considering this chaotic situation, it would not be surprising that Reverend Ely did not have the opportunity to find a private moment with the President. Yet critics of the clergyman later offered another explanation; they insisted that he did indeed intend to speak with the President but, at the last moment, lacked the courage to raise a matter which was sure to irritate and anger a man who was famous for his temper tantrums and rage at those who dared to disagree. However, safe in his ministerial study in Philadelphia, Reverend Ely did not hesitate or mince words in his strongly worded letter to the President. In his view, it was, after all, a matter of great importance which concerned the Christian morality of the nation. His subject and perceived threat to the public morality was Peggy O'Neale Eaton, the wife of Jackson's newly appointed secretary of war.

In his long and carefully composed letter, Reverend Ely argued that for the sake of his administration, his country, and himself, the President should not allow Mrs. Eaton such an exalted position in the government; she had, Reverend Ely stated, a long-standing "bad reputation." The implication was obvious; he was suggesting that Andrew Jackson fire his secretary of war! Knowing that Jackson would not be likely to countenance such a suggestion without persuasive arguments, Ely marshaled all the ammunition he possessed. Everyone in Washington, he claimed, knew what Andrew Jackson did not: that Mrs. Eaton was known to be a dissolute woman shunned by the virtuous ladies of Washington. Worse, while her first husband had been on sea duty as a naval officer, she had been intimate with her present husband, Major Eaton, and become pregnant with his child. After

The behavior of Andrew Jackson's supporters on his inauguration day shocked and dismayed many in the Washington establishment who feared that democracy would inevitably lead to social disorder and political chaos. (Library of Congress)

the suicide of her first husband and before her marriage to Eaton, Mrs. Eaton had, said Reverend Ely, traveled alone with Eaton, even recording their names as man and wife on hotel registers in New York. Not only was all this evidence irrefutable, argued the clergyman, but the President's own wife, the recently deceased but still beloved Rachel, had held the "worst opinion" of Mrs. Eaton. In the light of all this overwhelming evidence, Ely hoped the President would follow the only Christian moral course and dismiss Secretary Eaton from the Cabinet, thus preventing an example being set that would undoubtedly lead to the decline of public morality.

As anyone who knew Andrew Jackson could have predicted, this letter sent "Old Hickory" into a ferocious rage which none of his advisers or friends could contain. Its culmination came two years later with the resignation of the entire Cabinet, an event unprecedented in the history of the United States government. In the intervening two years the normal affairs of government—foreign affairs, tariffs, taxes, appointments to official office—were relegated to secondary importance as Andrew Jackson became obsessed with proving Peggy Eaton's chastity and virtue. Not only was almost every letter Jackson wrote concerned to a greater or lesser degree with her, but he sent government agents to interview witnesses and collect written evidence which could then be presented in legislative and Cabinet meetings. Peggy Eaton became *the* political litmus test of loyalty to the Democratic party. Belief in Peggy's virtue meant loyalty to Jackson, while anyone who let slip the slightest doubt was banished. Even the President's nephew and niece, acting as his personal secretary and official hostess in the White House, were dismissed and sent back to Tennessee when they refused to socialize with Mrs. Eaton. Although historians have dismissed the "Eaton Malaria" (Martin Van Buren's term) as trivial and unworthy of the President's attention—"sheer madness," said one—to Andrew Jackson himself it was the most pivotal and significant issue during the first years of his presidency.

Jackson's initial response to Reverend Ely was a long, impassioned letter castigating the clergyman for trafficking in vicious rumors and gossip. "If you had come to see me," said Jackson, "I could have given you information that would at least have put you on your guard with respect to anonymous letters, containing slanderous insinuations against female character. If such evidence as this is to be received," continued the President, "I ask where is the guarantee for female character, however moral—however virtuous?" There was real danger here, argued Jackson, since women require special protection.

> Whilst on the one hand we should shun base women as a pestilence of the worst, and most dangerous kind to society, we ought, on the other, to guard virtuous female character with vestal vigilance. Female virtue is like a tender and delicate flower; let but the breath of suspicion rest upon it, and it withers and perhaps perishes forever.

It was a sentiment with which most men and women of the time would have agreed. Where many would have disagreed with Jackson was his assumption that Mrs. Eaton belonged with virtuous women rather than with those "base" women who should be shunned as a "pestilence."

Furthermore, said Jackson, "I have not the least doubt but that every secret rumor is circulated by the minions of Mr. Clay, for the purpose of injuring Mrs. Eaton, and through her, Mr. Eaton. . . ." Although Jackson was to change his mind several times about just who the villains were—after Clay, he blamed a conspiracy by clergymen and females and finally settled on his own Vice President, John C. Calhoun—he never doubted that the ultimate target was not Mrs. Eaton or Mr. Eaton but he himself, the President of the United States. His conviction was not shared by most of his friends and supporters. They urged him to avoid becoming involved in the petty squabbles of the ladies of Washington for fear he would appear ridiculous. The President was oblivious to their pleas, insisting that his own character and the integrity of his entire administration were at stake. From Jackson's perspective, on Peggy Eaton's chastity or the lack thereof depended the respectability and integrity of his presidency.

Before Andrew Jackson immortalized Mrs. Eaton by making a political issue of her sexual behavior, she would not have appeared a likely candidate for such public attention. Born in 1799, the daughter of tavern keeper William O'Neale, Margaret O'Neale had grown up with Washington. Although she was commonly referred to as "Peggy," the tavern keeper's daughter who served her father's customers with much more than drinks and food, Mrs. Eaton indignantly denied the rumors. Insisting that she had never been called "Peggy," that her parents and friends had always referred to her as Margaret, Mrs. Eaton, in her autobiography, defended her upbringing as very respectable and middle-class.

> My father kept a tavern, and called it the Franklin House. I recollect distinctly as a little girl watching the swinging sign which bore the portrait of the Philadelphia printer and swung in front of our door to let travellers know that we kept a public house. When I approached young womanhood my father took down that old sign and turned his residence into rather a first-class boarding house for first-class people; but I am not ashamed to say that I was born in the Franklin House and

This picture of "Peggy" Eaton was taken later in her life, considerably after the scandal which rocked Washington during the first years of Andrew Jackson's administration. This portrait of a staid Victorian matron belies her reputation as a siren endangering the morals of the young nation. (Collection of Pauline Wilcox Burke)

that my father was a tavern-keeper. I have always been superior to that petty American foolery.

Margaret Eaton's family was not alone in struggling to achieve respectability in the new capital city of Washington. Located on low muddy ground, the government buildings—the Capitol and the President's house—were still unfinished and primitive in appearance when Eaton was growing up. She described the city in her youth as a "wilderness." But it was a wilderness where all the important people of the fledgling republic came to exert their influence and make their reputations. Senators, congressmen, generals, clerks, and diplomats converged yearly on the raw, muddy streets, where very little housing was available. As a result, when Congress convened every year and representatives arrived from all over the country, they took up rooms in boardinghouses like the one owned by Margaret O'Neale's father.

> . . . from my earliest years, I became acquainted with all the distinguished men in the nation. I was always a pet. I suppose I must have been very vivacious. . . . Amongst my earliest recollections of distinguished people who stayed at my father's house are those of Gov. Lloyd of Maryland and his family, and of Senator Gore of New York.

Margaret Eaton's autobiography makes it clear that from a very young age, she was keenly aware of her own attractiveness and intelligence. She soon found that she could carry off a witty repartee with the most distinguished of her father's guests and became more and more confidant in her ability to charm them. "While I was still in pantalets and rolling hoops with other girls I had the attentions of men, young and old, enough to turn a girl's head," Margaret wrote, but ". . . the fact is, I never had a lover who was not a gentleman and was not in a good position in society. No low mean man ever dared from my earliest childhood to intrude himself upon me." This young woman was clearly set on improving her situation in life by marrying a man of respectable social status. After several false starts on relationships with men who turned out to be inappropriate, Margaret met and married John Timberlake, an officer in the U.S. Navy. Unfortunately, although Timberlake was a respected naval officer with the social status Margaret longed for, he drank heavily and was financially improvident. The young couple, soon with two young children, continued to live with Margaret's father, and when Timberlake was away at sea, his young wife helped out in the boardinghouse.

It was during these years that Margaret became acquainted with Major John Eaton and Andrew Jackson, as well as many of the other congressmen and senators from Tennessee and other surrounding southern states. Eaton was a regular at the boardinghouse, where he formed a firm friendship with Margaret and her husband, as well as her parents and children. Andrew Jackson, as an elected representative from Tennessee, was there for two congressional seasons, one year with his wife Rachel and the other by himself. Ordinarily, wives tended to stay at home, and the congressmen who stayed in the boardinghouses made up what they called a "mess"—a term which meant more than just eating together. It also indicated a voting block, because representatives from the same geographic regions talked over political strategies and formed a kind of community away from home. Several times Eaton and Jackson accompanied Margaret and her family to a nearby Presbyterian church, and both commented in their letters home that they regarded her parents with respect and found Margaret herself quite charming, especially when she entertained the company with her piano playing in the evenings.

Still, many people were not so kind in their assessment and persisted in the assumption that Margaret at best flirted with the male guests and at worst had indiscriminate sexual relations with them. Indeed, some of the guests, cronies of Jackson and Eaton, assumed that Margaret's status as a serving girl in the boardinghouse made her fair game to pursue. Richard Call, a representative from Tennessee who stayed at the boardinghouse with Jackson and Eaton one year, made an awkward attempt at seduction when he was alone with Margaret in the parlor. Margaret responded by backing off and picking up a pair of tongs from the fireplace hearth, which she then used to threaten Call. With this lack of encouragement, Call desisted in his attempts to seduce Margaret, but thenceforward he became her enemy, at every opportunity reinforcing the rumors that were already circulating. Just after the fire tongs incident, Margaret sought Andrew Jackson's protection by confiding the story to him; she clearly hoped that Jackson's sense of patriarchal honor could work in her favor. In this she was absolutely right, for Jack-

Although his frontier background and campaign rhetoric made him seem to be a "man of the people," Andrew Jackson was so entrenched in an authoritarian and patriarchial style that it undermined his commitment to democratic ideals. (Corbis-Bettmann)

son warned Call not to approach her again. However, he did not reject Call as a friend; the two were to remain very close, and Jackson did not mention the incident to anyone else until years later, when Margaret was under fire from all Washington. At that time, Call wrote to Jackson to support Reverend Ely's accusations against Margaret, insisting that he knew her to be dissolute and free with her sexual favors. Jackson's reaction was to roar like an enraged lion. "You of all people," he wrote, "have reason to know of her virtue!" Suitably chastened, Call retreated from Jackson and their friendship for several years.

In 1828 Margaret's husband committed suicide while away on sea duty. Rumors circulated that he had done it out of despair that Margaret was having an affair with Major Eaton, while others said he had stolen money from the Navy and was fearful of being found out. Still others insisted he had only stolen the money because Margaret, in addition to being a loose woman, was also a spendthrift. Whatever the truth was, Margaret and Major Eaton were soon courting, and by the fall of 1828 John Eaton wanted to get married. Still, he hesitated because of the political situation. In a long, slanderous political campaign, his best friend, Andrew Jackson, had been elected President of the United States, and Eaton's prospects for becoming a Cabinet member were very good. However, the President-elect was still smarting from the mudslinging of the campaign, which had been aimed largely at his wife, Rachel. Thirty-seven years before, when Andrew Jackson and Rachel Donelson had eloped, they both believed that Rachel's first husband had already obtained a divorce; later, documents surfaced to show that the divorce had not been final before she married Jackson. This made Rachel an adulteress and also implicated Jackson, since he had been a good friend of her husband. When all the accusations and counteraccusations were being flung about in the campaign, the religiously devout and publicly reticent Rachel was devastated. She had never liked being in the public view, never sought to be a high-fashion woman of society, and never wanted to move to Washington as first lady. Despite Jackson's repeatedly professed love and even worship of her, he ignored her wishes in this regard and pursued his public career. Perhaps some underlying sense of guilt made him all the more infuriated when the opposition made Rachel's virtue a campaign issue.

John Eaton had been through the campaign and all its ugly accusations as a friend and close political and personal adviser to Jackson. He was well aware that his marriage to Margaret Timberlake could only fan the flames of gossip surrounding the question of morality which plagued Jackson; it could also hurt his own chances for a high post in the administration. Eaton made a special trip to Jackson's plantation in Tennessee to talk over his desire to marry the new widow, but he also indicated his doubts about whether this was the appropriate timing. He requested Jackson's advice in the matter. Jackson's answer was unequivocal. Don't let the gossips intimidate you, urged Jackson. Marry her immediately, and that will have the effect of stopping the unflattering rumors. Jackson insisted that once Margaret was married to someone of high social and political standing and integrity such as John Eaton, her reputation would be safe. Delighted to have his mentor's blessing and encouragement (some say that Eaton considered Jackson a father figure), John Eaton married Margaret on New Year's Day of 1829.

Things began to go wrong for Andrew Jackson before he left the Hermitage for Washington for the inaugural festivities. Just days before they were to leave Tennessee, Rachel Jackson died; she was fifty-three years old and in poor health, but some said the dread she felt of going to Washington was a significant factor in her death. Another story has it that she had only recently discovered some of the obscene and malicious things that had been said of her in the campaign and that this was enough to precipitate heart failure. Jackson, in frequent pain himself from old wounds and a failing, aging body, mourned her loss with great emotion both in private and in public but did not delay his journey to the capital. In the spring of 1829 Jackson began announcing his choices for the Cabinet—choices which were not well received by either political party. Even Jackson's friends conceded that he had neglected better-qualified candidates for political hacks and his own cronies; this seemed especially reprehensible, since reform and the eradication of corruption in government had been major campaign issues. One of his most criticized appointments was that of his old friend John Eaton as secretary of war. While Jackson and the Democrats were busy defending the Cabinet, Washington's newly emergent high society, represented by some of the Cabinet and other officials' wives, began to ostracize Mrs. Eaton from the official round of social activities. Mrs. Calhoun, wife of the Vice President, refused to return a social call after Mrs. Eaton had left her calling card (a great insult), while other society leaders ignored her. Of all this, however, Jackson took no notice until he received the fateful letter from Reverend Mr. Ely of Philadelphia.

Andrew Jackson had always taken pride in his honor, his loyalty to his friends and family, and his position as a benevolent patriarch. Once convinced he was right on any issue, he demanded unconditional loyalty and would not countenance one shred of criticism, no matter how constructive and friendly it might be. Despite his long friendship with Ely and the fact that the minister had been held in high esteem by his beloved Rachel, Jackson considered him to have been duped by his

John Henry Eaton was not only a close political advisor to Andrew Jackson, he was a good friend and some said, almost like a son. Eaton expected to be appointed to Jackson's cabinet and was well aware that his marriage to Peggy O'Neale Timberlake could cause problems for the new administration. (Library of Congress)

political enemies. The possibility that Ely might, by virtue of his position as a Christian minister, have more credibility than Jackson himself on the issue of morality and female purity never occurred to the President. Margaret Eaton, Jackson informed the minister, was married to a man of important political status and unquestioned honor, and she had been accepted as a friend by the President himself. He also pointed out that all the men involved in the accusations—Margaret's first husband, Timberlake; her present husband, John Eaton; and Andrew Jackson himself—were all members of the Masonic order; they would never betray each other, for they had taken a secret oath of loyalty and friendship. No further proof, asserted Jackson, was required to demonstrate Margaret's sexual virtue.

Yet proof was what obsessed Jackson for almost the entire spring and summer of 1829. When he had assembled hundreds of pages of affidavits, statements, and testimonials from everyone even remotely involved, Jackson called an official meeting of the Cabinet to hear the evidence and, presumably, to vindicate Mrs. Eaton. To this meeting, held on September 10, 1829, Jackson also invited Reverend Ely and another Washington minister who had joined Ely in the accusations. With his stack of documents before him, Jackson proceeded to demolish each and every one of the charges against Margaret and John Eaton. Finally, as the Cabinet members sat in embarrassed silence, a squirming Reverend Ely admitted that there was no credible evidence against John Eaton. When a triumphant President bore down on him, shouting, "nor against Mrs. Eaton either," the shaken minister timidly replied, "On that I would rather not state an opinion." Enraged, Jackson shouted, "She is as chaste as a virgin!" Reminding the Cabinet members that if they and their wives refused to "admit" Margaret to Washington society by ostracizing her from social occasions, they would be, in effect, insulting the President himself. In his official family (the Cabinet), he insisted, he would, at all costs, have "harmony." Peremptorily dismissing the tribunal, Jackson considered the matter settled.

But Margaret's status in Washington's social hierarchy was far from settled. Respectable middle-class women were embarrassed by Margaret's boardinghouse manners, earthy language, and arrogant assumption of her new social importance. Her undeniable beauty, wit, and intelligence could not make up for a crude upbringing and suspected lack of virtue. They determined to resist their husbands and the authoritarian edicts of the President of the United States in this matter. One leader of Washington society whose husband edited a newspaper friendly to the Jacksonians proudly described the "stand" taken by the "ladies" of Washington.

> A stand, a *noble* stand, I may say, since it is a stand taken against power and favoritism, has been made by the ladies of Washington, and not even the President's wishes, in favor of his dearest, personal friend, can influence them to violate the respect due to virtue, by visiting one, who has left her strait and narrow path.
> With the exception of two or three timid and rather insignificant personages, who trembled for their husband's offices, not a lady has visited her, and so far from being inducted into the President's house, she is, I am told scarcely noticed by the females of his family.

Thus, the women of Washington took quite a different view than Andrew Jackson—one which had little to do with male honor or political conspiracies. Proud of their husbands and their own role in the new republic, these women were determined to defend their own respectability and social status; to accede to Jackson's demand that a compromised and lower-class woman was worthy to join their ranks was to demean all of them and nullify their credibility in the social and private sphere of society.

Not only did most of the Cabinet wives refuse to call on Margaret or invite her to their homes, but Jackson's own niece, Emily Donelson, who was acting as White House hostess, took her own "stand" alongside the "ladies" of Washington and against her uncle. Emily was only twenty-one when her Uncle Andrew, after the death of Rachel, asked her to act as his hostess. Her husband, who was her first cousin and Jackson's nephew, would also be in the White House as the President's personal secretary. Unlike her Aunt Rachel Jackson, Emily was

Although this cartoon appeared during Jackson's second administration and emerged from unhappiness with his political stand, it expresses the feelings of the "ladies" of Washington who were convinced that Jackson wanted to dictate activities and events in the social and private sphere of life—the sphere in which they claimed ascendency. (Library of Congress)

eager to go to Washington and occupy a place of importance in society. Her parents, like Andrew and Rachel Jackson, had been born on the frontier, lacked education, and lived most of their lives in primitive, often violent conditions. Emily and her siblings, however, had been raised in comfortable economic circumstances and sent to schools appropriate for genteel social status. Emily, like the frontier region itself, was eager for recognition by the nation. Her father was inordinately proud of Emily but incredulous at the family's good fortune. Soon after Emily and her husband were settled in Washington, the family back in Tennessee began receiving letters like this one from Emily's cousin who had accompanied her.

> The President's House is quite a Palace . . . I have a room, here, fit for a Princess, with silk curtains, mahogany furniture, a carpet such as you Tennesseans have in your parlour, and a piano.

Astounded at such descriptions of luxury in Washington and struggling to comprehend just how far the family had come, Emily's father reflected on the past in a letter to his daughter.

> When I take a view of things that have pass and the Situation you are now in I am astonished out of measures when I once thought that I was to have no other way to support your mother and my children but by my Dog and gun and you are now fixed in a Splendid room in the president's House. . . .

Young and inexperienced, Emily was anxious to please her uncle and make a good impression on the ladies of Washington. This created the first dilemma she faced, since it soon became apparent that she could not entertain Margaret Eaton as Jackson demanded and at the same time be accepted by the best social circle. Thus, in spite of her love for her uncle and gratitude to him for giving her the opportunity to leap up the social ladder, she very quickly decided that preserving her place in society meant that she must uphold the virtue of her sex by rejecting any association with Mrs. Eaton. Writing to her family in Tennessee, Emily reported:

> There has been a good deal of discontent manifested here about the cabinet and particularly the appointment of Maj. Eaton, his wife is held in too much abhorrence here ever to be noticed or taken in society. The ladies here with one voice have determined not to visit her. To please Uncle, when we first came here we returned her call, she then talked of her intimacy with our family and I have been so much disgusted with what I have seen of her that I shall not visit her again. I am afraid it is to be a great source of mortification to our dear old Uncle.

When Major Eaton complained that she was treating his wife unfairly and tactfully suggested that inexperience had led her to believe the slanderous rumors, Emily indignantly defended her behavior.

> As to the probability of my becoming a victim to the slanders of this or any other place . . . I hope I shall maintain my reputation as it has heretofore been unsullied, and at the close of my Life that I shall have the satisfaction of knowing that my character has not only been pure but unsuspected.

The "stand" chosen by Emily and her husband not only was a great source of "mortification" to their uncle but also caused him so much hurt and anger that his health, already fragile, worsened, as Andrew Jackson Donelson wrote to a close friend in Tennessee:

> You are aware of his sensibilities—how all absorbing they are when excited by friends and especially by such collusions as here. . . . They have been steamed to the highest point and have done more to paralyze his energies than years of the regular and simple operations of the Gov. ought to have done. . . .

Andrew Jackson was indeed "excited" and "steamed" but certainly not paralyzed when it came to insisting on obedience to his authority in his "official" family—by which he meant the members of his Cabinet and their families as well as his relatives living in the White House. To the three Cabinet members whose families still refused to socialize with Mrs. Eaton, Jackson, in January of 1830, sent a personal emissary. The President's messenger told the recalcitrant three that Jackson was much "excited" by their treatment of Margaret and that he "had come to the determination of having harmony in his cabinet." This was no empty threat, insisted the messenger, for the President had decided that unless Mrs. Eaton received visits from their families and was invited to their large parties, they would be removed from the Cabinet. Although Jackson subsequently retreated from this threat and made peace with the offending members for another year, the truce was an uneasy one. Jackson was not quite so accommodating when it came to his own household. After Emily snubbed Margaret on two different public occasions, Jackson decided to force the issue by giving a dinner party at which Margaret was an honored guest—he was determined that Emily should accept Mrs. Eaton. The

Emily Donelson was only 21 when she was asked by her uncle, Andrew Jackson, to act as his White House hostess. She yearned to be accepted by the "best" social circles in Washington but this desire conflicted with orders given by her uncle to socialize with Peggy Eaton. Her refusal to befriend Peggy led to painful divisiveness within her family. (Collection of Pauline Wilcox Burke)

invitation was sent out, but Margaret, who by now had been humiliated several times, sent her regrets.

> Circumstances, my dear Genl., are such . . . that under your kind and hospitable roof I cannot be happy. You are not the cause, for you have felt and manifested a desire that things should be different. . . . You meet to enjoy yourselves, but there would be none to me.

Jackson exploded once again, this time at his family, insisting that if Emily could not follow his wishes, then she should quit his household and return to Tennessee. This time the President did not relent as he had done with his Cabinet, and in the spring of 1830, his niece and nephew packed their bags for the long trip back to Nashville. In a letter later that fall, Jackson revealed just how hurt and angry he was at the betrayal by his own family.

> . . . and what was the most cruel thing of all my own connections included in this unholy wicked and unjust conspiracy against female character, by which I was to be reached, and the memory of my D'r wife who ought to have been dear to all her connections, indirectly or directly assailed. . . .

But Emily would not relent, and for all Jackson's efforts, the "harmony" he so desired, even demanded as his right, was nowhere in evidence.

More than a year since Jackson had taken office had now passed, and his administration was in disarray, the Cabinet polarized by the Eaton affair and also by political and social differences which had never been very far from the surface. The coalition which had elected Jackson to the presidency had always been an uneasy one, held together by tenuous agreements between Secretary of State Martin Van Buren of New York and Vice President John C. Calhoun of South Carolina. The two men, representing the northern and southern wings of the Democratic party, had long been enemies, and both had been opposed to Andrew Jackson in the election of 1824. In addition to their political differences with Jackson, they both came from a significantly higher social stratum than the frontier Indian fighter and worried that his appeal to the "common man" would lead to mobocracy rather than democracy. However, both recognized in 1828 that their chances of being part of a winning presidential ticket were nil unless they put aside their differences and supported General Jackson. Calhoun was rewarded with the office of Vice President on the assumption that he would be next in line for the presidency after Jackson had served his two terms; it even seemed quite likely that Calhoun might be President in four years, since Jackson's health seemed to be failing rapidly. Martin Van Buren became the secretary of state.

Predictably, the storm caused by the ladies of Washington in denying Margaret Eaton "admission" to their society reopened the barely concealed but already existing political divisions. As former President John Quincy Adams observed, political society was divided into "blue" and "green" factions, with Martin Van Buren the leader of the "frail sisterhood" and Calhoun the head of the "moral party." Van Buren adopted the cause of Margaret Eaton as his own, even throwing dinner parties in her honor when no one else would return her social calls. Perhaps the fact that Van Buren was a widower made his course easier than that of the married Cabinet officers, but whatever the reason, he soon became one of the

President's best friends. They frequently went horseback riding together, and Jackson began referring to him as Van or Matty. Calhoun took just the opposite position, supporting his wife's decision that she would not call on the Eatons. In so doing he was supporting the three members of the Cabinet who ostracized Margaret. Jackson soon came to the conclusion that it was not his old enemy Henry Clay or the "females and clergymen" who were conspiring against him but his own Vice President, John Calhoun.

This suspicion was soon reinforced by the revelation that years before when Calhoun was a member of President Monroe's Cabinet, he had conspired to undermine Jackson's actions as military commander in Florida. Jackson had always been notoriously sensitive on this issue and infuriated by any hint that he might have violated the government's policies. When in the fall of 1830 documents came to light that Calhoun had gone so far as to suggest Jackson's arrest for insubordination, the explosion from the President was predictable. By the spring of 1831, Jackson believed that the "villain" behind the attacks on Margaret Eaton was Calhoun. Attempting to undercut Calhoun's chances for the presidency, he wrote a secret letter in which he endorsed Martin Van Buren as his heir apparent. Still, he could find no solution to the disharmony in his Cabinet until one was slyly suggested to him by Martin Van Buren: that the entire Cabinet should resign, giving Jackson the chance to get rid of his enemies and reconstitute a more "harmonious" official family. Van Buren and Eaton submitted their resignations first, and then the President suggested to the others that they resign as well.

The mass resignations of the Cabinet caused a sensation in the press, raising fears that the government was in imminent danger of collapse. Amidst this widespread fear and confusion, the Eaton affair came to public attention. Gradually it leaked out that Margaret Eaton was the cause. Long letters sent to the press by the disaffected Cabinet members accused Jackson of "subserviency" to Margaret Eaton, in effect making her the President! Essentially, they charged, they had been dismissed because they would not socialize with a tavern girl. As soon as these charges appeared in print, John Eaton demanded satisfaction in the form of a duel for the slurs on his wife's virtue. He was contemptuously refused. Undeterred, Eaton armed himself with a pistol and went in search of several of the offending Cabinet members, in effect stalking them. When the former Cabinet members wrote to Jackson asking for protection, the President brushed them off and took no action. Luckily no actual violence ensued. Instead, Eaton issued a long statement to the newspapers defending himself and his wife and echoed Jackson's belief that since there was no real evidence against his wife, he could only conclude that Vice President John Calhoun was at the root of a conspiracy to destroy the Jackson administration. It was all the more diabolical, he claimed, because it also destroyed the reputation of a virtuous woman. Margaret became instantly infamous as press accounts began referring to her as "Bellona" (Roman goddess of war) or "Madame Pompadour," decrying the fact that a woman—and such a woman—held such influence over the President.

In the midst of all the publicity, the aristocratic and dignified John Calhoun, who had remained silent throughout the entire imbroglio, decided that the time had come to respond. In a long letter for publication in newspapers, Calhoun justified his response by saying that since Eaton had "gratuitously dragged my name into his controversy," he felt "compelled" to explain why his wife, with his support, had refused to exchange social calls with the Eatons. It was not, he claimed, due to "political motives," since "the road to favor and patronage lay directly before me, could I have been base enough to tread it." This was, of course, a barb aimed at Martin Van Buren for currying favor with Jackson by befriending Margaret. No, said Calhoun, he had approved of Mrs. Calhoun's decision

> though I foresaw the difficulties in which it would probably involve me: but that I viewed the question involved, as paramount to all political considerations, & was prepared to meet the consequences, as to myself, be they what they might.

The reason he was willing to sacrifice his political future, Calhoun argued, was that the high morals of the nation depended on the purity and virtue of women. The ladies of Washington, through their "high minded" independence, had achieved a "great victory" for the country which should not be "perverted" by Eaton's "false representations of the real question at issue." That question was the ability of virtuous women to "censor" their own ranks and thus preserve their purity and by implication the morals of the nation. Mrs. Calhoun had made it clear to him that Margaret Eaton had always been "excluded" from Washington society, and therefore it was not a matter of "the exclusion of one already admitted into society, but the admission of one already excluded." Thus there was no tawdry plan to besmirch a respectable reputation, only the upholding of moral standards. If political considerations, such as Jackson's demands that the ladies admit Margaret to their company, were to prevail, then "that censorship, which the [female] sex exercises over itself; and, on which, all must acknowledge, the purity and dignity of the female character mainly depend," could not function and the morals of the nation would suffer. "Happily for our country," concluded Calhoun, "this important censorship is too high and too pure to be influenced by any political considerations whatever." Jackson's attempt to politicize female purity and thus destroy the nation's morals could not be tolerated. On matters of purity and morality, Calhoun argued, he must defer to his wife's judgment. Ironically, while Margaret Eaton had found a champion in Andrew Jackson, the "ladies" of Washington had found theirs in John C. Calhoun.

With the Cabinet "purged," Andrew Jackson was free to assemble a new Cabinet. Fortunately for the new members, they would not be required to socialize with Margaret Eaton; in the wake of the scandal, Jackson appointed her husband governor of Florida, and Margaret left Washington. Emily Donelson and her husband returned to the White House, where they both resumed their respective positions as official hostess and private secretary. Andrew Jackson was eventually elected to a second term in office, after which Martin Van Buren, as Jackson's choice, became President. John C. Calhoun never fulfilled his dream of becoming President of the United States. After the Cabinet purge, Andrew Jackson may have thought himself the victor, but it was the "ladies and clergymen" who had carried the day, for it is their judgment about Margaret Eaton that has been accepted as the truth by writers and historians from that day to this.

AN INTERPRETATION

In the historiography of the Jacksonian era, phrases such as the "self-made man," "the rise of democracy," and "political equality" loom large. Although Jackson

himself was no "common man"—he owned a large plantation and many slaves—
he had at least had his beginnings as an uneducated frontiersman who seemed to
embody the hopes and dreams of ordinary men. In the expanding and expansive
new republic, Andrew Jackson's success was a symbol of a growing pride in na-
tionhood and the promise of equal opportunity. If historians have demonstrated
that his administration and his policies were not as revolutionary or even reform-
minded as he claimed, that does not diminish the reality that masses of people at
the time perceived him as the champion of honest, hardworking Americans against
the monsters he fought against: the bank, the Indians, southern nullification, and
corruption in government. For frontier farmers, artisans, and workingmen, Jackson's battles for economic and political reform held out the promise that they, too,
could acquire economic, social, and political status.

For women, however, the issues were quite different. The battles (Jackson
put his political reforms in those terms) for economic opportunity, political participation, and social status did not include them. Margaret O'Neale Eaton is a
good example. As a struggling tavern keeper's daughter, she did not have many
options for improving her social status despite her high degree of natural intelligence and quick wit. Not even her worst detractors ever claimed that Peggy
O'Neale was stupid, backward, or ignorant—had she been male, she could have
overcome her background by studying law as Andrew Jackson or John C. Calhoun
had done. Having completed a course in law and entered politics, she could have
been the match of either Jackson or Calhoun! As it was, Margaret was socialized
very early to realize that women improved their status and gained power and influence only through marriage to men of superior social standing. (Of course, men
used this method to improve their chances in life as well. Both Andrew Jackson
and John Calhoun married women who vastly increased their wealth and opportunities for success.) Margaret set out, using the one asset available to lower-class
women—their sexuality, to attract one of the "first-class" men who frequented her
father's boardinghouse. We know that she was not simply flirting with every man
around her, not only because she claims this to be the case in her autobiography
but also because there is evidence of her rejection of suiters who would not serve
her purposes, suiters such as Richard Call, whom she fought off with fire tongs.

Once married to John Eaton, however, Margaret assumed she was entitled
to recognition and respect. Because she also had the admiration and friendship of
Andrew Jackson, no one, she thought, could deny her the place in society she had
so long yearned for. Ironically, she never really desired to be a major influence in
politics, as her enemies charged. What she wanted was to be accepted as a Cabinet official's wife, to exchange calling cards with the "ladies" of Washington, and
to be invited to all their balls and dinners. Her biographer, in a book entitled
Democracy's Mistress, argued that Margaret challenged the failure of democracy in
the social world of women and thus should be considered as something of a hero.

Later in life when Margaret wrote her autobiography, she praised Andrew
Jackson for defending her and being the champion of her cause. She admired him
very greatly. Sadly, however, she also commented that she would have been better off had he never made such a public and politicized issue of her sexual character; he may have thought he was defending her, but he also made her infamous
in history. What Margaret may have recognized was that Andrew Jackson was more

obsessed with his own status, power, and honor as a family and national patriarch than he was concerned with her well-being. Jackson wanted desperately to be accepted among powerful and elite social groups and to become a part of the emergent middle class, yet he also had an older, more traditional view of family life and patriarchal honor. He assumed that the male head of family—and for him family included his extended kin group, slaves, servants, even close friends and advisers—reigned supreme and that he also could make judgments about character, honesty, and punishments and rewards among the group. That is why the possibility that some group or individuals beyond his patriarchal authority might judge Margaret Eaton an immoral woman or that his niece, Emily, might side with them rather than the head of her family was unbelievable and deeply hurtful to him. Almost pathetically, Jackson kept on reiterating the necessity for "harmony" within his family. He also never understood why anyone outside his kin group could seriously question his judgment of Margaret Eaton's chastity. The only reason that made any sense to him at all was that of a political conspiracy against him, having nothing to do with Margaret and her sexual behavior.

Jackson was old enough that he never quite grasped the seriousness of the values associated with the emergence of a middle class. Concurrent with the spread of a market economy, this emergent middle class took itself very seriously, adopting radically new sets of values regarding sexuality, women, family life, and religion. The new middle-class family included only husbands, wives, and children; if there were servants or slaves in the household, they were not part of the family. Within the confines of the family, women were regarded as superior in morality, religion, and culture. Although men still ruled economic and political life, middle-class women commanded respect because of their moral authority. This new platform of influence within the family gave women opportunities they had not had before, opportunities to exercise their moral influence in social matters outside the home. They became leaders in reform movements and in evangelical churches, forming organizations for benevolence based on their class status. In these efforts they were supported and encouraged by religious leaders, such as the Reverend Ely of Philadelphia, and together clergymen and middle-class women led the evangelical revival that was to sweep the country in the antebellum period. Eventually the evangelical movement became almost synonymous with the Whig and later Republican political parties, and although women never controlled politics, their influence as part of the reform wing of those parties was significant.

The dark side of this new power base for middle-class women was that it was based on class and sexual purity. Men only had respect for middle-class women whose sexual purity was, as Emily Donelson said, "unsuspected." To retain this newly found respect, middle-class women policed their own ranks. They would refuse to associate with unchaste women, and they, as a class, would make judgments as to morality or immorality, not men. Thus, Mrs. John Calhoun could with assurance simply announce to her husband that she would not visit Mrs. Eaton, even though it was a political disaster for him. This was a power that women as a group, independent of their husbands, had not previously exercised. Thus, it seemed to them a "noble" stand against the political demands made by Andrew Jackson. If some of their husbands thought the whole "petticoat war" a silly affair, there were enough like John C. Calhoun who recognized their right, even duty, to make such judgments. With the support of such husbands and the evangelical clergy, the "ladies" prevailed.

Sources: The best sources for this story are Margaret Eaton's *Autobiography* (New York: Scribner's, 1932) and the letters of the other participants. See the *Correspondence of Andrew Jackson,* edited by John Spencer Bassett, Vol. III, 1820–1828 (Washington, 1928); *The Papers of John C. Calhoun,* 20 volumes, edited by Robert L. Meriwether and Clyde Wilson (Columbia, S.C., 1958–); and *Emily Donelson of Tennessee,* by Pauline Wilcox Burke, 2 volumes (Richmond, Va. 1941). The scandal is also extensively treated by Martin Van Buren in his *Autobiography* in the *Annual Report of the American Historical Association for the Year 1918* (Washington, 1920), and by a contemporary society "lady" of Washington, Margaret Bayard Smith, in *The First Forty Years of Washington Society* (New York, 1906). Secondary accounts of varying quality may be found in Queena Pollack, *Peggy Eaton: Democracy's Mistress* (New York, 1931); Robert Remini, *Andrew Jackson and the Course of American Freedom* (New York, 1981); and Richard B. Latner, "The Eaton Affair Reconsidered," *Tennessee Historical Quarterly,* Vol. 36, No. 3 (fall 1977). A few sources that help put the affair in context are Norma Basch, "Marriage, Morals, and Politics in the Election of 1828," *Journal of American History,* Vol. 80, No. 3 (December, 1993); Jan Lewis, "The Republican Wife: Virtue and Seduction in the Early Republic," *William and Mary Quarterly,* Vol. 44 (October, 1987); the chapter on Andrew Jackson in Lewis Perry, *Boats against the Current: Revolution and Modernity 1820–1860* (New York, 1993); and Stephanie McCurry, "The Two Faces of Republicanism: Gender and Proslavery Politics in Antebellum South Carolina," *Journal of American History* (March, 1992).

11

CANAL WARS: THE MAKING OF THE CHESAPEAKE & OHIO CANAL

PETER J. WAY

The end of the War of 1812 signaled the beginning of a long period of economic change and growth for the United States. Trade and commerce with the European powers expanded, bringing profits to merchants who could then invest in the beginnings of a manufacturing system. But continued growth and movement of both agricultural and manufactured commodities required a much better transportation system than the muddy roads, stagecoaches, and farm wagons which existed at the time. As early as the post-Revolutionary period, leading politicians, landholders, and merchants had been advocating some method of "developing" the western part of the new republic. Home from the war, George Washington spent most of his time thinking about and proposing schemes that would allow western farmers (many of them renters on the lands he owned in western Virginia) to ship their grain and produce to coastal cities. His pet scheme was for a man-made waterway that he dubbed the Potomac Canal.

Washington never completed his canal, but by the 1820s canals were on the minds of many people. The state of New York was the first to commit state funds to the building of a canal that would stretch more than 300 miles, connecting New York City with the Great Lakes port of Buffalo. Begun in 1817 and finally finished in 1825, the Erie Canal provided a success story for others to emulate. Because of the Erie Canal, farmers in the lands being rapidly settled in Ohio, Indiana, and Illinois could ship their grain cheaply to New York City and the European ports beyond. The canal also enabled New York City to become the busiest, most profitable commercial center in the United States. With this example before them, other states began planning their own extensive and intricate systems of canals, all hoping that theirs would be as successful as New York's.

Peter Way's story about the building of the Chesapeake and Ohio Canal reveals another side to this tale of economic development and growth. The C&O, like the Erie Canal, was built before there were large-scale organizations to plan and carry out such huge projects, before there was machine technology, and before there was sufficient financial capital to assure success. Way's story reveals how these obstacles were overcome, but he is most interested in the labor force that actually built the canals. Canals were a labor-intensive enterprise, and it was a major problem to find enough

181

workers, men willing to perform manual labor for low wages. Not only were there too few men in the country to fill the workforce, but most native-born young men owned or hoped to own their own farms. In the culture of the new republic, respectability entailed independent status such as that of a craftsman who owned his own shop or a landowning farmer. Such men would avoid wage labor at all costs.

The solution to this labor shortage proved to be the attraction and utilization of immigrant labor—Irish immigrant labor. Coming from a desperately poor and factionalized country, the Irish were ready to take on any job for any pay in order to survive. It was they who built the canals and made the Transportation Revolution possible, and it is their experiences that Peter Way recaptures in the following essay.

John Brady worked and died on Maryland's Chesapeake and Ohio (C&O) Canal, murdered on November 9, 1834, in the home of his employer, Patrick Ryan, by the boss's wife, Mary. His unfortunate demise opens the lock gates of the past, allowing the story to flow of the many people who made the transportation network which powered America's economic expansion in the nineteenth century. Theirs is a tale drenched in blood, sweat, and tears.

Brady and the Ryans lived together in a hut right on the C&O at Middlekauff's Dam, which was north of Williamsport, a little village near Hagerstown nestled on a bend of the Potomac River 100 miles as the canal wends north of its Georgetown terminus, near Washington, D.C. Their shanty camp likely resembled one on the Erie Canal at Mohawk Falls, near Troy, New York, described by the British traveler Frederick Marryat as "a few small wooden shealings, appearing, under the majestic trees which overshadowed them, more like dog-kennels than the habitations of men." Undaunted, Marryat entered a "tenement about fourteen feet by ten" in which "lived an Irishman, his wife, and family, and seven boys as he called them, young men from twenty to thirty years of age, who boarded with him. There was but one bed, on which slept the man, his wife, and family. Above the bed were some planks, extending half way the length of the shealing, and there slept the seven boys, without any mattress, or even straw, to lie upon." The Ryan shanty, with its two rooms and sleeping loft, was hardly more commodious or comfortable. It was in such a world that John Brady and Patrick Ryan lived, rudimentary accommodations plopped down in the midst of a forest solely for the purpose of carrying on the business of canal construction.

The Chesapeake and Ohio was an artificial waterway that aimed to connect the Atlantic Ocean with the Mississippi via Pittsburgh and the Ohio River system, thereby drawing the agricultural produce of the hinterland to the eastern seaboard (at a cost to the producer, of course). Begun in 1828, over the next two decades the canal crawled up the Potomac Valley into the rocky heart of the Appalachian Mountains, ultimately ending at Cumberland, Maryland, some 180 miles to the northwest. It was an undertaking of gargantuan proportions which fell to the lot of men like the contractor Patrick Ryan and the worker John Brady, not to mention women such as Mary Ryan, and their stories are too often lost in the celebration of the "Transportation Revolution" which they wrought.

As a contractor, Patrick Ryan was responsible for overseeing most of the work in canal construction. These small builders were men of limited capital but with the requisite experience, contacts, and cash or credit to hire a gang of laborers and provide them with tools, housing, and food. They contracted to build a section of canal and often differed little from their employees in terms of either economic means or background. Many started out as skilled workers or even laborers, and some dropped back down into the laboring ranks as a result of their failed efforts at contracting. Most contractors in the early decades of canal building (1810s–1840s) came from Ireland like the men they hired. Patrick Ryan and John Brady, for example, shared not only a home and the rough hands of a hard worker but also the experience of being Irish, which entailed a communal past stretching back before their births involving English conquest of their homeland, the gradual breakdown of traditional peasant culture and Celtic ways, economic dislocation, and near forced migration to a nativist, anti-Catholic America, bringing these individuals to the Potomac wilderness, cultural baggage in hand. If not quite of the same blood, John Brady was akin to Patrick and Mary Ryan. Just a

Canallers lived in ramshackle shanties, thrown up either right on the canal line or in shanty camps in nearby cities and towns. Often this housing was provided for them by contractors or canal companies and was meant to be, because of its temporary nature, most basic. Families often lived with the male canallers in worker communities that were home to much drinking and fighting, as well as more benign forms of social interaction. (Frank Leslie's *Illustrated Newspaper,* Sept. 7, 1889)

little capital and a different county of origin within Ireland separated them, but this was sufficient to open the door to murder.

Like most other Irish people who came to America in the nineteenth century, Brady arrived with only his muscle power with which to survive. Many immigrants collected in eastern urban centers, but the limited jobs and harsh living conditions there pushed many out into the countryside in search of work, and the various canals under construction during the early stages of the great Irish immigration acted as a magnet. Brady likely heard of the employment opportunities available and gravitated to the C&O. But he had been at work on the canal for only three weeks when he came down with "the fever and ague," which rendered him unfit for hard labor. Patrick Ryan took Brady into his shanty and gave him the less onerous job of cook. His illness worsened, and on a Friday, Brady began bleeding from the nose and thus was prevented from helping Mrs. Ryan prepare food or wash dishes. This inability to perform his duties no doubt antagonized the contractor's wife, and blood would flow with greater profusion early in the morning of November 9.

A gambling party was held in the Ryan shanty on the evening of the 8th, canallers "hustling" with boss Ryan "keeping coppers for us" (i.e., acting as the bank). Brady, who was either "not very sober that night" or "not a drunken man" depending on the witness, played for a while and then withdrew into the kitchen, domain of Mary Ryan. An argument ensued and Brady struck Mrs. Ryan, for reasons unexplained. Hearkening to Irish regional animosities, the affronted woman swore that "if any county of Clare man or Fardoun, or any other man would strike her or offend her in her own shantee, she would hammer the life out of him," whereupon Mary "picked up a candlestick & struck Brady and kept striking him till Mr. Ryan told her to quit." Brady was heard to "hollow [sic] murder," but none of the gambling party went to his assistance. While no one saw Patrick Ryan strike Brady, the two were together in the kitchen when the latter again cried murder. Thereafter Ryan, telling his wife "that if she did not quit quarrelling she would drive all the men from their work," ejected Brady from the shanty. The stricken canaller stumbled around the camp fruitlessly appealing for help and begging Ryan to let him back in. A neighbor, Elizabeth Morris, awakened in the loft of her shanty by a "dreadful noise," first thought "Ryan was killing his wife," as "they had often quarrelled before," but soon heard Brady crying "Ryan don't kill me," followed by a sigh and silence. Her husband William, hearing a couple of "strokes" which he described as "a dead sound, as if on something soft," went down to investigate. He lit a candle and saw four or five men between the shanties by Ryan's place whom he could not identify but "was afraid to go out for fear of getting a stroke" such as Brady had, and because he "might get cold."

Finally allowed back into the shanty, Brady went up into his bunk in the loft, and in the morning he was "very dead." Doctor James McKee, called to see Brady, found the "deceased was perfectly paralytic, extremities cold, with symptoms of compression on the brain—examined the head after death, and after removing the skull found a large collection of blood on the left side of the brain sufficient to destroy life." Doctor J. J. Beatty also examined the corpse and noted "a great deal of swelling on jaw and left side—several cuts over his head and one or two marks of violence on each side of the windpipe." He concluded that there was "external violence sufficient to produce death," as Brady was "cut through to the bone in several places . . . dreadfully beaten on the face and head" and these "wounds must have been inflicted with a heavy instrument."

Patrick and Mary Ryan were tried for and acquitted of Brady's murder. The public perception that violence was endemic on canals and among the Irish workers no doubt helped save the Ryans, for, as one witness put it, "such disturbances are common in shantees." The contractor's record of service to the canal also influenced the decision (he was described by canal engineer Thomas Purcell as "an excellent contractor—a fair man"), as did the testimony of a militia major that Ryan had taken "the side of laws" and turned out with the troops when a "war" broke out among the Irish canallers near Williamsport in January 1834. This conflict will form the next chapter in our story. Admittedly unpremeditated and to a degree provoked, the Ryans' killing of Brady went unpunished. Regardless, it is clear that Mary Ryan had battered Brady repeatedly with a "very large" candlestick, while circumstantial evidence (such as the bruising on the neck) suggests that Patrick had assaulted him. It is somewhat surprising that the newspaper reports did not draw attention to the fact that the alleged murderer was a woman, this being an age in which women were to be all things pure and whose hands were not to be sullied by hard work, let alone blood. But Mary Ryan's purity was tainted by her service to men who were not her kin, her hands hardened by the labors she performed, and her character compromised by her nativity, the Irish assumed to be brutes. Thus, she was allowed to escape the cult of domesticity that prevailed and was excused from the moral restraints this imposed on middle-class women.

Brady's murder nonetheless excited "more than common interest . . . in the public mind" and a detailed report of the trials in the *Hagerstown Torchlight*. This was likely due to the "Irish war" that had convulsed the canal ten months earlier and necessitated the calling in of federal troops, a "story" widely covered in regional newspapers. This series of clashes involved two opposed Irish factions, the "Fardouns" (also known as Fardowners, Connaughtmen, or Longfords, from the province of Connaught on Ireland's west coast) and the "Corkonians" (from County Cork, in the southwest province of Munster). Such factions grew out of a tradition of county rivalries in Ireland rooted in a long-term experience with social and economic violence, which may have resulted from conflict between agricultural workers of one county and transient laborers from another who competed for limited harvest jobs. Despite the hazy historical roots, the Irish tradition of faction fighting and clandestine agrarian violence crystallized on British and North American public works, with the first reports of such clannish conflict appearing in the early 1830s just as canal construction was beginning to take off and when the workforce was dominated by Irish immigrants. Corkonians typically congregated in their own shanty communities, while Connaughtmen also clung together. Contractors often came from or led the same faction, and work decisions—who was hired, who got which contract—could take into account these allegiances. Throughout the 1830s a faction sought to control its section of the canal, and when times were tough, it could attempt to usurp the territory of its rival. On the C&O in 1834, Corkonians clustered north of Williamsport around Middlekauff's Dam, near the site of the Ryans' shanty, while the Fardouns tended to live and work to

the south. And from the testimony at the trial, it would appear that the Ryans belonged to the former faction, while John Brady was associated with the latter. Thus,
while the Cork-Fardoun conflict in the Ryan-Brady case was contained within one
shanty, ten months earlier it had encompassed an entire region with proportion-
ally graver consequences.

Hostilities in the "Irish war" opened on Thursday, January 9, 1834, ten
months to the day prior to John Brady's murder. John Irons, like Brady a Fardoun,
was attacked and beaten by a group of other canal workers, with fatal results. The
inquest into his murder reported that "he came to his death from blows received
on several parts of his body and head from persons unknown." But this was not
just a simple matter of murder, unlike the Brady case, for Irons's demise set off a
"kind of guerilla war" involving "Armies" of Irish canallers numbering in the hundreds. The *Williamsport Banner* reported that "there are two national parties
among them, composed respectively of those from the North and those from the
South of Ireland. The former are designated the *Fardouns* and *Longfords;* the latter, *Corkonians.* " Irons's crime was being a Fardoun at the mercy of Corkonians.

Early on Monday the 13th, the Fardouns took their revenge when about 200
men, some with firearms, attacked a number of their opponents who were working on the canal six miles south of Williamsport. The Corkonians, "having no
warning of the approach of the enemy . . . were routed and dispersed, four or five
were badly bruised and wounded." A "company of mounted citizens, in aid of the
civil authority," among them Patrick Ryan, marched to the spot and took fifty prisoners before a justice of the peace, who committed thirty-five to prison in Hagerstown. In ensuing days, "great commotion has existed among the hands. Very little work has been done, and a state of alarm and warlike preparation has taken its
place." On Thursday the 16th, a party of Corkonians "committed excesses" on
the canal north of Williamsport, and the next morning a small party seen approaching the town from above were met at the aqueduct and driven back. The
citizens armed themselves; nonetheless, on Friday a force of about 300 Fardouns,
armed with guns, clubs, and pick handles, marched up the canal, crossed the aqueduct, and were joined north of the village by 300 to 400 of their brethren. They
spilled onto a field at Middlekauff's Dam, where the Corkonians were "in battle
array, drawn up on the top of a hill, about three hundred in number, and armed,
in part, with military weapons." A "challenge to combat" was issued, and according to the *Banner:*

> Volleys of shot were exchanged; some men were seen to fall, and the party above
> began to fall back and disperse before the superior forces of the enemy. A pursuit
> ensued through the woods, where frequent firing was heard, and no doubt many
> lives were taken. Persons who traversed the field after the battle was over observed
> five men in the agonies of death, who had been shot through the head; several
> dead bodies were seen in the woods, and a number wounded in every direction.—
> Those who observed the battle described it as one of great rage and most deadly
> violence.— All the deaths and wounded are said to be of the *Corkonians.*

That night, the victorious Fardouns passed quietly through the streets of
Williamsport and returned to their shanties below town.

The "public peace" having been outraged, citizens of Williamsport called out
the volunteer companies from Hagerstown and requested "a sufficient federal

force" from Washington "to preserve order among the laborers." Two companies arrived from Baltimore, the first time federal troops intervened in a labor dispute, and remained for the rest of the winter. However, a peace conference between the two factions held on the 27th produced a treaty signed by the workers' delegates promising: "That we will not, either individually or collectively, interrupt or suffer to be interrupted in our presence, any person engaged on the line of the Canal, for or on account of any local difference, or national prejudice, and that we will use our influence to destroy all these matters of difference growing out of this distinction of parties, Known as Corkonians and Longfords." Furthermore, they agreed to inform on those breaking this pledge or inciting a riot, and each delegate posted a $20 bond to keep the peace. Calm returned to the canal for the time being.

The Chesapeake and Ohio was part of a wave of canal construction that began with the Erie Canal (1817–1825). Canals were artificial waterways meant to fa-

The rock cut on the Erie Canal near Lockport, New York, involved excavating a channel twenty-seven feet wide, thirty feet deep, and two miles in length through a mountain ridge. Blasting was done with gun powder packed in hand-drilled holes, while horse-operated cranes line the lip of the cut at seventy-foot intervals to lift the spoil from the lock beds. Many injuries resulted from such work. This engraving portrays the workers as an undifferentiated mass of man and beast toiling away in the pit, receiving directions from a more clearly-drawn management figure. (The Metropolitan Museum of Art, Dick Fund, 1941)

cilitate commercial exchange with the expansive hinterland, which heretofore had
been inhibited by natural impediments like the Appalachian Mountains, the lack
of roads, and the subsequent expense of haulage. Building in this "Transportation Revolution" peaked in the mid-1830s, with 1277 miles of canals completed
by 1830, more than doubling to 3326 miles in the ensuing ten years. About 35,000
people worked in the industry at this time, and canal projects became bureaucra-
tized, becoming extended management structures of directors, engineers, sur-
veyors, maintenance superintendents, and locktenders needed to build and operate transportation networks that could measure hundreds of miles in length. Such
considerable business ventures required millions of dollars in investment and
thousands of paid workers. They were initially carried on by joint-stock companies, with private investors buying shares in speculation of future profit. When such
private capital proved insufficient, states often stepped in, either by providing funds
for private companies or by creating government agencies—canal commissions or
boards of works—to oversee the building of "public works" at the state's expense.
The C&O Canal was a joint-stock company that relied on private investment and
whatever credit banks and bond dealers were willing to allow it. But increasingly
the company became dependent on the Maryland state government for funding;
it received a $2 million loan from the state in 1835 and a $3 million stock subscription the next year, and it borrowed another $1.65 million in 1839.

   While canal companies and state governments supplied the cash on which
the industry operated, it was contractors like Patrick Ryan who assumed much of
the economic risk of canal building. These independent builders put up the initial capital and only received full payment upon completion of their "section" of
the line to specifications established by the engineer. In the meantime, men had
to be hired, tools and food provided for them, and roofs put over their heads, and
this all cost money. This situation was exacerbated by the competitive nature of
the bidding process for contracts, which meant that contractors had a narrow profit
margin, and continuing financial problems pushed many into the red. Insolvent
builders did not have the wherewithal to give workers their earnings, and worker
discontent was a recurring presence on the C&O. The problem emerged almost
immediately upon the opening of construction. The proposed canal route was divided into sections on which prospective contractors made bids. Company policy
was to accept the lowest responsible bid, which placed great pressure on contractors to cut their estimates to a minimum, as sharp competition for contracts
prevailed. The first letting of thirty-four sections in 1828, for example, received
almost 500 proposals. This system opened the door to shoddy workmanship and
shady business dealings, a danger exacerbated by the method of payment. Builders
were paid monthly on the basis of their set scale of prices, minus 20 percent retained by the company to ensure satisfactory work, meaning that they never were
paid in full until completion. This system was in continual crisis throughout the
1830s as the company's financial problems increased and its ability to pay on
schedule declined. Contractors were forced to resort to credit to push work along,
often leaving themselves overextended. As Lee Montgomery, a contractor who will
figure prominently in this story, complained, "a man . . . in the Imploy of the company is doomed to distress and distruction." He was speaking of builders, not
workers. "The truth is," admitted the chief engineer, Benjamin Wright, "that *we*

know the prices of these contractors are very low, and that it yet remains doubtful whether they can sustain themselves." When debts grew too large to be redeemed by future construction, contractors often fled the line, abandoning their contracts and leaving their creditors and unpaid workers to scramble for whatever property and outstanding money they left behind. In May 1829, the contractor on section 19 of the C&O absconded with the last estimate, leaving his unpaid laborers "in a pitiable condition . . . sick, without money, medicine, provisions or the power of attaining any." And when Ford and Company bailed out the following year, they owed their workers and masons $150 to $200 in total, in some cases $15 to $20 to married men with families dependent on the wages, while in 1833 Thomas Walsh fled "poor, common labourers," each of whom he owed between $15 and $42. Contractors on the C&O were again caught in a spiral of inflation and failures in the mid-1830s, no doubt putting additional pressure on builders like Patrick Ryan to get the most work possible out of their men.

At the same time, the small scale of their job meant that a contractor forged close ties to his hands, often providing food and shelter and living and working alongside them, much as Ryan did. C&O chief engineer Charles Fisk asserted in 1838 that "every contractor has his followers, labourers who go with him from one part of the country to another." In this situation, paternalistic relations naturally arose, with the contractor a father figure to his men, while his wife, if present, played the mother. As with real families, however, all was not sweetness and light, and conflict was a common occurrence; in this way, John Brady's death can be seen as the consequence of domestic violence and but an extreme manifestation of the dangers faced by canallers on a regular basis.

Workers on the C&O in the 1830s usually numbered between 2000 and 3000, a very large industrial workforce at the time, and labor shortages prevailed until the late 1830s. The company competed with other public works, as well as different industries and agriculture's harvest demands for wage workers. C&O President Charles Mercer lamented during the first of many labor shortages that "labourers are difficult to be had, at high prices . . . besides their board and whiskey and a supply of necessary tools." While contractors were generally responsible for finding, hiring, and paying workers, the sheer numbers required by the entire canal project meant the company often played a part in labor recruitment so as to ensure a supply of hands for builders to employ. The board of directors advertised for workers, sent out recruiting agents, and petitioned Congress unsuccessfully for 1000 federal troops to work on the canal's mountain section. Increasingly the company looked to Europe to satisfy its hunger. "Meat, three times a day, a plenty of bread and vegetables, with a reasonable allowance of liquor, and light, ten, or twelve dollars a month for wages, would we have supposed," the company president, Charles Mercer, wrote in 1829, "prove a powerful attraction to those, who, narrowed down in the circle of their enjoyments, have at this moment, a year of scarcity presented to them." The C&O recruited through company agents and notices in European newspapers advertising 10,000 job openings, over three times what was needed. The canal was so desperate to tap this labor market that it even sought to revive indentured servitude, with prospective workers promising to exchange two to three months' labor for passage to America. In all, several hundred men emigrated under this scaled-down indenture, some with their families. But during the passage, the laborers were fed too little, and what they got was often rotten, leading "these clouns" [sic] to threaten the company's agents and attempt to break into the ship's storeroom to "gratify their own ingovernable appetites." Contractors complained that the laborers arrived "destitute of the comforts of life, and we have been compelled to clothe them." Through such orchestrated immigration and by the individual initiative of immigrants who found their own way to the canal, the workforce increasingly was dominated by migrant Irish, leading President Mercer to proclaim: "The greater part of them are transient foreigners; sometimes on the Pennsylvania Canals; sometimes on the Baltimore and Ohio Rail Road; sometimes at work on our canal."

The life they encountered on the canal was a difficult one, marked by rudimentary living conditions. In urban shantytowns workers and their families lived in rented housing or buildings of their own construction in so-called bog settlements. The husband was often away at the canal, returning home during slack periods. More common were work camps, rude collections of shanties that mushroomed along the canal line, home to tens to hundreds of people. These makeshift villages were predominantly male enclaves—men outnumbered women by more than 5 to 1 in an 1850 C&O work camp—but the working population was inflated by family members, both women and children. Bunkhouses in which congregations of men lived communally prevailed when work sites were some distance from settlements or when the majority of the workforce were young and single. The men slept in bunks arranged in tiers around the walls, shared a communal hearth, and had their cooking and cleaning performed for them. The number per shanty could vary widely; barracks housed up to twenty-two residents in the 1850 C&O camp. Some shanties were family dwellings, a husband, a wife, and children living with a number of boarders, not unlike the traditional farm household. The common feature linking bunkhouse and family shanty was their spartan character; for example, the Ryans' shanty, just a two-room shack with a loft, was home to both employer and hands. Those that had windows rarely had glass or screening, an open invitation to mosquitoes and blackflies. A cooking pot or crude hearth usually sat in the center of the building, with a hole in the roof overhead as a chimney. Beds were commonly mere planks, sometimes cushioned with straw.

Women played a key role in the domestic sphere of shanty camps, but one distinctly different from that of their middle-class sisters. They worked as cooks, cleaners, and laundresses for canallers, usually in the pay of the company or contractors at wages considerably below those of men. Nellie Butler and Susan Jackson, for instance, cooked for the C&O in 1829–1830, while Mary Adlum and her daughter Rachael did the same for a contractor in 1834. The experience of Mary Ryan as a domestic drudge was therefore hardly unique. Women also ran their own boardinghouses in which canallers stayed. Many others lived off work camps back in some city to which their men would return during the off-season, where they worked at sweated labor as seamstresses to support their families or took up domestic service, both difficult, poorly remunerated jobs. While performing tasks traditionally associated with females, it was hard work to the canalling sorority, not a divine vocation.

Working conditions for canallers were equally rough. Construction was powered by man and beast using traditional tools, shovels, picks, wheelbarrows, and carts. Canallers labored twelve to fifteen hours a day in all kinds of weather, often in water. Digging was the basic toil, but blasting, quarrying, and skilled masonry also were involved, all strenuous forms of labor, especially when performed at an unremitting pace. Accidents were commonplace, with blasting being particularly dangerous. Three Irish workers were killed while blowing rock on the C&O in June 1830; having lit the slow fuse to a powder charge, but not hearing the expected blast, they returned just as it exploded. The laborer Felix O'Neal said that he was "by the will of the Almighty god disabled by a blast, which unables me at the present to support Meself, which said Blast, broke my thigh bone, and injured my hand most surprising." And a mason, John Miller, was injured "without fault of his owen" while quarrying stone in October 1838, making it necessary "that his limb was on the spot amputated." John Brady would have confronted similar dangers before sickness led him into Mary Ryan's kitchen.

Brady's "fever and ague" was but one of many illnesses that plagued canals. Typhoid and dysentery were caused by food or water contaminated by excreta, conditions promoted by unsanitary and poorly drained work sites. Malaria and yellow fever were spread by mosquitoes common to the swampy or bushy land near canals. The months from July to October were generally known as the sickly

The finished locks on the Erie Canal at Lockport give an indication of the engineering feat achieved. A series of steps, the locks allowed canal barges to, in effect, climb a mountain ridge and to complete the journey along the canal from the Hudson River to Lake Erie. In this later photograph, it can also be seen how canals, as the key transportation routes of their era, became magnets for industrial and commercial development. (American Heritage Picture Collection)

season, and the Potomac Valley was notorious for its fevers. The first few sum-
mers of construction on the C&O decimated the ranks of workers, causing a labor
shortage and driving up wages. Wracked with fevers, unable to work, and without a Patrick Ryan to take them in, many hands turned up destitute on the streets
of Frederick, Georgetown, and Washington, where they were cared for in public
poorhouses. Dr. John Little, in his role as a trustee of the poor for Georgetown,
received "daily, almost hourly calls to relieve the laborers coming into town, from
the line of the canal, sick and destitute of the means to procure medical aid or the
common necessaries of life."

Cholera was the most dreaded scourge that ravaged canals, however. Brought
from Europe by immigrants, the disease spread throughout eastern North America, making its appearance on the C&O near Williamsport in June 1832. Seven
cases appeared in three days, five of them proving fatal. In September, a contractor near the village again reported that "the collery is on our work . . . a grate dale
of excitement provales a mongst the people thay are flying to and frow." Thirty
deaths occurred in a few days opposite Shepherdstown, Virginia, and "the poor
Exiles of Erin are flying in every direction," leaving the line between Point of Rocks
and Williamsport virtually deserted. How Patrick Ryan dealt with this scourge is
unclear, but President Mercer tried to grasp the point of view of a John Brady:
"imagine the panic produced by a mans turning black and dying in twenty four
hours in the very room where his comrades are to sleep or to dine." Panic and
flight were natural responses. Thomas Purcell, the resident engineer, reported that
"men deserted by their friends or comrades, have been left to die in the fields, the
highways, or in the neighbouring barns & stables." Frances Trollope wrote
poignantly of encountering such a debilitated canaller:

> a poor creature, who was already past the power of speaking; he was conveyed to
> the house, and expired during the night. By enquiring at the canal, it was found
> that he was an Irish laborer, who having fallen sick, and spent his last cent, had left
> the stifling shantee where he lay, in the desperate attempt of finding his way to
> Washington, with what hope I know not. He did not appear above twenty. . . . I
> saw him buried under a group of locust trees, his very name unknown to those
> who laid him there . . . but no clergyman attended, no prayer was said, no bell was
> tolled.

This life of hard work, rough conditions, looming injury, ever-present illness,
and—above all else—elusive pay contributed directly to the "Irish war" of January 1834. Throughout the winter of 1833–1834 the C&O tottered on the brink
of insolvency. Lacking money to pay builders, the company made frantic efforts
to secure loans from local banks; those contractors without adequate capitaliza-
tion faced economic failure and the wrath of their employees. These anxieties
seeped down to the laborers, who feared that work would be abruptly halted and
wages would be lost. The canal threatened to be swamped in either a sea of debt
or a wave of violence, and the dam was breached when a contractor owed money
by the company discharged his men without fully paying them upon the completion of his section. These disgruntled laborers, being of the same Irish faction,
joined together to plot strategy. Unable to grasp the real culprits, the canal company and contractor, they turned on members of the other faction. "The cause of
the difficulty," the *Hagerstown Torchlight* reported, "is said to have been, either the

suspension of work, or of payment, on one or more sections of the canal." John Irons was thus an unwitting victim of the canal's economic crisis and the so-called Irish war a natural by-product. Armies marched, the battle of Middlekauff's Dam was fought, and troops descended on the canal to calm the waters. Engineer Thomas Purcell felt that more than mere interethnic hostility was at play, however; instead, the disturbances were "the result of a regular organization . . . the ultimate object being to expel from the canal all except those that belong to the strongest party and thus secure for the remainder higher wages." These initiatives were eventually lost in the mushrooming factional conflict and ultimately squelched by military intervention. Fearing further disorder, the state of Maryland took out an additional subscription of company stock in March 1834, which financially revitalized the C&O and temporarily obviated the need for workers to fight over employment.

Our second chapter ends in the story of factional and ethnic violence on the Chesapeake and Ohio Canal, but the book is not closed. Irish canallers were forced to act out the same plot time and again throughout the 1830s, with economic and social problems fueling violence. The animosities between Corkonians and Fardouns which saw Mary Ryan lay low John Brady and which, stoked by economic uncertainties, flared in the wake of John Irons's death reignited regularly. But increasingly individual factions waged war against contractors and the canal company. At the same time, Irish canallers attacked workers of different ethnic extractions, as happened in 1839 with a raid on the village of Little Orleans, when Fardouns again marched along the canal and people once more lost their lives, Germans this time instead of their usual Corkonian foes. This battle of Little Orleans and the events leading up to it form the next installment in our story.

The peace treaty that had formally ended the January 1834 conflict was quickly forgotten and the infusion of money from the state soon dissipated, once more making employment and payment uncertain. Workers were again at each other's throats when the same two factions battled near Point of Rocks south of Harpers Ferry in June 1834, leaving three people dead and necessitating the calling in of the militia. In early February 1835, laborers turned out (struck) for higher wages, and operations were interrupted for fifteen days until a horse and rifleman company drove them back to work. In January 1836—two years after the 1834 war and fifteen months after Brady's murder—Corkonians again fought Fardouns near Clear Spring, just north of Middlekauff's Dam, the scene of these crimes. Two shanties were burned, and several of the combatants were severely wounded. The following April, Irish workers joined together in a strike, drove a workforce of "Dutchmen" (Germans) and "country borns" from their jobs, and temporarily interrupted work before the discontented men left the line and an uneasy peace was restored. During this turnout, several contractors managed to keep construction going by using strikebreakers or "scab" labor, and their sections were the target of violence later in 1836. According to George Bender, a company engineer, secret societies among the workers were the source of these attacks. He reported that the area around Hancock, Maryland, upriver from Williamsport, was "the seat of a regularly organized society of these desperadoes." "The Society," he continued, "is believed to be but a branch of one in the City of New York, and that it has branches in all the States where internal improvements are in progress."

This organization used threats, vandalism, and beatings to get its way in the workplace by chasing off resisting contractors and laborers. Factions ruled the canal. Persisting economic troubles made workers feel insecure and prone to ethnic violence, while contractors were often caught in the middle without the means to satisfy their hands' demands. The result, carnage on the canal in the summer of 1839, hearkens back to 1834. Lee Montgomery, a Methodist parson as well as a contractor, was the key figure of authority in this bloody passage of our story.

Montgomery, who had built a tunnel on Pennsylvania's Union Canal, was chosen to oversee the mountain tunnel near Paw Paw in present-day West Virginia. He was a rough-and-tumble man who was close to his chosen hands, not unlike Patrick Ryan. But also like Ryan, he was ready to resist violent canallers and had managed to escape the turnout and violence in the spring of 1836 through a willingness to meet force with force. "Our Methodist parson contractor (Montgomery)" claimed "that his men were generally picked men, and had provided themselves . . . with some Guns and a few little sticks and as it was supposed they would use them rather than be intruded on, the rioters thought it best not to stop as they were passing by." George Bender confided of Montgomery: "The truth is that in a good cause few men would probably use a 'Little Stick' more effectively than himself, although he would *pray* at the same time." Such prayers could not hold back the tide of factional displeasure or ensure his own economic well-being.

The Paw Paw tunnel was the most daunting section on the canal, requiring a cut through 3118 feet of solid rock. Manpower, hand tools, and gunpowder were to move this mountain. Years of blasting lay ahead, with men at times working night and day. As each foot slowly receded, however, so did Montgomery's fortunes. In the end, his men suffered. Wages were frequently late, and work periodically ground to a halt. The tunnel camp was the source of much of the violence that flashed forth on the C&O and Montgomery the usual lightning rod.

On New Year's Day, 1838, four hundred men from the tunnel, unpaid by Montgomery for a month, flocked to Oldtown, 12 miles upriver, where they ransacked several buildings before the militia incarcerated ten ringleaders. On February 12, workers surrounded the office at the tunnel and threatened to destroy the completed works. Disorder persisted for two to three days until the men were pacified by promises of payment. But dollars were always short and tempers high. That summer the chief engineer, Charles Fisk, reported: "The laboring men & miners have obtained, or very nearly so, the mastery. There is unquestionably a regular conspiracy among the men to have the work carried on to their own liking. They permit no boss to remain, who endeavours to get full work out of them." On August 1, the C&O responded by blacklisting 127 workers, prohibiting their employment by any contractor. The whole line would benefit, it was felt, from the substitution of "more orderly and submissive labourers." Nonetheless, Montgomery's money problems grew. In May 1839—at a time when the company held $30,000 in retained percentage on his work and owed him upwards of $20,000 in payment on his estimates—Montgomery had to lay off most of his men because he did not have the means to buy essential gunpowder. Fisk reported that the idle miners and laborers joined with other workers and "have been marching up & down the line, three or four hundred in number with arms, threatening & using violence when opposed by those peaceably disposed." To prevent trouble from escalating, the company issued state-guaranteed bonds as security on a loan to pay off the money owed, but again this was only a temporary solution. By August, C&O managers were debating whether to suspend parts of the work or to cut the number of hands employed. As with the 1834 "guerilla war" around Williamsport, such economic anxiety bred factional conflict, which gripped the region for most of a month; the scene of action had just shifted along with the construction site, and this time the Fardouns terrorized all and sundry.

Montgomery, repeatedly in need of cash, was receiving advances from the company almost monthly, but never enough to pay his men fully. On August 11, 1839, about 100 armed Fardouns left the tunnel and moved downriver to a work camp near Little Orleans. There they "entered the Shantee's of the Contractor and Labourers, and beat and wounded them very much, took what money, watches, and everything else of value they could take away, and leaving a number of persons very much injured. The Contractor and Labourers on this Section are Germans." One man thrown into the fire later died from his burns, prompting a German priest, Father Guth, to confess of the Irish: "were I superstitious I would really believe they are incarnate Devils." The Fardouns then reportedly marched up the Potomac, breaking into farmhouses and shanties, before the militia was mobilized.

This rapid response did not entirely silence the canallers. As late as the end of September, a Hagerstown newspaper reported that "the line of the Canal from Oldtown to the South end of the Tunnel, has been, for some time past, the scene of the most savage and barbarous outrages." The militia officers "learned that there is a well organized society among the *Fardowns* or *Longford* men, and that they are well disciplined in the use of their arms; and from their movements, appear to have their officers to command." The society also was said to have a war treasury "to give bail for any of their party, who may be taken." As a result, it was virtually impossible to get incriminating evidence, as "no Contractor can appear against them, without abandoning his work; nor dare a Contractor even discharge one of the men, without incurring the displeasure of all his comrades." The *Herald of Freedom* insisted: "They are banded together with pledges of brotherhood, and have their secret signs or pass words." And pity those that should cross them, as "at a moment's warning, a leader will march, perhaps with 100 men, and in the most lawless manner, attack any of the other party, or any inoffending citizen against whom any prejudice exists."

The militia spent five days in sweeping the line, rather indiscriminately, of rioters and weapons. Working from a list of leaders provided by Father Guth, they arrested about thirty laborers, shooting eight to ten men in the process, killing one. At Fisk's directions, the troops destroyed workers' shanties and leveled grog shops, the ultimate source of disorder in company eyes. Thirty to fifty buildings in all were torn down, many reportedly belonging to innocent individuals. A lawsuit was launched against Fisk and two militia officers by those workers whose property was destroyed, claiming that they had not been involved in the riots and were law-abiding citizens. The court eventually decided that the officials had exceeded their authority, and it rendered a judgment of $2737 against them. The defendants unsuccessfully appealed to the company and the state for relief.

Fisk had always been frustrated by an unwillingness to drag rebellious canallers through to the end of the legal process. In the past, prisoners had been released from jail after the line had been quieted, and he felt that such treatment fostered conflict and effectively yielded authority to the secret societies, an evil he was determined to root out once and for all. The jailed laborers were to be prosecuted to the law's full extent, while assistant engineers were instructed to gather evidence against the leaders who had been jailed. As an added precaution, he placed a labor spy, James Finney, among the workers to ferret out information that could be used against the riot leaders. On the strength of the testimony of Finney and Father Guth, fourteen laborers were convicted on charges ranging from riot, robbery, and arson to assault with intent to kill and sentenced to the state penitentiary for from five to eighteen years. Nine, convicted on lesser charges, were punished by fine and imprisonment, while four were acquitted. Finney eventually received $100 for his service to the company. The company profited also, as the swift policing of the August disturbance and the prosecution of the labor leaders caused wages to fall from $1.25 to 87.5 cents a day in the aftermath. The threat

C.&O. CANAL

The end goal of canal construction was making a profit for the investors. Hauled along by mules at a clip of 5 miles per hour, barges brought the agricultural produce of the interior to eastern cities and lake ports, and carried many travelers into the American heartland; all for a fee. The C&O only made it to Cumberland, Maryland, however, and the warring workers were partly responsible for stemming its tide of development. The 180 miles of canal they constructed north from Georgetown nonetheless remain as a testament to their strength and endurance. (Library of Congress) of renewed violence was omnipresent, however, a fact brought home in 1840 when Maryland's governor pardoned those imprisoned for the August 1839 riot. Within days, there were reports that some of these men had returned to "their old haunts." A contractor complained that one had visited his section "threatening him with violence and destruction of property."

Turning the screw on workers did not solve the company's financial problems, however. Contractors still clamored for money the C&O did not have. Severe financial problems forced it to cut back on construction and the number of laborers employed. Promissory notes were issued in September 1839, in an effort to keep work going, but the company was almost $3 million in debt and the future looked bleak. Work faltered, contracts were declared abandoned, and the labor force dwindled as unemployed men straggled off to find work elsewhere. Lee Montgomery managed to pierce the mountain at Paw Paw but sank into a pool of debt and creditors' lawsuits before the tunnel could be finished. In 1841, there were only about 700 men on the line when construction finally ground to a halt. Work was renewed periodically only to peter out. But in 1850, the C&O finally reached Cumberland, Maryland, a compromise terminus to the canal some 180 miles up the Potomac from Georgetown, but far short of its envisioned Ohio River juncture.

Promoters of the Chesapeake and Ohio Canal dreamed of breaching the Appalachians and drawing the trade of the Ohio Valley down the Potomac, while at the same time opening up America's hinterland to the civilizing influence of the east. This great public work was thrust on the shoulders of laborers and contractors, largely of Irish origin. They tried to fashion others' dreams from mud and too often slipped into a swamp of debt. The C&O never realized its goal, and the contractors and canallers paid the price.

AN INTERPRETATION

Individual threads drawn out of a tapestry of experience, Brady's death and the multiple incidents of collective violence on the C&O canal in the 1830s are not intended to represent the sum of the canal experience; nor is the morbidity of the subject matter meant to shroud the complex and colorful life of canallers. Nevertheless, these acts of violence were not somehow separate from the fabric of existence in the shanty camps. They were natural by-products of the historical processes that gave birth to canal construction and the early industrial capitalism it represented. And for people like these canallers—unskilled, socially and economically marginalized, highly transient—the experience was a continuous one of hard work punctuated by repeated acts of violence, from interpersonal aggression such as that which leveled John Brady and John Irons to outright battles involving hundreds of participants like that which convulsed the canal in January 1834 and during the summer of 1839. Canal workers, contractors, and company officials alike were drawn into this spiral of violence.

The story of the Ryans and Brady, with the shanty camp at its core, was part of a great narrative that recounts the world's re-creation in the image of capital. Canal companies such as the Chesapeake and Ohio were early representatives of the large businesses that would dominate this world, and the work camp was a precursor of the many ghettos and company towns that would shelter this world's workers. As boss contractor and paid employee, respectively, Patrick Ryan and John Brady embodied the capital-labor divide that powered the system, while Brady's death symbolized in corporeal terms the alienation experienced by all workers. Conversely, Brady and the Ryans, like most other canallers and many other contractors, shared a common Irish immigrant background involving uprooting from the native land and transplantation to the not so fertile soil of America, where their ethnicity acted both as a means of communal organization and an excuse for their exploitation. Mary Ryan, while traveling the same path, shouldered additional burdens as a woman. In the course of trying to integrate her experiences as a female, a drudge for her contractor husband, and an Irish person, the tensions became too great and she lashed out. On her own, she was unable to hold the fragments of history together. But the stroke that felled John Brady, laying bare his skull and leading to his demise, also allows the historian to suture together the pieces of his life; the report of his death and the nature of his murder offer a glimpse behind the heretofore closed shanty door. At base a personal tale beyond complete comprehension from the present, Brady's murder nonetheless can be seen as an acting out of the gender, ethnic, and class tensions created by the economics of canal construction. Brady, the Irish worker, dies; and the Ryans, his employers, are exculpated, their alleged act excused on the one hand by the assertion that "such disturbances are common in shantees" and on the other by the characterization of Patrick Ryan as "an excellent contractor" and active participant in the suppression of the 1834 riots at Williamsport. Violence and death were part of the economics of canal building, and the social costs, in this case Brady's demise, were insufficient to effect a judicial balancing of the books.

To a degree, the Brady/Ryans story is also that of the faction fights and strikes that rocked the canal in the 1830s, in particular the battles of Middlekauff's Dam and Little Orleans. The Fardouns and Corkonians trod the same trail from Ireland to Maryland, where they were confronted with impromptu and often shabby living conditions, where disease and death seemed to ooze out of the mud along the canal bank, and where ostensibly high wages could melt away as quickly as ice water under a warm spring sun, through either contractor malfeasance or company incompetence. Backbreaking work and spirit-sapping economic uncertainty made for a disaffected labor force that, often with the stimulation of alcohol, repeatedly rose up to smite one another. But through the miasma canallers increasingly perceived the source of their problems and a possible resolution through collective actions. An inchoate understanding of their class exploitation fused with Irish cultural practices to produce incipient revolt. Utilizing terrorist tactics to scare off other workers, canallers sought to ensure employment for themselves. But individual or allied factions also waged war against contractors and staged strikes for full payment of wages or better pay and working conditions. A significant degree of conflict resulted. Irish workers on the C&O mounted at least ten riots or strikes and engaged in persistent labor unrest that led to six incidents of military intervention between 1834 and 1840. And on American canals as a whole, thirty-six riots and twenty strikes involving construction workers occurred from

1820 to 1849. In response, employers and canal officials drew together to punish workers and looked to the state to police canallers' collective actions. From 1829 to 1849, the military was called in fourteen times to put down worker uprisings, making the industry arguably the site of the most class conflict in the period and certainly the most heavily policed. Canallers thus formed the leading edge of the developing working class, at least in terms of exploitation, class struggle, and capitalist repression, as their experience on the C&O makes clear.

Such sustained militancy and swift state suppression indicated that something more than mere ethnic hostility was involved, although Irish workers usually were at its center. The struggle was rooted in the organization of work common to canal building—its methods of financing, work management, and labor recruitment and discipline, and the nature of work and consequent living conditions—unhinged on the C&O by economic problems that emerged virtually from the opening of construction. It was expressed in traditional cultural forms, but increasingly this conflict was turned to class ends, ultimately pitting workers against the interests of contractors and company. Canallers banded together into nascent labor organizations and sought to establish a certain amount of control over the workplace and their relations with their bosses. The Irish secret society acted as their model for mobilization. The resulting incidents of collective violence must be seen for what they were: coordinated maneuvers for job security and economic stability on a terrain of impending unemployment and recurrent nonpayment of wages. Unskilled immigrants with limited bargaining power, canal workers realized that organization and the threat of violence were the only means for them to establish some control over production and thereby better their conditions. True, canaller often smote canaller, Irishman killed Irishman. But in the end jobs were freed up, easing the victors' fears of unemployment; the company was repeatedly forced to issue money to contractors to repay the hands; and the state, while frequently rushing in troops to police the workers, was induced to funnel more cash into the canal to keep it afloat. The actions of these factions, however fratricidal, thus acted to enhance the economic security of canal workers.

A pattern is evident on the C&O that prevailed on most canals during this period. Canal companies' continuing financial woes undermined the contracting system and threatened the laborers' livelihood. In response, Irish workers joined together and used violence to establish control over jobs and wages, usually at the expense of fellow canallers. Their gains were limited and usually ephemeral, but this does not make the motivations of canallers any less real or compelling. The implicit aggression of the capital-labor relationship, with employers exploiting their workers, was acted out explicitly on canals, as violence was one of the few options open to laborers caught in a whirlpool of economic oppression and social fluidity. John Brady was murdered, John Irons beaten to death, Lee Montgomery chased to Washington, and an anonymous German laborer burned to death. But even in its seemingly most parochial forms, violence was generally precipitated and conditioned by the nature of the work environment: the exploitative character of the labor relationship and the fragility of community life this engendered. The story of canal laborers thus is an important one, and it is long since time that it was recounted.

Sources: This story is based primarily on the Chesapeake and Ohio Canal Company Papers, found in the Records of the National Park Service, Record Group 79, at the National Archives in Washington, D.C., especially Letters Received by the Office of the President and Directors (Series 190) and Letters Sent by the Office of the President and Directors (Series 194); another federal source was the United States Manuscript Census for 1850. Valuable company records were the *Annual Reports of the Presidents and Directors of the Chesapeake and Ohio Canal Company to the Stockholders* (Washington, D.C., 1828–1845). Another manuscript source consulted was the Peter Pitchlynn Papers of the T. Thomas Gilcrease Museum, Tulsa, Oklahoma. Newspapers used were the *Hagerstown Torchlight, Williamsport Banner, Niles' Register, BedfordGazette, Frederick Herald, Hagerstown Mail,* and *National Intelligencer.* Contemporary writings on canals were extracted from Frederick Marryat, *Diary in America* (1839), and Frances Trollope, *Domestic Manners of the Americans* (1832). The key secondary text on the C&O remains Walter S. Sanderlin, *The Great National Project: A History of the Chesapeake and Ohio Canal,* The Johns Hopkins University Studies in Historical and Political Science, Vol. 64 (Baltimore: The Johns Hopkins University Press, 1946). Other canal histories utilized were Thomas F. Hahn, "The Paw Paw Tunnel," in *The Best of American Canals,* No. 1, edited by William H. Shank (York: The American Canal and Transportation Center, 1980), p. 25; Richard B. Morris, "Andrew Jackson, Strikebreaker," *American Historical Review,* Vol. 55 (October 1949), pp. 54–68; W. David Baird, "Violence along the Chesapeake & Ohio Canal: 1839," *Maryland Historical Magazine,* Vol. 66 (summer 1971), pp. 121–134; David Grimsted, "Ante-bellum Labor: Violence, Strike and Communal Arbitration," *Journal of Social History,* Vol. 19 (fall 1985), pp. 5–19.

Portions of this article first appeared in "Shovel and Shamrock: Irish Workers and Labor Violence in the Digging of the Chesapeake and Ohio Canal," *Labor History,* Vol. 30 (fall 1989), pp. 489–517; "Evil Humors and Ardent Spirits: The Rough Culture of Canal Construction Laborers," *Journal of American History,* Vol. 79 (March 1993), pp. 1397–1428; and *Common Labour: Workers and the Digging of North American Canals, 1780–1860* (New York: Cambridge University Press, 1993). These portions have been reproduced with permission of the publishers, whom I would like to thank.

12

CELIA: SLAVERY AND SEXUAL EXPLOITATION

MELTON McLAURIN

Celia, the central character in Melton McLaurin's story, lived a short life—less than twenty years—that has all the elements of a tragedy. Because this young slave woman defended herself by murdering her master, her story became part of the public record, at least partially recoverable through diligent research in judicial and census records. Melton McLaurin has carefully pursued all the fragmented written documentation of her story and attempted to reconstruct it for us. On one level it shows what a remarkable young woman Celia was, and what an unusual one to take such violent action against an oppression that had no possible redress except in death. Although Celia escaped her master's exploitation, she herself was put to death for it.

Although Celia's response to her sexual exploitation is understandable, it was not one chosen by most black women in slavery. Perhaps the greatest tragedy revealed by Celia's story is that so many thousands of slave women regularly endured such treatment. If they thought about responding violently as Celia did (and it seems likely that they would have done so), perhaps they reminded themselves that such retribution would leave their children without a mother, their lovers or husbands without comfort, and their parents without a child. Killing a white master was almost like suicide, for it would bring certain death on the gallows. So Celia's story is fascinating because it tells the story of a woman who made an unusually dangerous choice, but it also reveals the daily suffering endured by many such women whose responses were quite different.

Celia's story also raises a host of issues about the human dimension of the institution of slavery, about relationships between people within a plantation household. True, the farm where Celia was enslaved was not a large plantation on which dozens of other slaves labored as well, but it raises similar questions about how this small group of people, both black and white, existed on such an intimate but unequal basis. The plantations and farms of the South were frequently isolated from urban centers and from each other. Wives of plantation masters, for example, rarely socialized with women on other plantations and were forced to rely for company on their daughters or their women slaves. White children played with black slave children and grew up with them as friends and playmates. Indeed, most white children had black women as their primary caregivers, women who were forced to abandon the care of their own children to care for the masters'. Masters of the plantation or farm were the most likely of its residents to travel on a regular basis, but when they were at home, they confronted daily the black slave women, with whom they at one time or another had sexual relations, often more accurately described as rape. Perhaps most difficult to understand are those daily confrontations with their own half black, half white children—children who would always be slaves and who might well be sold away to an unknown future.

Although Celia's story does not provide answers to all these questions about the human relations within the slave system, it does allow us to think more concretely, using evidence from this one probably typical household, about the way that individual actors caught up in such a terrible system chose to play out their roles. This is one story in which the facts are not as important as the window they open onto the emotions and feelings experienced by all those involved in Southern slavery.

On October 9, 1855, Sheriff William Snell delivered Celia, a nineteen-year-old slave already the mother of two children and probably pregnant at the time, to the Callaway County courthouse in Fulton, Missouri, to stand trial for murder. For an unlettered teenage slave girl from an isolated Missouri farm, the courtroom must have been a terrifying and hostile place. The courts of Missouri were not of her world. She knew about them only what her lawyers would have told her in preparation for her trial. Alone except for her lawyers, she faced the unavoidable stares of whites in the courtroom, among them the family and friends of the white man she stood accused of murdering. Celia's trial, its causes and consequences, confront us with the daily realities of slavery rather than with the abstract theories about the workings of that institution.

What we know of Celia's story begins with her purchase by Robert Newsom, who had migrated with his family from Virginia to Missouri in 1819. Sixty years of age in 1850, Newsom had become a prosperous Callaway County farmer. A widower, he lived with his family on an 800-acre farm, about half of which was cultivated and on which he raised primarily corn, wheat, and a variety of livestock, including swine, cattle, sheep, and horses. His family consisted of two grown sons—Harry, thirty-seven, and David, seventeen—and a grown daughter, Virginia Waynescot, thirty-one, who had three children of her own—Coffee, six; Thomas, four; and Amelia, two. Of Virginia's absent husband, there is no record. Also in the family was another daughter, Mary, fourteen. In 1850 Robert Newsom owned five slaves, all male, who helped provide the labor his large farm required.

In many ways Robert Newsom was typical of Callaway County's white residents. Located on the Missouri River in east central Missouri, Callaway was a prosperous county, its agrarian economy dominated by farmers rather than planters. Major crops were corn, small grains, livestock, and a wide variety of produce. Slaveholding in Callaway was widespread. By 1850 slaves constituted approximately 40 percent of the county's population. By the end of the next decade, Callaway ranked fourth among Missouri's counties in the number of slaves held. While many farmers held slaves (in fact, over half the county's white families did so); few individuals held large numbers of slaves. Rather, slaveholding patterns reflected the size of the average farm, and the majority of farms had less than 70 acres in cultivation. The average number of slaves held per master was quite low, something less than five.

Fulton, the county seat, reaped the benefits of the county's agricultural prosperity and enjoyed phenomenal growth during the decade of the 1850s. In 1850 the Presbyterians established Fulton Female Seminary in the town, and a year later they opened Fulton College, which was renamed Westminster College in 1853. The legislature placed the State Lunatic Asylum and the Missouri School for the Deaf in Fulton, and both institutions were operational by 1851. By 1855, possessed of the county courthouse, two Presbyterian colleges, and two state institutions, Fulton was a budding metropolis of some twenty stores and five churches, with a population of 1200 people, among them, according to a proud citizen of the era, "many old Kentucky and some Virginia families."

Although he was a prosperous farmer, surrounded by family and respected by his neighbors, Robert Newsom evidently missed female companionship. His wife had died sometime prior to the 1850 census, exactly when and by what cause we do not know. Newsom decided to remedy this deficiency in his life, and sometime in 1850 or early 1851, he traveled to neighboring Audrain County, where he purchased a young slave named Celia. Wasting no time in establishing the duties of his newest possession, he raped the fourteen-year-old girl during the trip home.

Although Newsom established Celia as the family cook, she continued to be sexually exploited by him, serving as a virtual concubine. Her special status was not without its material compensations. In return for her forced companionship, Newsom rewarded Celia with her own cabin, a one-story brick structure with a fireplace and stone hearth, surrounded by cherry and pear trees. During the five years of her residence on the Newsom farm, Celia bore two children fathered by her master, thus adding to Newsom's holdings in human chattel.

Celia's presence and relationship with her master seem not to have disrupted the Newsom household or to have threatened Robert Newsom's status within the community. Over the next five years after her arrival, little changed at the Newsom farm. Sons Harry and David married and moved with their wives to farms close by to their father's home. Virginia and her children continued to live with her father, as did Mary. There is no evidence to suggest that Newsom's standing in the community was compromised in any way or that his sexual exploitation of Celia altered Newsom's relationship with his adult children.

Robert Newsom's position as the patriarch supreme might have continued to go unchallenged. The adult sons undoubtedly expected to receive an inheritance from him, and it is reasonable to assume that he had helped both sons obtain their own homestead. Virginia, without husband and with no wealth of her own, was dependent on her father for her livelihood and for the support of her three children. Mary, barely older than her niece and nephews, was equally dependent on her father. At this juncture, however, basic human emotions touched off a chain of events that forced many of Callaway County's residents to face the harsh realities of slavery.

At some time during her stay on the Newsom farm, just when is unclear, Celia took a lover. George was his name, and he was yet another of Newsom's slaves. We know little about George, nothing of his age, his origins, his tasks and duties, or the length of time he had been owned by Newsom. We do know that his relationship with Celia was long-standing. It is probable that George was on the farm from the moment Celia arrived, since in 1850 Newsom owned four adult male slaves whose ages ranged from eighteen to thirty-one. We also know that in the spring of 1855, Celia again conceived, this time without certain knowledge of the father.

Aware that the child Celia carried might be his, George could no longer tolerate Newsom's sexual exploitation of Celia. Yet he could do nothing to prevent it without revealing his relationship to Celia and endangering both her life and his own. Rather than confronting Newsom himself, George placed the burden of action upon Celia. He informed her that "he would have nothing more to do with her if she did not quit the old man." How she was to accomplish this George evidently did not explain.

Given George's ultimatum, Celia adopted the least dangerous method of complying with her lover's wishes. She chose not to speak to Newsom directly but to appeal to the adult female members of the family, whom she implored to prevent their father from having intercourse with her. Whether the women believed her we do not know, but it is difficult to imagine that they were not already aware of the relationship between Celia and their father. Nor do we know if they attempted to intervene on Celia's behalf, although it is doubtful, for they were nearly as dependent on their father as was the servant who appealed to them. What is certain is that at this point a thirty-six-year-old mother of three and her unmarried nineteen-year-old sister were forced to confront what recent scholarship has shown to be for women both white and black one of slavery's oldest and most painful moral dilemmas. To do nothing meant that Celia would continue to be sexually exploited by their father. To confront their father meant threatening their material well-being and, in Virginia's case, the well-being of her children.

Whether or not his daughters attempted to intervene on Celia's behalf, Newsom's behavior did not change. At some point, driven by Newsom's continued sexual advances and George's demand, Celia directly confronted her master. Faced with rejection by her lover, she begged Newsom to leave her alone, using the excuse that she had been sick for the last few months as a result of her pregnancy. Newsom replied that "he was coming to her cabin that night." Desperately seeking some means of complying with George's ultimatum, a determined Celia threatened to hurt her master if he did so.

On the night of June 23, 1855, Robert Newsom had dinner with his family. After the meal Newsom read a book until the other family members retired. Then he left the house and walked the sixty steps to Celia's cabin, which he entered. Inside the cabin he was again confronted by Celia. Once more she begged him "to quit forcing her while she was sick," and once again Newsom refused. When he moved toward her, Celia grabbed a large stick she had obtained earlier in the afternoon for the purpose of defending herself should Newsom ignore her warnings. In an act of desperation and panic, she raised the oak stick above her head and brought it crashing down upon the face of the advancing Newsom. Staggered by the blow, the old man "sunk down on a stool or towards the floor," groaning and throwing up his hands as if to catch Celia. Afraid an angered Newsom would harm her, Celia struck her master again, hard, across the head, and he fell dead to the floor.

For an hour Celia sat stunned, watching the unmoving body of her master. She then decided to dispose of the corpse in a manner which would make it impossible to determine if Newsom had come to her cabin that night. She hit upon a plan both simple and ironic. She decided to cremate the body in her stone fireplace. Using dried hogshead staves which were piled outside her cabin and lightwood saved for fires during damp weather, she built a roaring blaze. She then doubled up Newsom's body, rolled it into the flames, and for the next four hours stoked the fire. The body consumed, Celia sifted through Newsom's ashes and removed the pieces of bone which had not burned. The smaller of these she crushed to bits on the hearth; the larger ones she hid beneath the hearthstones. Once she had obliterated Newsom's remains, she removed the last trace of her master's presence, scouring his blood from the cabin floor, and then went to bed.

The following morning, alarmed at Newsom's disappearance, the family began to search for him. They looked first in the fields and woods and then in the coves along the banks of the creek which bordered the farm. Celia, meanwhile, had spied Newsom's twelve-year-old grandson, Coffee Waynescot, perched in the

FIENDISH MURDER.

Correspondence of the Missouri Republican.

FULTON, June 25, 1855.

A most violent act was committed on the person of ROBERT NEWSOM, of this county, on Saturday night last, 23d inst., at his residence, eight miles South of this. He was murdered by one of his own slaves, a negro woman, in the kitchen—supposed, some time during the night—and his body entirely consumed by fire in the kitchen fire-place, and the ashes taken up next morning and deposited in the back yard. His body appears, so far as discovery can be made, to have been entirely consumed, except a few small bones, found in the pile of ashes, including a part of his skull bone and the extremities of some of his fingers. The murder was committed without any sufficient cause, so far as I can hear. Mr. NEWSOM was an old citizen of the county, about sixty years of age, and very active and energetic in his business. He possessed a valuable farm, and had accumulated a very handsome estate. The woman confessed to the murder on Sunday (yesterday) evening, and is in the hands of the law.

LATER.—Mr. NEWSOM, when the family retired, was left at his table reading a newspaper. None of the family heard any disturbance during the night, although the kitchen was within a few feet of the dwelling. He was absent at breakfast on Sunday morning, (yesterday) and the family, for the first time, became alarmed, and called in the neighbors, who continued to look for him until the afternoon, when suspicion fell on the woman, who confessed, and showed the ash pile, where the remnant of bones were found. The ash pile had not before been noticed, and would not have been, if she had not directed attention to it.

Report of Robert Newsom's death carried in the *Missouri Republican* (St. Louis) June 28, 1855. "Fiendish" was a term frequently used by the press of the nineteenth-century South to describe violent crimes committed by blacks. (St. Louis Mercentile Library)

limbs of one of the cherry trees that surrounded her cabin. In an act that revealed the depth of her hatred for her white owner and his family, Celia promised the boy "two dozen walnuts if I would carry the ashes out. I said good lick." And so young Coffee scooped his grandfather's ashes from Celia's fireplace, inevitably inhaling some of the tiny particles that would have swirled and danced in the cabin air, and then unknowingly carried his grandfather's remains in a bucket and "put them out alongside the path that led to the creek."

By this time neighbors had been summoned to join the search, and the family, beginning to suspect foul play, had identified George as the most likely suspect. Among the searchers was William Powell, a yeoman farmer who was himself the master of two slaves. Evidently told by Virginia and Mary of George's relationship with Celia, Powell interrogated George, accusing him of harming his master. Faced with these accusations, George chose to protect himself rather than Celia and denied any knowledge of Newsom's disappearance. It was a predictable response to the moral dilemma he faced, for, as we will see, Powell probably threatened George's life if he did not tell all that he knew. George also indicated that Celia probably knew about whatever fate had befallen Newsom. From George's statements, Powell concluded that Celia knew Newsom's fate and that it was likely that "he had been destroyed in the Negro cabin."

Accompanied by several others, Powell confronted Celia with George's accusations. She at first denied any knowledge of Newsom's disappearance, so Powell threatened to take her children from her unless she confessed. When she still refused, Powell threatened to hang her. At that point Celia confessed that she had killed Newsom and revealed the manner in which she had disposed of the body. Her confession resulted in an immediate search of the cabin and grounds, and the searchers soon discovered Newsom's charred bones beneath the hearth. From the ashes which Coffee Waynescot had dumped by the pathway the search party recovered yet more bone fragments and some metal buttons that Mary Newsom had recently sewn on her father's coat. George, who joined the search for evidence, contributed the fire-blackened knife of his former master.

The following day the township's two justices of the peace, at least one of whom was a slave owner, examined witnesses, issued subpoenas, and arranged for an inquest by a coroner's jury. A day later, six men of the township gathered at the Newsom farm to hear the evidence presented by the justices. Within hours they returned an indictment for murder, and Celia was carted off to the county jail in Fulton to await her trial, which was set for the ninth of October.

As often happened after other acts of slave violence, rumors of slave insurrection swept Callaway County, an occurrence which of itself speaks to the uneasy conscience of slaveholders. The Newsom family and others continued to believe that at the very least George had been involved in the murder, despite his continued denials. Some ten days after her original incarceration, Colonel Jefferson Jones, a prominent Fulton attorney, was sent to interrogate Celia to determine if she had acted alone or with accomplices.

Jones, who owned three domestic servants, questioned Celia repeatedly about George's involvement in the crime. In an effort to get Celia to implicate George in Newsom's murder, Jones informed Celia that "George had run off" and advised her that "she might as well tell if he had anything to do with killing the old man." This information must have come as a psychological blow to Celia, even though she knew George had previously implicated her in Newsom's death. Yet despite Jones's repeated efforts to get her to acknowledge that George had helped her kill Newsom, Celia refused to implicate him. Throughout the interrogation she insisted that she had acted alone and on the spur of the moment and that she herself, without aid, had disposed of the body. To Jones's assertion that it was George who had "struck the old man from behind," Celia replied emphatically that George had not struck Newsom, knew nothing of his death, and was not at her cabin at any time on the night on which Newsom was killed. Given her desperate situation and Jones's obvious desire for her to implicate George, Celia's refusal to do so is a remarkable expression of her devotion to him.

At this juncture, Missouri's slave code brought John Jameson, Colonel Jones's uncle, into the case. In Missouri, as in other Southern states, a slave accused of a capital crime was entitled to a court-appointed attorney. To defend Celia the court chose Jameson, a prominent Fulton attorney, a former speaker of the Missouri House of Representatives, a three-term former Democratic congressman, and the father of four children, three of them girls under the age of sixteen. The congressional career of the fifty-five-year-old Jameson had been less than mediocre. His chief concern in each of his three nonconsecutive terms seems to have been maintaining a western military force adequate to prevent Indian attacks, a preoccupation that resulted from his brief service as a noncombatant in the Black Hawk War. He had the reputation of occasionally imbibing "a little too freely," and his professional contemporaries judged him "not profound." He deplored "the labor and research" of his profession. As a jury advocate, however, his colleagues deemed him "not excelled by anyone in central Missouri, and by few if any, in the State."

Possibly because of Jameson's distaste for the mundane chores of legal research, circuit court judge William A. Hall appointed two assistants. Nathan Kouns, a college-educated twenty-two-year-old, had been admitted to the Missouri bar earlier that year. Hall also appointed to the defense another lawyer beginning his practice, twenty-six-year-old Isaac Boulware. Both young men came from prominent Callaway slaveholding families; Boulware was the son of one of Fulton's wealthiest men and largest slaveholders.

Judge Hall's appointment of such a prominent lead attorney to defend Celia seems surprising, unless the issue of slavery in the larger society is considered. During 1855 between June, the month Newsom was murdered, and October, the date of Celia's trial, Missourians were involved in a heated debate over slavery, one forced on them by the Kansas-Nebraska Act. The passage of that act, overwhelmingly favored by Missourians, had further divided Missouri's constantly feuding Democrats. One faction, led by Thomas Hart Benton, who sought to regain his seat in the United States Senate and control of the party, opposed the further expansion of slavery. Senator David Atchison, a supporter of the Kansas-Nebraska Act who was fast making a reputation as a pro-slavery spokesman, led the other. The act also split Missouri's Whig forces, but to a lesser degree, and Alexandre Doniphan, who was decidedly pro-slavery, retained the support of the majority of his party to replace Atchison when his term expired in 1855. The

Benton-Atchinson-Doniphan Senate contest so divided the state legislature that no man could obtain a majority, and the seat was left vacant until 1857.

This struggle within the legislature merely reflected the intense debate over slavery that swept Missouri when Kansas had been opened to settlement. Pro-

---

FULTON, Mo., July 29, 1855.

Editor Missouri Republican:

In your issue of July 3d, headad "Fiendish Murder," and dated Fulton, June 25th ult., an article in regard to said murder needs correction. It reads thus: "Mr. NEWSOM, when the family retired, was left reading a newspaper, at his table." *So far correct.* "None of the family heard any disturbance during the night," (correct) "although the kitchen was within a few feet of the dwelling." Now, I suppose the kitchen above alluded to is intended to mean the negro cabin where the process of burning and destroying the body of the murdered man took place. It is therefore incorrect. The negro cabin where the burning of the body of Mr. NEWSOM took place, is distant from the dwelling about fifty yards, and surrounded by cherry and pear trees. One door, only half fronting the dwelling, and no windows, the building of brick, one story and low. This, although unintentional on the part of your Fulton correspondent, is calculated to give a wrong impression to the public mind, and I hope, in justice to the family, you will make the correction.

Yours,   H. NEWSOM.

Harry Newsom's response to the *Missouri Republican*'s story on his father's death. Note that Newsom is concerned only with assuring readers that the family knew nothing of the incident and the formal manner in which he refers to his father. His letter appeared in the August 2, 1855 edition of the *Republican*. (St. Louis Mercantile Library)

slavery forces were incensed by the efforts of the Massachusetts, later New England, Emmigrant Aid Society to finance the settlement of free-soil farmers in Kansas. Increasingly, Missourians turned to violence to stop what they considered an abolitionist invasion which threatened both their security and their slave property. By the end of 1854, slaveholders in the state's western counties had organized associations to protect their slave property and begun a campaign of intimidation against those suspected of abolitionist sentiment. Kansas became the most heated issue in the Missouri legislative session of early 1855, and the press joined what was rapidly becoming a general furor. Two days before Celia killed her master, Missouri newspapers warned their readers that abolitionists in Lawrence, Kansas, planned to forcefully overthrow the official pro-slavery territorial legislature and to steal Negroes in Kansas and then invade and colonize Missouri. By August, more vigilance committees and patrols had been formed in some of Missouri's counties with large slave populations, especially those counties near the Kansas border.

Predictably, reports of violence against abolitionists and those considered abolitionists soon appeared. In some communities suspected abolitionists were jailed; in others they were physically assaulted. A group of pro-slavery Missourians almost killed an abolitionist minister from Maine who attempted to reach Kansas aboard a river steamer. In Morley, Missouri, a group of "Atchinson ruffians" broke into a church and attacked and threatened to kill a minister of the northern branch of the Methodist Church, which like other Protestant denominations had been divided by the slavery issue. Only the congregation's pleas for mercy saved him.

In early July James Shannon, president of the University of Missouri, contributed to the increasing vehemence of the slavery debate. Prompted by the desire to prevent abolitionist teachings from corrupting his students, Shannon sent the state's newspapers an emotional defense of slavery which most editors published, even though some opposed his views. Shannon predicted that "unless the swelling tide of anti-slavery fanaticism be beaten back," the Union would be destroyed within five years. Slavery, he continued, was "sanctioned by the Bible, the Laws of nature, and the Constitution of the United States." Shannon's statement, which was also picked up by the abolitionist press, created a sensation in Missouri. Some hailed Shannon's wisdom; others saw him as a bigoted fanatic.

Its timing suggests that Shannon issued the letter to support the efforts of some of Missouri's most influential advocates of slavery to promote a pro-slavery convention scheduled in Lexington on the twelfth of July. Opponents portrayed the convention, composed primarily of representatives from counties with large slave populations, as an effort to promote Atchinson's Senate candidacy, although both he and Doniphan were invited and attended. Convention proponents saw it as a response to Northern efforts to "abolitionize Kansas and nullify federal slave policy," thereby threatening "the rights of the Southern States and the welfare of the Union."

In session from July 12 to July 14, the convention produced a rather predictable set of resolutions which upheld states' rights in all areas pertaining to slavery and condemned the efforts of northern states to deny admission of additional slave states to the Union. They also expressed the fears of Missouri slaveholders that their property would be threatened if abolitionists controlled Kansas. Finally, the resolutions called upon the people of Missouri to employ all "suitable and just" actions to eliminate this threat. As was to be expected, the work of the convention met with a mixed reception. Those who had favored its calling praised the resolutions. Its critics, however, saw in the resolutions "treasonable designs."

Under such circumstances, it is reasonable to assume that Judge Hall appointed John Jameson as Celia's lead attorney precisely because Jameson had not become involved in the debates about slavery then sweeping the state. Jameson was a respected attorney, a well-known and admired political figure. He had never taken a strong public stance on slavery, although he was a slaveholder, the owner of at least two domestic servants. In addition, as the father of three daughters, he might have been considered sympathetic toward the accused. Yet Newsom's continued relationship with Celia, despite the presence of two adult daughters in his household, indicates that a Southern male's attitude toward the sexual exploitation of female slaves was not necessarily influenced by any concern about the possible effects such actions might have on his daughters.

From the point of view of a judge seeking to prevent Celia's trial from being used in the slavery debates, Jameson seemed the perfect choice. If this was the judge's reasoning, he overlooked a significant factor in Jameson's background. Jameson had recently undertaken the study of theology and become a minister in the Christian Church. As events would prove, he took seriously the moral dilemmas of slavery which were so crucial to Celia's case.

Celia's trial was held on a single day: October 9, 1855. Jameson and the defense did not dispute the facts of the murder. Jefferson Jones, William Powell, Harry Newsom, and Virginia and Coffee Waynescot testified for the state. The five witnesses related the story of Newsom's murder, with heavy emphasis on actions and little concern for motive. Celia's confession, signed with an "x," was also entered as evidence by the state. In his cross-examinations, however, Jameson focused on motive, which was the key to his defense. In his cross-examination of both Virginia and Coffee Waynescot, he established the fact that Newsom had not slept in his bed on the night of the murder. He also obtained from Virginia the admission that Celia had been ill for some time. From both Powell and Jones, he obtained testimony that Newsom had habitually forced Celia to engage in sexual relations with him and that she had begged him to cease doing so, using her illness as an excuse. He also obtained from Powell testimony that Celia had not meant to kill Newsom when she struck him, only to prevent him from having intercourse with her. Powell's statement about intent underscored similar testimony Jones had given while testifying for the prosecution.

Jameson continued to emphasize motive with the witnesses he called, although he first made an unsuccessful attempt to challenge the state's physical evidence. He then produced his star witness, Thomas Shoatman, another of Newsom's neighbors, who had been present in July when Jones had questioned Celia. Like Powell and Jones, Shoatman testified that Celia had not meant to kill Newsom, only "to keep him from having sexual intercourse with her." However, he added that after Celia first struck Newsom, the old man did not stop his advances. Rather, he testified, "the reason she gave for striking him the second blow was that he threw his hands up towards her to catch her, that she was afraid he would catch her."

Clearly Jameson was attempting to establish a case of self-defense for his client with Shoatman's testimony. While Southern states recognized the right of a slave to use force to repel a threat on her life, such threats were difficult to prove. As a slave, Celia was barred by Missouri law from testifying against a white man, even a dead one. Thus self-defense could be established only if a white person were willing to testify in Celia's behalf, and no white person had witnessed Newsom's death.

Faced with the difficulty of proving self-defense, Jameson adopted a novel and daring defense strategy. He contended that Celia possessed the legal right to use deadly force in the defense of her honor. The audacity of such an argument is revealed by the fact that no Southern state made a crime of the rape of a slave by any male, black or white, free or slave. In Missouri, as in most other Southern states, sexual assault on slave women by white males was considered trespass, not rape, and an owner could hardly be charged with trespassing upon his own property.

Jameson's assertion that Celia was justified in killing Newsom in defense of her honor depended on a unique interpretation of Missouri's general statutes. He argued that two general statutes applied to Celia's case, although she was a slave and as such did not enjoy the rights and privileges the free population held. The first made it a crime to take "any woman" against her will. The term "any woman," Jameson argued, applied to Celia, despite her slave status. The second specifically stated that even first-degree murder was justifiable if it was committed "in resisting a person attempting to commit a felony on the individual, or in the individual's house." If these statutes applied to slaves, then Celia was doubly protected by them.

Jameson's entire defense rested on the instructions that he requested that the presiding judge give the jury. His instructions allowed the jury to find Celia not guilty if they found that she had acted to prevent Newsom from having sexual relations with her, or if they found that she had not intended to kill him but acted in the heat of passion. The instructions he proposed specifically requested the jury to acquit Celia if they found the pertinent general statutes "to embrace slave women as well as free white women." Each of the instructions based on this concept Judge William Hall refused to deliver to the jury. Instead, he complied with the request of the state's attorney to deliver a set of instructions that made it clear that if the jurors found that Celia had killed Newsom, for whatever reason, they were to return a verdict of guilty.

While Judge Hall's refusal of Jameson's requested instructions to acquit if Celia had acted to protect her life is unusual, his denial of Jameson's instruction to acquit because of Newsom's sexual assault was practically a foregone conclusion. Had he done otherwise, he would have extended the protection of the general statutes to Missouri's slave population, in effect nullifying what one historian has identified as a primary characteristic of slave codes: the effort "to confine the content of slave law to the situation of slaves alone." Jameson's contention that the state's general statutes on rape applied equally to slaves and whites was, therefore, a much more radical concept than that advanced by proponents of Dred Scott, whose celebrated case was even then making its way through the courts. At least from the perspective of Missouri, the central issue in the Scott case was that of comity. The United States Supreme Court would uphold this view in 1857. Scott's contention that his residency in a free territory made him a free man entitled to the protection of the federal Constitution did not threaten slaveholders' actual control over their individual slaves. Jameson's claim that a state's general statutes on rape applied to the female slave population did, by essentially transferring control of the slave woman's sexuality, including reproduction, from the slave master to the female slave.

Jameson's assertion that a slave woman was entitled under the law to resist the sexual advances of a master, to the extent of using deadly force, also challenged a fundamental premise of the sexual dynamics of slavery. Its radical nature is revealed by the fact that recorded cases of rape against female slaves in the South are practically nonexistent. While it was possible to charge a male slave with raping a female slave, such cases were extremely rare and convictions rarer. Criminal charges against whites for raping slaves simply were not lodged. A search of the most extensive compendium of slave cases reveals not a single case in which a white male was charged with raping a slave, although cases of male slaves charged with raping white women are easily found. Yet the literature on slavery makes it abundantly clear that white males regularly abused female slaves sexually, with one scholar estimating that over one quarter of all female slaves were sexually exploited. Thus Jameson, in his requested jury instructions, threatened a basic assumption in the actual operations of the institution of chattel slavery: that white men enjoyed unrestrained access to slave women, as well as property rights to the offspring of such unions.

Denied the ability to acquit on grounds of self-defense, the jury returned a guilty verdict, and Judge Hall sentenced Celia to be hanged on the sixteenth of November. Jameson immediately moved for a retrial, a motion the judge denied. Jameson then appealed the case to the Missouri Supreme Court, which had just begun its fall session in St. Louis. According to Missouri law, it was within Judge Hall's jurisdiction to issue a stay order to prevent the possibility that Celia would be executed before the Supreme Court could consider her appeal. The current debate over slavery may have influenced the judge to see the sentence executed quickly, just as it is probable that he believed Celia received an impartial and proper trial, according to existing statutes. Whatever his reasons for it, and none are recorded, Judge Hall's decision was fraught with moral overtones, the more so since he had previously revealed to a daughter his fears that a female domestic slave had attempted to poison him. He refused to issue the requested stay of execution order. Celia, meanwhile, had delivered a stillborn child, an event that removed the last possible obstacle to her execution being carried out as originally ordered. Only the Missouri Supreme Court could intervene.

Hall's refusal to issue a stay of execution order placed Celia's fate at the mercy of the speed with which the Supreme Court heard appeals. As the date of her execution approached and no word had arrived from St. Louis, some Callaway residents took a desperate gamble. On the night of November 11, five days before her scheduled execution, Celia "escaped" from jail. If not involved in Celia's escape, Jameson was certainly aware of it, for in a personal appeal to the Supreme Court dated December 6, he left little doubt that her escape was arranged. Celia had escaped execution, he wrote, only as a "consequence of her escape from prison, or in other words, taken out by some one. . . ." He explained that she was recaptured well after the original date of execution but that another day, December 21, had been set by the trial court. Worried that Celia might yet be executed before the Supreme Court could rule on her appeal, he urged the justices to review the record of Celia's case and to issue a stay of execution order "until the case can be tried in the Supreme Court in January next." He admitted "more than ordinary interest in the case" because he believed Celia acted only "to prevent a forced sexual intercourse on the part of Newsom." He also noted that "the greater portion of the community here are much interested in her behalf." Jameson's admission that Celia was broken out of her jail cell to prevent her execution before the Supreme Court could act is further supported by the fact that Matt, a black man also under sentence of death who escaped with her, was "returned" the morning following the escape.

On December 14, the Missouri Supreme Court responded to Jameson's plea for action, but not as he had hoped. It ruled that "upon examination of the record and proceedings of the Circuit Court of Callaway County in the above case, it is thought to refuse the prayer of the petitioner. It is therefore ordered by this Court that a stay of execution in this case be refused."

This decision sealed Celia's fate. After a brief period of freedom which raises a number of questions for which the record supplies no answers, Celia was recaptured and returned to custody by none other than Harry Newsom. Whatever her circumstances in that brief period, it is a reasonable assumption that only concern for her children, also the children of Robert Newsom, could have drawn her back to the farm of the master she murdered. On the afternoon of December 21, she was brought to the gallows. There she made her final statement, insisting once more that she alone had killed Newsom. Again she maintained that she had not

> HANGING A NEGRESS.—CELIA, a negress, who has been under sentence of death since the 14th of October, for the murder of her master, ROBT. NEWSOM, in June last, was executed near this place on the 21st ult. The evening previous to her execution, and while under the gallows, she made what she said was a full confession of the crime. She has, at various times, implicated several persons; but, by her dying confession, all of them are exonerated from any participation in the murder. She said that on the evening of the occurrence she procured a large, stout stick, (much larger and heavier than that before described by her,) and took a position behind the door, leaving it slightly ajar; that her master came to the cabin, pushed the door open and entered; as soon as he entered she struck him with the stick, felling him to the ground. She did not, at first, intend to kill him, but she said, "as soon as I struck him the Devil got into me, and I struck him with the stick until he was dead, and then rolled him in the fire and burnt him up." She denied that any one assisted her, or aided or abetted in any way. She was hung at 2½ o'clock, on Friday, 21st of December last. Thus has closed one of the most horrible tragedies ever enacted in our county. —*Fulton (Mo.) Telegraph, Jan. 4.*

The story of Celia's execution as carried in the *New York Times* of January 16, 1856. Copied from the *Fulton Telegraph* of January 4, 1856, it is the only extant reference to Celia's death. (*The New York Times*)

intended to do so. According to a Fulton reporter, she claimed that "as soon as I struck him the Devil got in me and I struck him with the stick until he was dead and then rolled him in the fireplace and burned him up." At 2:30 P.M. the trap was sprung, and Celia fell to her death. The reporter ended his story of Celia's execution with a final note of unintended irony, which but underscored the nature of slavery as a moral dilemma. "Thus closed," he wrote, "one of the most horrible tragedies ever enacted in our county."

Where Celia's remains are interred, much like the events of her life before her purchase by Robert Newsom, is not recorded. Nor are there any records of what became of her children. For a time they probably remained the property of Robert Newsom's legal heirs. It is unlikely that they would have long remained in the Newsom family, for their presence would have been a bitter reminder of the tragic events of the summer of 1855, although there is a possibility that the nine-year-old slave girl Harry Newsom owned in 1860 was Celia's child and his half sister. Surviving Celia by little more than a year, John Jameson died suddenly in 1857 and was laid to rest in the family cemetery in Fulton. Robert Newsom was buried beside his wife in the family cemetery on the farm they had carved from the Missouri wilderness. His gravestone still stands in a field just off a rural road in Callaway County.

AN INTERPRETATION

What, in the end, does this tragic case tell us about slavery and the South's defense of it? At one level it gives us an excellent example of what Thomas Jefferson and others recognized as an inevitable consequence of slavery, the brutalizing of both slave and master. The patriarchal nature of Southern society, combined with the almost absolute control of the master over his human chattel, resulted in widespread sexual exploitation of female slaves. Such exploitation violated even the professed code of the male patriarch, which portrayed the patriarch as the protector of all members of his extended family, including his slaves. It demeaned basic human relationships between male and female slaves and created underlying tensions within many slaveholding families.

Celia's trial also demonstrates how the law was used in the antebellum South to protect the rights of slaveholders. Southerners insisted that the law uphold the master's property rights, while recognizing that as human beings slaves possessed certain rights, including an inviolable right to life. Yet as Celia's case demonstrates, the inevitable conflicts between even the recognized human rights of the slaves and the property rights of masters, with rare exceptions, were settled in favor of the masters, just as the law was designed to control the behavior of slaves, not of their masters. Celia's trial also shows how the South used the law to create the illusion that slaves possessed certain human rights, an illusion which served to ease the conscience of white Southerners and refute abolitionists' charges of slave mistreatment. Procedurally, Celia's trial was correct, yet procedure prevented any consideration of Newsom's violation of Celia's most basic human rights.

At yet another level, Celia's case demonstrates the inevitability of personal moral decisions about slaves and the treatment they received. Her story is a study of what the historian Charles Sellers referred to as "the fundamental moral anxiety" that slavery produced. This fundamental moral anxiety and the moral dilemmas that produced it were at the very heart of the institution of slavery. Try as they might, Southern whites, both slaveholders and nonslaveholders alike, could never completely escape the moral dilemmas of the peculiar institution. Abstract defenses of slavery were always possible, yet again and again the routine operations of the system gave them the lie.

Celia's case also dramatically illustrates the impossibility of divorcing such local incidents from the national debate over slavery. It is a safe assumption that for some of Fulton's residents in the summer and fall of 1855, Celia's trial and execution lent greater significance to the political debates on slavery then raging across the state and in the nation.

The major significance of the case and of the thousands of other such personal moral dramas which were played out in the South, however, was their long-term effect on the viability of the institution of slavery. The South eventually sought to solve the political problems of slavery by secession, which it also saw as the answer to a variety of problems of an agrarian economy based on slave labor. And to some degree, stung by abolitionists' attacks, the South began an effort to reform slavery, to remove or control the more flagrant abuses of slavery, although extending protection from rape to female slaves was not among the reforms proposed. Secession might well have solved a Southern nation's immediate political and economic problems. It could not have solved, however, the moral dilemma inherent in slavery. So long as the South retained its cultural links with Western society and its values, slavery, because of its moral dimensions, would have remained a cancer eating away at the foundations of whatever society an independent South might have attempted to construct.

Sources: An in-depth study of this topic may be found in Melton McLaurin's book *Celia: A Slave* (Athens: University of Georgia Press, 1987). Also see A. Leon Higginbotham Jr., "Race, Sex, Education and Missouri Jurisprudence: *Shelly v. Kraimer* in Historical Perspective," *Washington University Law Quarterly,* Vol. 67 (1989), p. 673; and Hugh P. Williamson, "Document: The State of Missouri against Celia, A Slave," *Midwest Journal,* Vol. 8 (spring/fall 1956). Newspaper articles include those in the *Missouri Republican* (St. Louis) of June 28 and August 2, 1855, and the *New York Times* of January 16, 1856, p. 2, col. 6.

13

THE BIRTH OF A STATE: WEST VIRGINIA AND THE CIVIL WAR

JOHN ALEXANDER WILLIAMS

"I thought the day of sectionalism had passed!" exclaimed a delegate when politicians from northern and southern West Virginia clashed during the state's first constitutional convention in 1862. But he was wrong. Sectionalism is a staple of American politics. The geographic distribution of resources and population creates differences within most states, leading politicians from one section to promote policies which benefit their part of the state and which are opposed by the leaders of other sections. Disputes of this nature were especially common in the first half of the nineteenth century and affected states as diverse as Virginia, Illinois, Tennessee, and California. Often sectional quarrels were punctuated by threats to divide the state (this happens even today—in California, for example). But there were always forces promoting compromise as well as division: there were statewide institutions, such as the courts and political parties, and central sections whose interests and leaders overlapped the extremes. This was the case in Virginia. For three generations before the Civil War, leaders of eastern and western Virginia quarreled over who should have the right to vote, over the apportionment of the legislature, over transportation improvements and where to put them and how to pay for them, and over various policies relating to slavery, which was deeply entrenched in the plantation economy of eastern Virginia, the oldest part of the state, but which was progressively less important as one moved westward through the Appalachian mountains and valleys to the farming, mining, and manufacturing economy of northwestern Virginia. There were compromises as well as quarrels, however, and during the 1850s many sectional issues appeared to be fading except among a frustrated minority of leaders in the city of Wheeling and nearby places in the extreme northwestern part of the state. Then in 1861 came the crisis provoked by the secession of seven Deep South states. The secession crisis reawakened sectionalism in Virginia and especially the western resentment that easterners always seemed ready to subordinate western and statewide interests in order to defend the institution of slavery. This time sectional conflict ended in the creation of West Virginia as a separate state embracing roughly a third of Virginia's 1860 population and territory. How this actually came about provides one

of the most fascinating episodes in the political, military, and social history of the Civil War era.

R arely has history in the form of war and politics intruded into the lives of ordinary Americans the way it did in western Virginia in the year 1861. "We occupied the place of Hawthorne's unfortunate man who saw both sides," Rebecca Harding recalled of her hometown of Wheeling during the months preceding the outbreak of the Civil War. "Sectional pride or feeling never was so distinct or strong there as in the New England or lower Southern States . . . the great mass of the people took no part in the quarrel . . . busied with their farms or shops, the onrushing disaster was as inexplicable [to them] as an earthquake." The election statistics bear out Harding's observation. In the presidential election of 1860, western Virginia voters gave most of their votes to candidates who promised sectional peace. But the largest bloc of voters comprised those who stayed home from the polls. Again in February 1861, when Virginia voters were called upon to elect delegates to a convention to deal with the crisis provoked by the Deep South's secession, over a third of the electorate failed to vote. The long and suspenseful debates of this convention led to excited crowds in Virginia's capital city of Richmond and to urgent consultations among politicians, but most people busied themselves in their early spring tasks. Then, on April 12, Confederates attacked Fort Sumter in South Carolina; on April 15, President Abraham Lincoln called upon the loyal states to furnish volunteer troops to suppress the rebellion. Governor John Letcher of Virginia indignantly rejected Lincoln's call; instead, on April 17, the Richmond Convention adopted an ordinance of secession by a vote of 88 to 55. In theory, this ordinance had no effect until it was ratified by the voters at the spring election scheduled for May 23, but officials began acting as though the

Scene near Parkersburg, Virginia, 1859, as painted by Lefevre J. Cranstone. (Lilly Library, Indiana University)

matter were settled. On May 1, Governor Letcher mustered the militia into state service, and Colonel Robert E. Lee, newly installed as commander of Virginia's troops, ordered western militia commanders to occupy the principal junctions along the Baltimore & Ohio (B&O) Railroad. Negotiations got under way leading to Virginia's membership in the Confederacy, while Unionist politicians from the west, some of whom had barely escaped being roughed up by the Richmond mobs, made their way back across the state to rally supporters at home.

"The elders of the family, as a rule, sided with the Government; the young folks with the South," Harding recalled. There were many exceptions to this rule, but it held true among many of western Virginia's "best" families, where fathers remained loyal to the Union while their sons slipped away to fight for the Confederacy. In Wheeling, where the crowds that gathered outside newspaper offices were against rather than for secession, the young "bloods" who went south told the tailor who made their matching gray uniforms that the gear was for use in a wedding. Younger men were generally the first to confront the necessity of choosing sides. Before 1861, joining the county militia meant little more to most young men than a chance to socialize with other fellows and to show off for the girls. But with the militia called up to state service, a great many young western Virginians found themselves taking steps that eventually led to their enrollment in the Confederate army. In Upshur County, for example, the sixty-seven militiamen who reported for duty on May 7 were soon marching north toward the key railroad junction at Grafton. Soon they would be mustered into Confederate service as the "Upshur Grays" while a volunteer contingent of Unionist "Upshur Blues" began drilling at home. In the "Pan Handle" counties, constituting a narrow sliver of Virginia territory centered on Wheeling and wedged between Ohio and Pennsylvania, the militiamen generally refused Governor Letcher's summons and instead provided nuclei of volunteer Union outfits. The first such unit, commanded by Benjamin F. Kelley, a railroad man with military training, began drilling on Wheeling Island and prepared to move east in the direction of Grafton as soon as the May 23 election was decided. Meanwhile, on the evening of May 22, the crisis claimed its first casualty, when a state militiaman posted as a sentry on the railroad near Grafton exchanged shots with two local Union volunteers. The sentry was wounded, and one of the Union men, T. Bailey Brown, was killed and later memorialized as the first official Union casualty of the Civil War.

"Things fall apart," wrote a poet of another country on the verge of civil war, "the center cannot hold." The political center had been occupied in western Virginia by leaders known to historians as "conditional" Unionists; that is, they opposed Virginia's secession but denied the right of the federal government to hold seceded states forcibly in the Union. Fifteen western members of the Richmond Convention eventually signed the secession ordinance, including two who had initially voted against it. The ordinance posed a special problem for officeholders. The two congressmen from northwestern Virginia refused to resign from the House of Representatives as other Virginia congressmen did, but state officials from western Virginia generally decided that their duty required them either to follow Virginia into the Confederacy or to retire into neutrality. Prominent men whose age or exposed property counseled prudence often became neutrals or Unionists, while their sons joined the rebel army. Such was the case with William P. Thompson, one of the young men who went south from Wheeling in those matching gray uniforms; his father was the only Virginia state supreme court justice to remain loyal to the Union. Western Virginia's most prominent political family, the Jacksons of Clarksburg and Parkersburg, splintered in several directions. General John Jay Jackson, Sr., spoke out promptly for the Union. One of his sons, James M., engaged in a fistfight with a secessionist cousin, Judge William L. Jackson, at a mass meeting in Parkersburg on April 18, with the older but fitter judge coming out on top. On April 29, another cousin, Thomas J., assumed command of the Virginia troops that had seized control of the federal arsenal at Harpers Ferry. Within a year, the fortitude and military skill of this Jackson earned him the nickname "Stonewall" and made him, with General Lee, one of the two most celebrated Confederate commanders of the war. This had unfortunate implications for Judge William L., who acquired the nickname "Mudwall" when he, too, took the field as a general in the rebel army later in 1861.

"Now is the time for a new separate state of West Va, to stand 'now and forever' under the 'glorious Stars and Stripes," wrote a Wheeling Unionist on April 23. If Virginia could leave the Union under the theory of secession, then why couldn't western Virginia secede from Virginia? This threat had first been raised by one of the Jackson ancestors in 1802 and had been repeated many times since. Now the division of Virginia into two states was again discussed in mass meetings in many western counties during the spring of 1861. On May 11, acting in response to a call issued by Unionist members of the Richmond Convention, some 430 westerners—some self-appointed and others selected by mass meetings in their

William Lowther "Mudwall" Jackson, Parkersburg jurist and rebel general. (Courtesy of Blennerhassett Island Historical State Park)

hometowns—gathered in Wheeling to chart a course for the western counties should the secession ordinance be ratified on May 23.

This "First Wheeling Convention," as it later became known, gathered in a meeting room in Wheeling's Washington Hall. From the top floor of this building, the delegates could have had a clear view of their dilemma. The smoky factory town of Wheeling sat next to the Ohio River, which formed Virginia's western boundary and a traditional dividing line between the South and Midwest. The river, together with the B&O Railroad and a famous suspension bridge carrying the National Pike across the river into the state of Ohio, formed the city's lifelines of trade. The convention delegates watched Kelley's volunteers drilling on the large flat island facing the city, but they weren't the only ones watching. Along the river's opposite shore in the state of Ohio, Union troops and volunteers were also gathering, held in check only by President Lincoln's desire not to take the first step until the fate of the secession ordinance was formally decided on May 23.

No one in the convention had to be told that northwestern Virginia lay on an invasion route. Fully half of the section's 250,000 people lived on or near the borders of Ohio or Pennsylvania. East of the Allegheny Mountains, which separated the northwest from the rest of Virginia, the Baltimore & Ohio Railroad followed the Potomac River, which like the Ohio had now become the boundary between Confederate and Union states. Almost as ruinous as the military prospect was the possibility that these rivers might become international boundaries: "we have no commercial relations with the south," wrote Waitman T. Willey of Morgantown on May 6; ". . . by being dragged into (or rather hitched onto) a southern confederacy, surrounded by Ohio and Penna., and Maryland, as *foreign* countries, our trade and commerce would be destroyed." Almost all of the counties represented at the May 11 meeting sold the products of their farms, mines, factories, and workshops to the Northeast or Midwest. Consequently, "the people here," a Wheeling man predicted, "except for a little handful of secessionists, are all ripe for a [separate statehood] movement . . . , but they lack a bold, prudent and skillful leader."

The boldest leader of the moment was Congressman John S. Carlile, who wanted to move swiftly and decisively to create a new state, to be called New Virginia, out of the two northwestern Virginia congressional districts. If the convention acted quickly, Carlile urged, there might be time to get Virginia's permission—required under the U.S. Constitution—for the formation of a new state from its territory. But was Carlile's plan prudent as well as bold? Other leaders were less hopeful than he that Virginia secessionists would cooperate. And what about the Lincoln administration and Congress? Would a government that denied the right of southerners to secede from the Union turn around and grant the northwest the right to secede from Virginia? General John Jay Jackson, Sr., opposed Carlile's plan as "premature, . . . revolutionary, and altogether unwise." Willey, who with Carlile and Jackson was one of the few experienced politicians in attendance, warned the delegates against "insurrectionary or unconstitutional means of accomplishing an object which he thought could be accomplished according to law." Deferring action on Carlile's plan, the convention instead appointed a committee, whose job was to coordinate the campaign against ratification of the secession ordinance and to organize a second convention, whose members would be chosen in a more regular fashion, to assemble in Wheeling a month later should the ordinance be rat-ified on May 23.

Francis H. Pierpoint was a member of this committee. A lawyer from Fair-mont, Frank Pierpoint was a man who had finally come into his own. His law prac-tice was flourishing thanks to patronage from the B&O Railroad, which had linked Fairmont with Baltimore and Wheeling in 1853. In 1854, he opened the area's sec-ond coal mine in partnership with James O. Watson, and that same year he was mar-ried at age forty to a beautiful young woman, Julia Robertson. In the spring of 1861, Pierpoint was now a family man, with four young children. As he stepped forward to a leadership role in Wheeling, his wife was in the midst of redecorating their house, and all of their children had whooping cough. Young Captain Thompson, with boots and plumes to set off his new gray uniform, had already been to their home, osten-sibly to recover a state-owned musket in the possession of one of the housepainters. Julia Pierpoint sent him away empty-handed, and Frank returned home safely on May 18. Then during the night of May 22, awakened by his children's coughing and alert to every nighttime noise in the little town, Pierpoint discovered a neigh-bor keeping watch over his house, fearful that Pierpoint's life was in danger. Early the next morning, his partner Watson roused him to warn of a secessionist plot to seize him and transport him to Richmond; entrusting his family and business to Wat-son's care, Pierpoint slipped out the back of his house and caught the early morn-ing train to Wheeling. Thus it happened that the future "Father of West Virginia" did not get to vote in the secession referendum of May 23.

As elections went, the vote of May 23 was anticlimactic. Intimidation of vot-ers was widespread, in Union strongholds as well as in the rest of Virginia. No statewide returns were ever certified, but historians estimate that roughly two-thirds of the voters in what is now West Virginia rejected secession, with all but 2000 voters ratifying it in the rest of Virginia. Since secession was thus approved by a wide margin, it set in motion a rapidly unfolding set of events. The federal troops that had been held in check at the border now moved across the Ohio River at Wheeling and Parkersburg on May 26 and followed Kelley's troops east along the B&O. The outnumbered and outgunned secessionist army abandoned the junction at Grafton and moved to Philippi, some thirty miles south, where the first battle took place on June 1, resulting in a Union victory. Six weeks later, follow-ing a series of panicky rebel retreats, Union troops commanded by General George B. McClellan won a decisive victory in the battle of Rich Mountain on July 11. A parallel invasion of the Kanawha Valley soon followed, leading to further Con-federate defeats. By early August, the Unionist heartland in northwestern Virginia lay safe behind federal lines. General Lee came out in person in August to try to reverse these results but was unsuccessful.

The Union victories made the work of the Second Wheeling Convention that assembled on June 11 less risky but not less complicated. Delegates rehashed the arguments of the first convention, with Carlile moving for immediate "dismem-berment" of Virginia into two states, Willey arguing for a less revolutionary pro-cedure, and another bloc of delegates opposing the idea of a new state as inexpe-dient during the wartime emergency. Willey's proposal to "restore" the government of Virginia provided a compromise. Accordingly, the convention summoned all duly elected members of the Virginia General Assembly who would swear allegiance to the Constitution of the United States and to the "vindicated and restored" Virginia government. Forty-nine members of the House of Delegates and eleven state senators answered the call on these terms and gathered in Wheeling on July 1 to reclaim Virginia's place in the Union. Certifying the election of Unionist congressmen in the May 23 vote, this "Loyal" legislature filled

West Virginia Union volunteers. Drawings by Joseph H. DissDebar. (West Virginia Department of Culture and History, Archives and History Division)

three of Virginia's nine congressional seats and chose Carlile and Willey to complete the terms of the resigned U.S. senators. Meanwhile, after a private caucus of convention delegates, Frank Pierpoint was elected governor by a unanimous vote on June 20, 1861. Pierpoint promptly borrowed $5000 on his personal note to get the new government started, took over the U.S. Customs House in Wheeling as his capitol, and bought himself a new suit of clothes. On June 21, he wrote to President Lincoln in his official capacity as the governor of Virginia. Lincoln quickly acknowledged Pierpoint as such, and so did federal military commanders at Wheeling and in the field. On July 25 the U.S. Senate accepted Carlile and Willey's credentials by a vote of 35–5, thus lending the loyal government the stamp of congressional approval.

How much of these developments can be attributed to behind-the-scenes maneuvers by the Lincoln administration? There is no clear-cut answer, but the record suggests that official Washington gave full encouragement to the project of restoring Virginia's government while sending mixed signals on the idea of dividing the state. Pierpoint's address to the loyal General Assembly on July 2 attributed the secession crisis and outbreak of war to "a great conspiracy" which, through the instruments of subversion, "terror," and "intimidation," had destroyed the lawful government of Virginia. Thus the restoration of that government should be judged not by the proportion of Virginia's population or territory that the loyal government commanded or the number of previously elected officials who were willing to take the Wheeling convention's oath, but by the fact that the government in Richmond had removed itself from the protection of the U.S. Constitution by perverting the will of the people and engaging in armed rebellion. This theory fitted in nicely with the official view in Washington that the Confederacy represented a "slave conspiracy" rather than the free choices of most southerners. "The President . . . never supposed that a brave and free people, though surprised and unarmed, could long be subjugated by a class of political adventurers always adverse to them . . . ," a cabinet member wrote Pierpoint. The actions at Wheeling also provided a model through which constitutional government could be restored to other southern states as the rebellion was suppressed, as Lincoln's attorney general, Edward Bates, wrote approvingly. But don't complicate things, Bates urged, by moving to divide the state. "The formation of a new State out of Western Virginia is an original, independent act of Revolution. . . . Any attempt to carry it out involves a plain breach of the constitution, both of Virginia and the Nation."

Pierpoint's initial concern as governor was defense, not dismemberment. The summer victories and McClellan's ascent to overall command of the Union armies had diverted both soldiers and attention from western Virginia, as did the expiration of enlistments by men who had signed up for three months of duty in the spring of 1861. Pierpoint was moderately successful in filling Virginia's quota of three-year volunteer enlistments in the fall of 1861. Eight Virginia Union regiments were raised, most of them detailed for duty guarding the B&O Railroad, the Union's most direct link for men and supplies between the eastern and western theaters of the war. Joshua Winters, an eighteen-year-old farm boy from the Pan Handle whose father had been one of the self-appointed delegates to the First Wheeling Convention, was one of those who answered the call, signing up on September 23, 1861, and shipping out after some training at Wheeling to the upper Potomac front on November 8.

The early battles and skirmishes had given many young men a new appreciation of the realities of warfare. "[V]olunteering in Monongalia moves very tardily," a Morgantown resident wrote Pierpoint in August. "Each man thinks he is not the one to do the fighting but would rather do the talking." "Josse" Winters's older brothers and brothers-in-law held back, waiting until a year later, by which time the governor had stimulated lagging enlistments with threats of a Union draft. "I don't know what Peerpont ment when he sent speakers to tell the peapel that they was a goin to draft," Josse's mother, Eliza, wrote to him in September 1862. "If it hadent a bin for the draft Isaac nor Jim woodent a went but so it is and I cant help it." Things were not much different on the Confederate side. Many of the militiamen who marched off in May 1861 were ready to come back home by August but found themselves in a ticklish position if their homes lay behind federal lines. Returning rebels faced harassment, arrest, or worse when they came back to their families and could purge suspicion only if they volunteered to fight on the Union side. A substantial number of western Virginia soldiers ended up serving in both armies, either as volunteers who changed opinions during the course of the war or because they were called up first as Virginia militiamen and then returned home to get caught in the Union draft. Then there were the men like the slave owner's son from the Greenbrier Valley whose actions were described years later by one of his father's former slaves. After his first taste of combat, this young rebel came home "sceered to death," got himself a crutch, and hobbled around on it until the war was over, obviously not fooling as many people as he thought.

Western Virginia Confederates cut off from their homes frequently became "partisan rangers," guerrillas who operated in the no-man's-land that existed in what is now central and southern West Virginia. The campaigns of 1861 had established firm Union control north of the B&O and in a Kanawha Valley region centered on Charleston. There were also Union outposts east and south of these lines, but these were easily bypassed by guerrillas operating on familiar terrain and enjoying substantial support from the local population. Capturing horses for the Confederacy (or stealing them, as federal authorities saw it) and burning bridges on the B&O were the principal activities of these fighters, who operated under the authority of the government in Richmond but were detached from the regular Confederate command and regarded as common criminals by Unionists. The lines of the main armies remained stable through the first two years of the war, with the Union holding northwestern Virginia and Confederates holding the Greenbrier Valley and the rest of southwestern Virginia. Well-organized raids broke the stalemate periodically, with rebels moving westward toward the Ohio River, while federal raiders tried to reach and cut the Virginia & Tennessee Railroad in the southwest. Two large Confederate raids did extensive damage in 1862 and 1863, including one that briefly captured Pierpoint's hometown, where the raiders burned the governor's library in front of his law office as well as the B&O bridge over the Monongahela. But the dominant feature of the fighting in western Virginia was a genuine civil war, literally pitting brother against brother and neighbor against neighbor. This "bushwhacker's war" involved all the bitterness and brutality that such fighting usually entails.

The irregular character of partisan warfare gave young women more opportunities to participate than might otherwise have been the case. At least nine women partisans were imprisoned at Wheeling at some time during the war. One of them was Mary Jane Green, who was arrested initially as a spy at Sutton in August 1861; later that year, she was taken to a Wheeling prison, where she made life miserable for guards and other inmates. "General Rosecrans had her brought

Citizen homeguards scouting for guerrillas and horse thieves during the "bushwhacker's war." Drawing by Joseph H. DissDebar. (West Virginia Department of Culture and History, Archives and History Division)

before him when she abused him with her tongue and he ordered her back to jail," reported the provost marshal (chief of military police):

> [later] General Rosecrans directed me to send [her] to her home in Braxton County with the hope and expectation that some Union troops would shoot her . . . in a short time she was returned to me having been caught in the act of destroying the telegraph line near Weston, Lewis County. She is an ignorant creature, but at times has the ferocity of a perfect she-devil about her. I cannot advise her release. . . .

Although the charge against these women was treason, none of them was shot, as was often the fate of male guerrillas, but their jailers found them "hard cases" to deal with. Pierpoint initially ordered some of the women sent to Camp Chase, a larger prison near Columbus, Ohio, and then devised a scheme to turn them over to Confederate authorities in eastern Virginia, only to be informed that "Wearing soldier's clothing in camp is not an offense for which they can be sent South and if that is all that is against them, they must be disposed of in some other way." Another female partisan, Nancy Hart, rode at the head of one of the most notorious guerrilla bands, the Moccasin Rangers, with her boyfriend, Perry Connolly. A teenage beauty who could charm her way out of tight situations, Hart continued fighting after Connolly was killed in 1862. Later she teamed up with another partisan, Joshua Douglas, and after the Moccasins were destroyed by federal "snake hunters" in 1863, she moved with him to a remote location in the mountains.

Women were confined to more conventional roles in secure areas. Ladies in Wheeling, Parkersburg, and other cities volunteered as nurses in military hospitals, made bandages and flags, and prepared foods for ceremonial occasions. Laura Jackson Arnold, the devoted sister of Stonewall but as ardent a Unionist as he was a rebel, befriended and nursed soldiers at the federal advance post at Beverly. Farm women had no choice but to take over male tasks when men were absent. "I chopped wood yesterday till I had a blister on my hand," wrote Annie Winters, Josse's sister. "You don't believe how lonesom we are. We just have one man left. . . ." Men in turn learned to do for themselves things they had formerly depended on women to do for them. On January 1, 1863, for example, boxes from home provided the six men in Josse Winters's tent with a New Year's dinner worth writing home about: "we had turkey and pound cake and pies, appels. chicken. and ever thing that is good for diner and a nuff left for two days yet. . . . o yess I forgot we had wine too but thair was no girls hear for to wate on the tabell."

Meanwhile, the project to divide Virginia gained momentum. The Second Wheeling Convention adopted a "dismemberment ordinance," which was put before the voters for ratification in a referendum on October 24, 1861. This ordinance proposed to take thirty-nine counties out of Virginia and into a new state to be known as "Kanawha." The ordinance was approved by 18,408 to 781 in an election in which few, if any, secessionists or antistatehood Unionists bothered to vote. Then a Third Wheeling Convention gathered on November 26 to draft a constitution for the new state and continued in its deliberations until February 13, 1862. On May 13, 1862, the loyal legislature voted its approval, as required by the U.S. Constitution; a few days later, at the regular spring election, Governor Pierpoint was elected governor of Virginia by 14,824 votes, less than a third of the number voting in western Virginia in the 1860 election but sufficient to the purpose, since Pierpoint was running unopposed.

The Third Wheeling Convention changed the name of the new state to West Virginia by a vote of 30 to 9 for "Kanawha"; this gave the new state a familiar name but also created an identity problem that has not been easy to live with. Other features of the new constitution were not so easily decided. First, there was the question of how much of Virginia the new state should include. The traditional dividing line between eastern and western Virginia was the Blue Ridge Mountains, which divided Virginia almost in half. Another possibility was the dividing ridge of the Alleghenies, which separated the watersheds of rivers flowing westward toward the Ohio from those of rivers that flowed east to Chesapeake Bay. But either of these "natural" borders would have taken in a large number of rebels and slaves from the

Nancy (Peggy) Hart, Confederate spy, railroad-track wrecker, and friend of Captain Perry Connolly. (Courtesy of Blennerhassett Island Historical State Park)

Shenandoah Valley and southwestern Virginia while leaving out much of the railroad that linked Wheeling and Parkersburg to the Northeast. In the end the convention came down on the side of expediency. Recalling what the United States had done in its western expansion, a Kanawha County delegate explained that "wherever a territory becomes essential to the prosperity and safety of a State, it may purchase it if it can, and if it cannot, it may take it." And so the border of West Virginia was extended south and east of the Unionist heartland, taking in five southwestern counties that were still behind Confederate lines and six additional counties, creating a second panhandle extending east along the Potomac River to the point where the B&O Railroad crossed safely into Maryland. Referenda were prescribed to give these extensions the sanction of lawful procedures, but like the other elections held since fighting broke out, this voting produced lopsided margins and small numbers of votes.

The most heated controversies were stirred by the issue of slavery, which was at best a moral blind spot for most white western Virginians. Westerners had criticized slavery through most of Virginia's history, but from an economic rather than

Western Virginia women as sketched by Joseph H. DissDebar, 1846–1850. (West Virginia Department of Culture and History, Archives and History Division)

a human rights perspective. "We were, so to speak, on the fence, and could see the great question from both sides," wrote Rebecca Harding, who gained literary fame during the war for her exposure of working and living conditions among Wheeling factory workers. "Abolitionism never was a burning question in our part of Virginia." "We do not want to be connected any longer with the miserable one-idea negro policy that has cursed us all the days of our lives," the *Wheeling Intelligencer* editorialized on the eve of the constitutional convention. "We have had enough of it and want to get clear of negroes." Reflecting such views, the new constitution left the institution of slavery undisturbed but prohibited any new settlement by African-Americans, slave *or* free, in the new state. Congress refused to accept this provision, however, and made the admission of West Virginia to the Union conditional on the abolition of slavery. Senator Willey accordingly brought forth a compromise in the form of a constitutional amendment that prohibited any new slaves from entering West Virginia and provided for the gradual emancipation of those already there. The majority of statehood advocates accepted this "Willey Amendment," but a furious minority headed by Carlile opposed it and engaged in various attempts to sabotage the statehood movement. The antistatehood Unionists failed in Congress and at the referendum which accepted the Willey Amendment, but President Lincoln's cabinet split evenly on the issue when the West Virginia statehood bill came to the President's desk. Attorney General Bates led the opposition on constitutional grounds, objecting to the "revolutionary" nature of the state-making process. Salmon P. Chase, secretary of the treasury and a former governor of Ohio, spoke for statehood in the cabinet. "It would have been as absurd as it would have been impolitic to deny the large loyal population of Virginia the powers of a State Government" in deference to the claims of elected officials who had become rebels. Since Pierpoint's Virginia government was constitutional, it

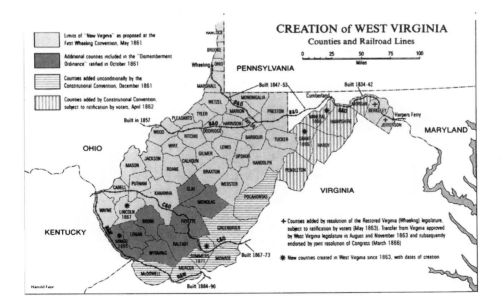

could therefore give West Virginia the constitutional permission required to become a separate state. "The case of West Virginia will form no evil precedent," since similar conditions were unlikely ever to be encountered in another state, Chase concluded. After reviewing these arguments, at practically the last minute on the last day of 1862, Lincoln accepted the pro-statehood position and signed the West Virginia bill. On June 20, 1863, having met Congress's conditions and chosen a new slate of officials, West Virginia became the thirty-fifth state and stitched its star to the national flag. The occasion was marked by parades, flags, and speeches. Thirty-five little girls sang the national anthem. Governor Pierpoint delivered his valedictory address, and the new West Virginia governor, Arthur I. Boreman, spoke his inaugural. "I recon thair was a grate fus in Wheeling," wrote Joshua Winters from his guardpost out on the railroad on June 21.

Not long afterward, Governor Pierpoint moved the loyal Virginia government's headquarters to Alexandria, close to Washington, D.C. The railroad over which he traveled was now protected by an expanding system of log blockhouses extending from Parkersburg east into Maryland. The railroad's greater security permitted Joshua Winters and his unit to move south into the guerrilla country and then east of the Alleghenies as fighting in Virginia intensified during 1864. Winters fought in the Shenandoah Valley campaigns in April and May 1864 and then, wounded in the hand on June 5, spent the summer "a bummin in the hospital" in Parkersburg. In September, Winters was back with his unit for further combat in the Valley, and then in November his three-year enlistment was up. His discharge paper issued at Wheeling on November 20, 1864, describes him as "Six feet 0 inches high, fair complexion, grey eyes, dark hair, and by occupation, when enrolled, a farmer." On November 28, Josse made the last entry in his diary and headed home to Sand Hill: "I AM FREE ONCE MORE."

Scene near Parkersburg in November 1859. Painted by Lefevre J. Cranstone. (Lilly Library, Indiana University)

Rebecca Harding, admitted by success and marriage into the highest literary circles in Boston late in the war, was shocked by how little people there knew about the conditions she had left behind in West Virginia. "The histories which we have of the great tragedy give no idea of the general wretchedness, the squalid misery, which entered into every individual life in the region given up to the war," she wrote later. "Below all the squalor and discomfort was the agony of suspense or the certainty of death. But the parsnip coffee and the empty purse certainly did give a sting to the great overwhelming misery, like gnats tormenting a wounded man." Lizzie Grant, an ex-slave, had similar recollections. "When that war was over lots of money had been spent, nothing won, but a lot of new graves, widows and orphan children suffering—their homes all wrecked." Grant and her husband stayed on the Kanawha Valley farm of their former masters, working for a year at $2.00-a-month wages to repair the buildings and fences the armies had destroyed. "I guess I expected the government to give us negroes a home and mules as we had made Maser all he had but no sir, we were not given a thing but a hard deal." Eventually, Grant and her husband left West Virginia for Texas.

Those who stayed in West Virginia stopped making history and resumed their ordinary lives. Joshua Winters returned to his family's farm, married his prewar sweetheart, and lived there the rest of his life. The ex-guerrillas Nancy Hart and Joshua Douglas started a family, and their backwoods hideout became just another mountain farm. William P. Thompson moved to Parkersburg and made money in the oil business, although not so much as some who had stayed out of the fighting. Judge and now General William L. "Mudwall" Jackson also came home to Parkersburg but moved on to Louisville, Kentucky, where he prospered as a lawyer. Laura Jackson Arnold's elderly husband divorced her after the war, accusing her of romantic entanglements with the Union officers she had befriended. Pierpoint's erstwhile partner, James O. Watson, grew rich in the coal industry, but the ex-governor did not share in this prosperity. His personal fortunes limped along, never recovering from their wartime neglect. Later in life he got interested in genealogy and changed the spelling of his last name to Pierpont. That was how the state of West Virginia spelled it when it installed a statue of Pierpont in Statuary Hall of the U.S. Capitol in 1910.

AN INTERPRETATION

Both Congress and the U.S. Supreme Court affirmed the creation of West Virginia after the Civil War, but the constitutionality of the process remained subject to debate by historians. Did the consent given by the loyal Virginia government at Wheeling really meet the test of constitutionality? Did the various referenda that punctuated the state-making process really express the will of the people? Was the creation of West Virginia the logical outcome of the long history of sectional battles between eastern and western Virginia? Or was the new state, as a bitter Virginia politician proclaimed after the war, "the bastard child of a political rape?" We could answer these questions more readily if the entire electorate had participated in the referenda or if we could sort out western Virginia military enlistments into precise numbers of Union men and Confederates, but this is not possible. The irregular nature of guerrilla warfare and especially its blurring of the lines between patriotic and criminal behavior make it even harder to determine exactly who stood where in western and West Virginia during the period 1861–1865.

Ultimately the interpretation of these events is a matter of values as much as facts. The West Virginia statehood movement was democratic in spirit and involved farmers, preachers, teachers, businessmen, and many others who had rarely had a voice in Virginia politics. On the other hand, lawyers and veteran politicians did most of the talking and made most of the decisions in the three Wheeling conventions. Similarly, the constitution of 1863 was promulgated by undemocratic means during the war, but it was a much more democratic document than the Virginia constitution it replaced or the West Virginia constitution that ex-Confederates wrote after they won control of the new state in 1870. Which matters most—democratic form or democratic substance? In ideal circumstances, one would say both, but conditions were hardly ideal in a mountainous border region in time of civil war.

The creation of West Virginia was, in effect, the only successful example of secession in U.S. history. But there are many such examples in world history, including some that make headlines today. In Canada, for example, the French-speaking province of Quebec threatens to secede from the Canadian confederation, but the leaders of the native peoples of northern Quebec have warned—as western Virginia Unionists did during the American secession crisis—that if Quebec leaves Canada, the north will leave Quebec. Quebecois nationalists deny the propriety of this countersecession, just as Confederate Virginians did. Where does justice lie in such circumstances? At what point should the principle of minority self-determination yield to the principle of majority rule? How can that point be determined without violence? These were the issues at stake in 1861 in the United States at large and in more concentrated and localized form in the two Virginias. If these issues arise again in Canada, the details may differ, but we can confidently expect to hear our northern neighbors repeat most of the arguments heard in Richmond and Wheeling in the spring of 1861.

In the former Yugoslavia and in Ireland, federalists and nationalists are divided by religious traditions, while in Canada language provides the point of division. In West Virginia, however, the antagonists on both sides were overwhelmingly white, English-speaking, and Protestant. What else then divided them? Some contemporary observers offered a class analysis—the rich and poor for secession and Virginia, the middle class for the Union and West Virginia—but it does not hold up to close scrutiny. Middle-class folks were good Confederates in the Greenbrier Valley and other places behind rebel lines, and there were many examples of poor mountaineers helping the federal army when it operated in Confederate territory. Nor do prewar political alignments explain choices made in 1861, although prominent state-makers such as Pierpoint and Willey were more likely to have been former Whigs than Democrats. A statistical analysis of voting in 1860 and 1861 shows that secession sentiment in Virginia increased proportionately with the number of slaves in a given county, but loyalty to slavery does not seem to have been as much a factor in explaining western Virginia secessionism or antistatehood Unionism as outright hostility to black people—white racism, in other words. A detailed examination of military enlistments in two counties, one each in northwestern and southwestern Virginia, shows that a man was more likely to fight for Virginia and the South the longer his family had lived in the state and that, conversely, recent arrivals—even from states farther south—were more likely to become Unionists.

Social, economic, and demographic factors combined with matters of age, gender, and personal temperament to explain a given individual's choice in 1861, even when—it must be remembered—the great majority of western Virginians didn't want to choose sides at all but wanted instead to go on with their everyday lives. It is important to remember also that a fluid and fast-changing military situation forced choices upon them. The significance of the Union army's conquest of northwestern Virginia in the spring and summer of 1861 is obvious if we compare the experience of Virginia with that of Tennessee. Tennessee, like Virginia, had a long history of sectionalism and a staunch uncompromising Union movement during the secession crisis. But in contrast to northwestern Virginia, eastern Tennessee lay deep within Confederate territory; as the war began in earnest, Union men there had to flee north for their lives or go into hiding. East Tennessee did not come under federal control until 1864, by which time Unionists had controlled the state government at Nashville for nearly two years, "reconstructing" it on the same basis that the Pierpoint government had used in Virginia. Once they controlled the entire state, East Tennessee Unionists dropped their demand for its dismemberment. It was therefore the military situation more than any other factor that explains why "East Tennessee" today remains a geographic expression, while "West Virginia" became the name of a state.

Sources: The basic documents of West Virginia statehood and Civil War history can be found in Virgil A. Lewis, ed., *How West Virginia Was Made* (Charleston, W.Va.: News-Mail Printers, 1909); Charles H. Ambler, Frances H. Atwood, and William B. Mathews, eds., *Debates and Proceedings of the First Constitutional Convention of West Virginia*, 3 vols. (Huntington, W.Va.: Gentry Brothers, 1939); and U.S. War Department, *The War of the Rebellion: The Official Records of the Union and Confederate Armies* (Washington: U.S. Government Printing Office, 1890). Daniel W. Crofts, *Reluctant Confederates: Upper South Unionists in the Secession Crisis* (Chapel Hill: University of North Carolina Press, 1989), is essential for understanding the prelude to war and statehood. John Alexander Williams, *West Virginia: A History* (New York: W. W. Norton and Company, 1976), pp. 57–75, offers a convenient summary of the fighting in western and West Virginia; Elizabeth Davis Swiger, ed., *Civil War Letters and Diaries of Joshua Winters, A Private in Company G, First Western Virginia Volunteer Infantry* (Parsons, W.Va.: McClain Printing Company, 1991), is the most entertaining and informative of the published soldiers' diaries. Rebecca Harding Davis, *Bits of Gossip* (Boston: Houghton, Mifflin & Company, 1904), provides brief and insightful recollections of the war years. H. E. Matheny, *Wood County, West Virginia, in Civil War Times, With an Account of Guerrilla Warfare in the Little Kanawha Valley* (Parkersburg, W.Va.: Trans-Allegheny Books, Inc., 1987), is one of the best local histories. Charles H. Ambler, *Francis H. Pierpont, Union War Governor of Virginia and Father of West Virginia* (Chapel Hill: University of North Carolina Press, 1937), and Richard Orr Curry, *A House Divided: Statehood Politics and the Copperhead Movement in West Virginia* (Pittsburgh: University of Pittsburgh Press, 1964), offer opposed views of the statehood movement. John E. Stealey, III, "In the Shadow of Ambler and Beyond: A Historiography of West Virginia Politics," in Ronald L. Lewis and John C. Hennen, Jr., eds., *West Virginia History: Critical Essays on the Literature* (Dubuque, Iowa: Kendall/Hunt Publishing Co., 1993), especially pp. 1–14, reviews their debates and those of other historians. Lewis and Hennen provide a useful collection of documents in *West Virginia. Documents in the History of a Rural-Industrial State* (Dubuque, Iowa: Kendall/Hunt Publishing Co., 1991).

14

THE BURNING OF CHAMBERSBURG

EVERARD H. SMITH

When, after the South fired on Fort Sumter in April of 1861, President Abraham
Lincoln called for troops to preserve the Union, there was no shortage of volunteers.
Despite the well-known fact that Northerners were almost as prejudiced against
African-Americans as Southerners were, thousands of young men rushed forward to
be counted in the struggle. In every town young men had their pictures taken, said
good-bye to their sweethearts and families, and paraded out of town to the tune of
martial music and a shower of flower petals. Similar spectacles took place in most
secessionist states, where a multitude of young men, most of whom owned no slaves
nor had any hope of ever owning slaves, seemed anxious to volunteer for the glory of
defending the "peculiar" institution. Both sides seemed to be convinced that the war
would be both glorious and short.

    None of the men who marched so blithely off to a grim future could have had any
way of knowing the horror and brutality that lay before them. True, some of the older
men who were to become officers had fought in the Mexican War fifteen years before,
but that had been a war against a much weaker and unprepared enemy, involving
much smaller armies; and it was won in a short period of time. Most of the men who
were volunteering for the Civil War were children at the time and did not even have
family members who could tell them about it. And even if they had heard stories about
past wars, none of those stories could have prepared them for the carnage on a massive
scale that was to characterize the Civil War. In the Mexican War, the size of an army
was about 2000 men; in the Civil War it could reach 100,000. At the end of the
Mexican War, the American death toll was about 3000; at the end of the Civil War, it
was 600,000! Not only were the numbers dramatic testimony to the change in
warfare, but so, too, were the tactics of warfare. The Mexican War had been fought in
the same style as eighteenth-century warfare; that is, armies met on discrete
battlefields and, since weapons did not have particularly long-range accuracy, engaged
in face-to-face combat. Honor was gained, for officers, by riding one's horse directly
into battle, while infantrymen marched straight at the enemy, finally engaging with
bayonets. Battles were usually brief and did not involve civilians. In the Civil War
both sides sent thousands of young men charging straightforward into the deadly fire
of long-range, accurate artillery and against an entrenched enemy that could easily

pick them off by the hundreds. At Gettysburg, Robert E. Lee ordered 13,000 men to make such a charge and lost three-quarters of them, or over 9000 men. In the campaign called "the Wilderness" a year later, Ulysses Grant sent 55,000 to their deaths under similar conditions. As historian Charles Royster has said, the Civil War was the most "destructive" in the nation's history.

In this essay about the burning of Chambersburg, Pennsylvania, Everard Smith explores another aspect of warfare that was changed by the Civil War: the involvement of civilian populations. In previous conflicts, the war was between armies, not between civilians. Battles were fought, armies marched, and treaties made on the basis of what happened between armies; if civilian bystanders were hurt, it was because they were inadvertently in the way or caught in the cross fire. At the beginning of the Civil War, it seemed as though that pattern might continue; General Lee was the epitome of the Southern gentleman, devoted to the preservation of his own and Southern honor, while the North's General McClellan behaved quite timidly in order to avoid suffering casualties among his own men, never mind civilian bystanders. By the end of the war, however, General William Tecumseh Sherman planned quite explicitly to march his army of 50,000 troops from a conquered Atlanta to the sea, intimidating and terrorizing the civilian population as he went. Demoralization of noncombatants, he thought, was the best way to win the war. Not only that, he reasoned, it achieved justice, since Southerners should be punished for supporting the rebellion. In the following essay, Everard H. Smith explores how this kind of thinking emerged in the minds of Confederate soldiers and officers in the little town of Chambersburg.

Т he spring of 1863 was high tide for the Southern Confederacy. In the politically significant Eastern Theater, the hundred-mile stretch of territory between the rival capitals of Richmond and Washington, D.C., General Robert E. Lee's Army of Northern Virginia had just won its second dramatic victory over the Army of the Potomac in less than five months. On the bloody battleground of Chancellorsville (April 30–May 5), the invading Union army had been driven from the field in humiliation—outgeneraled, outmaneuvered, and outfought by a force less than half its size. In the wake of this battle, many observers considered the Confederates unbeatable.

With federal troops banished yet again from Virginia's soil, Lee turned his attention to a recurrent dream: an invasion of the North that would carry the war to the enemy and, perhaps, lead to the foreign recognition the South so desperately sought. Once before, the previous summer, Lee had led his mighty host across the Potomac River into western Maryland, only to see his plans undone when a copy of his orders mistakenly fell into Union hands. This time, he confidently predicted a more favorable outcome. By the end of May, Lee had gained the approval of President Jefferson Davis for what he intended to be the decisive campaign of the war. Reorganized and reinforced, his command totaled 75,000 men.

The Army of Northern Virginia reflected both the geographic region and the larger American nation that produced it. All eleven Confederate states were represented on its rosters, though several (Texas and Louisiana, especially) had only small contingents of troops present for duty. While statistics are imprecise, the average rebel soldier was similar in age, outlook, and experience to his Yankee adversary. Typically, he was a young man between the ages of eighteen and twenty-six, a farmer by profession. Illiteracy rates were high—perhaps 50 percent in some rural units from the Deep South—but most soldiers had enough education to read and write. Their letters and diaries often displayed poor grammar and spelling but were vividly expressive of their thoughts and feelings. Most of these youths had never traveled outside the county of their birth before joining the army. Their values included strong allegiances to home, church, and community.

Although the South had introduced conscription as early as 1862, the majority of its soldiers were volunteers whose decision to join the military had been motivated by patriotic considerations. They perceived themselves as defenders of the South's right to liberty and independence. Because troop units were raised locally, many soldiers lived and fought with friends and relatives whom they had known since childhood. This sense of community contributed to the high morale that characterized the army and later sustained it through decline and defeat. In 1863, Lee's men were still riding high as a consequence of their many victories, and their self-confidence was unbounded, even to the point of arrogance. Indeed, some historians have detected a touch of *hubris*—the exaggerated pride that precedes a downfall—in the attitude these troops displayed on the verge of the campaign that culminated at Gettysburg.

In Robert E. Lee, the army possessed a commanding general who was determined to implement a military policy characterized by idealism and elevated moral principles. Lee's objectives were diplomatic and political as well as military. One important goal was to display Confederate virtue to the outside world, contrasting it with the destructive behavior that Yankees were presumed to have displayed in the South. In conversations with Southern officials while his strategic planning was under way, Lee promised "to carry on the war in Pennsylvania without offending the sanctions of a high civilization and of Christianity."

As Lee undoubtedly realized, such a policy was politically advantageous, for it not only preserved morale and discipline but helped influence public opinion, especially overseas, where slavery had cost the South the moral high ground in the contest for foreign approval. Yet there is little doubt that the general also believed wholeheartedly in the principles he advocated. A seventh-generation Virginian, the son of a Revolutionary hero and state governor, Lee was a deeply spiritual man inculcated in the values of the eighteenth century. Patience, kindness, and forgiveness were all central to his code of moral law, which was rooted in an ethic of Christian humility. "The forbearing use of power," he once wrote, "does not only form a touchstone; but the manner in which an individual enjoys certain advantages over others, is the test of a *true gentleman*. The power which the strong have over the weak . . . the forbearing and inoffensive use of all this power or authority, or a total abstinence from it, when the case admits it, will show the gentleman in a plain light." The invasion of Pennsylvania put this magnanimous policy on view for all to see. On June 21, Lee issued General Orders Number 72, which forbade injury to private property and set orderly procedures for requisitioning supplies. Six days later, in the midst of the campaign, he outlined his principles even more specifically in General Orders Number 73:

The commanding general considers that no greater disgrace could befall the army, and through it our whole people, than the perpetration of the barbarous outrages upon the unarmed and defenseless and the wanton destruction of private property, that have marked the course of the enemy in our own country. . . .

It must be remembered that we make war only upon armed men, and that we cannot take vengeance for the wrongs our people have suffered without lowering ourselves in the eyes of all whose abhorrence has been excited by the atrocities of our enemies, and offending against Him to whom vengeance belongeth.

To the modern observer, such sentiments might seem naive, even hypocritical. But Lee's magnanimity appealed to the high-minded elements in the Southern

The magnificent photographs of the Civil War era captured the character and personality of their subjects for posterity. General Robert E. Lee, the personification of Southern idealism, wore full-dress uniform, gold-embroidered sash, and presentation sword for this portrait. During his invasion of the North in 1863, Lee attempted to shield civilians from unnecessary suffering. "The forbearing use of power," he wrote," . . . is the test of a *true gentleman.*" (Cook Collection/Valentine Museum)

self-image. Southerners customarily asserted that they guided their lives by strong ethical principles. The Confederate captain who recorded a prayer in his diary "that I may leave the low, sordid, selfish and mean and strive after the honorable, just, noble, and generous" was typical of thousands of soldiers who expressed such expectations with complete seriousness. With few exceptions, Marse Robert's men applauded the moral tone of his military policy. Unrecognized at the time was one of history's small tragic ironies: General Orders Number 73 was issued while the army was headquartered in a small Pennsylvania town called Chambersburg.

In many important respects, the cultural values expressed by Southern soldiers were indistinguishable from those displayed by the young men they were fighting. Whatever their political differences, even in the midst of a divisive civil war, all Americans shared a common heritage and traditions. But there were important differences as well. The most important distinction between the South and the rest of the United States was slavery. Although less than a quarter of the white population owned slaves, the average Southerner wholeheartedly supported both the institution and the racist assumptions on which it was based. In the decades before the war, the Southern way of life had come under increasing criticism from the rest of the nation. Southerners had responded by defending slavery as a positive good and by suppressing internal dissent that might suggest otherwise. Not surprisingly, this intolerance exercised a strong influence on the way they thought about, and acted toward, the outside world.

One of the most important—and explosive—components in the Southern value system was the concept of honor. This ancient complex of beliefs, with deep roots in the Indo-European tradition, contributed far more to the antebellum South than the courtesy and gentility with which the word is usually associated. Honor provided both a personal moral code and a social system that created communal order. It divided the population into leaders and followers, whose mutual duty was to uphold core values that were unquestionable. An elaborate social code, founded on deference, defined their relationships. In theory, at least, this code functioned without friction, because people knew their proper place and deferred naturally to their betters. Southerners often proclaimed the superiority of this way of life to what they saw as the egalitarian pretension of the rest of the nation and the unseemly disorder it produced.

In reality, an honor-based society was enormously oppressive, for its basic purpose was to uphold the status quo and the supremacy of the ruling elite. The ideology of the Old South was an ethic of white male power, created by the dominant race, class, and gender for the dual purpose of protecting slavery and defending its own place in the social order. In pursuit of these goals, Southern leaders systematically excluded everyone but themselves from participation in the power structure. Black slaves were their most obvious victims, but in fact their definition of inferiority was much broader and included practically anyone who was not white, male, native-born, and Protestant. The maintenance of this value system rested not on voluntary cooperation but on brute force. Anyone who dared question the existing order was subjugated, often violently.

Male dominance was especially important to the protection of the slave regime, for masters who demanded absolute obedience from their servants quickly realized they must require it of their families as well. To be sure, Southern men often treated women with exaggerated courtesy. But their definition of "ladyhood" restricted women to the exercise of submissive virtues, thereby ensuring that they would be at least outwardly subservient to male will. By the middle of the nineteenth century, women in other sections of the country were beginning to question gender stereotypes with increasing insistence. Northern feminists frequently based their quest for equality on comparisons with the slave's lot. In the Land of Dixie, however, such challenges could be extremely dangerous. The identification of feminism with abolitionism only increased its unacceptability.

Apologists for Southern culture clearly spelled out the risks incurred by any woman who flouted conventional behavior. In *Sociology for the South; or, the Failure of Free Society* (1854), George Fitzhugh argued that respect between races and sexes flourished only in a state of dependency: "A man loves his children because they are weak, helpless, and dependent; he loves his wife for similar reasons. . . . He ceases to love his wife when she becomes masculine or rebellious." Lest his readers miss this thinly veiled threat, Fitzhugh explained it in detail:

> So long as she is nervous, fickle, capricious, delicate, diffident, and dependent, man will worship and adore her. . . . In truth, women, like children, have but one right, and that is the right to protection. The right to protection involves the obligation to obey. A husband, a lord and master, whom she should love, honor, and obey, nature designed for every woman. . . . If she be obedient, she is in little danger of mal-treatment; if she stands upon her rights, is coarse and masculine, man loathes and despises her, and ends by abusing her. Law, however well-intended, can do little in her behalf.

If one carried the implications of this remarkable statement to their logical conclusion, a woman's failure to display appropriate submissiveness to the self-styled gentlemen around her was not merely impudence but a direct challenge to the Southern world view. Disobedience stripped women of the protection they would otherwise enjoy as ladies, justifying their punishment.

Like women, foreigners were regarded as a suspicious and potentially subversive element in the population. In the United States at large, the mid-nineteenth century was a time of considerable anxiety over immigration. Its steady growth, especially the large increase in the Irish and German populations, had triggered a nationwide backlash. The American, or Know-Nothing, Party, a short-lived political organization that deliberately pandered to antiforeign, anti-Catholic sentiments, had strong support in the South during its brief heyday in the 1850s. It controlled an estimated 29 percent of the Southern delegation in the House of Representatives and influenced politics in several states. Although relatively small, the German population in the South was particularly vulnerable to persecution. While Germans had lived in America since colonial times, many recent refugees had fled central Europe in the late 1840s following unsuccessful liberal revolutions that had attempted to bring reform to the ruling monarchies. This association made them deeply suspect to Southern nativists.

In the event of subversion, whether by slaves, foreigners, or uppity women, the Southern ruling class had methods at hand to stamp it out. Closely associated with honor was a common instrument of group violence and social control: the *charivari,* or "shivaree." This festive, almost ecstatic rite mingled justice with bacchanalia. The charivari punished social evil and defended traditional mores, equated, of course, with the precepts of the honorable society. Feminine virtue and family sanctity were especially potent calls to community action. Sanctions against offenders ranged from mild shaming to deadly vengeance and were frequently accompanied by raucous, inebriated celebrations. By sacrificing unworthy victims, the participants purified themselves, reconfirmed their own virtue, and made an example of anyone who might be tempted to challenge the system. Social leaders often condemned the charivari, and a few progressives even attempted to interfere with it, but the majority endorsed its activities through either their participation or their silence. Once in a while, as in a lynching or the aftermath of the Nat Turner slave rebellion in Virginia in 1831, the charivari exploded in anarchy. Most of the time, as in the case of a tar-and-feathering, it expressed itself in stylized, almost formal rituals whose principal purpose was punishment and humiliation rather than death.

Thus, the Army of Northern Virginia began its invasion in a divided state of mind. Southern honor was a tense, volatile value system, wracked by internal inconsistencies that could be resolved only within a narrow range of behavior. On the one hand, it often instilled great personal virtue in the individual. Thousands of Confederates entered Northern territory determined to emulate General Lee's noble example. Yet, paradoxically, the vices embodied in this ethic were also capable of undermining the very virtues they were supposed to maintain. Even as they claimed that they guided their lives by the highest ethical standards, Southerners practiced intolerance and inequality. In their hands, the concept of honor was fully capable of becoming an instrument of violent oppression against anyone who dared to oppose them. This tendency the Confederates also took with them to Pennsylvania.

Lee's gray-clad legions began moving north in the middle of June, crossing the Potomac River into Maryland. By June 15, the cavalry advance guard had reached the Mason-Dixon line, the border between Maryland and Pennsylvania and, traditionally, the symbolic dividing point between North and South. Beyond lay territory that was alien in more senses than one.

The Cumberland Valley of southwestern Pennsylvania had been settled by Scotch-Irish and German immigrants in the first half of the eighteenth century. The German majority imparted a strong ethnic flavor to the region that continues to characterize it even today. These settlers, often members of close-knit Protestant religious groups, were distinguished by their hard work, pacifism, and commitment to traditional Germanic folkways. Native-born Americans called them the Pennsylvania Dutch, a corruption of the word *Deutsch*. To the invading Southerners, this culture would have appeared profoundly foreign. It would also have symbolized Yankee society and Yankee institutions, which Southerners were conditioned to regard as inferior.

In keeping with their commander's high-minded expectations, the Confederates entered Pennsylvania in an idealistic mood, determined to vindicate their self-image. The publication of General Orders Number 72 and 73 produced widespread support that was reflected in the personal letters and diaries of soldiers of all ranks. "Gen. Lee has issued very stringent orders about private property," noted Lieutenant Colonel Franklin Gaillard of South Carolina in a letter written home to his brother. "He is very right. . . . [W]e must not imitate the Yankees in their mean acts." Preston H. Turner, a noncommissioned officer from North Carolina, echoed these sentiments: "I think it is right to show them we are gentlemen." With more attention to propriety than to spelling or punctuation, one Georgia infantryman outlined his thoughts as follows: "I feel like retaliating in the strictest sense. I don't think we would do wrong to take houses; burn houses; and commit evry [*sic*] depredation possible upon the men of the North. I can't vindicate the principle of injuring, or insulting the female sex, though they be never so disloyal to our Confederacy and its institutions. Could I ever condescend to the degrading principle of taking from a female's person, a piece of jewelry?, Shall I ever become so thoughtless of my character or forgetful of my raising,? God forbid."

Throughout the invasion, Lee's men tried hard to be magnanimous conquerors. Commercial destruction was kept to a minimum. The Confederates gleefully burned the Caledonia Iron Works, owned by the notorious abolitionist Thaddeus Stevens, but this was a legitimate industrial target, vulnerable under any definition of the laws of war. Military seizures, including thousands of horses and cattle, were carefully repaid in Confederate currency or government requisitions. Major General Jubal A. Early, an infantry commander with a reputation for harshness, levied a ransom of $100,000 on the town of York but allowed the town fathers to escape with a payment of $28,000. Occasional crimes against the inhabitants were promptly punished under military law. Most looting involved petty seizures of hats, shoes, fence rails, vegetables, fruit, and other articles that officers and enlisted men regarded as fair prey.

Describing their own behavior, the Confederates waxed self-congratulatory, even smug. "[Y]ou may believe that the people was very near skird to death but wee treated them with respect," one North Carolinian proudly wrote home to his family. "I have heard of no case of outrage to person or property," averred a Virginia staff officer. "Such is Genl Lees order. . . . And what Genl Lee says the army does down to the lowest private because they say 'I reckon he knows.' " In York, even as the Confederate ransom was under way, one officer called the townspeople together to remind them of how courteously the rebels were behaving. "You can see for yourselves we are not conducting ourselves like enemies today," he lectured the residents. "We are not burning your houses or butchering your children. On the contrary, we are behaving ourselves like Christian gentlemen, as we are. . . . Are we not a fine set of fellows? You must admit that we are."

This legend of rectitude only grew in the retelling. By postwar times, it had reached truly preposterous extremes. In his memoirs, written years after the war, General Early advanced the improbable claim that his men had not touched so much as a single fence rail. Early's subordinate, Brigadier General John B. Gordon, admitted to the destruction of one fence but maintained that he had personally returned the horse his men had tried to steal. In their own minds, at least, the Confederates' policy of forbearance was an unquestioned success.

Yet as the long gray columns wound through the countryside, passing through such picturesque villages as Mercersburg, Shippensburg, and Greencastle, it quickly became apparent that the local citizenry did not appreciate the considerate treatment they were receiving. Instead of displaying respect or gratitude, they insulted their conquerors with irreverent, provocative behavior. The worst offenders were the women who openly jeered the passing soldiers' ragged condition, held their noses at the smell of unwashed men, turned their backs to the street, sang Union songs, and waved Union flags with enthusiasm. To one young Confederate, the people "looked mad & sullen at our appearance[. A] great many closed doors; stores all closed." Another enlisted man complained: "I often felt as if I was amidst heathen[. T]hey all looked grim and angry[. N]ot a wave of Hankerchief was made for us [by any of the women] after we left Maryland."

Stung by this unexpected hostility, Lee's men responded with increasing contempt. Their comments took on a more menacing tone. "Here you find none of that grace of manners, high-toned sentiment, or intellectual culture that you find in old Virginia," a Catholic chaplain grumbled. "Indeed, with all their wealth they [the Yankees] appear little advanced in civilization." A disturbing common theme emerged in many letters: the supposed contrast between the beauty of the countryside and the inferior foreign population that inhabited it. A Virginia artilleryman wrote that his unit had been "marching constantly & through the finest country I ever laid my eyes on, inhabited by the hardest looking set of people— *abolition Dutch.* We have passed through such a number of little towns that I can't remember the names of half of them but the principal ones were Chambersburg & Shippensburg. The former is a place of about 10,000 inhabitants, all Dutch & the meanest looking white people I ever saw." A North Carolina lieutenant expressed a similar opinion: "[T]his is a fine country the fields all covered with the finest Wheat I ever saw. . . . And the People Generly Ugly. [T]hey are a mixed people, Dutch, Irish, &c." Colonel Collett Leventhorpe, a fellow Tarheel, was even more blunt: "This is the best farming country I almost ever saw. But such stupid, boorish people—genuine Dutch!"

Ominously, the Confederates reserved their harshest and most bitter comments for the women:

> This is a most magnificent country to look at, but the most miserable people. I have yet to see a nice looking lady. They are coarse and dirty, and the number of dirty looking children is perfectly astonishing. A great many of the women go barefooted and but a small fraction wear stockings. I hope we may never have such people. . . . Their dwelling houses are large and comfortable . . . but such coarse louts that live in them. I really did not believe that there was so much difference between our ladies and their females. I have seen no ladies.

> What a race of people! Until yesterday when we reached this place [Carlisle] I have seen nothing approaching to good looks in the women. Real specimens of the Dutch boors. The heavy brutish lips, thick drooping eyelids indicate plainly the stupidity of the people.

> The people in the towns seem to stir about as much as usual or more, and behave pretty well, except that now & then the women turn their backs on us, or bring up a decided pout, which as they are naturally very much uglier & coarser than ours doesn't improve them, in fact it is a trial their faces are not up to.

> I believe I never told you any thign [*sic*] about the Girls of Pennsylvania. Neither is it necessary that I should, for they are the ugliest set of mortals I ever saw, long faced bare footed big nose and every thing else that it takes to constitute an ugly woman. I do not say this out of any disrespect, but because it is the truth.

On the surface, these comments might seem simply amusing, the petulance of conceited young men spurned by patriotic Northern women. In fact, it was a far more dangerous development. Describing one's foes as subhuman, a process called depersonalization, is a psychological technique that has been practiced by warriors since ancient times. By stripping the enemy of human fellowship, it rationalizes retaliation and lessens inconvenient feelings of guilt. Wartime dehumanization often precedes an increase in violence.

While this disturbing trend was under way, the Confederate army continued its advance. As its point of concentration, General Lee had picked the small crossroads town of Chambersburg. Founded in 1764 on Falling Spring, a tributary of the Conococheague River, Chambersburg was the seat of Franklin County and a prosperous commercial center of 6000 whose assets included a foundry, an edged tool factory, a paper mill, one bank, two breweries, and four hotels. Unfortunately for the residents, its location on the Cumberland Valley Railroad, and on the main turnpikes leading north and east through South Mountain, made it a logical campground for the invading Southerners. Here Lee could rest his weary men while keeping a wary eye on the movements of the Army of the Potomac, somewhere east of the mountains.

The first troops to reach Chambersburg, Brigadier General Albert G. Jenkins's cavalrymen, clattered into town on June 15 and remained two days before leaving to scout the army's advance. One week later, Lieutenant General Richard S. Ewell, commanding the Second Corps, occupied the town and established headquarters in the courthouse. Two of his infantry divisions camped nearby; the third, commanded by General Early, camped along a parallel road 10 miles east. On June 26, as Ewell's men departed north, headed toward Carlisle, Lieutenant General A. Powell Hill's Third Corps arrived from the south. With Hill came General Lee, who pitched his tent in the woods just outside town and remained there directing the army's operations for the next four days. By June 28, with the arrival of Lieutenant General James Longstreet's First Corps, six Confederate infantry divisions held positions in the immediate vicinity, a total of more than 60,000 men for whom the town was forced to play unwilling host.

The reception these troops encountered was as negative as it had been elsewhere. "Passed through Chambersburg. . . ." a Virginia surgeon wrote in his diary. "Stores closed but streets & windows filled in with men and women, the latter very common looking, not to compare with our Southern females. . . . Some of the women were very impudent." One group of women blocked a Confederate column by standing defiantly in the roadway, refusing to move. The officer in charge ordered his men to break ranks and march around the human barricade. As Francis Warrington Dawson, a British soldier of fortune, rode through town, his horse stumbled on the cobblestones, sending him sprawling. Dawson was irked to hear a female voice exult: "Thank God, one of those wicked Rebels has broken his neck."

Even foreign observers noted the hostility of the townspeople. Lieutenant Colonel James Arthur Lyon Fremantle, an officer in the Coldstream Guards who was visiting the Confederate army, felt that the natives regarded the troops "in a very unfriendly manner." He described Chambersburg women as "viragos" and recorded that they "were particularly sour and disagreeable in their remarks." The colonel remarked on "the singular good behavior of the troops towards the citizens" but added that "I heard soldiers saying to one another that they did not like being in a town in which they were very naturally detested." He concluded that the residents seemed "not the least thankful" for Confederate forbearance.

Major General Lafayette McLaws, one of Longstreet's division commanders, summarized the hardening Southern attitude:

> At Green Castle on the road to Chambersburg, several young ladies were assembled engaged in scoffing at our men as they passed, but they were treated with contempt or derision. I heard of nothing witty said by any of them. It was made evident however that they were not ladies in the Southern acceptation of the word. . . . The people of Chambersburg are decidedly hostile. The men dare not show it but by their looks. The women tried to be sarcastic on various occasions but succeeded in being vulgar only. They are a very different race from the Southerner. There is a coarseness in their manner and looks and a twang in their voices, which grates harshly on the senses of our men.

However strong the impressions it created, the occupation of southern Pennsylvania lasted less than a week. On June 29, having learned that the Union army was advancing, Lee began a reconcentration of his forces 25 miles farther east, at Gettysburg. Most of his army departed Chambersburg soon afterward. Major General George E. Pickett's division, designated the rear guard, remained in the town until July 2, a circumstance that delayed its arrival on the battlefield and determined its employment in the climactic third day's assault, ever afterward known as "Pickett's Charge."

At Gettysburg, Lee's hopes for a decisive Southern victory ended in bloodshed and defeat. For three days he aimed sledgehammer blows at the Army of the Potomac, trying to break its ranks. The Union army stood firm. Following the repulse of Pickett's Charge on July 3, the Army of Northern Virginia had no recourse but to retreat. During the third week in July, it slipped back across the Potomac River into Virginia. Never again would the Confederates pose a major threat to the North. In the judgment of many historians, the Battle of Gettysburg may well have been the military turning point of the war.

Along with the unaccustomed shock of defeat, Lee's disgruntled troops took with them their unpleasant memories of the North, many of which were now focused on one Cumberland Valley town. Nearly a month after the army returned to Virginia, resentment still lingered in Colonel Gaillard's comment that the Pennsylvanians "looked at us with sour faces, long faces, and indifferent faces." Such recollections festered long after the campaign ended.

The following summer, the Confederates returned to Chambersburg.

Much had changed during the previous twelve months. The tide of victory, which seemed to be flowing so strongly in the South's favor, had now reversed its course. In Georgia, Major General William Tecumseh Sherman had begun the campaign for Atlanta that was to make his name a legendary byword for cruelty. In Virginia, a new Northern commander, Lieutenant General Ulysses S. Grant, had undertaken a campaign of attrition that had backed Lee's army into the defense of Petersburg, a vital railroad center south of Richmond. In an effort to distract Grant's attention, Lee dispatched a small diversionary force commanded by Jubal A. Early into the Shenandoah Valley with orders to threaten Washington,

D.C. Though technically still under Lee's command, Early was for all practical purposes an independent commander with the right to determine policy in his theater of war.

Unlike Lee, General Early was not committed to humanistic principles of warfare. By nature he was an entirely different personality, almost a mirror opposite of his courtly superior. Whereas Lee was tall, handsome, and always impeccably groomed, Early was grizzled, twisted by arthritis, and handicapped by a speech impediment that caused him to stutter. Lee was invariably courteous, the perfect gentleman; Early had served as district attorney in his native Franklin County, Virginia, and was renowned for his abrasive tongue and sarcastic sense of humor. Lee was a pillar of conventional rectitude, happily married with numerous children; Early was a misanthropic bachelor who flouted traditional morality by living for years with a mistress.

Like Grant, Sherman, Philip H. Sheridan, Nathan Bedford Forrest, and many other leaders who rose to prominence during the second half of the war, Early was a modern warrior with little patience for half measures. His ransom on York during the Gettysburg campaign was typical of his approach to warfare. From the beginning, his expedition was characterized by a spiraling cycle of violence and

As though in deliberate contrast to the elegantly tailored Lee, Lieutenant General Jubal A. Early posed for his portrait in shabby uniform and unkempt beard. His attitude toward warfare was similarly unromantic. "If I had had an opportunity," he wrote following the war, "I would have done much more burning in the enemy's country." (Cook Collection/Valentine Museum)

by increasing ferocity toward civilians. Among many other incidents, the Confederates extracted a "contribution" of $200,000 from Frederick, Maryland, by threatening to burn it. Early also extorted smaller sums of $5000 from Middletown and $20,000 from Hagerstown. In revenge for these depredations, a frustrated local Union commander torched three private homes owned by Southern sympathizers in Jefferson County, West Virginia.

On June 28, Early placed Brigadier General John McCausland in charge of two mounted brigades and an artillery battery, a force that included General Albert Jenkins's former cavalry command and was familiar with the route into Pennsylvania. A tough West Virginia mountaineer, McCausland was an ideal foil for his combative commander. Early's written orders, all copies of which later disappeared, instructed McCausland to occupy Chambersburg and to demand of its inhabitants the sum of $500,000 in "greenbacks" (federal paper money) or $100,000 in gold as compensation for the three houses that had been burned. In default of payment, McCausland was commanded "to lay the town in ashes."

In a series of postwar statements, Early blandly defended his course of action and his choice of Chambersburg as a target. The size of the ransom, he claimed, was equivalent to the value of the private property destroyed; Chambersburg was selected for the reprisal "because it was the only one [town] of any consequence accessible to my troops." The general maintained that he bore the community no grudge and that he set his levy at a reasonable figure to offer the residents a genuine chance to save their homes. None of these claims stands up under analysis. The three homes for which the ransom was supposedly retaliation could not possibly have been worth so large a sum. Several other Pennsylvania towns, equally prosperous, were within striking distance of the raiders. The ransom demanded of Chambersburg, a town of 6000 with one bank, was more than twice as large as the amount extorted from Frederick, a community of 8000 and five banks. Most revealing of all, perhaps, was Early's comment in an unpublished postwar letter to the owner of one of the houses: "If I had had an opportunity I would have done much more burning in the enemy's country." Taken together, the evidence suggests that Chambersburg's fate was sealed the moment McCausland departed on his terrible mission.

After riding through the night, the Confederate troopers reached their destination at dawn on Sunday, July 30, 1864. Once again, as they had done the year before, the residents acted defiantly. The town council refused even to meet with the invaders. While some citizens urged the cavalrymen to lower their demands, others taunted the Southerners, unable to believe they would actually carry out their threat. In any event, the issue of compliance was moot: warned in advance of the approaching raiders, the town's bankers had escaped during the night, taking their cash assets with them. After waiting an interval variously estimated at three to six hours, during which his troopers openly prepared for their grim task, McCausland put the community to the torch.

The morning was sultry, not a breath of fresh air stirring. The plumes of smoke from individual fires rose lazily and straight into the air, first one, then another, blending inexorably into a single lurid column that overspread the sky. Around it long streams of flame wrapped themselves, twisting and writhing into a thousand fantastic shapes. The burning mass formed fearful whirlwinds that swept through the streets, early versions of the firestorms that ravaged European and Asian cities following aerial bombardments during World War II. One gust passed over a collected pile of apparel, sending clothes shooting nearly a hundred yards into the air and scattering them far and wide. The roar and surging of the flames, the crackling and crash of falling timbers, mingled in terrible dissonance with the cries of hogs, cows, and horses trapped helplessly in their pens.

The flames appeared momentarily to converge on the Diamond, as townspeople called their central square, and then shifted, racing eastward along Market Street. They devoured every building save four along the west side of Main Street for a distance of three blocks; roared up New England Hill a total of five blocks more; consumed Queen Street from the town market to Huber & Company's edged tool factory, including the foundry that stood parallel to Falling Spring; and leaped erratically from building to building on Second Street as far as the doors of the Methodist Church. Later, distraught citizens assessing the damage found that the entire central business and residential district—twelve square blocks surrounding the Diamond—had been gutted. Here and there a few isolated piles remained standing, some by intention, the majority by inadvertence. Only the outskirts of the community survived relatively intact.

Squads of Confederates fanned out through the thoroughfares, breaking open doors with axes and turning out terrified families into the streets. Most victims were given ten minutes or less to save their possessions. Few managed to save anything more than the clothes on their backs. Singular acts of cruelty accompanied these proceedings. At one home, soldiers locked a woman into an upstairs bedroom while they set the dwelling on fire beneath her. At another, they poured gunpowder under an elderly invalid's chair, swearing they would teach her to walk. Neighbors managed to rescue both victims before the flames reached them. At a third house, where the owner's wife had just died in childbirth, the soldiers interrupted the wake, forcing the mourners to bury the body in the garden to save it from the flames. One sick child was rushed to safety on a shutter.

As the fire spread, many Confederates lost all sense of military discipline. Officers found it impossible to control their men. The soldiers pillaged freely, robbing citizens of sums large and small. As they moved from house to house, they systematically ransacked bureaus, wardrobes, and trunks before setting fire to the contents. The bartender at Montgomery's Hotel lost $700, his life savings, as he attempted to flee his room. Another resident was hustled into an alley and relieved of $1.60. Some rebels extorted their own individual ransom payments to protect houses. More often they simply pocketed the money and then applied the match.

Fleeing to safety, the family of Jacob Hoke was accosted by an officer on horseback who entreated one of the women to mount behind him, shouting wildly that he was done with military service. No sooner had he disappeared than another materialized, demanding the family's carpetbags. Around them, in the smoke-shrouded streets, drunken cavalrymen reeled along the sidewalks "in every possible disguise and paraphernalia." Screaming women and children ran frantically to and fro, desperately seeking relatives or possessions. "I never witnessed such a site in all my life," wrote one soldier to his wife. "Nancy, the poor wim-men and children and also gray heard men was runing in every direction with a little bundle of cloths under there arms crying and skreaming."

A few courageous soldiers resisted their orders or found ways to avoid car-rying them out. One officer, stationed in the southeastern quarter of town, kept his troops so busy evacuating people that they somehow never found time to apply the torch. Another, in quiet disgust, unbuckled his sword, the cherished symbol of field command, and left it standing against the wall of a ruined house. William E. Peters, a Virginia colonel, refused outright to participate in the destruction and was placed under arrest for his courage. The day after the raid, all charges against him were dropped. But individual acts of compassion were submerged in the gen-

Only the shell of the Franklin County Courthouse remains standing after the destructive Confederate raid in July of 1864. The structure was later rebuilt. This photograph was made by a local firm, the Zacharias Brothers. It was originally re-leased in stereo format, which gave a three-dimensional effect when seen in a spe-cial viewer. (Minnesota Historical Society)

eral cataclysm. In his official report, Brigadier General Bradley T. Johnson, who commanded the second of the two participating brigades, lamented the breakdown of order: "I tried, and was seconded by almost every officer of my command, but in vain, to preserve the discipline of this brigade, but it was impossible; not only the license afforded was too great, but actual example gave them excuse and justification." Added the local Presbyterian minister: "The ferocity of the Rebel soldiers during this affair seems almost incredible. With all their fierce passions unrestrained, they seemed to revel, as if intoxicated, in the work of destruction."

Miraculously, despite numerous close calls, no citizen died in the conflagration. McCausland reported his loss at one man killed from ambush on the trip back to Virginia. Townspeople later claimed to have executed an officer whom they caught stealing personal possessions, but the individual they identified actually survived the war and lived to a ripe old age, calling this assertion into doubt. The extent of damage to the town was incontrovertible. When the incendiaries finished their task on the afternoon of July 30, more than half of Chambersburg's population was homeless. The fire destroyed 266 houses and businesses, 98 barns and stables, and 173 outbuildings of various kinds: a total of 537 structures valued at $783,950. A state commission later evaluated the total damage to real and personal property at $1,628,431. Pennsylvania appropriated $900,000 to reimburse the sufferers, but other claims, including those filed against the federal government for its failure to protect the citizens, were never resolved.

J. Kelly Bennette, a Virginia hospital steward, was among the many Confederates in McCausland's brigade who exulted at Chambersburg's downfall: "[W]hen reason had time to regain her seat I believe that they all thought as I thought at first; that it was Justice & Justice tempered with mercy. . . . That *burning per se* is wrong no one can deny. . . . But there may be circumstances under which it is not only *justifiable* but becomes a duty—stern it is true but nevertheless binding." Bennette equated the reprisal with the protection of Southern womanhood: "We are in this war to defend the *women*—if we try one expedient & it fails we are recreant in our duty if we persevere in that expedient instead of changing the prescription." He acknowledged that "there were some who having become drunk seemed to glory in destruction," but he pleaded strong provocation in their behalf.

By 1864, unfortunately, such sentiments were probably shared by many Southern leaders. One looks in vain for criticism from the apostle of moderation, General Lee: his writings during and after the war contain not one word of disavowal or regret. General Early later cited Lee's silence as tacit approval of his actions: "I gave the order on my own responsibility, but General Lee never in any manner indicated any disapproval of my act, and his many letters to me expressive of confidence and friendship forbade the idea that he disapproved of my conduct on that occasion." Had Lee abandoned his principles or concluded that his earlier policy was a mistake? The record is eloquently silent. In his bulky two-volume memoirs, published two decades after the war, former Confederate President Jefferson Davis simply quoted Early's version of events without further discussion. In the words of one historian, such bitterness was an unhappy commentary on the last year of a struggle that had turned base and desperate, a conflict in which incidents such as Chambersburg had become "a sad, minor theme to accompany the major chords."

AN INTERPRETATION

The events that occurred in Chambersburg in 1863 and 1864 suggest that its tragic destruction was the result of both social tensions present in Southern society and the brutalizing escalation of the Civil War itself, which had undermined traditional humanitarian considerations toward civilians.

Like warriors everywhere else, the soldiers of the South expressed cultural beliefs and assumptions through their conduct. During the Gettysburg campaign, their attitudes were consistent with the values of their society, which had constructed a complex, highly convoluted value system to protect its most sensitive subject, slavery, from internal dissent. The Southern code of honor required the ruling elite to act toward others in a courteous, genteel fashion. However, this behavior was conditioned on the expectation that the nonelite (a comprehensive category) would acknowledge their inferiority through deferential conduct and their willingness to leave important issues to their betters. Failure to know one's place canceled any obligation on the part of the leadership to behave politely. All too often, the consequence was the orderly but violent repression exemplified by the charivari.

Lee's men entered Pennsylvania confident that the local population would appreciate their moral superiority. When it did not, the Confederates reacted with surprise, shock, and then deep anger and bitterness. It was, no doubt, unrealistic for the troops to expect Northern civilians not to express their feelings about the occupation. But the Southern response was sharpened by the concept of honor, which aggravated resentment and focused attention on those supposedly responsible for the provocation. The rebels responded sullenly to such inoffensive acts as the absence of waving handkerchiefs, while more overt forms of resistance triggered a wave of ugly depersonalization. Given the themes present in the prevailing ethic of their society, the careful distinction drawn by Confederate soldiers between "Southern ladies" and "Northern females" was fraught with fatal significance. Such bizarre overreactions were comprehensible only in the context of a society in which foreigners or women were not expected to have opinions about anything important and could be punished if they did.

In 1863, military discipline and the example of General Lee were still strong enough to prevent immediate reprisals against the townspeople. By the following year, those constraints had eroded. When the Confederates returned to Pennsylvania in 1864, they finally settled scores with the community most strongly identified with enemy values. Indeed, what happened to Chambersburg may be seen as a charivari in which an entire town was called to account, punished, and humiliated for its conduct. Numerous reports testify to the breakdown of military discipline and to the atmosphere of dark carnival that attended the event. The formal, ineffective protests by some Confederate officers, the silence of General Lee, the drunken celebrations, the revelry in destruction, the mingling of the twin themes of justice and saturnalia, the association of ladyhood with the need for retaliation, and even the limitations of the reprisal itself (in which property was unhesitatingly destroyed but no one was killed or raped) all fit the tragic pattern of the charivari and support the interpretation that the Southerners viewed their requital in social as well as military terms. This belief would have had the advantage of rationalizing their behavior, thereby mitigating any sense of guilt they might have felt and even permitting them to emerge from their grim work with a renewed sense of virtue.

Honor explains the manner in which Chambersburg was targeted for vengeance and the process through which the reprisal eventually occurred. But the soldiers of the Army of Northern Virginia were also shaped by the tendency of warfare to brutalize its participants. Regrettably, this was an influence to which human beings have always been vulnerable. Dehumanization, for example, is as old as recorded history. It can be found in the writings of early Greek historians such as Herodotus and Thucydides. In extreme form, it has rationalized many of the most horrible genocidal events of the twentieth century, including the Holocaust during World War II. Sadly enough, the Civil War is far from the only case study of depersonalization at work in the United States, for American soldiers have surrendered to these impulses in other wars as well. During the Philippine Insurrection, United States troops referred to their Filipino adversaries as "niggers" and wrote comments home such as the following: "I am probably growing hardhearted, for I am in my glory when I can sight my gun on some dark skin and pull the trigger" (see Stuart Creighton Miller, "Empire in the Philippines: America's Forgotten War of Colonial Conquest," in Volume II of *True Stories from the American Past*). In a similar spirit, American propaganda toward Japan in World War II was highly racist, while Americans in Vietnam referred to both their allies and the enemy as "slants" or "gooks," an attitude that contributed to atrocities such as the My Lai massacre.

Some historians view the Civil War as a watershed in the development of such savage forces. During the first half of the nineteenth century, warfare underwent a profound and terrible transformation, with results that affected world history. The democratic nationalism of the French Revolution, sustained by deadly new technology and modern techniques of industrial production, swept away many old European conventions. The eighteenth-century concept of limited war, which minimized bloodshed and destruction, was supplanted by total war, which mingled social, political, and strategic objectives in a ruthless new ethic. Total war engaged the full resources of the nation-state and its population in a life-or-death struggle for survival.

In the wake of the Napoleonic conflict, foreign experts tried to assess its implications. In his famous treatise *On War* (1832), the Prussian military theorist Carl von Clausewitz speculated that the perilous combination of democracy and total war would unleash mankind's basest passions, thereby leading to what he called the "absolute perfection" of warfare—a state of pure violence, unrestrained by the ordinary conventions of peacetime society.

Alexis de Tocqueville, who toured the United States during the same period and observed its institutions in action, reinforced these observations by pointing out that American democracy was especially vulnerable to these forces. Americans, he predicted in the second volume of *Democracy in America* (1840), would fight with irresistible determination in time of conflict because of the totality of their involvement: "War . . . in the end becomes the one great industry, and every eager and ambitious desire sprung from equality is focused thereon."

Clausewitz and Tocqueville were among the first to suspect that the pressures of total war would brutalize the participants and ultimately reflect their most negative characteristics. Unfortunately, the course of events in the Civil War proved them right. Northerners and Southerners alike began the conflict as an affirmation of high American ideals. Both sides suffered an escalation in violence; both sides gradually gave way to vengeful impulses that undermined their commitment to principle and unleashed ugly passions that simmered under the surface of their societies.

Thus, the burning of Chambersburg may also be interpreted as a consequence of the deterioration of a society waging a terrible war for survival and acting with increasing desperation to achieve it. In 1863, the dominant influence in the Confederate army was still General Lee's moderate policy of forbearance. But by 1864, Northern leaders such as Grant and Sherman were scourging the Southern countryside, the Confederacy faced not only military defeat but the complete destruction of its value system, and the attitude of the typical soldier was perhaps best represented by General Early, who shamelessly destroyed an entire city and regretted only his inability to punish the hated Yankees further. Under these circumstances, the violent proclivities of Southern society were much more easily unleashed. Even Lee, through his silence, appears to have accepted the new order of things. Whether or not the outcome might have been different had Lee personally been in charge—and his moral stature among Southerners remained great—it is noteworthy that the perpetrators were never disciplined by their own commander.

To be sure, Confederate satisfaction at the destruction of Chambersburg was short-lived, for it only intensified the escalation of violence and the punishment of the South. The news roused Abraham Lincoln to fury and brought a new Union commander, Philip H. Sheridan, to the Shenandoah Valley promising a scorched-earth policy that, in Grant's famous phrase, would force crows to carry their own rations. Sheridan's army trounced Early in the autumn of 1864, ending Confederate supremacy in this region of Virginia. Farther west, General Sherman cited Chambersburg as a justification for his own firestorm of retribution in Georgia. Some of his soldiers used the town as their rallying cry when they set fire to Atlanta just before starting the March to the Sea.

Thus did the South pay dearly for its brief moment of vengeance. In later years, many Southerners recognized their error. As William C. Oates, a former infantry colonel, regretfully acknowledged in 1905, "It never pays to do wrong to spite some one else for having acted likewise. This is true of armies as well as individuals." Tragically for all concerned, the South absorbed its lesson far too late. Will Americans in future wars learn from history or repeat the mistakes of the past?

Sources: A scholarly version of this article first appeared in *The American Historical Review* (April 1991) as "Chambersburg: Anatomy of a Confederate Reprisal." The unpublished letters and diaries of Confederate soldiers provide the best insight into their thoughts during and after the Gettysburg campaign. These letters are preserved in archives by the tens of thousands. Two major repositories used in the research for this article are the Southern Historical Collection at the University of North

Carolina at Chapel Hill and the Manuscripts Department of Duke University. Edward B. Coddington, *The Gettysburg Campaign* (1968), and Frank E. Vandiver, *Jubal's Raid: General Early's Famous Attack on Washington in 1864* (1960), provide a context for these two operations. Recent secondary works that explore the complex interrelationship of Civil War soldiers and their society are Gerald F. Linderman, *Embattled Courage: The Experience of Combat in the American Civil War* (1987), and Reid Mitchell, *Civil War Soldiers* (1988). Both authors argue that the idealistic virtues of soldiers North and South were undermined by their wartime experience. Bertram Wyatt-Brown, *Honor and Violence in the Old South* (1986), is a provocative investigation into the strange synergy of violence and antebellum Southern culture, a topic that has intrigued many historians.

15

AN INSURRECTION THAT NEVER HAPPENED: THE "CHRISTMAS RIOTS" OF 1865

STEPHEN NISSENBAUM

At the end of the Civil War there remained the unresolved question of what was to be done about the more than three million African-Americans who had been freed from slavery. White Southerners were fearful about their own economic futures, to say nothing of fears for their physical safety if their former slaves united in retribution. Freed slaves had every reason to expect that a government which had been willing to sacrifice over 300,000 lives to end the slave system would also be willing to provide them with the essential economic means—land—to allow them to become contributing members of society. Yet the fate of both white Southerners and freedmen and freedwomen was in the hands of Northern politicians who had never been able to agree that the rights of freedpeople were a high priority in the war. What was universally celebrated at war's end was the subjugation of the South and the preservation of the Union. Considering that so many lives had been sacrificed, it was almost inevitable that the Union had become a "holy" cause, couched, by the President himself, in terms of a religious cleansing that would lead to a sanctified nation.

This emphasis on the preservation of the Union rather than the rights of African-Americans was clear from the beginning of the war right through to the end. Lincoln's Emancipation Proclamation, for example, was a very controversial, politically sensitive document. The President stood to lose much of his support for the war if he were to issue it in the early stages; such a proclamation only became feasible when the Union was in a militarily strong position after the bloody battle of Antietam. Even then the proclamation did not free slaves in slave states that had sided with the Union—Delaware, Maryland, Kentucky, and Missouri. In the South, of course, with the Confederacy in control, the proclamation had no effect until the military situation changed. Another example is the decision to use African-American troops in the Northern army. Northerners demonstrated their racism by initially denying the right of free blacks in the North to fight for the Union cause. Even when it became clear that enthusiasm for the war was waning and conscription was necessary to fill the ranks of the army, there was resistance to allowing African-Americans to fight. Only because of that shortage of men combined with extensive politicking and lobbying on the part of African-American leaders such as Frederick Douglas did black regiments become grudgingly acceptable to Northerners. Despite the not inconsiderable accomplishment of ending slavery as an institution, the still rampant racist attitudes in the North made the future of African-American freedpeople in the South very precarious.

Stephen Nissenbaum's story of the rumored Christmas insurrection reveals much about the immediate aftermath of the Civil War, when the hopes of freedpeople soared and white Southerners' fears reached almost hysterical proportions—emotions that were exacerbated by contested and ambiguous Northern policies. But this story also explores the nature of human relations in the plantation South before the war, the human give-and-take that was impossible to avoid, even though whites attempted to deny the essential humanity of their slaves. Embedded in the rituals of Christmas was reinforcement of the unequal and oppressive power hierarchy juxtaposed with the potential for resistance and the ultimate destruction of that hierarchy. What we know now is that despite the sacrifices of the Civil War, the Reconstruction era was not to overturn the hierarchy at all; that would have to wait another hundred years.

This is the story of an insurrection that never happened—a revolt that was never even planned. It is a story that would never have taken place at all except for the convergence of three elements, each involving a different kind of "history." The first element, one of *military history,* was the defeat of the South at the end of the Civil War. The second element, one of *political and economic history,* was the liberation of slaves and a new federal policy that promised them their own land. The third and final element, one of *social and cultural history,* was Christmas.

It is that final element, Christmas, which requires the most explanation. The Christmas season had long been a special occasion in the American South for both white and black people. And for the most part the season did not involve what we might expect—church services, or elegant balls, or Santa Claus. Instead, this was a season of hard drinking, noisemaking, and generally rowdy behavior. (It can best be considered as a New Year's Eve, Mardi Gras, and Halloween, all rolled into one.) Christmas was a time when the ordinary rules that governed social behavior simply ceased to operate, or when those rules were actually turned upside down. Children were allowed to demand gifts from grown-ups, women from men, and the poor from the rich. This was an occasion when "the world turned upside down." And those who really controlled Southern society—wealthy adult males— were generally willing to go along with this topsy-turvy state of affairs: they knew it would only last a short time.

As early as 1773, one visitor recorded in his diary on Christmas day that "I was waked this morning by Guns fired all around the House." In 1823, a rural white Southerner attacked the Christmas season for being a "general scene of dissipation and idleness." Some folks spent the time making "rough jokes." "Apprentice boys and little negroes" fired guns and crackers. And everyone—"parents, children, servants, old, young, white, black, and yellow"—drank hard. "And if you inquire what it is all for, no earthly reason is assigned . . . , except this, 'Why man! It is Christmas.' " More than three decades later, a teenage Virginia girl named Amanda Edmonds was awakened "by the repeated blows of the firecrackers, and the merry voices shouting 'hurr[a]y for Christmas,' and then the nog was on the wing until the eggs were foaming, in went the milk and all ingredients poured together; lastly it was foaming in our glasses, till they were drained of the contents."

Everybody commented at the time about how much Southerners drank during the Christmas season. It is clear that people—women and even children among them—commonly began drinking at breakfast. Teenager Amanda Edmonds began Christmas day in 1857 drinking "glass after glass" of spiked eggnog. Once again, in 1861, the first thing Edmonds did in the morning was to have "a joyful eggnog drink—I really got tight. The first signs of Christmas that I've seen."

The American South was not unique in celebrating the Christmas season in such a fashion. In much of the North, and in Europe, too—in most early agricultural societies—late December was taken as a time of carnival. Here was the one time of the year in which there was fresh food and drink aplenty from the recently completed harvest and an extended period of leisure in which to consume it— leisure that followed hard upon months of grueling and intensive labor. (In a way, it was much like the same holiday season in modern college communities, in which the conclusion of final examinations is similarly celebrated with boisterous drinking and letting off steam.)

But in one important particular, Christmas in the antebellum South was unique. For, in that society, all those carnivalesque holiday rituals extended across the color line—they encompassed black slaves as well as their white masters. If Southern society was "turned upside down" at Christmas, that inversion involved not simply age, class, and gender (as it did in other places); above all, it involved race.

First of all, Christmas in the slave quarters meant *freedom*—for a little while. Christmas was the one time of year when slaves were released from the obligation to work, usually for several days in a row. Slaves became, in a sense, free— free from labor, free to do whatever they wished, free even to travel off their masters' property. One Northerner, living on a plantation as a tutor to the owner's children, reported that "[t]hroughout the state of South Carolina, Christmas is a holiday, together with 2 of the succeeding days . . . especially for the negroes. On these days the chains of slavery . . . are loosed. A smile is seen on every countenance."

Slaves employed their freedom in a variety of ways, from visiting friends and family members to participating in religious meetings. But perhaps the activities that were most often reported involved revelry: eating, drinking, dancing, making noise, and making love. Solomon Northup, a free black who was kidnapped into slavery in Louisiana, later wrote of Christmas as "the times of feasting, and frolicking, and fiddling—the carnival season with the children of bondage . . . the only days when they are allowed a little restricted liberty, and heartily indeed do they enjoy it." A white Southerner used the same term, calling Christmas "the time of the blacks' high carnival," while another white man described the period as "times of cramming, truly awful. [T]hey stuffed and drank, and sang and danced." The wife of ex-U.S. President John Tyler wrote in 1845 that the family's slaves "have from now a four days' holiday and have given themselves up completely to *their* kind of happiness—drinking, with nothing on earth to do."

It seems clear that sex was involved in all this, too. More than one visitor explicitly described the slave Christmas as a modern version of the old Roman Saturnalia, an orgiastic occasion. One writer who did so employed language whose euphemisms were not intended to conceal the author's meaning: "From three to four days *and* nights are given as holiday, during which every indulgence and license consistent with any subordination and safety are allowed."

Christmas misrule entailed even more than leisure and "liberty." It also meant a symbolic turning of the tables between masters and slaves. Christmas was the one occasion of the year when slaves were actually allowed to demand gifts from their masters, even to do so in an aggressive fashion that might have led to a whipping at any other time of the year. One common seasonal ritual was termed "Christmas Gift." "Christmas Gift!" usually amounted to a boisterous wake-up call combined with a demand for presents. A former slave described one version of the ritual: "The cock crowing for sunrise is scarcely over when the servants steal into the Big House on tiptoe so they can catch everybody there with a shouted 'Christmas Gift!' before the kitchen fire is even started or the water put on to boil for the early morning coffee." In response, each member of the white family who is thus "captured" must hand over a gift to the slave who has "caught" her. Years later, a planter's daughter, Susan Dabney Smedes, described the game with nostalgic affection:

> On Christmas mornings the servants delighted in catching the family [i.e., the owner's family] with "Christmas giff!" "Christmas giff!" betimes in the morning. They would spring out of unexpected corners and from behind doors on the young masters and mistresses. At such times [she adds in explanation] there was an affectionate throwing off of the reserve and decorum of every-day life.

Young Amanda Edmonds, the same teenager who got tight on eggnog at breakfast, wrote to her diary in 1857 that " 'Christmas Gift' was heard from every tongue this morning before we hardly saw the first gleam of morning in the far east." The recollections of a one-time slave, a Georgia field hand named James Bolton, suggest that the custom was not always limited to house servants: "We runned up to the big house early Christmas morning and holler out, 'Morning, Christmas Gif!' Then they gave us plenty of Santy Claus, and we would go back to our cabins to have fun till New Year's Day."

Christmas was the one occassion of the year on which plantation owners would formally offer presents to their chattel slaves. It was a rare planter who did not give something to his slaves at Christmas. At a minimum, the gifts were small—the kinds of things we might dismiss today as "trinkets" but which the slaves had good reason to value: sugar, tobacco, or hats, along with ribbons, bandannas, and other decorative items for the women. Some slaveholders distributed money. An especially lavish (and ostentatious) example of this practice was reported by Richard Jones, a former slave from South Carolina, whose account also reminds us how demeaning such ritualized generosity could be:

> Marse allus carried a roll of money as big as my arm. He would come up to de Quarter on Christmas, July 4th and Thanksgiving, and get up on a stump and call all the chilluns out. Den he would throw money to 'em. De chilluns got dimes, nickels, quarters, half-dollars and dollars. At Christmas he would throw ten-dollar bills. De parents would take de five and ten dollar bills in change, but Marse made dem let de chilluns keep de small change. I ain't never seed so much money since my marster been gone.

Dressing for the Carnival (1877). The great American artist Winslow Homer painted this large oil canvas while traveling in southern Virginia at the very end of Reconstruction. An immensely respectful and dignified portrayal, it shows a man being dressed for the John Canoe Christmas ritual by his wife and another woman as the children watch in fascination. (Metropolitan Museum of Art Amelia B. Lazarus Fund, 1922).

On many plantations slaves were asked to approach the Big House to receive their gifts in person from their master and his family (along with the family's best wishes). More often, it was masters and their families who visited the slave quarters to attend the slaves' own party there. But wherever these scenes took place, in the quarters or the Big House, some planters and their families used the occasion to make elaborate gestures of deference to their slaves. Oftentimes they joined in the festivities themselves, at least symbolically. Just as often, they prepared the party meal themselves, or they personally superintended its preparation. Occasionally, a master even made the ostentatious gesture of serving part of the meal to the slaves himself. One North Carolina slaveholder centered his version of the ritual on the preparation and distribution of eggnog: after the drink was "pronounced right," it was ceremoniously placed out on the piazza (on a beautiful mahogany table that came from the Big House). At this point the slaves assembled and were ceremoniously handed one glass apiece:

> My grandfather knew every one of his negroes, big and little, by name; and his greeting was always personal to each. They came up in couples, according to age and dignity, and the unvarying formula was: "Sarvant, Master; merry Christmas to you, an' all de fambly, sir!" "Thank you, Jack; merry Christmas to you and yours!"

Whites were aware of the symbolic significance of these gestures of deference, gestures that demonstrated that they were playing their part in the expected seasonal ritual in which the world was briefly and symbolically "turned upside down." They would refer to the unprecedented degree of "familiarity" between masters and slaves on this occasion. One Tennessee slaveowner claimed that at Christmas his "people" were "as happy as Lords." Another man wrote: "Here all authority and all distinction of colour ceases; black and white, overseer and bookkeeper, mingle together in the dance." Another planter stressed how different Christmas was from the only other holiday he permitted his sixty slaves—the Fourth of July: "The one in July is celebrated with a dinner and whiskey. The Christmas holiday is a very different thing. It lasts from four to six days, and during this *jubilee* it is difficult to say who is master. The servants are allowed the largest liberty."

"It is difficult to say who is master." That was surely an exaggeration. But it was also the very point at which the meaning of Christmas in the slave South became potentially *political*—the point at which, under certain circumstances, slaves might think about becoming their own masters for real. In fact, some black people used Christmas to take *permanent* control of their lives. For example, the season offered unique opportunities for escaping slavery altogether by running away, taking advantage of the common Christmas privilege of freedom to travel (and along roads that might now be crowded with unfamiliar black faces). Christmas also presented a tempting occasion for more aggressive forms of resistance. Sanctioned disorders could always step across the bounds and edge over into violence, riot, or even revolt. A striking number of actual or rumored slave revolts were planned to take place at Christmas—nearly one-third the known total, according to one historian. Reports of Christmas insurrection were especially rampant in 1856; in that year revolts were reported in almost every one of the Southern states.

That was in slavery times. But the most serious rumors of planned insurrection at Christmas (rumors that amounted, in the end, to very little) came just *after* the slaves were finally emancipated, with the end of the Civil War, in December 1865. Here was the point at which the memory of the traditional rituals of the Southern Christmas converged with a moment of serious political crisis in the lives of both black and white Southerners.

Some political history, then. If ever there was a time when the hopes of African-Americans were at fever pitch, it was in 1865. Those hopes had been raised by a set of executive orders and congressional acts, passed during the war itself and for essentially military purposes. The Union army of General William Tecumseh Sherman had marched irresistibly through Georgia late in 1864, finally taking Savannah in late December. (Sherman telegraphed President Lincoln a famous message, offering him Savannah as a "Christmas present.") Sherman's march had created a refugee army of slaves, tens of thousands of newly liberated slaves who were now impoverished and homeless and who turned for assistance to the Northern troops. To deal with the army of refugees, in January 1865, General Sherman issued a proclamation that would have important consequences: Special Field Order No. 15. This proclamation set aside for the freedmen any lands (in the area of his recent march) that had been confiscated by the Union army or abandoned by their white owners. These lands, to be divided into 40-acre lots, included some of the best real estate in Georgia and South Carolina.

A few months later, in March 1865, the U.S. Congress established a new federal agency, the Freedmen's Bureau, designed to deal more systematically with the difficult but imminent transition to freedom. The Freedmen's Bureau adopted Sherman's policy and extended it to the entire Confederacy. In late July, the head of the Freedmen's Bureau, General Oliver O. Howard, issued to his staff Circular No. 13 (a circular was a memorandum designed to circulate to all agents of an organization). Circular No. 13 contained a set of procedures that would divide abandoned or confiscated Southern plantations into 40-acre lots and distribute them to black families. Each of these families would receive a written certificate of possession. (The policy became associated with the catchphrase *forty acres and a mule*).

But in the summer of 1865, with the war over and Andrew Johnson in the White House, federal priorities in Washington underwent a significant change. President Johnson decided that the most important task facing the United States was not that of dealing with the freed slaves but rather that of reestablishing the loyalty of white Southerners. To do so would involve "restoring" abandoned lands to their former owners. The President now instructed General Howard to reverse his policy and to withdraw Circular No. 13. The Freedmen's Bureau was ordered to persuade the former slaves to abandon their hopes for land—and to sign labor contracts for the coming year with their former masters.

Both blacks and whites knew this was a crucial issue. Each side knew that the key to the future lay not just in legal freedom from slavery but also in the linked questions of land and labor. Whoever was able to own the one would also be able to control the other. Without working on land that belonged to them (or that they could later purchase), the freedmen and their families would be at the mercy of their former owners. And both sides knew that plantation owners would never voluntarily sell their land to blacks. Without land reform, the freedmen could never control their own labor. They would be working under conditions almost identical to those imposed by slavery itself.

The situation was profoundly muddled during the fall of 1865. Most agents of the Freedmen's Bureau (but not all of them) dutifully spent the fall of 1865 trying to extinguish the very hopes they had earlier helped to spread. In reality the cause of land reform was lost. But many freedmen could not bring themselves to believe that they were being betrayed by the very people who had just liberated them.

At this time of mixed and confusing messages, large numbers of Southern blacks came to pin their lingering hopes on the coming Christmas season. Word passed through the African-American community, often spread by Union soldiers, that when Christmas arrived in 1865, the government would provide them with land and the other necessities of economic independence. An ex-slaveholder from Greensboro, Alabama, wrote to his daughter that the Union troops who were stationed near his plantation had assured his former slaves "that our lands were to be divided among them at Christmas," and he added in frustration that they had already ceased doing any work. "Almost all are living along thoughtless of the future" and paying no attention to "what they will do after Christmas, when all will be turned adrift."

Black Refugees Crossing the Rappahannock River, 1862. Even relatively early in the Civil War, before emancipation, many African-American slaves fled their legal places of residence, especially in areas such as this one in northeastern Virginia, where Union troops were located nearby. Note the heavily laden cart drawn by oxen in this photograph. (Library of Congress).

It should not be surprising that the freedmen chose to hold such high hopes for the Christmas season, since for African-Americans Christmas had long been associated with the symbolic inversion of the social hierarchy—with grand gestures of paternalistic generosity by the white patrons who had always governed their lives. In 1865 those white patrons happened to be the government of the United States. To intensify black hopes still further, the Thirteenth Amendment to the U.S. Constitution (abolishing slavery) was due to take effect on December 18, one week to the day before Christmas.

By mid-November 1865, Southern newspapers were publishing stories about these Christmas dreams. One story (titled "The Negroes at Christmas Time") reported that blacks throughout the South entertained expectations of "being furnished, about Christmas, by the Government, with the necessaries of 'housekeeping' . . . waiting in a life of ease and idleness, for the jubilee. . . ." A newspaper in Mississippi reported that "wildly credulous and wildly hopeful of men are . . . awaiting the millennium of the 25th of December, who expect a big division of land and plunder on that day." And the *New Orleans Daily Picayune* editorialized that "it has seemed to be impossible to eradicate from their minds the belief that about Christmas they were to have lands partitioned among them; and their imaginations have been heated with the expectation of becoming landholders, and living as their old masters used to do without personal labor."

Without personal labor . . . a life of ease and idleness . . . awaiting the millennium . . . waiting for the jubilee. For white Southerners these were also code words. What they meant was that many blacks had not returned to work for their old masters at war's end (in fact, the crops of the 1865 season had gone mostly unharvested) and that they were refusing to sign degrading labor contracts with their former masters for the coming season. Alabama landowner Henry Watson reported that "Not a solitary negro in the country has made a contract for next year. The soldiers told them not to make them, that if they did they would be branded and become slaves again!" Their refusal posed a serious threat to the regional economy and especially to the well-being of the planter class.

It also indicated that the freedmen might be politically organized. Whites tended to interpret the hopes of the freedmen as aggressive and threatening, a sign that they were ready to turn to violence. And whites, like blacks, looked to the Christmas season as the time when matters would finally come to a head. Interpretations varied as to precisely how, and for what reason, violence would break out. Some whites thought it would happen spontaneously. An Atlanta newspaper warned that the holiday might start out as a "frolic" but that it would soon turn into something considerably more menacing. Emboldened by alcohol and encouraged by "bad white men," the blacks could be easily "persuaded to . . . commit outrage and violence." A planter from South Carolina told a visiting reporter that "some families will be murdered and some property destroyed," and he concluded ominously, *"It will begin the work of extermination."*

The fears of the one race were commingling in volatile fashion with the hopes of the other. As December approached, an increasing number of Southern whites became convinced that the freedmen were actively plotting an organized insurrection. All across the South, "apprehensions" of such a planned insurrection during the Christmas holidays were reported (and spread) by newspapers. In mid-November a Louisiana newspaper reported that "there is an increasing dread of what may turn up in the future. The negroes are, by some means, procuring arms, and are daily becoming more insolent." Toward the end of the month the *Cincinnati Daily Enquirer* headlined a story "A Negro Conspiracy Discovered in Mississippi" and explained that "a conspiracy had been organized among the blacks, extending from the Mississippi River to South Carolina, and that an insurrection was contemplated about Christmas." Such stories were printed and reprinted by newspapers throughout the South. Some of the rumors were quite detailed. A letter printed in the *New Orleans True Delta* cited a "reliable" report that blacks would collectively revolt "on the night before Christmas" and "wreak their vengeance" on whites whose names had already been chosen. The victims were to be identified to their attackers "by signs and marks placed on each house and place of business"—these marks would consist of coded numbers, as well as the letters X and O "set in chalk marks."

It was largely to the Freedmen's Bureau that there fell the task of persuading the freedmen that Christmas would not be ushering in the "jubilee," that further disruption of the Southern economy would harm them as well as whites, that the signing of labor contracts was now their best available recourse—and that insurrection would be futile. Under orders from President Johnson himself, the head of the Freedmen's Bureau, General O. O. Howard, spent the late fall touring the South in order to communicate these points. On November 12, General Howard sent a policy statement to his staff:

> It is constantly reported to the Commissioner and his agents that the free[d]men have been deceived as to the intentions of the Government. It is said that lands will be taken from the present holders and be divided among them on next Christmas or New Year's. This impression, wherever it exists, is wrong. All officers and agents of the Bureau are hereby directed to take every possible means to remove so erroneous and injurious an impression. They will further endeavor to overcome other false reports that have been industriously spread abroad, with a purpose to unsettle labor and give rise to disorder and suffering. Every proper means will be taken to secure fair written agreements or contracts for the coming year, and the freedmen instructed that it is for their best interests to look to the property-holders for employment. . . .

On another occasion, General Howard warned the freedmen directly that there would be "no division of lands, that nothing is going to happen at Christmas, that . . . [you] must go to work [and] make contracts for next year. . . . [I]nsurrection will lead to nothing but [your] destruction." Most agents of the bureau dutifully (if reluctantly) passed along the word that the freedmen's Christmas hopes were nothing but a pipe dream—or, as a Memphis newspaper put it, "a la mode Santa Claus." Colonel William E. Strong, the bureau's inspector general, addressed a group of Texas freedmen in plain language:

> I have been sent here from Washington, to make a speech to the colored people. I have little to say, and that is in plain words. Winter is coming on—go back to your former masters, work, be obedient, and show that you are worthy of freedom. You expect the Government to divide your late master's lands out to you, and about the first of January you will get buggies and carriages; but you are mistaken. You

will not get a cent. It all belongs to the former owners, and you will not get anything unless you work for it. It is true that rations have been given to some of you,
but you will not get any more. You have had good masters, I know. I have been
through here long enough to find out for myself.

But white Southerners were skeptical about whether such a cautionary message would be heeded by the black community. What was needed, one newspaper argued (in a sarcastic reference to the abolitionist leanings and the New
England background of many Freedmen's Bureau officials), was straight talk
from "imposing" men "who were born at least one thousand miles distant from
Cape Cod." Of course the planters themselves reiterated the message to their
ex-slaves. But the slaves would not heed *their* warnings, either. As one Mississippi newspaper conceded, "It amounts to nothing for former masters and mis-
tresses to read these orders to negroes. . . . They do not believe anything we can
tell them."

Some whites consciously manipulated the fear of an insurrection as a way
of convincing state and federal authorities to allow Southern whites to rearm
themselves—and to disarm (and harass) the freedmen. An Alabama official used
just such an argument in a letter to the governor of that state: "I am anxious to
organize the local company. It is feared the negroes will be troublesome about
Christmas unless there is some organization that can keep them in subjection."

But many whites were truly fearful. The mistress of one plantation near Columbia, South Carolina, later recalled how she was terrified by the nocturnal
singing that came from what until recently had been her slave cabins—singing that
evoked "expectations of a horde pouring into our houses to cut our throats and
dance like fiends over our remains."

It is possible that some African-Americans were indeed harboring thoughts
of (if not making plans for) a Christmas revolt. But those plans could hardly have
amounted to a coordinated conspiracy. What is far more likely is an explanation
that places both white fears and black hopes in the context of the intense expectations that normally surrounded Christmas on the slave plantation. For if Christmas was a time when slaves expected gestures of paternalist largesse, it was also
a time when slaves were used to acting up. (In that sense, the Atlanta paper may
have been shrewd in suggesting that the Christmas insurrection might begin as a
"frolic.")

What was happening in late 1865 was that a serious, contested set of political and economic issues—issues involving the radical redistribution of property
and the radical realignment of power—chanced to converge with a holiday season whose ordinary rituals had always pointed, however symbolically, to just such
a redistribution of property and just such a realignment of power. On both sides
of the color line there was a shared mythos about Christmas that made the holiday loom with ominous weight in the watershed year of white defeat and black
emancipation.

There was no insurrection. Confrontations, yes—even, in a number of cities, violent riots. The most serious of these was in Alexandria, Virginia, where two people were killed. But it soon transpired that the Alexandria riot was actually initiated by whites and that both victims were black. By December 28 or 29, it was

clear that the danger had subsided. "The *ides* of Christmas are past," one Southern paper proclaimed, "without any insurrection of the colored population of the late slave holding states. There is no probability of any combination of freedmen for hostile purposes; neither are they likely to combine, at present, for political or industrial objects." Another paper simply reported that "some cases of collision between blacks and whites occurred on Christmas, but there was no organized demonstration on the part of the former."

It was now possible to reinterpret the events of December 25, to put them back into the old, familiar antebellum categories. Newspapers reassured their readers that such "collisions" as did occur were "isolated" events and that they were not even political in nature but merely a function of old-fashioned Christmas rowdiness—occasioned by alcohol, not ideology. The Virginia correspondent of a Washington newspaper reported with relief that "a few brawls in Norfolk and Portsmouth were the result of whiskey, and had no political significance whatever." "Too much whiskey," claimed one paper; "much bad whiskey," added another; "some colored men, very much under the influence of bad whiskey," chimed in a third. And the newspapers now reported arrests for drunkenness and disorderly conduct by placing their notices in the police log, not the political columns. The racial identity of the offenders now hardly mattered. The *Richmond Daily Whig* reported on December 27 that "Christmas was celebrated in this city with unprecedented hilarity."

> It was more a street than a home celebration. "King Alcohol" asserted his sway and held possession of the town from Christmas eve until yesterday morning. Liquor and fire-crackers had everything their own way. A disposition was manifested to make up for lost time. This was the first real old fashioned Christmas frolic that has been enjoyed in the South for four years. The pent up dissipations and festivities of four Christmas days were crowded into this one day. . . .

By December 29, the *New Orleans Daily Picayune* even chose to use humor as a way of marginalizing the racial content of the violence that had indeed erupted in that city on Christmas day. Under the heading "Every one ought to be eloquent in his own defense," the paper reported that one white man, arrested on Christmas for rowdy behavior, testified in his defense: " 'Your honor, I am charged with being a disturber of the peace. It is a mistake, your honor. I have kept more than a hundred niggers off the streets these Christmas times. May it please your honor, I have a bad cold.' " The man's case was dismissed.

The crisis passed, it was now possible for white Southerners to return to the underlying problem—the collective refusal of the freedmen to work for their old masters. That would take care of itself, the *New Orleans Daily Picayune* explained, as the freedmen came to understand that their "true friends" were the Southern planter class, not the Northern demagogues who had falsely promised them land. When that truth at last dawns upon them—as it inevitably will—"they will learn where to learn their own true interest and duty."

The same editorial went on to explain bluntly just what that would mean:

> As the season passes by, without bringing them the possessions they coveted, and the license to be idle, which they expected with them, and they learn that they must look for support to themselves—for the government will decline to help those who do not help themselves—the relations of labor to capital will begin to be freed

from one of the most perplexing of the elements that have kept them unsettled; and to adjust themselves upon the natural basis of the mutual dependence of planter and freedmen on justice to each other for their mutual prosperity.

In other words, the freedmen would soon be forced back into virtual slavery. A newspaper in Richmond even resorted to a nostalgic evocation of the old interracial Christmas rituals, along with a rueful acknowledgment that the planters were unable to perform the part of patrons in the gift exchange. Not only would the freedmen fail to receive their masters' land, but they might even have to do without the "usual presents" they customarily received on this occasion. However, that was an aberration, indicating only that the planters were temporarily impoverished, not that race relations had changed:

> Heretofore every one of these four millions of beings expected and received a Christmas present, and partook of the master's good cheer. Now, alas, that former master is penniless, and he who depended upon his bounty is a homeless wanderer. The warm blanket, the cheerful fire, the substantial fare, the affectionate greetings, and the gifts they have been accustomed to receive at the hands of old and young will, we fear, be sadly missed.

Emancipated Negroes Celebrating the Emancipation Proclamation of President Lincoln. Like the bleak illustration on page 8, this woodcut-it appeared in March, 1863, in a French magazine, *Le Monde Illustre.* It shows African-American refugees accompanying an ox-drawn wagon (there were also two horses behind the oxen). But the few months that had passed since that earlier photograph made all the difference in the world to these refugees: they were now legally free. (*Le Monde Illustre,* March 21, 1963)

The Richmond editor summed up the prospect by referring to the eclipse of an old tradition—a tradition we have already encountered at the beginning of this story: "The familiar salutation of 'Christmas gift, master,' will not be heard." (That was the ritual in which slaves awakened their masters' families with a demand for gifts.) But the real object of nostalgia here was the *master's* loss, not the disappointment of his former slaves. That point came across clearly enough in the editor's concluding shot, an expression of hope that in another year or so things would be back to normal for the freedmen—"that their future condition may be better than their condition is at present, and that the next Christmas may dawn upon a thrifty, contented and well regulated negro peasantry."

Even now, with the Civil War lost and the black population legally free, the capital city of the Confederacy was continuing to link rituals of Christmas misrule with the maintenance of the antebellum racial hierarchy. A "contented and well regulated negro peasantry" was, after all, just what was needed to sustain a prosperous class of white planters. The cry of "Christmas gift!" would be music to their ears.

AN INTERPRETATION

The story of the "Christmas Riots" of 1865 is a microcosm of the entire period that became known as Reconstruction, the years between 1865 and 1877. It was a period of great hopes for the freedmen, hopes that were dashed, then raised, and then dashed once again.

As we have seen, with the war over, President Johnson quickly placed his highest priority on restoring the states of the late Confederacy to their former place in the federal Union. The new President rescinded Field Order No. 15. With his tacit encouragement, the Confederate states attempted to act as if little had been changed by their military defeat. They passed "Black Codes," requiring freedmen to sign annual contracts (those who refused were subject to arrest by any white man) or stipulating that unemployed blacks had to pay a "vagrancy" fine—and if they were unable to pay the fine, they could be bound out to work for anyone who paid it for them.

The South seemed to be reestablishing slavery in all but name. The defiance of a few states was especially brazen: Mississippi and Texas would not recognize the Thirteenth Amendment, and South Carolina actually refused to nullify its secession ordinance. When the South held elections at the end of 1865 to choose men who would go to Washington to serve in Congress (once again, with President Johnson's approval), the men they chose included former Confederate leaders: more than fifty members of the old Confederate legislature, nine Confederate generals, six members of Jefferson Davis's cabinet, and even the vice president of the Confederacy, Alexander Stephens!

This time they had gone too far, and there was a Northern backlash. To begin with, the Republican-dominated Congress simply refused to seat the newly elected representatives of the ex-Confederacy. Soon President Johnson completely lost control of the process, and Congress itself took charge. Beginning in 1866 it embarked on a program that became known as "Congressional Reconstruction" (to distinguish it from the brief preceding period of "Presidential Reconstruction"). The President vetoed several of the bills that reached his desk, but Congress passed them over his veto. By 1868, Johnson's authority was so low that he was actually impeached by the House of Representatives, and the Senate fell only a single vote shy of the two-thirds majority necessary to convict him, and thereby remove him from office!

The first three years of Congressional Reconstruction, from 1866 to 1869, were the most militant. Bolstered by the 1866 elections, which brought large majorities in both houses for the Republicans (majorities that were, of course, enhanced by the absence of representatives from the Confederate states), Congress embarked on a program designed to make certain that the states of the Confederacy would have to make radical changes before they were readmitted to the Union. Over President Johnson's veto, it passed a Civil Rights Bill and a law granting broader power to the Freedmen's Bureau. The following year, 1867, Congress passed the Fourteenth Amendment, which guaranteed the right of American citizenship to the former slaves and barred states from depriving any citizen of "life, liberty, or property without due process of law." In 1867, too, Congress passed a series of new laws designed to rein in the defiant South. The Old Confederacy was now divided up into five military districts, each overseen by a U.S. general. This military occupation was to be the cornerstone of the new process by which the individual states would be readmitted to the Union. First, the occupying armies were given the task of registering all eligible voters—adult white males who had not been disenfranchised by the Fourteenth Amendment, together with all adult black males. Next, those voters would choose delegates to constitutional conventions, conventions that would draft new state constitutions (those constitutions would be required to ratify the Fourteenth Amendment and to guarantee blacks the right to vote). Third, the new constitutions would be ratified by popular vote. Finally, then—and only then—could regular elections be held for representatives and senators who would at last be admitted as members of the U.S. Congress.

This was the process by which, one by one, the states of the Confederacy actually reentered the Union. By 1869, with black voters playing a central role, every one of the Confederate states had been readmitted—all with Republican majorities. That same year Congress passed the Fifteenth Amendment, which explicitly granted the right to vote to all adult black males. For the first time in Southern history (and, as it happened, the last time for another century), black people were exercising real political power. The African-American community greeted the suffrage with as much fervor as they had earlier greeted emancipation itself. They voted in large numbers, and many of them were elected to office. All in all, fourteen black men were elected to the U.S. House of Representatives and two to the Senate. (On the state level, though, the situation was different: not a single state had a black governor during the Reconstruction years, and only in South Carolina was there ever a black legislative majority.) Still, even this degree of black political power represented a startling change in Southern—and American—life.

Such radical change came about in part because many Northern Republicans were truly concerned with the rights of African-Americans. But it also depended on the support of *other* Northern Republicans, so-called moderates whose support for black suffrage came chiefly from the desire to punish the South for the terrible war it had waged or to make sure that when the Southern states finally *were* readmitted to the Union, the political power of the national Republican party would not be weakened by the election of Southern Democrats. These moderates knew that almost 80 percent of the Republican voters in the South were African-Americans.

In part for this reason, Congressional Reconstruction had its limits. Above all, it addressed not at all the one issue that had been responsible for rumors of the "Christmas Riots" of 1865: the confiscation and redistribution of lands formerly belonging to wealthy white slaveowners. Instead, the legislation of the period of Congressional Reconstruction was focused on black political equality. Despite the efforts of more radical Republicans, it ignored the need for black economic rights. No laws like Field Order No. 15 or Circular No. 13 were ever passed—even though one proposal that would have provided the freedmen with rights in land nearly managed to make it through Congress, only to be dropped at the very end.

In any case, Reconstruction was not to last or even to generate much enduring change. In one state after another during the 1870s, political power fell back into the hands of the Democratic party—into the control of "unreconstructed" Southern whites. The term used by Southern whites to name this process was *redemption* (a word ordinarily used to refer to the ransoming of hostages or, alternatively, to the salvation of souls). But the "redemption" of the South meant the restoration of power to wealthy ex-slaveholders and the subsequent denial of political rights to the black community.

Reconstruction ended for a variety of reasons. In most Southern states, blacks did not amount to a majority of the population. Three of these states—Tennessee, North Carolina, and Virginia—were "redeemed" as early as 1870. And where blacks were more numerous, they were systematically intimidated, notably by the Ku Klux Klan. The Klan (founded in 1866) directed terror attacks against black schools and churches and also against black economic and political leaders. The Ku Klux Klan was responsible for many hundreds of political murders across the South. These attacks were not random; instead, they were part of an attempt to undermine black autonomy and to destroy the infrastructure of the Republican party in the South.

In several states, election times regularly produced something approaching civil war. In Mississippi, the situation in 1875 was so tense that the state's Republican governor asked for federal military help. But by now most Northern Republicans had wearied of the battle. Former Union general Ulysses Grant (who had succeeded Andrew Johnson as President) refused to intervene in Mississippi, declaring that "the whole public are tired of these annual autumnal outbreaks in the South." The result was that the Democrats regained control of Mississippi. By the beginning of 1876 only South Carolina, Florida, and Louisiana remained in Republican control.

The presidential election of 1876 put a final end to Reconstruction. The two major candidates, Republican Rutherford B. Hayes and Democrat Samuel J. Tilden, ended up in an electoral deadlock (Tilden actually won the popular vote). Hayes finally managed to win the election by agreeing to remove all the remaining federal troops from the South—in exchange for the disputed electoral votes of three crucial Southern states. With the implementation of that bargain in 1877, the South was at last fully "redeemed."

Let this story end on a personal note. When I myself was in graduate school, during the 1960s, one of the first books I was assigned to read was about the end of Reconstruction. It was a well-known and respected book with an inspiring title, *The Road to Reunion*. On the front cover of this book was a picture that showed two hands entwined in a mutual handshake. The hands represented, of course, the two sections of the United States that had so recently been at war with each other: the North and the South. What I failed to notice, until a classmate pointed it out, was the color of those two hands. They were both white.

Sources: There is no full-fledged study of the "Christmas Riots"; this story was written mostly from contemporary newspapers. The one article on the subject is Dan T. Carter, "The Anatomy of Fear: The Christmas Day Insurrection Scare of 1865," in *Journal of Southern History,* vol. 42, 1976, pp. 345–364. Useful books include William McFeely, *Yankee Stepfather: General O. O. Howard and the Freedmen* (New Haven: Yale University Press, 1968), and Claude F. Oubre, *Forty Acres and a Mule: The Freedmen's Bureau and Black Land Ownership* (Baton Rouge: Louisiana State University Press, 1978), especially pp. 1–89. The Civil War origins of a potential land-reform policy are discussed in LaWanda Cox, "The Promise of Land for the Freedmen," *Mississippi Valley Historical Review,* vol. 45, 1958, pp. 413–440. A splendid study of the entire period is Eric Foner, *Reconstruction: America's Unfinished Revolution, 1863–1877* (New York: Harper & Row, 1988).